D1223491

Global Evangelization Movement: The AD 2000 Series

COSMOS, CHAOS, AND GOSPEL

A chronology of world evangelization from Creation to New Creation

David B. Barrett

Birmingham, Alabama

Titles in print in the AD 2000 Series:

World-Class Cities and World Evangelization, by David B. Barrett, 1986
World in View by R. Keith Parks, 1987
Unreached Peoples: Clarifying the Task, by David B. Barrett and Harley Schreck, 1987
Evangelize! A Historical Survey of the Concept by David B. Barrett, 1987
Cosmos, Chaos, and Gospel, a Chronology of World Evangelization from Creation to New Creation by David B. Barrett, 1987

Titles under development:

Urban Mission in the World's 3,000 Metropolises
Biblical Light on Global Mission
300 Plans to Evangelize the World
Reaching the World for Christ: a Dialogue
A Bibliography of Evangelism and World Evangelization
Measuring the Unfinished Task: Ways of Quantifying World Evangelization
Evangelize in 180 Dimensions: an Analysis of Today's Richest Christian Word
A Dictionary of World Evangelization

Also:

The Great Commission: A Biblical Exegesis
Bold Mission Thrust, 1948-2000: A History
Computers and Networks for Global Evangelization
Megacities Need Megaministries

Published by New Hope, P.O. Box 11657, Birmingham, Alabama 35202-1657.
Printed in the United States of America.

Library of Congress Catalog Card Number: 87-061098
ISBN: 0-936625-18-X

CONTENTS

AUTHOR'S PREFACE

This book is the fourth to be published in a sequence called 'Global Evangelization Movement: The AD 2000 Series'. In the series we recognize the existence today of a vast, relatively unorganized global movement concerned to further the evangelization of the modern world. It embraces all churches, all denominations, all Christian organizations. It covers all countries, all peoples, all languages. Our series attempts to provide a wealth of new materials, new research, and new data to assist this movement to achieve its goals.

I am grateful to the four editors of this series for their assistance in evolving these materials. In particular, Dr. Bill O'Brien, executive vice-president of the Foreign Mission Board, Southern Baptist Convention, has written a short commentary on this chronology from his standpoint as a mission executive working daily with personnel, colleagues, and contacts in 200 countries across the world. Our aim has been to keep our materials relevant to the realities of mission in the contemporary world around us.

David B. Barrett
Richmond, Virginia
April, 1987

COMMENTARY: MYSTERY AND KINGDOM

William R. O'Brien

Alpha and omega are human verbal markers that measure for us entry and exit, beginning and ending. How near or how distant those points are from each other may be related to how narrow or how expansive is our thinking.

A group of traveling religious leaders from the West recently asked Bishop K.H. Ting in China, 'What are your personal goals for the next five years?' His reply, in contrast to the question, was, 'Our goals are to train leaders, laying the foundation for the next five hundred years.' The answer not only reflected a difference in the perspective of time, but also a perception of the Kingdom of God, its mission on earth, and its transcendent permanence.

The Kingdom of God provides both the context for our existence and the reason for our living. It is simultaneously our core and circumference. It is cosmically dynamic, embracing unity and diversity, complementarity and paradox.

Missions toward the twenty-first century and beyond must become increasingly comfortable with a mixture of paradox, complementarities, and the balancing of opposites that are indigenous to such 'cosmos':

theoretical—practical	masculine—feminine
immediate—long-range	mercy—justice
traditional—non-traditional	church—kingdom
unilateral—multi-lateral	sign—agent
unitary—ecumenical	focus—scope
centrifugal—centripetal	patience—urgency
left-brain—right-brain	

Obviously, this is a partial listing. At any given moment one of these elements may be the dominant one for some good reason, but its counterpart is necessary to the rhythm of inhaling-exhaling. In atomic terms the behavior of light or electrons may sometimes be like a wave and sometimes like a particle, i.e. wave-particle duality. The physicists tell us it is impossible to observe both aspects simultaneously. Together, however, they provide a fuller description than either can alone.

Neither tunnel vision nor rigid presuppositions will provide adequate insight, much less direction, for any endeavor, be it scientific investigation or missions strategy. Since physics is more a matter of faith than an exact science, how much more the Kingdom and mission of God. Therefore, we must never succumb to 'psychosclerosis'—that is, a hardening of the mind that keeps one from seeing 360 degrees.

In this chronology of world evangelization, *Cosmos, chaos, and gospel,* David Barrett offers an antidote for tunnel vision. His chronology provides the necessary 'wave-particle' duality needed by serious missions planners.

Its 5,000 entries range across a broad spectrum. Taken as a whole, this chronology is not a synthesis of data, but rather a parathesis of scenarios and data; the juxtaposition of multiple strands of information. These many entries, standing alongside each other as they do, evoke a range of responses—from 'What if ...' to 'No way!' to 'Eureka!'

Both the prehistoric and the futurology sections of this work offer a multiplicity of scenarios that challenge present-tense thinking. While the historical section may feel like it is on more familiar footing, it may be debatable because of the interpretations some are disposed to bring to history.

Those concerned today with world evangelization, the Missio Dei, know from experience that it is impossible to arrive at viable, effective strategies for the future apart from objective study and the willingness to grapple with both the uncommon and the familiar. Like the principle of complementarity, both must be taken together to provide adequate descriptions of purpose, direction, and action.

At the very least, the struggle checks the normal tendency to place too little distance between the alphas and omegas in our limited understandings. As a whole, however, the scope of this chronology greatly expands the 'awe factor' each person brings to his perception of God. It challenges the tendency to settle for too small a perspective on God's creation. Further, this wealth of data opens us to many more options than normal cultural and philosophical parameters allow. Such options force one into the hard choices between security and vulnerability.

Jesus told a parable of the stewards and the money given each one. The heart of the story relates to action—not amount. The strongest language Jesus used in recorded Scripture was spent on the manager who chose security. He buried the money and presented it back to the owner, one hundred cents on the dollar. 'You wicked and slothful servant,' countered the owner. Western Christian cultures tend to define 'wickedness' as related to breaking any of the last five commandments given to Moses. How tragic it would be to keep all the last five, but break the first one by idolizing security.

As both objects and subjects of God's mission, the one option we do not have is that of burying new insight in order to safeguard that revelation against the King's return. Vulnerability is servant to a larger cause. Ultimately, then, risk and promise provide a safer context for missioning than do security and condemnation.

The realities of the coming twenty-first century can only intensify the struggle and the risks. Weighed against the role of the church and the scope of the task we will gladly struggle with the issues. The bottom-line issue for world evangelization is the chasm between Good News haves and Good News have-nots. How will a pilgrim covenant community on mission with God relate to those who have never heard the Good News?

From her death bed in 1915 Baptist missions education pioneer Fanny E.S. Heck said, 'Plan not for the year, but for the years. Think long thoughts.' *Cosmos, chaos, and gospel* is an instrument that can help us stretch our minds and think long thoughts, asking both WHAT IF? and WHY NOT? But the chronology alone is only half a complement. The counterbalance for *chronos* is *kairos*. As those entrusted with Kingdom priorities let us be sensitive to those moments of *kairos* that intersect our pilgrimage. If they change us and our direction, so be it. Of such is the mystery of the Kingdom!

William R. O'Brien
Executive Vice President
Foreign Mission Board
Southern Baptist Convention, USA

HOW TO UNDERSTAND THIS CHRONOLOGY

David B. Barrett

Chronologies do not replace history. Rather, they present us with a very compact, condensed form of history. Their great advantage is that they can pack a vast amount of factual information on a massive subject into a small and manageable space. With a minimum of essential interpretation, the subject can thus be covered within the covers of a single book.

This chronology attempts to do justice to the immense subject of God's purposes and plans in our Universe. It provides a historical and futurological background to the study of Christianity, global mission and world evangelization. It does this in the context of world history and world prospects in the future.

This secular context forms an indispensable background for understanding the unfolding drama of salvation. To understand mission and evangelization we must first understand God's Creation, in the past, the present, and the future. To understand the lightning spread of the gospel after the Day of Pentecost, we need to know how God had providentially prepared the Greek *koine* language and the Roman system of roads and mails. To understand the challenge to global mission in the year 1900, we need to know that John R. Mott in his classic *The evangelization of the world in this generation* described in detail secular developments facilitating the spread of the gospel such as navigation, shipping routes, telegraphy, length of railway track in the world's non-Christian countries, and so on. And to think out what possible alternative futures might await the Christian world mission from now into the future, we need to know the whole background of secular futurist forecasts in science, technology, and society.

All such secular material will be found here distributed throughout the chronology. The reader can thus see how it related to salvation history in the past. This will help him to work out for himself what this background secular context means for the mission of Christ today and in the future.

Evidence needs to be weighed

The chronology presents its evidence by bringing together a large number of facts, events, and scenarios. These are derived from experts in many different spheres—astronomy, cosmology, physics, archeology, paleontology, geology, history, linguistics, and the futurology of all these and other subjects and disciplines. Great care has been taken to ensure the accuracy of all the entries, especially of every historical event in the sequence up to the year 1987. But it should be clearly understood that these entries—prehistoric, historical, or futuristic—do not necessarily represent my personal views or opinions. I am simply the compiler or reporter, not the originator or protagonist.

Compiling the facts and interpretations of specialists in this way does not mean that we Christians have to accept them uncritically. I myself as a Christian believer do not accept the truth or likelihood or probability of a number of these items both in the past and in the future. The entries on the first page of the chronology, for example, describe the origin of the Universe as understood by contemporary astronomers, astrophysicists, and cosmologists. The entries on the second page describe the evolution of species as paleontologists and biologists understand it. But Christians have a prior authority in the Holy Scriptures, which we have found to be divinely and fully inspired. We can only accept secular findings if they do not contradict the Scriptures' clear and basic teachings about God, the world, and the human race. This means that we Christians are free to listen to the evidence adduced by experts in whatever subject, to weigh that evidence, and then to come to our own conclusions. We should therefore feel free to accept or discard entries in this chronology if they do not appear consistent with our faith in Christ.

God as Creator of all

The Scriptures teach that the God and Father of our Lord Jesus Christ was responsible for the creation of all things. God the Redeemer is also God the Creator. God as past, present, and future Creator is a fundamental theme running throughout the Scriptures. God created the Universe, as expounded in the Book of Genesis chapters 1-2. God has created life at every stage. God began the New Creation in Christ, and God will create, when the time arrives, the ultimate, perfected New Creation, the New Heavens and the New Earth.

Christ as central figure

Jesus Christ is the central figure in this chronology because he is the central figure in the whole drama of the Cosmos. He is the central figure as Logos in Creation; as Savior in Jerusalem; as Risen Lord of the church; as Messianic King in the Millennium; as Cosmocrat in this and future universes. At the close of the vision on Patmos, Christ declares: 'I am the Alpha and the Omega, the first and the last, the beginning and the end' (Revelation 22:13). Biblical insight on this is clear and detailed: Jesus Christ is 'the first-born of all creation; for in him all things were created, in heaven and on earth, visible and invisible, whether thrones or dominions or principalities or authorities—all things were created through him and for him. He is before all things, and in him all things hold together'. (Colossians 1:15-17, Revised Standard Version).

Three themes, yet a single theme

Our depiction of the drama of God's unfolding purposes is based on 3 words from biblical Greek: *cosmos, chaos,* and *euangelion.* Each embodies a major theme in its own right. But together also they embody a single theme, namely the story of God's creation and its vicissitudes over the aeons. Let us briefly look at these 3 words.

Chaos: abyss, primal waters, disorder, confusion

We start with chronologically the first of the 3 words, the Attic Greek word *chaos.* According to Liddell and Scott's *Lexicon,* it meant 'infinite space', 'infinite darkness', 'the expanse', 'the nether abyss', 'the first state of the Universe'. *Webster's 3rd new international dictionary* defines its English transliteration as a 'state of things in which chance is supreme', 'the confused unorganized state of primordial matter before the creation of distinct and orderly forms'.

Chaos is a biblical word, occurring in the Septuagint (Greek Old Testament, abbreviated to LXX). In its English form, it occurs a number of times in several leading English versions of the Bible. In Zechariah 14:4 (LXX), *chaos* is the vast chasm or abyss that will cleave the Mount of Olives in two when the Messiah returns on the future Day of the Lord. In Luke 16:26, the Latin Vulgate of AD 404 uses the Latin word *chaos* to translate the Greek *chasma,* and so the 1582 Rheims English New Testament reads: 'Between us and you there is fixed a great chaos'. And in the New American Bible (1970), Acts 19:32 portrays a vast assembly 'in chaos' over Paul's preaching. *Chaos* is synonymous with *abyssos* (abyss) which occurs frequently in the Bible (35 times in the Septuagint, 9 times in the Greek New Testament).

In the Bible, a whole range of words, concepts, and names surrounds the chaos-confusion-abyss concept. These include: disobedience, confusion, disorder, rebellion, rejection, sin, original sin, sinners, wicked, guilt, estrangement, alienation, selfishness, despair, punishment, evil, demons, devils, Satan, Abaddon, destruction, death.

Ancient Near Eastern peoples personified this concept as Tiamat, the primordial dragon or chaos monster of the undifferentiated primal waters. In Hebrew, the parallel word was *tehom,* as in Genesis 1:2, where it is translated in English as 'the deep' (KJV/AV), 'the abyss' (NEB). The Old Testament portrays God as victorious over this chaos monster, who is there named in addition either Rahab or Leviathan.

In Genesis 1:1-3, we read: 'When God set about creating the heavens and the earth, the earth was in a state of chaos and darkness was upon the face of the deep', or, 'When God began creating the heavens and the earth, the earth was at first a shapeless, chaotic mass' (The Living Bible). Or, in another translation, Genesis 1:2 reads 'The earth was without form and void, with darkness over the face of the abyss' (New English Bible). R. Young's *Analytical concordance to the Bible,* in print from 1879 to the present day, states: 'Genesis 1:1ff should be rendered: "When God began to create heaven and earth—and the earth was in a chaotic state and darkness was over the primordial ocean".' God's work of creation did not destroy the chaos and darkness but pushed them back and held them in check.

Chaos did not disappear after the Creation. Chaos imagery recurs throughout the Old Testament, especially in poetic contexts. Chaos still surrounds the habitable world on every side. In modern scientific terminology, the term entropy stands for this word chaos, the tendency for everything in the Universe to lapse irreversibly from order into disorder, to run down, to decline towards death.

Cosmos: order, the orderly Universe

The creation narrative of Genesis is paralleled by the creation epics of many other prehistoric peoples such as *Enuma Elish* of the Babylonians. Near Eastern peoples believed that our Universe resulted from the injecting of order (*cosmos*) into chaotic primordial beings or matter, 'the primeval emptiness of the Universe', 'the original state of things'. English poet John Milton perpetuated this thesis in his *Paradise Lost* (1667:1.10), describing 'In the Beginning how the Heav'ns and Earth Rose out of Chaos'.

The next of our 3 words is therefore *cosmos. Cosmos* is a Greek word meaning the idea of order in the Universe, or the ordered or orderly Universe. Cosmos is the opposite of Chaos. Cosmos means the intricate and subtle way in which the Universe is put together. In BC 600, a scientific revolution on the Greek island of Samos explained the Universe as Cosmos which arose out of Chaos. This was a new concept in the world of learning, telling mankind that the Universe is knowable. This ordered and admirable character of the Universe was called Cosmos. (See historical narrative in C. Sagan, *Cosmos,* 1980).

Not surprisingly, Cosmos is a major biblical and Christian concept. It occurs in Genesis 2:1 (LXX), proclaiming that God created not just the visible heaven and earth but also the entire Cosmos. The word also occurs 29 more times in the Greek Old Testament and it occurs 187 times in the Greek New Testament. Its meaning is the same as in classical Greek—the Universe as God's ordered Creation—but with additional insights. First, it is the human race's historical sphere, the context of its social relationships. Second, the Cosmos is to some degree a fallen world, to some extent under the dominion of evil powers and characterized by enmity to God.

Gospel: good news

The third of our 3 words is *euangelion* (evangel, gospel, glad tidings, good news) which occurs 6 times in the Greek Old Testament and 76 times in the New. It stands for the good news that although chaos reenters God's creation, God's redemption and salvation and healing in Christ are available.

A major occasion linking 2 of our key words occurs in the giving of the Great Commission: 'Go to every part of the world (*cosmos*) and proclaim the Good News (*euangelion*) to the whole creation.' (Mark 16:15, New English Bible).

Cosmos, chaos, and gospel

These 3 terms together, therefore, explain the theme of this chronology and the title of this book. Firstly, out of the chaos of unordered primordial matter, God creates Cosmos, the ordered Universe. Secondly, the Cosmos nevertheless reverts to chaos in numerous ways—widespread galactic violence, collisions, and mind-boggling explosions take place from earliest times to the present day; sudden mass extinctions of major species of life on Earth take place with startling regularity and frequency; the human race falls into rebellion against God. Thirdly, Christ becomes incarnate to save the human race from chaos, and his gospel or the good news of deliverance is announced to the world and to the Cosmos. Christ founds his church and then wins 8 billion followers into it over 20 centuries. Chaos nevertheless remains widespread. This huge church fails to obey Christ's Great Commission, Christians selfishly spend 97% of the world's riches on themselves, the world murders over 40 million Christians as martyrs over 20 centuries, sin and violence and chaos in the world reach frightening proportions.

These 3 themes—cosmos, chaos, and gospel—permeate the chronology from beginning to end. One cannot understand God's purpose and plan without understanding all three.

God's mission arises out of God's creation

Another trilogy of terms describing this drama would be: creation, mission, consummation. We live today in the era of God's global mission, but we cannot understand it fully without first knowing the details of God's prior creation and God's eventual consummation. This is the justification for the detailed treatment of Creation in the first 3 pages of the chronology, also for the last 3 or so pages in the future. At first sight these 6 pages look like merely 'secular' material, but on reflection we realize that these past and future events are profoundly religious, even profoundly Christian. They reveal to us fundamental aspects of Christ's preexistence, activity, and purpose.

Three cosmic eras

For all these reasons, we have divided our chronology into 3 major phases that we call 3 cosmic eras. These are here named: (1) The Prehistory of World Evangelization, (2) World Evangelization in Christian History, and (3) The Futurology of World Evangelization. The first takes us from the Creation to the Incarnation of Christ, the second from the Incarnation through the initial stages of the New Creation in Christ, the third from this unfolding New Creation to its final Consummation in Christ.

The first cosmic era: from Creation to Incarnation

Cosmic Era I, The Prehistory of World Evangelization, begins with God's Creation of the Universe and continues up to the Incarnation of Christ. It details the rise of religion and of God's special revelation as recorded in the Old Testament; it deals with the First Creation and what Christians call the First or Older Age. Our record of this first phase incorporates scientific data and prehistoric scenarios on the origins of the world and of the human race. It also incorporates biblical data from the Old Testament on the origin and development of Heilsgeschichte (salvation history). As we understand it, the scientific data do not contradict the biblical data; rather, they support and supplement them, as well as providing their context.

On the Christian worldview, God created the Universe and has been in control of the entire creation process from remote past to present and on into the remote future. Christians are creationists—that is, they affirm God as Creator. The exact details as to how long ago God created the Universe are understood by Christians in a variety of ways. Some Christians follow the 16th-century archbishop James Ussher, who was the first person to construct a mathematical model of reality and the first to compile a serious biblical chronology. Using the only evidence available at that time, namely the genealogies in the Book of Genesis, Ussher computed the year of Creation at BC 4004. By AD 1700, scientists faced with mounting geological evidence were reckoning the age of the Earth at 9,000 years, and many Christians today accept their estimated Creation dates of BC 7300, BC 8000, or BC 10,000. These dates all reject biological evolution as a factor in the origin of life.

Other Christians, equally committed to the primacy and plenary inspiration of the Bible, believe that God created the world utilizing the mechanisms that astronomers and paleontologists are now describing for us. For these Christians, the fact that cosmologists and astrophysicists indicate that the original Creation may have taken place from 10 to 20 billion years ago in no way alters the fundamental Christian affirmation that God has always been in full control of the whole process. Instead, it fills out and gives glimpses into the awesome omnipotence, omniscience, and omnipresence of God the Creator.

Each of these scenarios of the Earth's past is noted and incorporated in the chronology. (Note also that in a number of places throughout the whole chronology, dates (years) are preceded by a lowercase letter *c*. This stands for 'circa' (approximately) and means the year is an approximate estimate only).

The last part of Cosmic Era I deals with the revelation of God's redemption through Abraham, Moses, and the Old Testament prophets down to the end of the inter-Testamental period.

The second cosmic era: from Incarnation to New Creation

Cosmic Era II, World Evangelization in Christian History, deals with the First Advent of Christ the Son of God, and details the history of Christianity and its spread across the ages and across the globe up to the present day. It shows the First or Older Age overlapping with what Christians call the New Creation which is the Last or New Age in Christ. There is a case for holding, as we do here, that the origins of the New Creation go back to the time of Abraham in BC 1950, and that the New Creation then goes on to span both Cosmic Era II and also on to its consummation either during or at the end of Cosmic Era III.

The chronology illustrates this analysis of Cosmic Era II by listing a selection of the major or more significant events in the origin, growth, and spread of Christianity across 20 centuries and across the world; in evangelism; and in the evangelization of peoples and nations across the globe, with particular emphasis on statistical enumeration. It sets forth the 10 major epochs or pulsations in Christian history (shown as sub-titles in capital letters) using terminology coined by the historian K.S. Latourette and modified and expanded here; the origin of the 7 major ecclesiastical blocs and over 150 ecclesiastical traditions detailed in the *World Christian encyclopedia* (1982); the founding of Christian work in every continent, nation, country, and territory; the conversion or christianization of whole peoples; notable foreign missionary enterprises to other lands; the founding of major missionary boards, societies, and orders; statistics of Christian expansion; revival and renewal movements; major recessions or setbacks to Christianity, schisms and apostasies; church unions, mass movements into the churches; major international evangelistic campaigns; translations of the Bible into the world's languages; major technical innovations facilitating evangelization; predictions of theologians and churchmen over these 2,000 years concerning the anticipated imminent advent of Christ and also of the Antichrist; background data on science, scientific discoveries, and science fiction of importance and relevance to world evangelization; and other significant events in the history of the spread of Christianity. A majority of these Christian events are noted or further explained in the wider Christian context in the above Encyclopedia in its Tables 2 or in the texts on countries in its Part 7.

The presentation and language used here are standardized to a large degree. Note in particular that the spelling '1st', '2nd', '3rd', etc refers to the official titles of a series of regular conferences, whereas the spelling 'First', 'Second', 'Third', etc refers to other types of situation.

In Appendix 1 is a statistical table showing the numerical expansion of both evangelization (evangelized peoples) and of Christianity (total Christians) across the continents of the world throughout these 20 centuries, at regular intervals through historical time. These statistics are repeated in Cosmic Era II of the chronology at 29 historical turning-points or watersheds at which we summarize the *Global status* (printed in boldface type for quick identification) of Christianity and world evangelization.

The chronology and its format in Cosmic Era II are designed to display with clarity 3 particular emphases: (1) expansion of Christianity over time, i.e. over the whole period of Christian history, illustrated by the 10 major epochs or pulsations in Christian history; (2) expansion in numbers, i.e. the numerical growth of evangelization and of Christians, churches, dioceses, movements, et alia, especially for those few occasions before the year 1800 where detailed statistics were collected; and (3) geographical expansion to all nations and peoples. To give an overview of this latter emphasis (3), Cosmic Era II gives in *italics*, once only, the name of every country in the world (as existing in 1987, with names and frontiers as today) with the year when Christianity first reached it and ongoing or definitive evangelization began (i.e. arrival of the first resident Christians or missionaries, excluding any earlier temporary or short visits), giving details in parentheses of the agents involved.

The third cosmic era: from New Creation to Consummation in Christ

Cosmic Era III, The Futurology of World Evangelization, projects past and present trends into the future and examines alternate futures and possible scenarios. It presents an eschato-scientific overview of the future, in 2 parts.

First is given the Christian eschatological schema of the biblical End-time. For this, no future dates are possible nor can any be suggested. No exact apocalyptic timetable can ever be proposed. Christians of all confessions are agreed that the Parousia or Second Advent of Christ could occur today, or tomorrow, or in a year's time, or 100 years, or 1,000 years, or a million years, or a billion years. On this subject, the final word is: 'It is not for you to know times or seasons which the Father has fixed by his own authority.' (Acts 1:7, RSV).

Second is given a religio-scientific composite scenario of alternative futures, for both secular and religious concerns. It includes both optimum scenarios, and worst-case scenarios. For these, numerous future dates suggested by experts are given. The combination describes the future age, the New Age, the Last Age, the New Creation as it moves toward its consummation, against the background of the secular world. From our point of view as Christians, these materials help us to view the future and to think out what the meaning is of that central biblical affirmation 'God will sum up all things in Christ'.

The reader who wishes to make sense of the method and the material of this venture into both biblical and secular futures should be sure to read the separate explanations given at the beginning of Cosmic Era III. The introduction to part (a) concerns the Christian eschatological schema. The introduction at the start of part (b) concerns the religio-scientific composite scenario.

Our main approach to futurology is that espoused by the mainline discipline known as futurology, future studies, or futures research—forecasting using alternate futures. That is to say, we draw up not one single scenario but a range of scenarios taking into account the various possibilities that might emerge. This forecasting is not the same as prophecy, nor prediction, nor predestination, nor soothsaying, nor divining, nor fortune-telling, nor horoscopy (drawing up horoscopes), nor clairvoyance, nor crystal ball-gazing. (Note, however, that we do include notable cases of both biblical and extrabiblical prophecy and prediction).

As mission futurists, then, we are not claiming any special insight into the future. We don't know any better than our non-futurist colleagues what will happen in the future. But we should know better than non-futurists what could happen. We are therefore speaking only in terms of probabilities, possibilities, options, and consequences. We are simply exploring multiple future options and alternatives, in any of which we ourselves can become directly involved if we so wish.

Futurology speaks mainly about corporate life and society. It does also say a great deal about your future life as an individual. But it has clear limits. The United Nations' 2-yearly publication *World population prospects* tells us the probable mortality rate every 5 years up to AD 2025, in every country of the world. It tells you how many people will die in your country in 38 years' time. But it cannot tell you, the reader, what you yourself will be doing in 5 years' time, nor when you will die. Before too long, however, even that may be possible as medical researchers examine your genes in great depth.

Futurology today has become a professional science which has built up over 150 techniques including the delphi method in which the opinions of a variety of experts on some futurist topic are separately polled and analyzed by computer. It also gives plenty of scope to common sense, group discussion, research, and such activities as 'blue-skying'—the art of conjecture, speculation, thinking, and discussing in 'What if...' terms on the particular topics we are interested in.

Let us consider a concrete situation in the future, namely: Could the world become fully evangelized by AD 2000 with North American foreign missionaries alone accomplishing the task?

First, the futurist considers this future situation and thinks about 3 different kinds of future: (1) the possible future, (2) the probable future, and (3) the preferable future. For each, he then thinks out not just a single future but at least 2 alternate futures.

Regarding (1), one alternate future is that this task would be impossible for North Americans alone. The logistics of evangelizing in 7,000 different languages would surely defeat them. At the other extreme, it could be regarded as *possible* that North Americans might finish the task alone but only if certain conditions were met. Thinking it over, the futurist would write down the conditions: there would have to be greatly increased missionary enthusiasm in North America, continued expanding financial and logistical support from the churches, continued tolerance of their missionaries abroad, continued permission from non-Christian governments for them to reside in their countries, and a number of technological breakthroughs in communication in those 7,000 languages.

Regarding (2), this AD 2000 goal may well be possible but not probable; 67 countries are closed to resident foreign missions today, and this total is increasing by 3 more countries every year. If this residence barrier were overcome, it might then become *probable;* otherwise, it seems improbable.

Regarding (3), even if the AD 2000 goal were both possible and probable, it might still not be *preferable.* Such an important task should not be left to only one part of the Christian church. It would be much better if foreign missionaries from Third-World countries and Communist countries also had their full share in completing world evangelization.

This latter aspect of futurology emphasizes that the future is not predestined or deterministic; to a considerable degree, we can control the future. We can create a better world if we have the will and make the effort.

There is a distinction, too, between 2 equally important types of scientific conjecture or science forecasting: (a) scientific probabilistic predictions, and (b) science fiction. Examples of the former are an astronomer's forecast that the Sun has 8 billion more years of life left, or the incredibly detailed scenarios that cosmologists now think probable for the end of our Universe's life (described here for the dates between AD 8 billion and AD 10^{100} years). By contrast, science fiction is less concerned with probable futures and more concerned with speculating about possible futures. The first science fiction that has survived was penned in BC 414 by the Greek dramatist Aristophanes, who was also the first known writer to use the Greek word *euangelizesthai* (evangelize). Many Christians down the ages have written noteworthy science fiction; today, many writers are physicists, or astronomers, or other scientists; several are even Nobel laureates. Science fiction has been called 'the most significant literature of our day', even 'the only worthwhile literature of the 20th century'. This genre of literature helps to stimulate people's imagination concerning the future, and so a number of the more outstanding works are included in the chronology.

Note that the chronology includes at least one entry for every individual year from AD 1830-2030. Also, for the period 1960-2000, within each year many conferences and events are given their exact month and even days or dates, in which case they are arranged chronologically within that year. Other undated entries are also arranged approximately chronologically within their years.

At the end of the whole chronology, the diagram in Appendix 3 sets out the patterns of fission and fusion which have characterized Christianity over its 20 centuries of history, and sets out also 4 scenarios concerning its likely or possible development in the future.

7-phase typologies of Creation

There are many ways in which the data in this chronology could be divided up or classified into categories. Cosmic Era II does this by dividing the history of the Christian church into 9 epochs based on the ebb and flow of the fortunes of Christianity. In the same way, the entire chronology, which is the story of Creation itself—past, present, and future—can also be divided and classified in this manner.

As with any research situation, we can clarify our thinking by asking the 7 basic questions concerning the situation: What? When? Where? How? Whence? Whither? Why? If people are involved, we can ask a further question: Who?

Our chronology aids this process of understanding by incorporating 3 interestingly parallel ways of classifying the entire creation process. These are set out below. Further details on these phases or levels can be found in the chronology under the dates or references given below in parentheses.

(a) *Seven Days of Creation.* From the perspective of biblical revelation, the Book of Genesis, chapter 1, speaks of God's creative acts under the category of 7 Days (or eras, or epochs, of indeterminate length). On these Days God created the following (referenced here not by chronological dates but by reference to Genesis 1):
1. Light (Genesis 1:3-4).
2. Firmament, heaven, atmosphere, waters (Genesis 1:6-8).
3. Dry land, seas, plants, vegetation, fruits (Genesis 1:9-13).
4. Sun, Moon, stars (Genesis 1:14-16).
5. Living creatures, fish, birds, reptiles (Genesis 1:20-23).
6. Land animals, insects, domestic animals, mankind (Genesis 1:24-27).
7. Sabbath rest (Genesis 2:2).

(b) *Seven Stages of Creation.* Modern science recognizes a number of stages in which differing material was created or began after the Big Bang, as follows:
1. Energy, matter, antimatter, atoms, particles (BC 19 billion).
2. Light, quasars, galaxies, stars, dark matter (BC 17 billion).
3. Solar System, planets, Earth, Moon (BC 5 billion).
4. Life on Earth: algae, bacteria (BC 3.5 billion).
5. Species: 500 million varieties (BC 400 million).

6. Mind: the human race (BC 5.5 million).
7. Community, history, culture, philosophy, art, religion (BC 5 million to 500,000).

(c) *Seven Levels of Evolution.* Protagonists of evolution—whether evolution by a host of miniscule steps or evolution by a few massive quantum leaps—speak of 7 levels of evolution beginning at the dates shown in parentheses:
1. Energy (BC 19 billion).
2. Matter (BC 19 billion).
3. Life (BC 3.5 billion).
4. Mind (BC 5.5 million).
5. Supermind (AD 2030).
6. Galactic Mind (AD 500 million).
7. Cosmic Mind (AD 5 billion): universal consciousness.

These 3 schemes cannot yet be equated or combined. Each is looking at Creation from a differing standpoint. But the idea of a 7-fold progress in God's creative activity is common to all three. They provide a striking indication of the value of these differing standpoints.

Sources

Over 90 percent of the 5,000 entries in this chronology have sizeable bibliographical support in the literature. They are therefore not speculative, nor unverifiable; they are adequately documented and based on acceptable and accepted evidence. For each there is at least one reference, that is a significant book or article documenting its validity.

So, for example, the 2 sections at the end of Cosmic Era II headed 'STATUS OF THE COSMOS, 1988' and 'STATUS OF THE WORLD, 1988' give the best thinking of experts, and the most accurate data currently available, on a whole variety of subjects impinging on global mission and world evangelization. These 2 sections do not incorporate futures thinking; they deal with the actual, factual situation today, with the latest available statistics. The fact that we here have no room to document the sources should not be allowed to undermine their credibility.

In the same way, this formidable documentary support is true even of apparently legendary, controversial, or speculative material. Consider the legend of the lost continent of Atlantis (see BC 12,000, 10,500, 9350). Some Christians regard it as the site of the original Garden of Eden. The story of Atlantis has been supported since Plato in BC 390 by a vast corpus of literature. Up to the present day, this now totals over 5,000 books, of which some 4,000 argue the case for Atlantis' authenticity.

Likewise, consider the medieval Christian prophet, Nostradamus. He was the most widely read seer of the Renaissance. In 1547 he produced a volume of End-time prophecies which has been continuously in print ever since up to the present day. That work stands second only to the Bible in the vast number of translations, commentaries, and analyses it has generated over the centuries.

It is the same with a majority of the entries dealing with the future. Many future items reported here under Cosmic Era III as only a 2-line or 3-line miniscenario are in fact based each on a sizeable book or published article which develops the scenario in full.

In this compilation we list sources, in or after each entry, only in a handful of cases where we judge it especially important to do so. These include Genesis chapter 1 and other major biblical references, a small number of especially significant books, a few science fiction classics, and some of the major volumes that trace the development of the concept of evangelization.

A computerized database

The chronology has been developed on computer media for a variety of other uses in addition to this printed book version. Words, phrases, names, persons, subjects, themes can all be tracked, traced, and displayed instantly through global search options. Each entry is described by geographical, political, ecclesiastical, confessional, demographic, statistical, and other indicators so that one can examine reduced or specialized versions of the entries on any subject. All entries are also related to the main database dealing with the global status of Christianity in the context of 100 world religions, 9 continents, 254 countries, 3,100 large metropolises, 7,000 languages, 11,000 ethnolinguistic peoples, 18,000 Christian parachurch agencies, and 22,200 Christian denominations.

The uses of this material are thus limited only by the imagination and creativity of the user. From these data he can create statistical totals, statistical tables, statistical analyses of trends over time. He can generate multicolored graphics or maps. He can project them directly from a computer screen to a large wall screen at the moment he creates them. He can animate them. And the end product is: greater insight into the whole incredible story of world evangelization.

A macrothesaurus and macroindex

A printed index version is being developed for publication which will, among other things, list every single subject, name, place, and concept in a single alphabetical listing. Each would then be followed by all dates (years) in which it occurs in the chronology.

Conclusion

Such, then, is the drama of the Creation—the past, present, and future activity of God the Creator. This is the drama, too, of the ever-present threat of chaos. And this is the drama of the gospel, the good news that Jesus Christ is, in the final analysis, in control of the entire process. The kingdom of God has arrived, is arriving today, and will arrive tomorrow. And towards that goal we are invited to follow as disciples of Christ.

SELECT BIBLIOGRAPHY

This is a short selection from the vast range of books consulted during the compilation of this chronology. The selection gives the flavour of the subject. The listing of titles within each of the 3 Cosmic Eras follows approximately the unfolding of ages and subjects in the chronology itself.

A technical feature about this bibliography should be noted. It concerns our manner of presenting titles of books and articles. The usual practice in English bibliographies is to capitalize all nouns and adjectives in the titles of books and articles. This practice gives us no additional information but instead imparts a false significance to individual words in those titles. More serious, it hides the English language's valuable distinction between proper nouns (names, places, countries, organizations, campaigns) and those which are not proper nouns. Titles in English have in fact gradually moved in this direction over the last 200 years, abandoning a few capitalizations every decade. We therefore follow a different practice, and one that has growing support in the academic and publishing worlds.

Throughout our material in this book, it is essential to know whether a phrase like 'World Evangelism' is a proper noun (in this case, the title of the World Methodist Council's agency to evangelize the world) or whether it is simply a concept, in which case it should remain uncapitalized as 'world evangelism'. Hence our practice below, and in the chronology itself, is to capitalize only (1) the first word of each book title, (2) all proper nouns, and (3) adjectives and other words when part of an existing name. The only exceptions are books published before 1850, when titles were usually fully capitalized.

A similar practice is followed in the chronology for titles of conferences, themes, programs, and other activities. There, however, in a number of cases we leave a title's wording capitalized where that existing usage seems sufficiently significant.

A related practice is that, in bibliography and chronology, we use single quotation marks ('...') throughout for titles, articles, quotations, etc. This is because the normal practice of double quotes ("...") overloads the printed page when there are a very large number of quotations, as in the present book.

COSMIC ERA I: THE PREHISTORY OF WORLD EVANGELIZATION

(This section covers Creation, cosmology, prehistory of man, the rise of religion, and God's redemptive activity as recorded in the Old Testament).

The moment of Creation: Big Bang physics from before the first millisecond to the present Universe. J.S. Trefil. New York: Scribner's, 1983. 234 pages. (This book and the next describe the scientific evidence for the detailed scenario of the initial moments of Creation given on the first page of our chronology after the date BC 19 billion).

In search of the Big Bang: quantum physics and cosmology. J. Gribbin. New York: Bantam, 1986. 414 pages.

God and Creation. P.J. Flamming. Nashville, TN: Broadman, 1985. 167 pages. (A masterly and highly readable treatment of the Christian doctrine of God as Creator. Surveys the history and literature of the subject: biblical exegesis, philosophy, creationism, evolution, redemption, astronomy, current debates, et alia).

The red limit: the search for the edge of the Universe. T. Ferris. New York: Quill, 1983. 286 pages.

The new astronomy. N. Henbest & M. Marten. Cambridge, UK: University Press, 1983. 240 pages. (275 color pictures with vivid new imagery illustrating quasars and other cosmological themes).

Cosmos. Carl Sagan. New York: Random House, 1980. 365 pages. (A classic, based on a 13-part television series).

The extraterrestrial encyclopedia: our search for life in outer space. J.A. Angelo Jr. New York: Facts on File Publications, 1985. 254 pages.

Entropy: a new world view. J. Rifkin. New York: Viking, 1980; Bantam, 1981 (302 pages). (The place of entropy/disorder/chaos in ecology, economics, society as well as in physics).

Black holes and warped space-time. W.J. Kaufmann III. New York: W.H. Freeman, 1979. 221 pages.

Origins: what new discoveries reveal about the emergence of our species and its possible future. R. Leakey & R. Lewin. New York, Dutton, 1982.

Cosmos and history: the myth of the eternal return. Mircea Eliade. New York: Harper, 1954. 176 pages.

The encyclopedia of religion. Ed Mircea Eliade. New York: Macmillan, 1986. 16 volumes including index. (The most important 20th-century English-language reference work on religion from Paleolithic times to the present day).

The interpreter's Bible. Ed G.A. Buttrick. New York: Abingdon, 1951-57. 12 volumes. (KJV/AV and RSV text, exegesis, and exposition. First 6 volumes deal with the whole Old Testament revelation and its meaning).

COSMIC ERA II: WORLD EVANGELIZATION IN CHRISTIAN HISTORY

(This section covers the history and status of Christianity, mission and evangelism over the last 20 centuries.)

The evangelization of the Roman Empire: identity and adaptability. E.G. Hinson. Macon, GA: Mercer University Press, 1981. 332 pages.

A history of the expansion of Christianity. K.S. Latourette. New York: Harper, 1937-45. 7 volumes.

The new international dictionary of the Christian Church. Ed J.D. Douglas. Exeter: Paternoster, 1974. 1,074 pages.

Encyclopedic dictionary of religion. Eds P.K. Meagher et al. Washington, DC: Corpus, 1979. 2 volumes. (Very detailed on Christian history, personages, martyrs, missions).

World Christian encyclopedia. Ed D.B. Barrett. Nairobi: Oxford, 1982. 1,010 pages.

Exploring evangelism: history, methods, theology. M. Taylor. Kansas City, MO: Beacon Hill, 1964. 620 pages. (A comprehensive history of evangelism by a Church of the Nazarene theologian).

History of evangelism: 300 years of evangelism in Germany, Great Britain and the USA. P. Scharpff. Grand Rapids: Eerdmans, 1966. 373 pages. (Written from the standpoint of German Pietism).

The evangelization of the world in this generation. J.R. Mott. New York: SVMFM, 1900. 245 pages.

Evangelism for the world today. J.R. Mott. London: International Missionary Council, 1938. 295 pages. (World survey, with correspondence from 125 Christian leaders, for 1938 IMC Conference in Tambaram).

Operation World: a day-to-day guide to praying for the world. 4th edition. P. Johnstone. Bromley, Kent: STL, 1986. 501 pages.

COSMIC ERA III: THE FUTUROLOGY OF WORLD EVANGELIZATION

(This section covers secular futurism, secular methodology, classics of science fiction, biblical and extrabiblical prophecy, and the future of Christianity and religion. A fuller treatment of the latter subject will be found in the 3-page table 'Evolution of the futurology of Christianity and religion, 1893-1980', in *World Christian encyclopedia*, p. 854-6, which lists 280 distinct titles.)

The study of the future: an introduction to the art and science of understanding and shaping tomorrow's world. E. Cornish. Washington, DC: World Future Society, 1977. 308 pages. (The classic introduction to the subject; highly readable).

The future: a guide to information sources. 2nd edition. Washington, DC: World Future Society, 1979. 722 pages.

Arthur C. Clarke's July 20, 2019: life in the 21st century. A.C. Clarke. New York: Macmillan, 1986. 282 pages.

The encyclopedia of science fiction: an illustrated A to Z. Ed P. Nicholls. London: Granada, 1979. 672 pages.

Dimensions of science fiction. W.S. Bainbridge. Cambridge, MA: Harvard University Press, 1986. 278 pages.

The science in science fiction: does science fiction foretell the future? Ed P. Nicholls. London: Michael Joseph, 1982. 208 pages. (Lavishly illustrated discussion and explanation of a vast range of scientific subjects).

2010: Odyssey Two. A.C. Clarke. London: Granada, 1982. 297 pages. (This novel and the next 2 titles are probably the 3 most brilliant, convincing and suggestive recent examples of classic science fiction).

Contact: a novel. Carl Sagan. New York: Simon & Schuster, 1985. 432 pages.

The songs of distant Earth. A.C. Clarke. New York: Ballantine, 1986. 257 pages.

The Third Millennium: a history of the world, AD 2000-3000. B. Stableford & D. Langford. New York: A.A. Knopf, 1985. 224 pages. (This convincing and well-illustrated book elaborates on a fair number of the entries in our chronology for the period AD 2000-3000).

The future of the Universe: a cosmological forecast of events through the year 10^{100}. D.A. Dicus et alii, *Scientific American*, 248, 3 (March, 1983), 90-101. (By 4 high-energy physicists/cosmologists).

Encyclopedia of Biblical prophecy: the complete guide to scriptural predictions and their fulfilment. J.B. Payne. Grand Rapids, MI: Baker, 1973. 754 pages. (Lists 8,352 predictive scripture verses (1,711 in the NT) containing 1,817 distinct biblical predictions (1,239 in OT, 578 in NT). Calculates 27% of all Bible verses are predictive; this is 21.5% of NT, 28.5% of OT).

Eschatus: future prophecies from Nostradamus' ancient writings. B. Pennington. Limpsfield, UK: Dragon's World, 1976. 91 pages. (Contains 60 full-color pages of apocalyptic imagery vividly illustrating the biblical End-time. The cover portrays the Four Horsemen of the Apocalypse surveying a devastated Europe).

The future of religion: secularization, revival and cult formation. R. Stark & W.S. Bainbridge. Berkeley, CA: University of California, 1985. 571 pages.

The future of global nuclearization: world religious perspectives. Ed T.R. McFaul. New York: Joint Strategy & Action Committee, 1985. 131 pages.

The Church at the end of the Twentieth Century. F.A. Schaeffer. London: Norfolk, 1970. 190 pages.

The future of the Christian world mission. Eds W.J. Danker & W.J. Kang. Grand Rapids: Eerdmans, 1971. 181 pages.

The future of the Christian Church. A.M. Ramsey & L.-J. Suenens. London: SCM, 1971. 87 pages.
The shape of the church to come. Karl Rahner. London: SPCK, 1974. 136 pages.
The church of the future: a model for the year 2001. W. Buhlmann. Maryknoll, NY: Orbis, 1986. 207 pages. (Describes and discusses the churches of 6 continents and how they relate now and in the future).

COSMIC ERA I: THE PREHISTORY OF WORLD EVANGELIZATION

GOD'S ETERNAL PRE-EXISTENCE

Uncreated, eternal existence of Triune God: Theos, Logos, Pneuma.

OSCILLATING UNIVERSE SCENARIO

Before creation of our Universe, several successive small cosmic explosions (Small Bangs) occur, each leading to a larger universe with short but progressively longer life; each short cycle so far has collapsed before life can evolve, and new bang occurs. (Landsberg-Park model of a universe bigger with each successive bounce).

GOD CREATES COSMOS OUT OF CHAOS

BC

19 billion Zero of cosmic time: creation of Universe in primordial monobloc with explosion and universal fireball (the Big Bang theory), continuously evolving and expanding; physically 9-dimensional (according to superstring theory) although only 3 dimensions develop significantly. (Genesis 1:1).

GOD CREATES ENERGY, MATTER, ANTIMATTER, ATOMS, PARTICLES

Universe passes rapidly through 7 eras or stages (freezings of matter or force) after Big Bang: (l) before 10^{-43} seconds (= Planck time), supersymmetry era; (2) before 10^{-35} seconds (temperature 10^{26} degrees K), GUT era (grand unified theory); (3) 10^{-35} to 10^{-10} seconds (at which temperature is 10 quadrillion degrees), electroweak era (freezing of electrical and weak forces), with sudden rapid 'chaotic inflation' or exponential expansion of Universe (then packed entirely within one Planck length of 10^{-43} cm) by up to $10^{1,000,000}$ times in less than 10^{-30} seconds, producing order (cosmos) out of primordial chaos; (4) 10^{-10} to 10^{-3} seconds, quark era (first form of matter); (5) 1 millisecond to 3 minutes, particle era (formation of hundreds of types of particles from sea of hot quarks); (6) 3 minutes (at temperature of 1 billion degrees) to 500,000 years, nucleogenesis (plasma and nuclei) era; and finally (7) at 500,000 years, hot expanding plasma freezes into hydrogen atoms, with massive release of microwave radiation as present (atomic) era begins. (Genesis 1:3).

After first millisecond from Big Bang, total darkness prevails throughout Universe for next 2 billion years before light bursts forth. (Genesis 1:2).

Universe has been radiation-dominated for its first thousand years (First Level of Evolution: energy), now becomes matter-dominated (Second Level of Evolution: matter), with total of 10^{80} elementary particles (protons, neutrons, electrons) in observable Universe.

By a million years after Big Bang, enormous clouds of hydrogen (75% of Universe) and helium (25%) form, later condensing into protogalaxies and then into giant protostars.

GOD CREATES LIGHT, QUASARS, GALAXIES, STARS—AND DARK MATTER

17 billion Creation of light with eruption of a billion blazing quasars (stupendously exploding or colliding protogalaxies with massive central black holes, emitting huge quantities of light, radio waves, X-rays and gamma rays) which then evolve over next 17 billion years into galaxies of which 2% have violent nucleuses. (Genesis 1:3).

16 billion Formation of first galaxies, eventually producing over 100 billion galaxies, all receding from each other, each containing from 1 million to 1,000 billion stars (grand total 10^{22} stars, shining because of nuclear fusion) and each with a huge black hole at its center; by 20th century AD, 99% of Universe consists of holes (spherical voids hundreds of millions of light-years across and empty of galaxies), with vast metagalaxies and superclusters of galaxies (lengthiest being 1 billion light-years long) around their edges; widespread galactic violence, collisions, explosions and chaos.

Luminous matter thus created amounts to 20% of Universe's total mass; 80% continues as cold dark matter (invisible, nonluminous) consisting of either neutrinos, axions, photinos, or cosmic strings.

15 billion Emergence of our Galaxy (Milky Way), 70,000 light-years in diameter, situated within our Local Group or cluster of 21 galaxies (12 being ellipticals, rest spiral or irregular). (Genesis 1:3).

14 billion Immense globular clusters of stars arise across Universe.

9.5 billion First massive stars in our Galaxy emerge as globular clusters eventually totaling 400 billion stars or solar masses (15% being white dwarfs and 1% red giants), 70% of which are binary pairs, and 10% of which later develop planets capable of supporting life; BC 7.7 billion, highly-evolved stars emerge. (Genesis 1:16).

7.5 billion Origin of all heavy elements as first-generation giant stars explode as supernovas, supplying raw materials of planetary systems and also cosmic rays which power all evolutionary processes.

GOD CREATES SOLAR SYSTEM, PLANETS AND EARTH

5.0 billion After nearby supernova explosion within Galaxy, our Sun (a 3rd-generation star) and our Solar System are created, with planets and asteroids; Sun rotates once round galactic center, 23,000 light-years away, every 250 million years. (Genesis 1:1,14-19).

4.7 billion Formation of Earth (and Moon) by condensation of hot gases, cold interstellar dust and rocks; in geological time, known as Pre-Cambrian Era up to BC 570 million, with 3 Periods: Azoic (Non-Life), Archeozoic (Primitive Life), Proterozoic (Early Life); BC 4.4 billion, Earth's oceans appear. (Genesis 1:10).

3.6 billion After 1.1 billion years of high-frequency bombardment of Earth by planetesimals from 2 to 20 miles diameter, frequency falls sharply to present level of one impact by extrasolar or galactic planetesimal of 3 miles diameter every 14 million years, and/or one of 10 miles diameter every 100 million years; these approximately mark ends of subsequent geological periods.

GOD CREATES LIFE ON EARTH

3.5 billion Life arises on Earth: first living organisms are free-living viroids; small, simple cells related to algae or bacteria, producing oxygen through photosynthesis (the major energy source for all life subsequently); remaining unchanged for 2.9 billion years; atmosphere largely carbon dioxide, methane and ammonia. (Third Level of Evolution: life).

Interstellar origin of life hypothesis: virtual uniformity of genetic code in all known forms of life is explained by either (a) Earth seeded with spores despatched in interstellar rocket from earlier civilization, or (b) Earth continuously bombarded with cosmic genes directed by a higher intelligence. (Biologist F. Crick, astronomer F. Hoyle, 1985).

3.4 billion Oldest known fossil traces of living matter: microfossils of blue-green algae (now with 25,000 species) and bacteria; BC 2 billion, oldest fossils of single-cell myxobacteria (active social micro-organisms, working as communities of microbes).

3.0 billion First multicellular organisms evolve.

2.0 billion Multicelled plants appear and flourish in seas on Earth; development of sexual reproduction by simple cells together with scheduled or programmed death as essential for improving life by evolution. (Genesis 1:11).

1.0 billion Proterozoic Period: sponges appear (5,000 species).

800 million Free oxygen accumulates on Earth as algae metabolize carbon dioxide.

Cambrian explosion of lifeforms

600 million Sudden, enormous proliferation in oceans of new multicelled organisms and great numbers of forms of life.

Vision with primitive eye-spots develops into image-forming eyes independently in marine worms, mollusks, and vertebrates; first arthropods appear (trilobites, equipped with a pair of compound eyes), hunting in packs on ocean floor.

First of 14 sudden mass extinctions of life on Earth (Great Dyings), occurring every 26 million years, selectively destroying species; others in 500 million (trilobites), 248m (marine), 243m, 225m, 215m (placodonts), 194m (clams), 175m, 163m, 144m (ammonites), 115m, 91m (sea urchins), 65m (dinosaurs), 38m (protozoa), 11m (mollusks); cause seen as bombardments of Earth by comets in Oort cloud of 100 billion comets surrounding Solar System as Sun's dim companion star Nemesis approaches every 26 million years.

570 million Lower Paleozoic Era, up to BC 395 million, with 3 Periods: Cambrian, Ordovician, Silurian; first invertebrates; marine animals with hard parts (shells, carapaces) appear, making possible their survival as fossils.

Infra-Cambrian ice age, followed in BC 280 million by Permo-Carboniferous ice age, then BC 3 million by Pleistocene ice age; 275-million-year periodicity due to Solar System entering massive belt of galactic dust.

500 million Cambrian disasters: sudden mass extinction of many species of segmented creatures (trilobites) which have dominated seas.

450 million Age of Fishes (first of the 5 vertebrates): jawless fish appear, also

first land plants. (Genesis 1:20).

410 million Jawed vertebrates (fishes) appear, also first land animals. (Genesis 1:11).

GOD CREATES 500 MILLION SPECIES OF ANIMALS AND PLANTS

400 million Dry land colonized on Earth; first of several hundred million distinct species arise (in sudden evolutionary bursts), 98% of which later become extinct with only 2% surviving until modern era (8 million species today); also early seed plants. (Genesis 1:24-25).

395 million Upper Paleozoic Era, up to BC 225 million, with 4 Periods: Devonian, Lower Carboniferous, Upper Carboniferous, Permian; first insects appear.

375 million Sharks appear, in Middle Devonian Period. (Genesis 1:21).

345 million Age of Amphibians (2nd of 5 vertebrates): at start of Carboniferous Period, first land vertebrates evolve from lobe-finned fishes; all meat-eating (no herbivores yet).

300 million Origin of shelled egg as method of reproduction among first reptiles, ensuring survival in drier climates.

280 million Permian Period, lasting 55 million years; climate becomes drier, swamps disappear; first major spread of true land-living animals (reptiles).

260 million First plant-eaters appear; large paramammals (primitive mammal-like cold-blooded reptiles) spread across globe and dominate Earth for over 70 million years.

248 million Permian cataclysm, biggest extinction of life ever: 90% of all marine species suddenly perish; 243 million, further mass extinction.

230 million Warm-blooded mammals appear (with high metabolic rate).

225 million Massive, severe and widespread extinction of most of Earth's 350,000 species (mostly marine creatures) at end of Permian Period.

Age of Reptiles (3rd of 5 vertebrates), found on all continents including Antarctica: Mesozoic Era, up to BC 65 million, with 3 Periods: Triassic (BC 225-190 million), Jurassic (BC 190-136 million), Cretaceous (BC 136-65 million); first lizards and flying animals. (Genesis 1:20,24).

215 million Sudden mass extinction of placodont species, et alia.

200 million Age of Dinosaurs: Euparkeria and later first true dinosaur Ornithosuchus and other intelligent bipedal (two-legged) carnosaurs (flesh-eaters) destroy all paramammals by BC 190 million, remain active for further 125 million years; herbivores also in every part of world, until sudden extinction of all dinosaurs.

195 million Whole of globe's landmass, previously in contact as single supercontinent Pangaia, begins to break up into Laurasia (in north) and Gondwanaland (in south); land-dwelling vertebrates flourish in all areas.

194 million Sudden mass extinction of clam species, inter alia.

190 million Jurassic Period, lasting 54 million years; sauropods (giant plant-eating dinosaurs) evolve, to a maximum weight of 100 tonnes (Brachiosaurus); also modern bony fishes arise.

175 million Jurassic sudden mass extinctions of species; also again in 163 million.

150 million First bird, Archaeopteryx, evolves from coelurosaurs (small dinosaurs).

144 million Sudden mass extinction of ammonite species, inter alia.

136 million Age of Birds (4th of 5 vertebrates): Cretaceous Period; birds radiate out into new environments; first flowering plants emerge.

120 million Evolution of first hadrosaurs (duck-billed dinosaurs), most successful and advanced of all dinosaurs; 35 distinct species; lasted 40 million years.

115 million Cretaceous sudden mass extinction of species.

100 million Continents of North America, South America, Africa and Europe begin splitting apart; total sauropod population now 40,000; first snakes (pythons) emerge, in Africa.

91 million Sudden mass extinction of sea urchin species, inter alia.

70 million Order of primates (social animals to high degree, and largely vegetarian, giving birth to their young singly) abandon ground living and take to insect-eating tree life in vast dense tropical forests of Africa and Eurasia, evolving over next 60 million years; BC 42 million, first higher primate Amphipithecus (near ape) arises in Asia and Africa as ancestor of all monkeys, apes and humans.

65 million Earth suddenly reverses polarity of its magnetic field.

Cretaceous-Tertiary boundary event, the Great Extinction, causing sudden disappearance and total extinction, without further trace, of all dinosaurs, pterosaurs and marine reptiles (after 6,440,000 generations averaging 25 years each), with 96% of Earth's entire species; probably due to giant asteroid or comet colliding with Earth, or to deadly radiation from a supernova; all mammals however survive, due to smaller size, so stage cleared for their evolution.

New Age of Mammals (5th of 5 vertebrates): Cenozoic Era, Tertiary Period, for 62.5 million years.

Paleocene Epoch, till BC 54 million; at least 60 genera of primates known.

50 million South America and India still islands, but moving towards their present-day positions.

Explosive evolutionary growth of the brain and cortex, with rapid and dramatic changes over next 50 million years.

40 million Anthropoids (Anthropoidea suborder): monkeys and anthropoid apes evolve from prosimians, in New World first then in Old; fruit-eating, requiring stereoscopic color vision.

38 million Sudden mass extinction of one-cell protozoa species, et alia.

Oligocene Epoch begins, lasting 12 million years.

30 million Hominoids (Hominoidea superfamily): apes (pongids, known collectively with later hominids as hominoids) evolve from monkeys: BC 28 million, Aegyptopithecus (Egyptian Ape).

27 million Climates over most of Earth become markedly seasonal; tropical belt shrinks towards equator.

26 million Miocene Epoch, lasting 19 million years; over 50 primate species in 20 genera.

20 million Dryopithecus (Woodland Ape): dryopithecines evolve, primitive ape-like animals inhabiting dense forests of East Africa (then an island) in vast numbers.

17 million Africa and Eurasia, isolated by shallow seas, become linked by land; various species pass from one continent to the other, resulting in explosion of evolutionary changes.

16 million World's climate begins to cool markedly, and its widespread huge tropical forests begin steady shrinkage, resulting in major pressures on dense-forest dryopithecines which become replaced by open-woodland ramapithecines.

14 million Hominoids begin to split into 2 quite separate lines: anthropoid-ape line (Pongidae family) and hominid (human) line (Hominidae family).

13 million First Ice Ages begin, with large glaciers covering Arctic and Antarctica.

First hominid (partly upright hominoid), the genus Ramapithecus (smallest of the ramapithecines) in Rift Valley, East Africa (hence originally termed Kenyapithecus), last common ancestor of apes and man; world population of these ancestral hominids then around 100,000, in Africa, Western Europe, Himalayas and Southeast Asia; gradual lengthening of period of childhood dependence due to increasing brain size.

11 million Sudden mass extinction of marine protozoans and mollusk species, inter alia.

10 million Asian apes (orang-utan, gibbon, siamang) split off from hominid line.

8,000,000 First Ramapithecine hominid with occasional upright posture, located in South Asia (Siwalik Hills, India).

The 'Fossil Void' in human prehistory: major gap of 3 million years in fossil record, disappearance of Ramapithecus and complete absence of hominid fossils up to BC 5 million.

7,000,000 Pliocene Epoch, lasting till BC 2,500,000.

African apes (chimpanzee with 400 cc brain size, gorilla with 500 cc) split off from hominids, leaving the latter then located only in Africa.

6,000,000 Ramapithecus diversifies into 3 different lines (genera) as environmental changes form new habitats: Australopithecus Africanus (Gracile Southern Ape), Australopithecus Boisei (Robust Southern Ape), and by BC 5,500,000, genus Homo (Man).

Over 90% of all known animal species become extinct by time of genus Homo.

5,500,000 Total hominid population born since ancestral hominid in BC 13 million: 45 billion.

GOD CREATES MIND: THE HUMAN RACE IN THE GARDEN OF EDEN

5,500,000 Genus Homo: hominid brain size increases from earlier level of 400 cc to 700 cc, often regarded as the threshold of humanness; origin of Homo line, located only in Africa (original Garden of Eden, Genesis 2:8) due to ecologically unique opportunities centering on change from forests to savanna, not by gradual evolving but in a dynamic state of evolution by series of relatively sudden quantum leaps (Fourth Level of Evolution: mind, i.e. self-reflective consciousness). (Genesis 1:26-27, 2:7).

Origin of noosphere (intellectual envelope over the Earth, the thinking layer of cultural heritage) out of biosphere (life without reflective thought); due to reflective man's sudden creation in one generation, 'he was suddenly there', appearing simultaneously at numerous points along a subtropical zone of Earth; the first inhabitants of the noosphere, the starting point of Point Omega (Teilhard de Chardin).

Origin of awareness of God, primitive worship, and prehistoric religion, the latter then a primordial monotheistic revelation of God, later degenerating into polytheism and animism.

Commission given by God to man: 'Be fruitful and multiply and fill the Earth' (Genesis 1:28); first foreshadowing of the later Great Commission.

First of 7 Biblical Dispensations covering human history: Innocence (Age of Adam and Eve) (Genesis 1:28), Conscience/Moral Responsibility (Genesis 3:7), Human Government (Genesis 8:15),

Promise (Genesis 12:1), Law (Exodus 19:1), Church (Acts 2:1), Kingdom (Revelation 20:4). (Scofield Reference Bible, 1909).

GOD CREATES COMMUNITY, LANGUAGE AND CULTURE

5,000,000 Rise of nomadic hunting-and-gathering mixed economy among Homo species in Africa, resulting in bands of 20-100 (averaging 25) members, establishment of base camps, food-sharing, division of labor (males hunting for meat, females gathering plants and rearing children), transportation of items in carrier bags, and ensuing cooperation.

4,500,000 Homo Habilis (Handy Man, Artisan Man) arises, with brain size of 750 cc and world population of 300,000 human hominids, all in Africa; emergence of first gestural language (with 700,000 distinct gestures possible).

First of God's 8 Covenants with man: Edenic Covenant, followed later by Adamic, Noahic, Abrahamic, Mosaic, Palestinian, Davidic, and New Covenant. (Scofield Reference Bible).

4,200,000 Origin of hominid habitual bipedalism (upright posture, walking and gait), the major step in human evolution, involving enormous anatomical change.

4,000,000 Australopithecus (Southern Ape-Man: bipedal vegetarian ape-men with 450 cc brain size) flourishes side-by-side with Homo Habilis, and Ramapithecus remnants, in Africa until extinction by BC 1,000,000, leaving only one hominid species on earth: meat-eating (30% of diet) hunter-gatherer socially-cohesive Homo, living only in Africa.

Origin of human culture: emergence of language and symbols

3,500,000 Emergence of spoken language (slow and clumsy rudimentary verbal communication) on part of Homo Habilis and other hominids, due to primates reaching out to inspect and analyze their 3-dimensional color world; emergence of symbols.

Origin of evil, on Judaeo-Christian worldview: Satan, the Adversary or Devil, an alien personal force in Universe, is cast down on Earth, attempts to destroy human reliance on God.

3,200,000 Earth starts getting colder; BC 2,400,000, glaciation begins; BC 1,500,000, sheets of ice cover parts of continents until BC 8000.

FALL OF MAN — 1: POLYTHEISM DISPLACES MONOTHEISM

3,000,000 Original monotheism, with right relations between God, man and whole creation, gradually degenerates into polytheism, animism, animatism, spirit-worship, shamanism, and religious chaos. (Genesis 3).

2,500,000 Quaternary Period (Age of Man) begins; Pleistocene Epoch (Later Ice Age), up to BC 8000.

First crude stone tools made and used, enabling hominids to eat meat from large animals; also origin of use of fire, cooking of food at campsites and family hearths (no trace of any human artifact in the archeological and fossil records before this date); Paleolithic culture (Old Stone Age), until BC 10,000.

2,300,000 Asteroid fragment 0.3 miles across strikes Earth in southeast Pacific at 45,000 mph with force of 10,000 megatons; dense debris clouds accelerate glaciation.

2,000,000 Origin of organized, planned, large-scale big-game hunting by Homo bands.

Global climate changes to cooler and drier conditions, enabling new species to emerge.

Separate continents of North and South America begin to link up.

Increasing brain power in Homo species, from Homo Habilis (cranial capacity now 800 cc) to Homo Erectus (over 1000 cc); new cultures emerge every 500,000 years.

1,750,000 Homo Erectus (Primitive Man, formerly termed Pithecanthropus, meat-eating [30% of diet] protohumans), with brain size increasing from 900 cc to 1100 cc over next one million years and world population of 500,000 human hominids increasing to 700,000 by BC 500,000; species represents a major quantum jump in culture, mental intelligence and self-awareness; species ends in BC 300,000 with 135 billion hominids and humans of all kinds having lived, most within Africa.

1,500,000 Acheulean tool technology (teardrop-shaped hand axes, larger tools, cleavers) arises with basic design persisting until BC 200,000 in Africa and BC 100,000 in Europe.

1,000,000 Major collision of Earth with planetesimal.

First large-scale human migration: small nomadic groups of black (dark-skinned) Homo Erectus move slowly (20 kilometers per generation, i.e. from Nairobi to Peking in 12,000 years) from Africa into Europe and Asia (but not America or Australia), changing from tropical to temperate-climate dwellers, thus becoming first Homo humans to exist outside Africa; due to ability to transport 4-fold commodities of food/water/fire/experience (via language).

800,000 Beginnings of organized ritual among hunting Homo Erectus populations from Africa to China (art, symbolism, body-ochre, burial and other rites, et alia).

600,000 Rise among Homo Erectus of organized, specialized, hunting way of life, characterized by large-scale hunts of animals large and small, systematic and controlled use of fire, controlled and patterned stone-tool manufacture, and continual geographical expansion into completely new regions.

500,000 Total human population born since origin of genus Homo in BC 5,500,000: 83.6 billion.

Origin of Homo Sapiens

Emergence, at numerous different centers, of new species Homo Sapiens, intelligent, self-aware, socially-aware, strongly cooperative, sharing, with extensive cultural traditions.

During periodic Ice Ages, 95% of all Homo Sapiens population and ancestors located in Africa, with only 5% in Eurasia.

436,000 Creation of world according to later Babylonian priest Berossus (BC 290).

300,000 First surviving non-utilitarian object (engraved art), found in France.

200,000 Complex Middle Stone Age technology emerges first in Africa (in Europe, BC 100,000), lasts until BC 35,000.

150,000 Regional forms of Homo species arise: Homo Sapiens Neanderthalensis (Neanderthal Man) in ice-gripped Europe and Near East, divided into many distinct tribes and cultures, with life expectancy 29 years); and Homo Sapiens Soloensis in Southeast Asia; most with large brain size of 1500 cc, sophisticated spoken languages, within world Homo Sapiens population of 1.4 million; both have disappeared by BC 33,000.

100,000 Great majority (90%) of Homo Sapiens world population of 1.5 million still located in Africa; differentiation into sub-species (human races) under way.

Organized religion now widespread: Mousterian industries flourish, accompanied by widespread signs of burials, grave offerings and cult objects.

c78,000 A disintegrating planetary civilization beyond Andromeda galaxy, 80,000 light-years from Earth, transmits intergalactic frantic plea for help as devastation spreads. (Claimed as received by Soviet astronomers in AD 1984.)

70,000 Final Ice Age begins, lasts 60,000 years until ice sheets begin shrinking in BC 15,000 and finally retreat by BC 8000.

60,000 Origins of herbal medicine, among Homo Sapiens Neanderthalensis; shamanistic ceremonial in burials at Shanidar, Iraq.

c47,000 Origins of earliest prehistoric civilizations including Atlantis and Lemuria, and the traditionally-first Cainitic urban civilization (with first city, Enoch) founded by Cain (Genesis 4:17); later these disappear and become lost without trace.

45,000 Final evolution of anatomically modern people/human beings, well differentiated into human races.

FALL OF MAN — 2: SHARING DISPLACED BY PRIVATE OWNERSHIP

45,000 Homo Sapiens Sapiens (Modern Man), with brain size averaging 1360 cc, emerges as the first fully modern man, with modern language capacity, same anatomy and intelligence as present-day humans; much more elaborate and complex social systems than hitherto; systematic control of vast game herds by manipulation and corralling; animal husbandry and domestication of horses and reindeer; together with use of symbolism, art (cave painting, carving and engraving), and ritual; new cultures emerge every 5,000 years.

40,000 All continents have almost reached their present-day geographical positions.

38,000 Colonizing of the Americas: first wave of Homo Sapiens immigrants enter North America from Eurasia via land bridge across Bering Straits, following herds of prey animals; second wave in BC 16,000.

35,000 Upper Paleolithic period begins, called Later Stone Age in Africa.

33,000 Cro-Magnon Man, discovered in Dordogne (France), oldest known fossil representative of Homo Sapiens Sapiens; possibly refugees over Atlantic land bridge from series of floods destroying earliest Atlantean civilization; rapid advances in hunting technology and culture; BC 28,000, first known musical instrument (bone flute, in France); BC 21,000, bone sewing needles, cold-weather clothes; BC 15,000, deadly spear-throwers; necklaces, jewelry.

Age of Art: emergence and rapid development of Ice Age prehistoric art, technology and creativity; intensive artistic activity mainly magic or hunting portrayals of animals in action, or of pregnant women (fertility rites); Venus figurines found across 3,000-mile swath from western to central Europe; for 25,000 years until sudden total disappearance of art in BC 8000.

30,000 Horses domesticated and ridden by humans.

25,000 First of several massive waves of advanced cultural immigration into Europe from the west (of Cro-Magnon or Aurignacian culture), coinciding with series of cataclysms overwhelming Atlantean civilization due to rising sea levels; later waves BC 14,000 (Magdalenian culture, with well-formed tribal and religious organization) and BC 9350 (Azilian culture).

Early trading networks among humans arise; beginnings of social-status hierarchy in hunter-gatherer communities.

Origins of nomadic pastoralism

20,000 Populations of (a) north China and (b) south China/Indochina become sufficiently differentiated to be designated respectively Mongoloid and Oceanic Negroid.

c20,000 First beginnings of pastoral nomadism (herding), with herds of animals owned by groups of humans and driven in cyclic migrations.

18,000 Northern Amerindians reach Central and South America.

Homo Sapiens migrates from Eurasia to colonize Australia, venturing 60 miles across Timor Straits in dugout canoes.

16,000 Maximum spread of ice sheets across globe, lowering sea level by 400 feet, exposing Beringia land bridge from Asia to North America, also Atlantic land bridge; BC 15,000 shrinking begins, sea levels rise; BC 8000, last glaciers retreat and melt.

c16,000 First localized beginnings of agriculture, in Zagros Mountains, Near East, though widespread agricultural revolution does not follow until 8 millennia later; nomadic life gradually gives way to settled existence and claims to private ownership of land.

c14,000 Legendary Hyborian age flourishes; millennia later as continent of Atlantis begins sinking, Conan the Cimmerian founds civilization of Aquilonia. (R.E. Howard, 1930 series of novels).

Japan: Pre-Jomon Ceramic culture; c12,000 Early Jomon; c4500 Mid-Jomon culture to BC 250; nomads, hunting and fishing, pottery.

13,000 Pacific Ocean port of Tihuanaco (Bolivia), with massive stone buildings, suddenly destroyed by being thrust up to 13,000 feet altitude in seismic upheaval accompanying melting of Ice Age glaciers.

c13,000 China: first cultivated or domesticated plants (millet, soybeans, later rice).

12,000 Climax of prehistoric art: cave paintings at Lascaux (southwest France), Altamira (Spain).

Global civilization allegedly flourishes on lost continent of Lemuria in mid-Pacific.

c12,000 Legendary antediluvian continent of Atlantis flourishes in Golden Age (in some accounts, colonized by extraterrestrials from outer space) as world's first global supercivilization (original Garden of Eden, Gardens of Hesperides, Elysian Fields, Paradise) and founder of all others: Egyptian, Sumerian, Akkadian, Lemurian, Hyperborean, Mayan, Aztecan, etc.; rise of human governments. (Total book titles on Atlantis: 5,000).

FALL OF MAN — 3: WEALTH INTRODUCES PERMANENT CONFLICT AND CHAOS

11,000 East Africa (Nairobi): first evidence of domesticated cattle; origin of cattle pastoralism.

Woolly mammoths, hunted by Stone Age man, suddenly disappear and become extinct.

10,500 Heyday of Atlantean world empire: population of 64 million; elephants, prehistoric monsters; golden-roofed stone cities with capital Cerne, ports, harbors, docks, vast network of canals; temple of Poseidon representing Cosmos, and Sun-worship as its original religion; armies of 1,250,000 men, navy of 1,200 ships; global commerce; first alphabet, ancient written laws; advanced mathematics and scientific knowledge including use of laser crystals, mass communication, land/air/undersea transportation; but eventually moral decline, materialism, perversion, torture, slavery and degeneration.

10,000 Formation of 5 modern human races completed after lengthy evolution: Australoid, Capoid, Caucasoid, Mongoloid, Negroid (or Congoid).

Post-glacial spread of wild cereal grains permits their storage and hence sedentary village life.

9800 Mesolithic (Final Upper Paleolithic) Period and cultures (Middle Stone Age arts and artifacts) beginning in northwestern Europe and Near East, up to BC 2700; final phase of hunting and intensified food-gathering, using a new technological advance, bows and arrows.

9350 Civilization of Atlantis destroyed by a universal catastrophe, last of series of global Deluges (the Flood, or series of continental Floods) as volcanic upheavals and melting glaciers and ice-caps raise global ocean levels by 500 feet, engulfing thousands of cities and Atlantean colonies across the world; remnants today Atlantic Ridge with Azores as its mountain tops.

9200 Near East: domesticated sheep appear.

Birth of permanent cities, agriculture and sedentary cultures

9000 Proto-Neolithic phase: origins of several highly-sophisticated civilizations in Near East in Anatolia; Neolithic Revolution, from food gathering to food producing; human dwellings evolve from caves to houses in neatly-constructed villages.

8900 World's first permanent city: sudden growth and explosive expansion of Jericho, to a population of 3,000, after introduction of cultivation techniques of wheat and barley; as commercial enterprise and trade (salt, sulphur) lead to wealth, city is fortified and surrounded by massive wall for flood protection; occupied for next 7,000 years until destruction.

c8500 Accumulation of wealth (money, possessions, land, herds, property, buildings, business deals) begins: acquisitiveness and demonic power of money (cattle, in Latin *pecus*, used at first) denounced as root of all evils, since accumulation is mainly at the expense of others; world becomes permanently polarized into powerful rich at one extreme and powerless poor at the other.

8000 Holocene (Recent) Epoch in geological history begins, up to present day; from standpoint of human history also called the Historical Period (begun 100 centuries ago).

Viet Nam pre-Neolithic Hoabinhian culture of Bac Son: domestication of buffalo, cultivation of rice.

Earliest date for creation of world, according to creationist theology (as expounded in 20th-century AD North America).

c8000 Agricultural Revolution (widespread and virtually instantaneous discovery and adoption of farming, wheat and barley crops, food production and food conservation), first in Near East (Anatolia, Fertile Crescent), then independently by BC 7000 in Europe, BC 5000 in northeast China and in Meso-America; diffused across world at rate of one kilometer per year; partially caused by end of Ice Ages and massive climatic change.

Three foundations of civilization now laid: (1) discovery of agriculture, (2) animal domestication and stock-breeding, and (3) fertility-rite cult of Mother Goddess as supreme deity.

Agriculture leads from nomadic life to sedentary existence, claims to private ownership of land and permanent ongoing conflicts, also to rapid growth of world population (then 5 million), and to rise and nurture of concentrated population centers, with development of complex division of labor.

China: first villages with pottery, in central interior.

FALL OF MAN — 4: WARFARE, KILLINGS, HUMAN SACRIFICE

7000 Neolithic Age (New Stone Age cultures): farming and stock-breeding well-established; rise of leisure, luxury items, cemeteries, trade, complex religious ideas, ancestor and fertility cults, arts and artifacts; first pottery (earthenware), in Anatolia.

Rise of organized warfare as social and political response to changed economic circumstances in wake of Agricultural Revolution due to ownership of land; Age of Confrontation in art, with portrayals of fights, disputes, aggression, fighting, confrontation, wars, killings, human sacrifice, chaos.

c7000 First vestiges of Indus valley civilization, which flourishes for 5,000 years until BC 2000; BC 4000, rise of Vedism; BC 2500, Mohenjo Daro and Harappa built as Indus valley's largest cities; Indus valley script similar to that of Easter Island, in Pacific.

6500 First large ships appear, in eastern Mediterranean and on river Nile.

c5800 First use of metals: copper, lead, gold; later, weapons and tools; 3200, international trade using gold and silver.

5600 Chalcolithic period: Early 5600-5000, Middle 5000-4000, Late 4000-3500.

5000 Development of temple towns, concurrent with human sacrifice, inflicted death, and religiously-related warfare; rise of city-states, specialized trades and industries.

Use of explosives known in India; BC 221, Carthaginian general Hannibal uses explosives against Rome; AD 673, Byzantine Greeks use 'Greek fire' to destroy Arab fleet.

c5000 Central America: riverine villages with rudimentary agriculture begin in Maya lowlands.

4600 Rudiments of Chinese logographic system of writing formed; widespread by BC 2000; Chinese literature begins BC c1400.

c4500 Mesopotamia: growth of polytheism in Sumerian pantheon of city gods; 4400, Ubaid culture in southern Mesopotamia leads by BC 3100 into Sumerian civilization (world's oldest urban literate culture); numerous cities, with monumental mud-brick temples as representations of the Cosmos.

4236 Egyptians adopt solar calendar, first use of hieroglyphics; copper and glass introduced; first nation to develop culture, and first to leave traditions to posterity.

4004 Date of Creation of world (at 9am on Sunday 23 October) as computed from Book of Genesis by Irish archbishop James Ussher of Armagh (AD 1581-1656; first person to construct a mathematical model to describe reality, and first serious biblical chronology).

Noah, told by God to build an ark, attempts to warn his generation until it becomes too late (Genesis 6).

4000 The biblical Flood (Deluge; Genesis 6-8): many massive local floods overwhelm Ur and lower Mesopotamia; Noah survives, with sons Japheth (father of Indo-European peoples), Shem (Semitic peoples), Ham (Canaan and African peoples); similar Flood tradition held by 90 other peoples worldwide including Babylonians, Assyrians, Persians, Egyptians, Greeks, Italians, Aztecs, Mayas, Incas, Mixtecs,

Zapotecs, and many others on 6 continents.
Second foreshadowing of later Great Commission, by God to Noah after the Flood: 'Be fruitful and multiply, and fill the earth' (Genesis 9:1, RSV).
Formal records begin (administration, storage, history), including first Table of Nations, or petty states (later recorded in Genesis 10, et alia).
Earliest roots of Vedism (Hinduism), in Iran and in Indus valley civilization; 2500, Aryan fire-sacrifice cult in Iran; 2000, Aryans begin migration to India; 1500, origin of Vedas in archaic Sanskrit; Hindu religion regards Cosmos as undergoing infinite number of deaths and rebirths, with a day and night of Brahma being 8.64 billion years long.

3800 Origin of counting and censuses, in Mesopotamia: systems of revenue control involving enumeration of persons capable of paying taxes; earliest mathematical calculations.

3700 Invention of wheel in Near East; BC 3000, wooden disc wheels on axles in use in Sumeria; BC 2000, spoked wheels on chariots in Syria and Egypt; BC 500 used by Celts in Europe.

3500 Early Bronze Age: rise of first literate civilizations in Mesopotamia and Egypt, as result of unlimited wealth due to irrigation and far-flung trade; c3200, Egypt changes suddenly and abruptly from a neolithic culture to an advanced one (copper tools, architecture, palaces, temples, written language, pyramids, etc.), with mathematical and scientific knowledge similar to Amerindian empires; all probably derived from survivals of Atlantean civilization.
World's largest city: Abydos capital of Egypt, with 20,000 population; then BC 3000 Memphis (40,000), BC 2240 Akkad, BC 2100 Lagash (100,000), BC 1990 Memphis (100,000, with 10,000 priests), BC 1770 Babylon, BC 1595 Thebes, then Memphis, BC 668 Nineveh (120,000), BC 612 Babylon (200,000), BC 479 Sravasti, BC 400 Rajagriha (capital of North India), BC 320 Alexandria (over 300,000), BC 300 Patna, BC 220 Hsienyang, BC 190 Changan, BC 170 Seleucia, AD 1 Rome.

c3500 Origin of acupuncture in China (earliest written reference BC 500); only healing system to have endured to present day unchanged over time.
First time-measuring device, gnomon (a vertical pillar); BC 800, sundial; AD 50, water-clock; later candle-clocks, sandglasses; AD c1250, first true mechanical clocks.

c3400 Invention of abacus in Mesopotamia (calculating board with manually-operated storage aiding a human calculator); widespread use in everyday life to present day; in universal use in Middle Ages throughout Europe, Middle East and Asia.

c3300 Origins in Mesopotamia of astrology, a pseudoscience postulating influence of planets and stars on earthly affairs in order to predict or affect destinies of individuals, groups or nations; first codified in Babylon c1750 in cuneiform text *Enuma Anu Enlil* devoted to celestial omens.

3200 Bronze Age, beginning in Greece (BC 1800 in China); average human life span 19 years, later increasing during Roman empire to 23, Middle Ages to 35, 1970s to 70 (in Western world), AD 2000 to 90, and by AD 2020 to 97 years.

3120 Beginning of Dark Ages (Kali Yuga, the final era), on Hindu calendar.

3100 Era of great empires in Mesopotamia: Sumerian (3100-2400), Akkadian (2400-2100), Sumerian Ur III (2100-2000), Old Babylonian (2017-1794), Assyrian (c1100-746), Neo-Assyrian (746-606), Neo-Babylonian (626-539).
Writing (expressing linguistic elements by conventional visible marks) first appears (logo-syllabic) among Sumerian (Akkadian) farmers in Mesopotamia, recording stock holdings on lumps of clay; cuneiform syllabaries; of world's 7 logo-syllabic systems up to present, 3 remain as yet undeciphered.
First united kingdom in Egypt under king Menes; kings buried in stone tombs.

c3100 City of Memphis founded by pharaoh Menes, with by BC 3000 a population of 40,000.

c3000 Proto-Indo-European, ancestor of English and other languages, is parent tongue of nomads roaming southeast European plains, and from Baltic to Iranian plateau; c2500, begins to break up, eventually producing Sanskrit by BC 2000, Greek by BC 800, and Latin by BC 500.
Rise of kingdoms: main function of the king is to ensure justice for all his subjects (Mesopotamia, Egypt), to restore balance between the rich and powerful and the poor and powerless; c2600, Mis-anni-padda king of Ur, first recorded ruler in Mesopotamia.
Egyptian logo-syllabic system of writing invented; in use up to AD 400; most Egyptian pharaohs however illiterate, relying on scribes.
Earliest books, papyrus rolls in Egypt; c2300, first libraries collected, in Egypt.
Phoenicians (Canaanites) settle in Byblos (Lebanon) as sea-traders and colonizers, develop farflung network of global commerce throughout area of old Atlantean empire, with 300 cities on west coast of Africa alone.
Minoan (Eteocretan) or Bronze Age (Aegean) sea empire and civilization in Crete; develops earliest form of written Greek; BC c1450, destroyed with its capital Cnossos by volcanic eruption and giant tidal wave.

c2900 Tower of Babel, a 7-story ziggurat symbolizing Cosmos according to Babylonian religious system centered on astrology, with 12 signs of the Zodiac on its top; mankind divided into separate peoples and languages and dispersed across Earth. (Genesis 11:1-9).

c2800 Invention of plough in Egypt and Mesopotamia, then Palestine, Roman and Greek empires, China; but not introduced into central Europe until AD c1050.
Mother goddess Inninn and son Tammuz worshipped as chief Sumerian deities (also for Egyptians, Hittites, Phoenicians, Scandinavians, et alii); c2200 in Egypt, resurrection cult of Isis and Osiris.

2680 Pyramids of Egypt built during Old Kingdom, over next 400 years; oldest, and only one remaining, of ancient Seven Wonders of World; c2500, Great Pyramid of Giza (Cheops, Khufu) with 2.3 million colossal stone blocks, whose interior is later held to be 'the Bible in stone', a divine prophecy of whole of 6,000-year history including Christian era to End of the World in either AD 1881, or 1936, or 1953, or 2001.

2600 Epic of Gilgamesh, oldest surviving creation narrative, in Akkadian language of Mesopotamia.

2500 Emergence of mathematics (numerical, algebraic, geometrical methods) in Babylonia.

c2500 Ink invented in China.
Use of metal as money introduced, in Middle East.
Concern for condition of the poor and needy appears in Middle East; origins of apocalypticism (the divine reversal of fortunes) in Babylonia, later in Zoroastrianism (c550) and in Hebrew prophecy.

2450 World's main cities: (Egypt) Heliopolis, Memphis, Abydos, Thebes, Aswan; (Mesopotamia) Sippar, Kish, Nippur, Erech (Uruk), Lagash, Ur, Eridu, Susa, Nuzu; (northern Syria) Byblos, Ebla; by BC 1750 Assur, Nineveh, Haran, Mari, Babylon, Asyut.

2350 Sargon the Great (reigned BC 2334-2279) conquers Sumerians, establishes first great empire known to history, from capital city of Akkad (Mesopotamia).

2200 Proto-Indic logo-syllabic system of writing invented in Indus valley.
Egypt ruled by Hyksos (Shepherd Kings), till their overthrow in 1550.

2150 Babylonian creation epic *Enuma Elish*: creation was due to conflict of deities, Tiamat goddess of darkness and chaos being slain by Marduk supreme god of Babylonians.

2100 Nomadic Amorites (Amurru, Martu) invade Mesopotamia, rule Babylon, and dominate Palestine for 600 years until defeated by Hittites and Kassites.

2003 Fall of religious center Ur of the Chaldees, capital of southern Mesopotamia, Sumeria, with its ziggurat of moon god (founded BC c3500, abandoned BC c350); Elamites capture city and end Ur's 3rd Dynasty.

2000 Large numbers of petty human states and governments emerge; warfare becomes widespread.
Earliest postal systems (mounted messengers, later posthouses) operate in Egypt and by BC 1000 in China under Chou dynasty; by BC 650 in Persian empire; then across Roman empire, Arab empire, and pre-Columbian civilizations of America.

c2000 First stirrings of urban-industrial mass society: vast bureaucracies rule Egypt and Babylonia, embryonic mass-production factories in ancient Greece and Rome, oil drilled in Greece in BC 400 and in Burma in AD 100.

GOD'S NEW CREATION BEGINS: GOD'S PLAN OF GLOBAL REDEMPTION

1950 Beginning of divine election of a chosen People of God to be repository of ethical monotheism; call of Abraham, first Hebrew patriarch, father of monotheism, who migrates (at age 75) as first missionary from Ur of the Chaldees to Palestine ('Go: in you all the families of the Earth will be blessed'), dies 100 years later; son Isaac has son Jacob who has 12 sons, ancestors of Twelve Tribes of Israel. (Genesis 12).
Beginning of God's self-revelation to human race (*Heilsgeschichte*, salvation history) as later recorded in Judaeo-Christian Scriptures; record unfolds around cities (1,230 references in Bible, with hundreds more on specific cities) with negative image of cities as evil from Enoch, Babel, Sodom (Genesis 4-19) on through to Great Babylon (Revelation 17), but later includes positive image from refuge cities (Joshua 20) to New Jerusalem (Revelation 22).
Biblical mandate for world evangelization begins, ultimately resting on 4 great commissions: (1) the commission to Abraham (Genesis 12:1-3: 'Leave', 'Go'), (2) the 'Great Commission for Israel' (Psalm 96:3: 'Declare my glory among the nations'), (3) the Great Commission of Jesus to the 12 ('Make disciples'), (4) the commission to Paul ('Bring about obedience to the faith among all nations', Romans 1:5).

c1900 Destruction of Sodom and Gomorrah by ear thquake, then covered by Dead Sea in Palestine. (Genesis 19).

c1800 Stonehenge megalithic monument erected in south Britain under Cretan influence as temple of sky worship and astronomical calendar clock.

c1780 Babylonian king Hammurabi (c1820-1750) issues comprehensive code of Sumerian laws; scholars use advanced mathematics.

1766 Chinese civilization develops under Shang dynasty (1766-1122) along Yellow river; script writing, bronze tools and weapons; succeeding Chou dynasty (1122-221) develops mathematics, astronomy, copper coins, silk textiles, iron tools and weapons.

1730 Joseph, great-grandson of Abraham, becomes adviser to pharaoh of Egypt.

1720 Descendants of Jacob enslaved in Egypt, 1700-1290.

1650 Emergence of 'the poor' (mentioned 245 times in Old Testament, under 6 main terms) as major category of God's concern throughout history ('the privilege of the poor' = God's preferential option for the poor).
1600 Origin of alphabet at Byblos: North Semitic (Canaan and North Phoenicia) with 22 letters; alphabetic Early Hebrew writing in ink develops soon after.
c1600 Myth of annunciation, miraculous conception, birth and adoration of Egyptian sky god Horus.
1595 Hittites conquer Babylonians and destroy Babylon.
1500 Vedas, holy writ of Hinduism, compiled from oral traditions (BC 1500-600).
c1500 Heyday of kingdom of Tartessus, 'Venice of the West', Atlantic Spanish port (biblical Tarshish—21 references), peopled by Tartessians, formerly colonized by Atlantis (with Rio Tinto copper mines, records and a literature both since BC 6500, and ability to sail Atlantic); prospers from trade with Phoenicians and Carthaginians; BC 533, destroyed by latter, vanishes without a trace.
Mycenaean (Late Helladic) prehistoric Late Bronze Age civilization in mainland Greece centers on Achaean Greek capital city of Mycenae, with Mycenaean as oldest known form of Greek language; mythology of Greek gods develops.
1468 Battle of Megiddo: pharaoh Thutmose III of Egypt invades Palestine and defeats Canaanites in first recorded strategic battle in history.
1375 Akhenaton (Amenhotep, c1400-1362), religious reformer and first recorded monotheist, rules as pharaoh in Egypt; succeeded by son Tukankhamen (1370-1352), later by Seti I (reigned 1318-1304).
1360 World's 5 largest cities: Thebes in Egypt (100,000 people), Memphis 74,000, Babylon 54,000, Chengchow 40,000, Khattushas (Hattusa) 40,000.
1300 Chinese logo-syllabic system of writing invented in China.
c1300 Climatic conditions reach catastrophically high temperatures worldwide.
God reveals himself to Moses (c1370-1250) in theophany of the burning bush and on Mount Sinai; God's name revealed as tetragrammaton YHWH (Yahweh, Jehovah). (Exodus 3:1-22).
1292 Rameses II (reigned 1304-1237) pharaoh of Egypt.
c1290 Planets Venus and Mars pass close to Earth disturbing its rotation, axis inclination, and magnetic field, causing many phenomena in the Exodus and subsequent Israelite history. (I. Velikovsky, *Worlds in collision*, 1950).

EXODUS OF ISRAELITES FROM EGYPT: GOD'S ENUMERATING BEGINS

c1290 Moses leads 72,000 Israelites out of Egypt after the Ten Plagues; 40 years' wanderings in wilderness; Moses receives the Law on Mount Sinai, dies at 120 years.
Mosaic covenant shows God giving special attention to the poor, humble and disinherited.
c1280 Ark of the Covenant, golden shrine of Presence of Yahweh (symbol of divine immanence), with golden mercy seat, containing 2 tablets of the Law, and located in Tabernacle (tent, portable sanctuary), travels from Mount Sinai to Jericho, Shiloh, finally to Solomon's Temple in Jerusalem; disappears BC c600. (Exodus 37, 2 Samuel 6:7; interpreted by E. von Daniken, *Raiders of the Lost Ark*, 1981, as electrical condenser used by Moses to communicate with alien spaceship).
c1270 Bible (beginning with 5 Books of Moses, Pentateuch) enumerates, in order to match up, 2 distinct entities: (1) the world of Gentile nations as harvest field (numbered at 70, see earliest ethnological Table of Nations in history in Genesis 10, etc), and (2) the People of God as harvesters, or harvest force, or people concerned with God's harvest plans—e.g. 70 descendants of Israel (Exodus 1:5), 70 elders (Exodus 24:1), censuses in Numbers, later Jesus' Mission of the 70 (Luke 10:1), etc.
1260 *Leviticus* and *Deuteronomy* contain detailed legislation to prevent accumulation of wealth, often linked in Bible with injustice and exploitation, as it leads to sin, pride, false security.
1250 Joshua leads first stage of invasion of Canaan, with fall of Jericho; later leaders known as Judges.
1150 Emergence of Olmecs, first pre-Columbian civilization of Meso-America on gulf coast of Mexico; stone monuments, picture writing; disappears by BC 800.
1100 Iron Age begins, in Europe and Near East.
Aramaic (Chaldean) comes into widespread use as lingua franca of Near Eastern official circles during Assyrian period, to BC 605; 850, Aramaic alphabet invented, replacing Early Hebrew; 550, serves as vernacular of Palestine (and so of Jesus) until 9th century AD.
1057 Great Comet in sky first noted, in Chinese literature, seen as harbinger of disaster and divine wrath; regular comet appearances seen thereafter, including BC 613, 467, 240, 12, AD 66, 1066, 1301, 1466, 1517, 1531, 1577, 1607, 1682, 1758, 1910, up to 1986 (Halley's returns every 76 years); held to explain Noah's flood, Star of Bethlehem, et alia.
c1030 Reign of Saul as king of united Israelite kingdom, 1030-1010, with population of around 500,000.
1010 Reign of David as king of Israel, 1010-970.
970 Reign of Solomon as king of Israel, 970-931; 959, first Temple built; at his death, split into Northern Kingdom (Israel) until 722 (all 19 kings being recorded as evil) and Southern Kingdom (Judah) until 586 (10 out of 19 kings being recorded as evil).
950 First full alphabetic system of writing derived by Greeks; later, alphabets invented for Aramaic, Classical Hebrew, Latin, up to several hundred by today.
Large-scale spread of urbanization through northern Chinese independent city-states.
880 Age of Hebrew prophets (with years of ministry): in Israel, Elijah (869-840), Elisha (855-795), Amos (785-750), Jonah (780), Hosea (760-735); in Judah, Isaiah (740-680), Micah (730-715), Zephaniah (628), Nahum (614), Jeremiah (626-580), Habakkuk (605); during Exile, Ezekiel (598-560), Daniel (570-535); after Exile, Haggai (520), Zechariah (520), Obadiah (490), Malachi (430), Joel (420).
870 Drought in Israel for 3½ years (the stereotyped period of evil and distress) under prophet Elijah. (Luke 4:25, James 5:17).
776 Two-decked ships originate in Tyre.
Olympic Games first celebrated, at Olympia, Greece; held at intervals until 290th Games in AD 390, then in 393 banned by emperor Theodosius; 1896, Olympiad revived in Greece as world's foremost amateur sports competition.
c 770 Amos and subsequent Hebrew prophets announce and proclaim a legal dispute or controversy between Yahweh and all pagan nations with their gods; in their trial, Israel's mission is as witness to Yahweh's character, activity and purpose in world.
c 760 Hebrew prophets take up defence of poor and needy, as victims of social crises; denounce poverty as an evil, attack all forms of economic and political oppression, taxes, fraudulent trade, seizure of land, injustice and violence.
753 Founding of city of Rome; year from which Romans subsequently reckoned dates (AUC, anno urbis conditae, or ab urbe condita).
733 Assyrian king Tiglath-pileser III plunders Israel, destroys Megiddo, raises Assyria to renown and power.
722 Fall of Samaria: end of Northern Kingdom of Israel; 27,290 leading citizens taken into captivity; disappearance of the Ten Lost Tribes of Israel.
c 700 Delphi Oracle, with major temple of Apollo, flourishes as center of Greek world and center of political prediction until finally eclipsed in AD 362.
650 World's 5 largest cities: Nineveh 120,000, Loyang 117,000, Yenhsiatu 108,000, Memphis 99,000, Chicheng 91,000.
c 650 Latin alphabet, adapted from Etruscan alphabet (invented BC 800).
c 631 Coined metallic money invented by Lydians (a Greek state in Asia Minor); 594, Greek silver drachma introduced; 450, coinage begins to be minted by Phoenicians; 269, Romans introduce silver denarius; AD c1800, paper money and banknotes spread widely.
623 Religious reform under Judean king Josiah based on Book of the Law (Deuteronomy) rediscovered in Temple; all foreign cults abolished; 609, Josiah killed at Megiddo.
606 Jewish youth Daniel taken captive to Babylon, interprets Nebuchadnezzar's dream (Daniel 2) as vision of the end-time with rise of 4 great powers, with interpretation varying down the centuries from the traditional view (Babylonian, Medo-Persian, Greek, Roman empires) to modern premillennial views (Hitler's Germany, USSR, Egypt [Islam], Iraq [Babylon, Assyria]; et alia).
600 Birth of Lao Tzu, traditional father of Taoism in China.
c 600 Egyptian navigators circumnavigate Africa under pharaoh Necho II.

Ionian Awakening: birth of science and technology

c 600 Greek island of Samos: Phoenician alphabet, literacy and mercantilism result in awakening of science across Ionia, teaching orderly nature of Universe as *cosmos*: Thales of Miletus (scientific worldview), Anaximander (astronomy), master engineer Theodorus (engineering), Hippocrates (medicine), Democritus (theory of atoms), Anaxagoras (experiments), Pythagoras (mathematics: Earth is a sphere, Cosmos is orderly), Aristarchus (heliocentric Universe); astrology widely regarded as a science; Attic Ionic, the literary language, becomes basis for Koine (Common Speech) of later Greek writing including New Testament; Ionian awakening finally destroyed BC c300 by its own slave-based economy.
597 First Babylonian destruction of Jerusalem, with looting of Temple; however, city not razed, walls remain, so further Jewish revolt later.
c 590 Persian religious reformer Zoroaster (628-551) replaces Iranian polytheism with worship of supreme god Ahura Mazda; 546, Zoroastrianism spreads under Cyrus.

EXILE OF JEWS IN BABYLON AND THEIR RETURN

586 Final fall of Jerusalem, obliterated by Nebuchadnezzar II (c630-562), Temple burnt and razed, walls broken down: end of Southern Kingdom of Judah; Jews exiled to Babylonia until 538 when Persian ruler Cyrus allows return.
575 Greek thinker and founder of astronomy Anaximander of Miletus (610-c540) develops first cosmology and first map of the world, believes in infinite number of worlds, all inhabited, all rising or falling.
557 Mahavira (c599-527), last of 24 Tirthankaras (prophets) who founded Jainism in India, attains *kevala-jnana* (highest knowledge) and advocates

nonviolence, vegetarianism and renunciation.

551 Birth of Confucius, dies 479; Confucianism remains ideology of ruling class and central core of Chinese religion for 2,400 years.

550 Greek philosopher and mathematician Pythagoras (c 580-c 500) develops number mysticism, becomes first to use word *cosmos* to denote well-ordered and harmonious universe.

Dawn of European science begins with philosophers of Greek city-states: Thales, Zeno, Plato, Aristotle, et alii.

Israel begins to transcend its nationalistic exclusivism; aided by apocalypticism, arrives at sense of God's mission to all peoples of the whole world; then progressively compromises its mission in the world through disobedience and unbelief.

Temple of Artemis (Diana) built at Ephesus by Croesus king of Lydia, 300 x 150 feet; 356, burned, later rebuilt.

c 540 Roman census of population founded by king Servius Tullius (578-534); 10 enumerations held before first formal census in BC 435 under direction of censorate, then elaborate censuses every 5 and a half years until time of Christ.

539 Fall of Babylon to Medo-Persians under Cyrus king of Persia; 538, first return of Jews to Jerusalem (under Zerubbabel/Sheshbazzar and Jeshua); 458, second return (under Ezra).

537 Foundations of new Temple laid; 515, completed under Zerubbabel; small and unpretentious.

528 Siddhartha Gautama (c563-483) becomes a supreme buddha (enlightened one) at Buddh Gaya, India; Buddhism spreads from India to central and southeast Asia, then to China, Korea, Japan, et alia.

520 First Celtic tribes (Gauls, Galli, Galatai, Galatians) advance into Italy; sack Rome in 387, then 386 Spain, Illyria; 275, widespread land seized; Celts unchecked throughout half Europe as far as Greece, Hungary, Romania and Galatia (Anatolia); 226, Carthaginians under Hasdrubal conquer southeastern Spain, Hannibal crosses Pyrenees and Alps.

519 Crucifixion introduced by Persians for rebels, pirates, slaves, religious agitators and criminals of lowest classes, with emperor Darius I crucifying 3,000 political opponents in Babylon; BC 260, introduced in Roman empire; AD 330, finally abolished by Constantine the Great.

500 Origin of Latin; BC 100, emergence of Classical Latin, holds undisputed sway until after AD 200.

486 Persian king Xerxes I (Ahasuerus; c519-465), husband of Jewish Esther, succeeds as king of Persia; 480, defeated by Greek fleet at Salamis.

447 Greek statesman Pericles (c 495-429) builds Parthenon as temple of Pallas Athene patron goddess of Athens, completed 432; houses Athene's giant ivory and gold statue.

445 Restoration of walls of Jerusalem under Nehemiah as governor on his first return; 432, his second visit.

430 Statue of god Zeus built at Olympia, over 30 feet tall, plated with gold and ivory; destroyed in AD 426.

World's 5 largest cities: Babylon 250,000, Ecbatana 200,000, Athens 155,000 (50,000 citizens, 100,000 slaves), Sravasti (Savatthi) 150,000, Champa 150,000.

414 Greek dramatist Aristophanes (450-388) writes *The Birds*, earliest work of science fiction known; is also first to use Greek verb *euangelizesthai* (as secular term meaning 'to carry good news'); term later used by Greek orator and statesman Demosthenes (384-322).

c 390 Athenian philosopher Plato (428-348) writes *Myths* postulating Sun's planets are home of departed spirits; also writes history of Atlantis.

PREPARATION FOR GOD'S MESSIAH: THE INTER-TESTAMENTAL PERIOD

387 Gauls defeat Roman army on the Allia, advance on Rome, burn it and besiege Capitol.

c 380 Oriental mystery religions arise, a plethora of fertility cults from Middle East featuring death-resurrection mythology, initiation, personal salvation now and bliss hereafter; notably cults of Dionysus, Cybele the Great Mother, Isis, Mithra; spread westwards through Greco-Roman world by means of migration, trade and military service; major syncretistic rivals to Christianity; died out by AD 480.

347 Greek philosopher, logician and scientist Aristotle (384-322) writes extensively on logic, art, ethics, politics, mechanics, zoology and the 4 elements doctrine; world's first and greatest scholar.

333 Palestine successively under Greeks (Alexander the Great); Ptolemies of Egypt, 323-198; Seleucids of Syria, 198-166.

c 300 Cursus Publicus, most highly-developed postal system and extensive messenger service of ancient Roman world, with relay stages covering 170 miles in 24 hours; persists until AD c820.

292 Colossus of Rhodes built over next 12 years: bronze statue of sun god Helios, over 100 feet tall.

290 Berossus, Chaldean priest of Bel in Babylon, compiles 3-volume history of Babylon and the world; first volume estimates time from Creation to Flood at 432,000 years.

c 290 Septuagint translation begun from Hebrew OT into Greek (LXX, from 70 or 72 Jewish translators in Alexandria); completed c150.

285 Great Library of Alexandria founded by Ptolemy kings of Egypt, finest in world, for all disciplines and subjects; first true research institute in history for study of the Cosmos; around 1 million handwritten volumes at its height; partially destroyed in BC 48 under Caesar, further destroyed as pagan by Christians in AD 411, finally destroyed by Muslim rulers in AD 642 with all volumes irrevocably lost without copies surviving.

280 Pharos of Alexandria, lighthouse built by Ptolemy II off Alexandria, over 440 feet high.

250 Gypsies emerge as Romany-speaking race in central India; AD 1000, begin emigrations out of India, taking Indic grammar and vocabulary; c1400, arrival across Europe.

246 Buddhism thrives in India under king Asoka, spreads into Ceylon.

232 Great Wall of China built, joining existing stretches into a continuous boundary for 1,920 miles, as defense against Huns.

200 Rise and spread of apocalyptic millennial beliefs and writings (as a solution to this-worldly triumph of evil) in Judaism and early Christianity until discredited by AD 450.

World's 5 largest cities: Patna (Pataliputra) 350,000, Alexandria 300,000, Seleucia 300,000, Changan 239,000, Loyang 189,000.

c 200 Human race enters Age of Pisces (the Fishes), according to zodiacal theory; a New Age leading to the Christian Era and lasting for 2,160 years.

Druids, learned priestly class among Celts in Gaul and Britain, with Hindu Brahmins in India, form last survivors of an ancient Indo-European priesthood.

167 Antiochus IV Epiphanes, Seleucid king of Syria, forces hellenization on Judaism, enters Jewish Temple (the Abomination of Desolation, or the Horrifying Blasphemy), attempts to replace worship of Yahweh by that of Olympian Zeus; crucifies lawbreaking Jews; origin and archetype of long series of antichrists throughout Christian Era.

166 Jewish revolt under Judas Maccabeus (died 161) reestablishes Jewish independence; his descendants, Hasmoneans, rule Palestine for next hundred years.

146 Destruction of city of Carthage (population 500,000) by Romans; only 50,000 survive to be sold into slavery.

103 Alexander Jannaeus (died 76) becomes king of Judea, culmination of Hasmonean dynasty; all hellenism destroyed; 90, Pharisees lead 6-year revolt against king, who crucifies 800 Pharisee rebels.

c 100 Vast majority of books in world are located in Great Library of Alexandria, with a million books, and about 50,000 more in China; all handwritten.

67 100,000 perish in rebellions in Palestine over next 40 years.

63 Roman general Pompey (106-48) captures Jerusalem, enters Holy of Holies but finds it empty; Palestine ruled by puppet kings including Herod the Great (BC 73-BC 4).

60 First Roman Triumvirate (informal): Pompey (assassinated BC 48), Caesar, Crassus.

58 Gaius Julius Caesar (BC 100-44), history's greatest general, studies ethnography and statistics of peoples of Gaul, then in 10 years of Gallic wars by BC 51 destroys 800 towns and villages of Gaul and kills or enslaves 3 million men; 44, assassinated.

48 Large part of Great Library of Alexandria destroyed by fire in Julius Caesar's wars.

46 Old Style or Julian Calendar devised by Julius Caesar; AD 1582, replaced by New Style or Gregorian Calendar introduced by pope Gregory XIII; 1986, Old Calendar still followed by Orthodox Churches of Jerusalem, Russia, Serbia and Bulgaria, also by Old Calendarist churches.

43 Second Roman Triumvirate: Anthony, Octavian, Lepidus; 31, Octavian defeats Anthony at battle of Actium.

c 40 Targums (parts of OT in Aramaic) circulate in oral form, later written down.

29 Theravada Buddhist writings compiled in Ceylon.

27 Octavian (Gaius Octavius, BC 63-AD 14) becomes first Roman emperor, with title Augustus.

19 Herod the Great begins massive rebuilding of Jewish Temple in Jerusalem; finally completed AD 64, but destroyed AD 70.

5 Augustus' imperial census; family of Jesus participate in Bethlehem; end of regular Roman 5-yearly censuses, followed only by ones in AD 14, 47 and 72.

4 Total Homo Sapiens population born from origin of species to BC 4: 33,994 million persons.

COSMIC ERA II: WORLD EVANGELIZATION IN CHRISTIAN HISTORY

FIRST ADVENT OF JESUS CHRIST THE SON OF GOD: TWO AGES OVERLAP

BC

4 Birth of Jesus of Nazareth, one infant among 6,600,000 born on Earth that year; the Incarnation of the Word of God.
Death of Herod produces violent unrest; Roman legate of Syria has 2,000 Jews crucified.

AD

1 Beginning of Christian Era according to Dionysius (AD 525).

6 Removal of Archelaus, son of Herod; Judea and Samaria placed under direct imperial rule.
Uprising under self-proclaimed Jewish messiah, Judas the Galilean, opposing first Roman provincial census of AD 6; Judas killed, 2,000 followers crucified.

9 Varian disaster in Germany: 3 Roman legions under P. Quinctilius Varus strategically ambushed by German Cherusci north of Rhine and annihilated.

14 Imperial Roman census under emperor Tiberius (BC 42-AD 37).

c 20 Essene ascetics (Jewish Zealots) of Qumran (Dead Sea, from BC 153-AD 73) write *Rule of the War of the Sons of Light and the Sons of Darkness*, showing considerable awareness of Roman military tactics; suicidal revolt of Zealots against Rome in AD 66, savagely suppressed by Titus in AD 68.

23 Total number of Roman imperial troops: 330,000 in 25 legions, rising gradually to 350,000 by AD 70; annual pay of legionary soldier 225 denarii per year.

25 Chinese emperor Kuang Wu Ti founds Eastern Han dynasty, conquers Viet Nam, dies in 57; Buddhism introduced into China.

27 Roman empire (33 million, 50% slaves) has 2.3 million Jews (7% of population) a large proportion being proselytes; in Palestine, 580,000 Jews and 220,000 Gentiles; average life-span then 23 years.

30 Baptism of Jesus by John the Baptist; beginning of public ministry of Jesus of Nazareth.

31 Jesus proclaims nearness and imminence of the rule of God: 'The Kingdom of God is at hand' (Mark 1:15).
Jesus chooses Twelve Apostles including 4 of his first cousins and 2 zealots (Patriots or Essenes), gives them power and authority, commissions them to go initially only to Israelites (Matthew 10:1-6); later commissions Mission of the 70 disciples to evangelize the 70 Gentile nations (Luke 10:1).

32 Jesus envisages lightning spread of the gospel to all nations within one single generation: 'This Good News of the Kingdom will be proclaimed to the whole oikumene as a witness to all nations. And then the end will come' (Matthew 24:14, Jerusalem Bible. Oikumene = Graeco-Roman inhabited world); 'the end' partly fulfilled in Fall of Jerusalem in AD 70.

33 Crucifixion of Jesus (Friday 3 April), followed by resurrection (Sunday 5 April) and ascension 40 days later; final stage in beginning of God's New Creation in Christ.

THE GREAT COMMISSION: 'GO THROUGHOUT THE COSMOS'

Appearances of Jesus over 40-day period: the Gospels record 50 commands (25 universal) of the Risen Christ, culminating in Great Commission.
Jesus reveals himself to over 500 disciples on one occasion in Galilee (1 Corinthians 15:6).
Jesus' Great Commission as spiritual counterpart of Genesis 1:28 with 2 components of evangelizing and discipling: 'Go forth to every part of the world (in Greek, *Cosmos*), and proclaim the Good News to the whole creation' (Mark 16:15, NEB); 'Go to all peoples everywhere and make them my disciples' (Matthew 28:19, GNB); Jesus' presence from now on is the ever-present Shekinah glory.
Jesus gives Great Commission in a number of different forms at different times during the 40 days to different groups, including individuals, emphasizing the 7 mandates: Receive! Go! Witness! Proclaim! Disciple! Baptize! Train!
Total human population of genus Homo born since origin in BC 5,500,000 (220,000 generations ago): 117,841 million persons. Total Homo Sapiens population born since origin in BC 500,000 (20,000 generations ago): 34,241 million persons. Total Homo Sapiens Sapiens population born since origin in BC 45,000 (1,800 generations ago): 12,791 million persons. Total People of God (Old Israel) since Abraham's call in BC 1950 (79 generations ago): 52.5 million persons.
Overlapping of 2 Ages or Epochs or Cosmic Eras now under way as the Church Age: (1) The Present Age or Old Age (Kingdom or Rule of Satan; a pseudo-New Age terminating at Second Advent), and (2) the Next Age or New Age or New Creation or Messianic End-Time (Kingdom or Rule of God; beginning at Jesus' resurrection and continuing after Second Advent).

Epoch I: CHRISTIANITY WINS THE ROMAN EMPIRE AD 33-500

AD 33-80 The Apostolic Age

33 **Global status:** during 40 days' Appearances of the Risen Christ, total of Jesus' disciples = about 4,000; total evangelized by Jesus as result of last 3 years' ministry = whole of Palestine (800,000).
Day of Pentecost in Jerusalem: 3,000 converted among Diaspora Jews and Gentiles from 'every nation under heaven', from North Africa to Persia.
Palestine. First Christians, in Jerusalem; Twelve Apostles become founder members of the Church, not primarily missionaries, evangelists, bishops or local pastors.
Israel. First Christians (from Jerusalem on Day of Pentecost) return to homes across Judea.
Egypt, Lebanon (then Phoenicia), *Jordan* (Transjordan), *Libya, Syria.* First Christians (returning from Jerusalem after Day of Pentecost).
Italy. First Christians (returned from Jerusalem after Day of Pentecost).
Large-scale people movement of families and villages into the church: 'More than ever believers were added to the Lord, multitudes both of men and of women' (Acts 5:14).

34 Apostles (the Twelve plus others) begin evangelizing widely: several remain in Jerusalem for a decade or two, several travel outside, but most evangelize only Jews until AD 38 (Peter), 43 (Paul), and after AD 50 (others).

35 Twelve Apostles, declining gradually in influence, appoint 7 deacons to administer relief for Hellenistic Christian community, while they concentrate on evangelism; 'The number of disciples multiplied greatly in Jerusalem, and a great many of the priests were obedient to the faith' (Acts 6:1-7).

c 35 Proliferation of 'signs and wonders' among early believers (listed 9 times in Acts); miracles and healings at this time an everyday occurrence and an essential part of proclamation of the gospel; 'power evangelism' thus one of the normal kinds of evangelism in the Early Church.
Turkey (then called Asia Minor). First Christians (in Antioch, returned from Jerusalem after Day of Pentecost).
Armenia (now USSR). First Christians (returned from Jerusalem after Day of Pentecost); c65, traditionally evangelized by Thaddeus and Bartholomew.

36 Martyrdom of Stephen the protomartyr; Jewish persecution of Early Church, especially of Hellenistic Christians; believers scattered throughout Judea and Samaria.
Dismissal of Pontius Pilate (Roman Samnite knight, procurator of Judea since AD 26); recalled to Rome, kills himself AD 39 on orders from emperor Caligula.
Sudan. First Christians; gospel taken to Nubia (Meroe) by Ethiopian eunuch baptized by Philip the Evangelist.
Mission extended to Samaritans by Philip; fresh persecution.
Conversion of Saul of Tarsus (age 24), a Roman citizen; departs to Arabia, then in 40 to Jerusalem and Tarsus; later renamed Paul.

37 Church throughout Judea, Galilee and Samaria multiplied (Acts 9:31).

38 After 5-year period of hesitation and partial obedience to Christ's Great Commission, first Gentiles are deliberately evangelized by the Twelve Apostles.
Commission to evangelize pagan Gentiles as Gentiles first forced on consciousness of Jewish church, through baptism by Peter of Cornelius, a God-fearer but not a Jewish proselyte (Acts 10:1-48).

c 38 Large influx of Italians (Cohors II Italica Civium Romanorum) converted through ministry of apostle Peter at Caesarea (Acts 10:48).
Twelve Apostles, after 5 years' hesitation, scatter across globe spreading the gospel, from Ethiopia (Matthew), to Armenia (Bartholomew) to India (Thomas); all martyred over subsequent 60 years.

c 39 Antioch (population 130,000): wider mission to Gentiles inaugurated.
Ethiopia. First Christians (returning pilgrims from Jerusalem present on Day of Pentecost); c80, Christianity known and openly practiced by merchants from Roman empire settled in Axum, Adulis and region.

c 40 *Greece.* First Judeo-Christians.
Holy See (at that time, Rome). First Christians in capital of Roman empire.
Mandylion of Edessa: king Abgar V of Edessa (BC 4-AD 50) obtains alleged portrait of Jesus (Icon of Christ); seized by Muslims in AD 944, surfaces in Lirey (France) in 1389, then regularly seen thereafter; now known as Holy Shroud of Turin.

41 Roman emperor Caligula (AD 12-41) attempts to set up statue of himself in Jewish Temple in Jerusalem; first to be regarded by Christians as the Antichrist; murdered soon after.

42 Mark the Evangelist (c10-68) works in Egypt; 61, arrives in Alexandria, organizes Coptic church.

Phoenicia, Cyprus, Antioch: 'A great number that believed turned to the Lord' (Acts 11:21).

43 Barnabas and Saul (later called Paul) at Antioch, new centre for Hellenistic Christians, 500 strong; believers first called Christians, in derision (Acts 11:26).

Romans begin conquest of Britain (population about 1,500,000).

44 Persecution in Jerusalem under king Herod Agrippa I (BC 10-AD 44); apostle James brother of John executed; imprisonment and escape of Peter.

Jewish revolutionary and messianic claimant Theudas arrives at Jordan with multitude; defeated by Romans, crucified, beheaded.

46 Paul's 1st missionary journey (45-48), with Barnabas: Antioch, Cyprus, Pamphilia, Pisidia, Lycaonia; develops strategy of urban evangelization and urban ministry, moving from city to city or town to town.

Cyprus, Northern Cyprus. First missionaries (apostles Paul and Barnabas).

47 Imperial Roman census under emperor Claudius I (BC 10-AD 54).

48 *Iran* (at the time Persia). First Christians (Assyrians); after 13 years' mission by apostles Judas (Lebbaeus) and Simon Zelotes in teeth of Zoroastrian priestly hostility, over 100,000 converted in the 12 Persian provinces (60,000 in Babylon alone).

49 Apostolic Council of Jerusalem: converts from paganism exempted from Jewish Law; Paul recognized as apostle to non-Jews.

Jews and Christians banished from Rome under Claudius.

c 50 *Iraq* (then termed Media, et alia). First Christians (Assyrians, with apostle Thomas, evangelizing Jewish colonies).

Assyrian Christians found Church of the East (later Nestorian).

Roman empire reaches its operational limit, with expansion everywhere halted by oceans, dense forest, desert or steppe; subservient client-states therefore established on periphery, nominally independent but subject to indirect rule.

For 15 centuries, the term 'missio' (mission) is used by the church only as a divine concept, the Triune God (Trinity) moving out into the world; only used of the church being sent since AD 1550.

50 Paul's 2nd missionary journey (50-52): Phrygia, Galatia, Greece, Athens (population 270,000).

Paul begins evangelization of 3 important Roman provinces: Macedonia, Achaia and Asia (Acts 16:6).

52 *India.* First missionaries (apostle Thomas, and others, in the south).

53 Paul's 3rd missionary journey (53-57): Ephesus (2 years, 3 months), Corinth, Macedonia, Philippi.

54 Martyrdom of apostle James the Less (James son of Alphaeus, one of the Twelve), stoned to death in Jerusalem.

55 Roman province of Asia (500 cities) evangelized from capital Ephesus, seat of proconsul; in 2 years, 'All the residents of Asia heard the word of the Lord' (Acts 19:10).

57 Paul's *Letter to the Romans* sent to about 3,000 Christians in 5 congregations in Rome (population 800,000).

Paul describes spread of the gospel: 'The sound of their voice went out to all the world; their words reached the ends of the earth (oikumene)' (Romans 10:18, GNB).

Greek (eastern) half of Roman empire already evangelized by Paul: 'From Jerusalem and as far round as Illyricum (1,800 miles) I have fully preached the gospel of Christ' (Romans 15:19).

58 Paul arrested in Jerusalem, imprisoned for 2 years in Caesarea; 60, sent for trial to Rome.

Revolutionary messiah Benjamin the Egyptian arrives on Mount of Olives with 30,000 followers; annihilated by Romans under Felix.

60 *Malta.* First missionary (shipwrecked apostle Paul, and others).

c 60 *Yugoslavia* (at that time Dalmatia, Illyricum). First Christians (among Diaspora Jews).

Martyrdom of apostle Philip (one of the Twelve), crucified in Hierapolis (Turkey).

61 Paul in Rome under military guard; gospel proclaimed in capital of empire.

Paul writes: 'The Good News which has reached you is spreading all over the world' (Colossians 1:6, Jerusalem Bible); 'The Good News, which you have heard, has been preached to the whole human race' (Colossians 1:23; Greek 'to all creation under the sky').

Britain (later UK). First resident Christians (Roman soldiers, merchants); origins of Celtic church.

Revolt against Rome by British queen Boadicea, who massacres 70,000 Romans, then dies with 80,000 Britons.

Apostle Simon Zelotes (Zealot, Patriot; one of the Twelve) martyred, sawn in two and crucified in Persia.

62 James the Just, brother of the Lord, ascetic bishop of Jerusalem, thrown off temple parapet and murdered by stoning in Kedron valley; successor Symeon (a first cousin of Jesus) crucified in AD 108; 13 successor bishops of Jerusalem up to AD 135 are all also Jewish Christians.

63 Paul freed in Rome, visits Spain, Greece, Asia Minor.

Spain. First Christians (Roman soldiers, merchants, evangelized by Paul).

64 1st imperial Roman persecution of Christians, under emperor Nero (AD 37-68); many heroic martyrs (put to death) and confessors (tortured but surviving); Nero seen by seer of Revelation as first archetypal Antichrist, the beast whose symbolic number is 666 (= 'Caesar Neron').

Great Fire of Rome; apostles Peter and Paul martyred, thousands of Christians burnt, impaled, crucified or otherwise killed by Nero.

Temple of Herod in Jerusalem finally completed.

Apostle Matthias (one of the Twelve) martyred, crucified in Sebastopol.

65 Prophecies of John the Divine: 'I saw another angel flying high in the air, with an eternal message of Good News to announce to the peoples of the earth, to every race, tribe, language and nation' (Revelation 14:6, GNB).

Four Gospels compiled, from earlier sources and eyewitness accounts: 65 Mark, 70 Luke, 75 Matthew, 90 John.

66 Evangelist Luke concludes his 2-volume narrative (Luke-Acts): The worlds of empire and Judaism have now been evangelized, the Gospel is now known to all peoples throughout them, and the Great Commission there largely completed.

Anti-Jewish riots and pogroms in Egypt: 50,000 Jews massacred in Alexandria, 60,000 elsewhere.

Apostles Judas Thaddaeus and (in 68) Bartholomew (Nathanael) martyred, former by mob in Ardaze (Armenia), latter by flaying and crucifixion in Albana, Derbend (Armenia), with a thousand believers.

67 Emperor Vespasian (AD 9-79) with 60,000 troops quells Jewish insurrection, reconquers Galilee; Zealot leader Menachem grandson of Judas the Galilean proclaims self Messiah, captures Masada and Antonian fortress in Jerusalem; Christians of Jerusalem flee to Pella.

68 Martyrdom of apostle Mark in Baucalis, near Alexandria.

69 All 4 million Jews throughout diaspora now evangelized, 'having been destined to hear the good news before judgment falls'.

Martyrdom of apostle Andrew (one of the Twelve), crucified at Patras, Achaia.

9,000 mounted Roxolani (Iranian) warriors raid Roman province of Moesia, retreat laden with booty, but then are intercepted and cut to pieces by Roman legion III Gallica.

70 **Global status:** One generation after Christ, world is 0.1% Christians (85% of them being Non-Whites, 15% Whites), 15% evangelized; with Scriptures translated into 5 languages.

Obliteration of Jerusalem by Titus (AD 39-81) with 4 legions, with 'desolating sacrilege' ('abomination of desolation', i.e. Roman eagles) placed in Temple before its destruction; 600,000 killed in Judea, 10,000 Jews crucified, 90,000 Jews taken to Rome as slaves; Jews and Jewish Christians scattered abroad; destruction of Jewish Christianity and end of Judaizers.

After fall of Jerusalem, Antioch becomes Christian center of eastern half of Roman empire.

c 70 *Albania* (then Macedonia). First Christians (among Diaspora Jews).

Martyrdom of apostle Matthew (Levi, one of the Twelve), beheaded in Persia.

72 Imperial Roman census under emperor Vespasian; no further censuses until Charlemagne.

73 Romans capture Zealot stronghold of Masada; no survivors after mass suicide pact.

c 75 'The End will come only after a predetermined number of souls is born' (Syriac Apocalypse/II Baruch 23:4-5, cf Yebamoth 62a).

78 Kushan or Kusana empire (BC 50-AD 400) from Afghanistan to river Ganges in northern India under nomad Indo-Scythian dynasty and king Kanishka I ranks among world's 4 top empires along with China, Rome and Parthia; Kusanas send Buddhist missionaries to Central Asia and China.

79 Eruption of Mount Vesuvius, destroying cities of Pompeii, Stabiae and Herculaneum; over next 1,900 years, over 80 more major eruptions.

Colosseum (Flavian Amphitheatre) built in Rome, for 50,000 spectators; large numbers of Christians thrown to beasts or otherwise martyred.

'Signs and wonders' (miracles demonstrating Kingdom of God) do not cease with end of Apostolic age, nor with later closing of New Testament canon, but continue throughout church history as waves of prophecy, healing, deliverance, tongues.

AD 80-130 The Sub-Apostolic Age

c 80 *Tunisia* (then termed Roman province of Africa). First Christians.

Missionary centre of Christianity shifts to Ephesus under apostle John.

France. First Christians (from Italy).

82 Martyrdom of apostle Thomas (Didymus, one of the Twelve), murdered in Mylapore, India.

83 Schism divides Jainism in India into Digambaras and Svetambaras.

c 85 Writings of Apostolic Fathers (Apostolici), Greek Christian writers from 85-150: Barnabas, Clement, Hermas, Ignatius, Papias, Polycarp.

Epistle of Barnabas predicts end of world: 'In 6 days, that is in 6,000 years, the Universe will come to an end.'

90 Rise of Gnosticism, a dualistic rationalistic heresy; apogee 135-160.

Canon of Hebrew Scriptures finally fixed, through Jewish elders at Jamnia; 170, first termed 'Old Testament' by Melito of Sardis.

c 90 First of a vast number of amateur scripture translations in Old Latin.

West Germany. First Christians (merchants and Roman soldiers).

First autonomous diaspora church, in Persia; composed of Syrian residents.

91 2nd imperial Roman persecution, partly due to emperor Domitian (AD 51-96; a devotee of astrology) demanding worship as Dominus et Deus (Our Lord and God); regarded by Christians as Nero Redivivus, the Antichrist; apostle John martyred in boiling oil (or, miraculously survives).

94 Clement bishop of Rome maintains that under apostle Paul the entire Roman empire became evangelized.

96 *Revelation of John* compiled by seer on Patmos: apocalyptic, astral concepts and symbols; total opposition to state cult of emperor-worship under Domitian.
Last judgment and final retribution will not come until foreordained number of the martyrs has been completed (Revelation 6:11).
Chiliasm (premillennialism) dominant in first 3 centuries; taught by Clement of Rome, Ignatius of Antioch, Papias, Justin Martyr, Hippolytus, Irenaeus, Tertullian, Cyprian, Commodianus, Lactantius, Methodius, et alii; later by Waldensians, Anabaptists, 19th-century Protestants (E. Irving, J.N. Darby, J.H. Brooks, N. West, D.L. Moody, W.E. Blackstone, C.I. Scofield); 1980, held by majority of USA Evangelicals inter alios.

98 Roman emperor Trajan (AD 53-177) extends Roman empire to include Arabia, Iraq, Armenia, Romania, Hungary.

100 **Global status:** 2 generations after Christ, world is 0.6% Christians (70% of them being Non-Whites, 30% Whites), 28.0% evangelized; with Scriptures translated into 6 languages; total martyrs since AD 33, 25,000 (1.2% of all Christians ever; rate 370 per year).
Buddhism spreads across China.
Rome the first and only metropolis in world to reach or pass 1 million population (until AD 1770); slaves number 60%; by 450 falls to under 250,000, and to under 19,000 by 1360 due to Black Death; then rises to 1 million by 1930.
Saudi Arabia. First Christians; later eradicated in 7th century by Islam.
World's 5 largest cities: Rome 1,100,000, Loyang 510,000, Alexandria 400,000, Seleucia 300,000, Changan 245,000.
Teotihuacan (Mexico) established as America's first urban civilization, built around massive pyramids of the Sun and Moon; 45,000 in AD 150, 90,000 in AD 350; at its height in AD 590, city contains 160,000 people and controls empire covering all Meso-America; other centers Tikal, Mochica, Zapotec, Uaxactun, Pachacamac, Monte Alban.

c 100 *Monaco.* First Christians (soldiers, traders).
Algeria (at that time Roman province of Mauretania). First Christians (Latin-speaking).
Romania. First Christians (in Roman province of Dacia).
Christianity predominantly urban, based on Roman cities, spreading from city to city along trade routes; later missions to Armenia, Ethiopia, China (under Nestorians) all center on capital cities.
Sri Lanka (then Ceylon). First Christians (Christians of St Thomas from India; Nestorians).

110 3rd imperial Roman persecution, under emperor Trajan; 111, severe persecution in Bythinia.
Armenia: persecution of Christians by Persian tyrant Artaxerxes.

115 Martyrdom of Ignatius bishop of Antioch.

116 Jewish uprisings in Palestine, Egypt, Cyrene, Cyprus and Mesopotamia.

117 Roman emperor Hadrian (76-138) codifies laws of Rome, establishes postal system throughout empire; executes 11,000 soldier Christian converts, also 2 bishops of Rome—Sixtus I, and Telesphorus.
Gnostic thinker Basilides of Alexandria is first to treat New Testament writings explicitly as Scripture.

c 130 Christianity spreads principally and normally, though not exclusively, through (as prevailing strategy) the planting of churches which then serve as missionary communities to evangelize their areas by continuing to attract and enlist converts; most converts are reached through casual contacts, witnessing a martyrdom, hospitality and care of strangers, et alia.
Christianity instils exclusivistic claims for Christ through initiatory procedures (catechumenate, baptism, eucharist), disciplinary procedures (safeguarding purity of the church, also restoration of offenders), Scriptures, creed, apostolic ministry; stressing Christianity's absolute covenant claims in areas of monotheism, morality, and mission.

AD 130-312 Pre-Constantinian Post-Apostolic Era

132 Second Jewish rebellion under alleged messiah Bar Kokeba; 134, second destruction of Jerusalem by Romans; 580,000 Jews killed in battle; almost entire Jewish population of Palestine dies or flees; final dispersal of the Jews.

136 Hadrian refounds Jerusalem as pagan city Aelia Capitolina; temple of Jupiter built on site of Solomon's Temple.

c 140 Hermas writes: 'The Son of God... has been preached to the ends of the earth' (*Shepherd of Hermas*).

140 Valentinus, failing to be elected bishop of Rome, writes Gnostic treatise *Gospel of Truth*.

140 Egyptian astronomer-mathematician Ptolemy of Alexandria (c100-c151) codifies Babylonian astrological tradition, writes *Almagest* (geocentric cosmology, geometry), also *Guide to geography*; holds Earth is a sphere at center of Universe; uses conical projection to map whole world from Britain to China.

143 Origin of popular communal Taoist religion in China.

144 Wealthy ship-owner Marcion (c85-c160) excommunicated, founds schismatic, heretical, rival religion throughout Roman empire, influential till c400; first to specify a closed canon of New Testament writings; c700, Marcionism finally dies out.

150 Minor persecution under emperor Antoninus Pius.

c 150 Four Gospels available written in Old Syriac as harmony or continuous narrative in *Diatessaron* of Tatian, a Gnostic.
Mandaeanism, a Jewish-Christian Gnostic syncretistic religion, begun in Iran.
Morocco (then part of Roman province of Mauretania). First Christians (4 bishoprics in Tangier-Rabat-Fez area before 200).
Bulgaria (at that time Roman provinces of Moesia and Thracia). First Christians (churches at Anchialus and Debeltum, and along Black Sea).
Portugal (then Roman province of Lusitania). First Christians (Romans).
Justin Martyr (c100-165) founds disciple-training school over a house in Rome, documents current 'signs and wonders' (exorcisms, healings and prophesyings), and writes: 'The first Apostles, twelve in number, in the power of God went out and proclaimed Christ to every race of men'; and 'There is not one single race of men, whether barbarians, or Greeks, or whatever they may be called, nomads, or vagrants, or herdsmen dwelling in tents, among whom prayers and giving of thanks are not offered through the name of the Crucified Jesus'; teaches that all orthodox Christians believe in a resurrection of the flesh and in a millennial reign in the New Jerusalem; martyred at Rome.
Latin now common language of Christian communities in West, replacing Greek as language of church of Rome for its first 100 years.

156 Death at the stake of Polycarp bishop of Smyrna, aged 87 years.
Phrygia: rise of Montanism under new convert Montanus (c120-c175), a puritanical, prophetic, charismatic, millennial, apocalyptic movement claiming to be a new age of the Holy Spirit; 206, Tertullian joins; 230, movement excommunicated by Synod of Iconium; continues underground until c880.

160 Numerous 2nd-century Christian apologists at work, including Quadratus bishop of Athens (*Apology*, addressed to emperor Hadrian), Aristides (Athens), Justin Martyr, Tatian (110-172), Athenagoras (Athens), Theophilus bishop of Antioch, Melito bishop of Sardis (20 works), Hegesippus (a converted Jew).

165 4th imperial Roman persecution, under learned Stoic emperor Marcus Aurelius (121-180); issues New Decrees prohibiting all new religious cults.

c 170 Portions of Scripture in Coptic translated.

174 *Austria.* First Christians.

176 Celsus writes attacking Christianity, Christ and Judaism; his *True Discourse* is first significant published attack, with Platonic defence of polytheism; derides Christianity for its inclusion of hoi polloi (common people).

177 Violent persecutions in Lyons and Vienne, France.

180 Christians now found in all provinces of Roman empire and in Mesopotamia.
First African Christians martyred in Carthage: Scillitans from Scilli, Numidia.

c 180 Pantaenus founds missionary training school in Alexandria (Egypt); visits India, reports Christian activity in Malabar; dies 190.
Irenaeus bishop of Lyons (c120-203) documents recent charismata (exorcisms, visions, prophecies), and teaches that Antichrist will be a Jew of the tribe of Dan, also Christ will inaugurate a literal millennium of 1,000 years.
Gnostic *Gospels* and *Acts of Thomas* written.
Basis for a Christian apologetic and appeals for conversion has now become 6 institutions: baptism, eucharist, disciplinary procedures, Scriptures, apostolic ministry, extensive charities; and other factors including rescue from occult powers.
Method of printing text discovered, empirically, in China, using ink (BC 2300), paper (AD 105), and texts carved in relief; c550, wood blocks in use; oldest known printed works are Buddhist incantations printed in Japan AD 764; first book 'The Diamond Sutra' in China, AD 868; c1041, Chinese invent movable type.
Lucian writes 'Icaro-Menippos', to debunk Greek view of religion with its multiple deities.

c 190 New Testament in Latin completed; Victor bishop of Rome becomes first Roman Christian to write in Latin.
Widespread turning to Christianity, with vast numbers, in North Africa.
Synod of Ephesus, convened by bishop Polycrates of Ephesus, fixes official date of Easter but it is repudiated by Roman pope Victor I.

c 195 Rise begins of episcopal confirmation separate from baptism, with infant baptism followed later by confirmation (laying on of hands).

197 Tertullian (c160-222) documents recent healings and exorcisms, also writes: 'Christ commanded them to go and teach all nations. Immediately, therefore, so did the apostles'; 'The blood of the martyrs is seed'; and 'There is no nation indeed which is not Christian'; 206, joins Montanist movement.

200 **Global status:** 6 generations after Christ, world is 3.5% Christians (68.0% of them being Non-Whites, 32.0% Whites), 32.0% evangelized; with Scriptures translated into 7 languages; total martyrs since AD 33 have been 80,000 (0.5% of all Christians ever; rate 480 per year).
Most of New Testament available in Sahidic Coptic (Upper Egypt), later in Bohairic/Memphitic Coptic (Coastal or Lower Egypt around Alexandria).

c 200 *Switzerland* (then called Roman province of Raetia). First Christians (Roman soldiers, merchants).

Sahara (later Spanish, Western). First Christians; eradicated during later Muslim rule.
Belgium. First Christians (during Roman occupation).
First permanent church buildings constructed (all worship previously in homes); only in cities, at first.
Edessa (now Urfa) first city-state to make Christianity its state religion; conversion of its king Abgar IX (179-216), first Christian political ruler; missionary center for eastern Syria.
Mahayana Buddhist traditions take literary form in India; *Mahabharata* and *Ramayana*, once secular epics, now sacred Hindu texts.
202 5th imperial Roman persecution, under Septimius Severus (146-211); 202, emperor issues edict prohibiting conversions to Christianity or Judaism; vicious imperial persecution in Egypt with thousands martyred, especially in Thebes (100 a day) and Upper Egypt; in Carthage, Perpetua and Felicitas martyred; imminent appearance of Antichrist widely expected.
c 205 First known Christian scholar and apologist Clement of Alexandria (c155-215) deals with problem of how Christian faith relates to Greek philosophy and culture, writes: 'The whole world, with Athens and Greece, has already become the domain of the Word'.
c 210 *Qatar* (then Persian province of Beit Qatraiye). First Christians (first documents AD 224).
c 215 Tertullian (and almost all Christians up to AD 313) totally prohibits Christian military service; Christians generally oppose army, forbid believers becoming soldiers, and condemn all military warfare, though all use military idioms and metaphors in teaching and preaching; but by AD 250 opposition to army service changes and custom falls into disuse.
217 Roman presbyter Hippolytus attempts to oust new pope Calixtus I, but fails; 235, martyred; first of 40 such antipopes over next 1,200 years.
c 220 Origen (c185-254) writes: 'The gospel of Jesus Christ has been preached in all creation under heaven, to Greeks and barbarians, to wise and foolish... It is impossible to see any race of men which has avoided accepting the teaching of Jesus'; 'The divine goodness of Our Lord and Saviour is equally diffused among the Britons, the Africans, and other nations of the world'; and 'The preaching of the gospel through the whole Oikumene shows that the church is receiving divine support'; but also 'Many people, not only barbarians, but even in the Empire, have not yet heard the word of Christ'; and 'The gospel has not yet been preached to all nations, since it has not reached the Chinese or the Ethiopians beyond the river, and only small parts of the more remote and barbarous tribes'.
220 First Buddhist missions from India to Viet Nam, 272 to China and Korea, 420 to Burma, Java and Sumatra, 552 to Japan, 650 to Tibet, 720 to Siam.
221 First Christian synchronistic history of the world, correlating pagan and Judeo-Christian data from Creation to 221 AD: *Chronicles*, in 5 books by Sextus Julius Africanus (c170-after 240), a native of Jerusalem; also an encyclopedia of general knowledge called *Kestoi* in 24 books; only fragments of both works survive.
224 In river Tigris area, over 20 episcopal sees; also revival of Zoroastrianism (Parsi religion).
225 Over 20 Assyrian bishoprics of Church of the East in Tigris-Euphrates region and to Caspian Sea and Bahrain.
230 Amillennialism (rejecting a literal millennium of 1,000 years) taught by Origen, Constantine, Augustine of Hippo, then replaces premillennialism as majority view in Church of Rome and later Protestantism to present day.
Armenia: violent persecution under Persian king Shapur I almost blots out Christianity.
235 6th imperial Roman persecution, under Maximinus (Thrax; died 238).
Origen writes his *Exhortation to Martyrs*; 254, dies as martyr himself after imprisonment and torture.
c 240 Gregory Thaumaturgos (c213-270) made bishop of Pontus, a majority pagan diocese; mass movement begins, 95% converted before his death.
241 Zoroastrianism (Parsiism) becomes official state religion of Persia under Shapur I.
242 Rise of Manicheism under Mani (216-276), a dualistic hierarchical rival religion to Christianity; bitterly persecuted; vast missionary expansion, spreads west to Spain and east to China, until final decline in 15th century.
244 Christian hierarchy already established in northwest Arabia.
245 Violent local persecution in Alexandria.
248 Cyprian (200-258) bishop of Carthage insists on rebaptism of all baptized outside Catholic church, and writes: 'Extra ecclesiam nulla salus' (Letters).
249 7th imperial Roman persecution, under military ruler Decius (c201-251): first universal and systematic state attempt to destroy Christianity; first persecution aimed directly at the clergy and bishops, with sizeable defections; first mass appearance of *lapsi, libellatici, sacrificati, traditores*.
Seven missionary bishops sent to peoples of Gaul by Cornelius of Rome: Gatien (Tours), Trophime (Arles), Paul (Narbonne), Saturnin (Toulouse), Denis (Paris), Martial (Limoges), Austremoine (Clermont).
250 Over 100 bishoprics in southern Italy, all centered in urbanized cities.
Latinization of Roman Christianity, and emergence of 'interpretatio romana'.
c 250 *Hungary* (at that time Roman provinces of Pannonia and Valeria). First Christians (Arian, Roman and Orthodox missionaries).
Church founded in Chersonesus (Sebastopol), Crimea, Ukraine.
Bahrain. First Christians, with a bishopric.
Peshitta (Simple), Syriac version of Bible, completed.
Luxembourg. First Christians (Roman soldiers).
Mayan civilization in Yucatan, Guatemala and Honduras flourishes until 16th century; every aspect dominated by religion, with time (regarded as divine) as majestic succession of cycles without beginning or end; world believed to be over 400 million years old, preceded by several earlier created then destroyed universes.
251 City of Rome: 45,000 Christians (4.5% of population of 1 million), 46 presbyters, 14 deacons, 42 acolytes, 52 exorcists, supporting 1,500 widows and persons in distress at cost of $90,000 (US dollars 1985 value) each year; by AD 300, church buildings in Rome increase to over 40.
Roman field army under emperor Decius destroyed at Abrittus (Dobruja) by Goths, killing Decius and son.
Novatian (c200-258), first learned Roman theologian to write in Latin, emerges as second antipope in papal history, founding rigorist (anti-lapsi) Novatian schism; documents contemporary charismata (prophesyings, tongues, healings, miracles, powers); martyred 258, but his sect spreads across empire and lasts until after AD 600.
252 Catastrophic plague epidemic strikes Mediterranean world, kills 25% of entire population of Roman empire over 20 years; 50% die in Alexandria; in Carthage, bishop Cyprian organizes medical aid; followed by debased coinage, financial disaster, then by famine, earthquakes, tornadoes, and huge tidal waves.
257 8th imperial Roman persecution, under Valerian (1st Rescript, against all bishops and priests); 258, 2nd Rescript, of increased severity; martyrdom of Cyprian and Roman pope Sixtus II; 260, death of Valerian.
259 Wide-ranging Barbarian incursions into Roman empire: Alemannic invasion of Italy, reaching also to southern France and Spain, finally defeated at Milan by emperor Gallienus; cities now acquire heavily-protected walls.
260 Edict of Toleration, under Gallienus (died 268); Christianity becomes a *religio licita* until Diocletian.
Number of Christians in Roman empire about 40%, increasing very rapidly.
c 260 Neoplatonist polemicist Porphyry (c233-305) writes, as most bitter and dangerous enemy of Christianity, 15 books *Against Christians*, and a more general *Prophetic apology for Christ*.
261 First basilicas (rectangular churches) built.
c 270 Rise of monasticism in Egypt, as direct challenge to lifestyle of the rich: (1) eremitical (Anthony of Egypt, c251-356), (2) cenobitic (Pachomius, c287-346); widespread over next 2 centuries, with many documented healings, exorcisms, miracles, signs and wonders; Egyptian monks travel widely, evangelizing in Europe, Britain, Ireland et alia.
275 9th imperial Roman persecution, under Aurelian (c215-275) who plans major escalation but suddenly dies.
c 280 First rural churches emerge, in northern Italy, and by 4th and 5th centuries in France also; Christianity no longer exclusively urban.
285 Baptism of converts at Lake Zurich (Switzerland).
287 Mass conversion of Armenia begins under Gregory the Illuminator (c240-332), provoking violent persecution from pagan king Tiridates II; 295, king baptized, Christianity declared state religion; 301, Gregory becomes catholicos of Armenia and consecrates 400 bishops.
290 Roman empire reorganized by emperor Diocletian (245-316) into 4 prefectures, 15 dioceses (secular areas governed by imperial vicars), 120 provinces; Christians begin to relate their ecclesiastical jurisdictions to these political boundaries.
295 David of Basra evangelizes in India.

300 **Global status:** 9 generations after Christ, world is 10.4% Christians (66.4% of them being Non-Whites, 33.6% Whites), 35.0% evangelized; with Scriptures translated into 10 languages; total martyrs since AD 33 now 410,000 (0.5% of all Christians ever; recent rate 1,540 per year).
Missionary activity under way in Georgia.
c 300 *Afghanistan* (then Khorasan). First Christians, with Nestorian bishop of Herat.
Areas of strongest Christian development in Roman empire: Syria, Asia Minor, Egypt, North Africa, also Rome, Lyons; chief numerical strength in east; no area in empire entirely unevangelized.
Over 200 Christian dioceses already established in Italy.
301 *San Marino.* First Christians, as Marinus and group of believers settle to escape persecution.
303 10th and last imperial Roman persecution, under Diocletian; aimed at clergy and bishops, with substantial defections; destruction of all church buildings and Scriptures ordered.
304 Diocletian decrees death penalty for all Christians:3,500 formal or official executions of church leaders including many bishops, with some further 500,000 Christians killed or executed in 10 years of systematic slaughter.
305 Total legions in Roman army 68 (up from 34 over period AD 6-231); a legion has now fallen from 6,000 to around 3,000 men who are both heavy infantrymen and also combat engineers; together with cavalry, scouts, frontier guards and other varieties of troops, total imperial armed forces 620,000 (64% frontier, 36% central reserve field armies).
c 308 Church of the Martyrs with 29 bishops in Egypt organized by bishop Meletius (died 325) of Lycopolis, in opposition to leniency towards *lapsi* favored by Peter I Ieromartyros (Seal of Martyrs) patriarch of Alexandria who is himself martyred in 311; Meletian sect is approved by Arians, lasts until c520.

c 310 Gaul still 70% pagan.
Eusebius of Caesarea (c265-339) writes apologetic works: *Praeparatio evangelica* (refuting paganism), *Demonstratio evangelica* (fulfilment of Hebrew prophecy in Christ); 314, completes his *Ecclesiastical History*, and *Martyrs of Palestine*; writes 'The doctrine of the Saviour has irradiated the whole Oikumene (whole inhabited earth)'.

311 Donatist schism in North Africa; rigorists, opposing leniency towards those who lapsed under persecution; by 330, 270 Donatist bishops rising to 310 by AD 394; 347, persecution under Macarius results in many Donatist martyrs; schism persists until Saracens destroy African church by AD 700.

Constantinian Era begins: Christianity becomes state religion

312 Constantine (c280-337) marches on Rome, sees sign 'In hoc signo vinces (By this sign conquer)'.

313 Constantine at Milan issues Edict of Toleration legalizing Christianity throughout Roman empire; 323, becomes sole emperor.
Episcopal sees in Gaul increase from 12 at accession of Constantine to 119 by AD 600.

314 Three Celtic bishops from Britain (population 2,000,000) attend council of Arles in France, as well as 14 Gallican bishops; 359, Celtic envoys attend Council of Ariminum (Rimini) to deal with Arian dispute.

318 Egyptian presbyter Arius (256-336) propounds Arianism (Christ a created being, not truly divine); held by some to be the Antichrist because he and it denied divinity of Jesus Christ; a major christological controversy, lasting into 8th century.

319 Pagan sacrifices prohibited throughout Roman empire.

325 Council of Nicea I (1st Ecumenical Council): Arianism condemned; also, council makes political province the basic unit for church's larger divisions, brings church's jurisdictional areas into line with secular dioceses and provinces of Roman empire.

327 Persian king Shapur II (309-379), supporter of state religion of Mazdaism (Zoroastrianism), becomes alarmed at Christianity's official sponsoring by Roman empire, and its spread across his empire, so orders forcible apostasy of all Christians; savage persecution ensues for 40 years.

329 Ascetic Egyptian monk Hilarion of Gaza (291-371), missionary to idolatrous pagans of Palestine, introduces monasticism and establishes first monastery, conducts widely-attested ministry of signs and wonders (healings, exorcisms).

330 **Global status:** 10 generations after Christ, world is 12% Christians (65.7% of them being Non-Whites, 34.3% Whites), 36% evangelized; with Scriptures translated into 10 languages.
Constantine moves capital of Roman empire to Byzantium, and renames it Constantinople; Christianity now overwhelmingly an urban phenomenon.
Origins of parochial system: dioceses begin to be subdivided into parishes; by 400, established in most cities along coast of Gaul; evangelization of rural Europe well advanced.

c 330 Catacombs in widespread use (till 10th century) as subterranean burial places and refuges for Christians under persecution; in Rome, they extend several hundred miles.

332 Ethiopia: shipwrecked Syrian slave Frumentius arrives in Axum; later becomes first bishop; origins of Ethiopian Orthodox Church.

339 Severe persecution of Christians in Persia, until 379, with 3 catholicoses martyred (341, 342, 346); intermittent brutal persecution by Sassanid rulers until 640 conquest by Islam.

c 340 Coptic Orthodox bishoprics under pope Athanasius (c296-373) number 100 in Egypt.

c 345 Persecution in East Syria and Persia drives 400 Nestorians with a bishop to settle in Malabar, India.

346 At time of Pachomius' death, over 500,000 monks (7% of population of Egypt) live in numerous monasteries (Tabennesis 7,000, Mount Nitrea 5,000, Arsinoe over 10,000).

347 Cyril bishop of Jerusalem (310-386) teaches that Antichrist will be a magician who takes over Roman empire, claims to be Christ, deceives Jews by rebuilding Temple, persecutes Christians, then is slain at Second Advent by the Son of God.
Vicious persecution of Donatist church with its 270 bishops, resulting in many martyrs.

c 350 *South Yemen.* First Christians (church built at Aden).
Nestorians on Socotra island, with own bishop from 5th to 15th centuries.
Sudan: Coptic Orthodox traders active from Egypt; on breakup of kingdom of Meroe over next 100 years, its 3 successor states become officially Christian.

350 *Ireland* (then Hibernia). First Christians (monks from Crete and Egypt).
Apogee of Arianism: whole of East now Arian.
Golden age of Buddhism in China (to AD 800); 401, Kumarajiva translates Sanskrit texts into Chinese.

c 360 8-volume *Apostolic Constitutions*, a Syrian collection of ecclesiastical law, makes frequent allusions to Great Commission of Jesus in Matthew 28:19-20.

361 Julian the Apostate (331-363) last emperor to attempt to replace Christianity throughout Roman empire by a revived polytheism; undertakes a full-scale restoration of pagan religion; his death signals final triumph of Christianity in both Eastern and Western empires.
World's 5 largest cities: Constantinople 350,000, Loyang 296,000, Rome 250,000, Patna 224,000, Ctesiphon 200,000.

363 Syrian biblical exegete Ephraem Syrus (c306-373), born in Nisibis, moves to Edessa, writes voluminously.

364 During reign of emperor Valens, conversion of Vandals to Arianism.

367 Canon of New Testament finally agreed on, the 27 books being listed in Athanasius' Easter Letter (367) for the East, by the Synod of Rome (382) for the West, and by the Synod of Carthage (397) for the entire church.

c 370 Ulfilas (311-381), an Arian, bishop of the Goths and later in Moesia II; creates German alphabet and translates Bible into Visigothic (first translation of Bible for specifically missionary purposes).

374 A layman, Ambrose of Milan (c339-397) acclaimed bishop by crowds; in his writings, documents current healings and glossolalia; later teaches Second Coming of Christ will be preceded by destruction of Rome and appearance of Antichrist on Earth.

378 Goths and northern Barbarians begin conquest of Roman empire.
Jerome (c345-419) writes: 'From India to Britain, all nations resound with the death and resurrection of Christ' (*Isaiam cliv, Epistol. xiii ad Paulinum*); estimates 1.9 million Christians to have been martyred since AD 33 (out of 120 million Christians, i.e. 1.6% or 1 in 60); documents numerous current 'signs and wonders' (healings, exorcisms, miracles).
Emperor Valens killed with an entire field army of 40,000 by Visigoths at Adrianople; Ambrose identifies Goths with Ezekiel's Gog, proclaims imminent end of world; Martin of Tours writes 'There is no doubt that the Antichrist has already been born'.

380 City of Antioch: of 150,000 population, 50% are Christians, increasing rapidly.
Theodosius I (347-395) emperor of the East makes Christianity state religion and decrees that all subjects of Roman empire must become orthodox Christians.

381 Council of Constantinople I (2nd Ecumenical Council); creed of Nicaea reaffirmed; Macedonianism and Apollinarianism condemned.
Constantinople recognized as first in rank among the eastern patriarchates.

388 First known case of burning of a synagogue by Christians, on orders of bishop Callicinon.

c 390 Collapse of Arianism throughout Roman empire, though it continues among some German tribes until c700.
Conversion of Fritigil queen of Marcomans through a slave; requests Ambrose for instruction in Christian faith by correspondence; evangelization of the northern Barbarians largely due to soldiers and slaves rather than to church-planting.

391 Roman emperor Theodosius I orders prohibition of pagan sacrifices and destruction of pagan idols and temples, including those of Isis and Osiris in Nubia.

392 Ascetic writer John Cassian (c360-435) enters Bethlehem monastery; 415, founds monastery in Marseilles; promotes spread of monasticism in West; much evangelization due to these itinerant evangelistic monks.

395 Roman empire permanently divided: Western empire ruled from Rome (sacked 410, 455, 476), Eastern from Constantinople.

397 Southern Picts of Scotland first evangelized by Ninian (Rigna, Trignan; c360-c432) bishop of Galloway.

398 John Chrysostom (c344-407) appointed patriarch of Constantinople, founds training school for native Gothic evangelists; writes, ' "Go and make disciples of all nations" was not said for the Apostles only, but for us also'; teaches that final Antichrist under direct inspiration of Satan will appear immediately before Second Advent of Christ in AD 430.

399 Pagans massacre 60 Christians in Sufes, Byzacena (modern Qasrin in Tunisia), as reprisal for toppling a statue of Hercules.

400 **Global status:** 12 generations after Christ, world is 18.6% Christians (64.0% of them being Non-Whites, 36.0% Whites), 39.0% evangelized; with Scriptures translated into 11 languages; total martyrs since AD 33 now 1,950,000 (1.0% of all Christians ever; recent rate 5,310 per year).

c 400 Persia (Tigris/Euphrates, and highlands) a strong Christian area: Persians now 25% Christians (Syriac-speaking, but no Persian liturgy or Scriptures).
Several millions of Christians known to have been buried in catacombs near Rome over 3 centuries by this date.
Spanish North Africa (Ceuta, Melilla; then in Roman province of Mauretania). First Christians (Romans).
Scriptures being translated into Ethiopic by monks from Egypt.

404 Vulgate or Common Bible (translation of Scriptures into Latin, common speech of educated mankind in Europe for a thousand years) completed by Jerome after 22 years' work from original Hebrew and Greek, living in Palestine.

405 Cyril of Alexandria expropriates all synagogues in Egypt; 412-444, serves as patriarch of Alexandria.

408 Western Roman emperor Honorius executes non-Christians for first time, in Gaul.

409 Arian Visigoths overrun Iberian peninsula.

410 Fall of Rome to Arian Barbarian Alaric (c370-410) and 100,000 Visigoth warriors; collapse of Western Roman empire.

Synod of Seleucia-Ctesiphon: national Persian church formed separate from church of Rome, with state-recognized catholicos in capital.

c 410 Alphabet and Bible in Armenian and also in Georgian completed by Mashtotz (Mesrob, c361-440), later patriarch of Armenia.
Founding of noted monastery at Lerins by Honoratus, produces succession of notable Gallic bishops.
Episcopate in Proconsular Africa, Numidia and Mauretania expands to 768 bishops; total episcopate across North Africa, including Egypt and Donatists, numbers 1,200 bishops.

416 Eastern Roman emperor Theodosius II excludes non-Christians from all public functions; 418, burns all non-Christian books and writings.

417 Orosius, young Spanish priest, encouraged by Augustine to write *Historia adversus paganos*, holding Rome will survive until the coming of Antichrist.

420 An Arab tribe in Arabia is converted to Christianity under sheikh Aspebet.
Long and cruel persecution of Christians in Persia for 18 years under king Bahram V.

424 Synod of Markabta: East Syrian (Assyrian) catholicos of Seleucia-Ctesiphon and Persian church become independent of Antioch and the Western church, with 30 episcopal sees in Mesopotamia, and 6 in Persia and the Gulf.

425 Nubia: Olympiodorus of Thebes observes that the Bejas and Blemmyes peoples (south of first cataract) are still pagans.

426 Augustine (354-430) bishop of Hippo completes in 13 years his treatise *The City of God* (De Civitate Dei), against background of Visigoth invasion of Rome; propounds allegorical millennialism, but also teaches that future final Antichrist will arise as Nero Redivivus; opposes emerging theory of cessation of charismatic gifts, as overreaction to excesses of Montanism et alia with the teaching that miracles and charismata ended with the Apostolic age; documents numerous recent miracles, exorcisms, healings and resuscitations.

430 British ruler Vortigern (c400-c440) invites Saxons to visit, settle and garrison strategic east coast areas, but in 442 Saxons rebel and seize power; 446, British make vain appeal to Roman military; widespread chaos till 500.

431 Council of Ephesus (3rd Ecumenical Council): Nestorius (c390-451) patriarch of Constantinople condemned as heretic, also Pelagianism.
Jewish messiah Moses appears on Crete ready to lead remnants of Israel dryshod to Land of Israel; date 440 widely believed for final coming of Messiah; over next 1,500 years, scores more Jewish charismatic claimants arise, attracting widespread followings, fanaticism, violence and martyrdoms, especially in 1087, 1117, 1127, 1160, 1172, 1295, 1502, 1528, 1648.
Palladius of Auxerre sent to Ireland as first bishop of the Scots by pope Celestine to combat errors of Pelagius; withdraws after unsuccessful mission.

432 Ireland evangelized by Patrick (389-461); plants 200 churches and baptizes 100,000; c440, many converts killed by soldiers.

434 Beginning of Attila the Hun's 19-year reign as 'Scourge of God'; greatest of the Barbarian rulers, destroys cities and towns and almost destroys Western empire; widely regarded as the Antichrist; defeated in Gaul, dies in 453.

438 Theodosian Code, codifying Roman law.

439 North Africa: fall of Carthage, persecution of Catholics under Arian Vandal kings Gaeseric (Genseric, 428-477) and Huneric.

442 *Isle of Man*. First Christians, under Patrick; by 600, island evangelized and christianized through bishop Conan.

c 450 Conversion to Christianity becomes mainly by communities, led by their kings or princes.
Liechtenstein. First Christians (merchants and Roman soldiers).
Six East Syrian (Nestorian) bishoprics in Arabia, under metropolitan of Kashkar.
Caucasus begins to be converted to Christianity.
Buddhism practiced in Burma, lower Thailand, Sumatra, Java; by 500, on wane in India.
Decline of 'Rule of the Secret', the 3-centuries-old rule that the mysteries of baptism and eucharist are not to be revealed to heathens (e.g. words of Lord's Prayer only revealed to converts on eve of baptism).
England occupied by Anglo-Saxon invaders, who over next 30 years wipe out Celts and Celtic church, destroying Christianity and Roman civilization.
Old English language flourishes, lasts till c1100, then succeeded by Middle English (1100-1500).

451 Council of Chalcedon (4th Ecumenical Council): Tome of Leo approved, definition of faith against Apollinarianism, Nestorianism and Eutychianism; confirms that ecclesiastical dioceses are equivalent to political dioceses; recognizes patriarchal status of diocese of Jerusalem; Dioscorus patriarch of Alexandria excommunicated.
After Chalcedon, Copts of Egypt divided, most becoming monophysites.

455 Sack of Rome by Vandals under Gaeseric, all ardent Arians.

457 Proterius, Melkite or anti-Monophysite patriarch of Alexandria replacing Dioscorus, assassinated by Copts.

458 Theological school established at Nisibis in Persian empire by Narses; 480, Barsumas bishop of Nisibis (assassinated 493) and reforming patriarch Mar Aba (assassinated 533) keep Persian church isolated from West.

c 470 Persia: Sassanid king Firooz massacres monophysite priests, crucifies bishop Babowi and others.

476 Sack of Rome by Barbarians under Odoacer (c433-493): end of Roman empire in the West, largely due to demographic pressure (overpopulation); Odoacer becomes king of Italy.

484 Christianity first divided clearly between East and West.

486 Council of Seleucia: Assyrian church in Persia declares itself Nestorian, opposing churches of Roman empire, with Seleucia under its catholicos Acacius proclaimed a patriarchal see on a par with Antioch and Rome.

490 Climax of first major epoch of advance: Christianity wins at least 80% of Roman empire.

491 Armenian church adopts monophysitism.

c 495 Nestorian metropolitan provinces in Persia number 7, with several bishoprics abroad (Arabia, India).

496 Clovis (c466-511) king of the Franks baptized with 3,000 warriors at Rheims.

498 Christianity spreading widely in Central Asia, with whole tribes converted; Nestorians active in Turkestan until eliminated c1350.

499 Task of translating Jesus' message into Greek and Latin cultures virtually completed, after 16 generations.

Epoch II: THE GREAT RECESSION (The Dark Ages) AD 500-950

500 **Global status:** 16 generations after Christ, world is 22.4% Christians (61.9% of them being Non-Whites, 38.1% Whites), 42.0% evangelized; with Scriptures translated into 13 languages; total martyrs since AD 33, 2,540,000 (0.8% of all Christians ever; recent rate 5,440 per year).
The so-called Dark Ages begin (AD 500-1000, early medieval period in Western Europe): no emperor in West, frequent warfare, virtual disappearance of urban life.
First Bantu cultivators, expanding from Nigeria, reach Africa's east coast, and in south cross river Limpopo.
The Nine Saints (Syrian Orthodox) establish monastery in northern Ethiopia and secure monophysite character of Ethiopian church.
Jewish sages compile Talmud.

c 500 *North Yemen*. First Christians, later eradicated by Islam.
During Dark Ages up to AD 950, decline of cities, Europe returns to village and town life; 11th century, revival of urban development.
Over next 2 centuries, scattered martyrdoms across Europe: Helier, Desiderius, Donnan, Emmeram, Bercharius, Lambert, et alii.

506 Church of Iberia (monophysite Church of Georgia) unites for 100 years with monophysite Church of Armenia, at Council of Dvin, capital of Armenia; 607, catholicos Kirion I of Georgia rescinds union, 627 monophysites in Georgia annihilated.

c 510 Irish Peregrini or Exultantes Christi (unorganized wandering hermits and preachers using *pugilatores scotorum* [Irish writing-tablets] as their major piece of equipment) begin to migrate across Europe for next 400 years, to the Alps, Germany, Danube, Italy, also to Orkneys, Faeroes, Iceland, converting much of Europe in one of great missionary feats of all time.
Scholar, theologian and statesman Boethius (c480-524) transmits classical texts and ideals into Middle Ages; precursor of medieval scholasticism; executed by Theodoric the Great, king of the Ostrogoths.

512 West Syrian church becomes formally monophysite under patriarch Severus of Antioch (c465-538); 518-565, monophysites violently persecuted in Antioch, with many bishops and clergy killed.

516 Conversion of Burgundians to Catholic Christianity.

520 Nestorians (Syriac evangelists) reported on island of Ceylon, with many converts, also in Malabar under a Persian bishop, in Ganges region, among Huns, Turks and Uighurs, in Tibet and Sumatra.

523 Massacre of 14,000 Arab Christians in Najran and Himyar (Arabia) by Jewish Arab king Dhu-Nuwas Masruq.

525 Christianity firmly established in Arabian peninsula until Islam conquers in 7th century.
Scythian monk Dionysius Exiguus invents Christian Era, dating from birth of Christ as AD 1 (later found to be 4 years too late), also new Easter tables; adopted in England at Synod of Whitby in 664.

526 King of Axum (Abyssinia) sends expeditionary force to Yemen to protect persecuted Christians.
250,000 including many Christians killed by earthquake in Antioch, Syria.

529 Justinian I (483-565) closes ancient schools of philosophy at Athens; 537, dedicates Santa Sophia basilica in Constantinople.
Benedict of Nursia (c480-547) founds Monte Cassino monastery, Italy; spread of his Rule and rise of Western monasticism.

533 Persia: persecutions under Khosrow I kill Mar Aba patriarch of the East, also 575 catholicos of the East Ahudemmeh.

534 Arianism disappears throughout North Africa, and becomes finally destroyed.

535 Cosmas Indicopleustes, Nestorian merchant missionary over most of world, retires to monastery and in 547 completes his global survey *Topographia Christiana* in 12 Books.

c 540 Emperor Justinian orders that all pagan tribes on periphery of Byzantine empire be converted to Christianity; 70,000 persons forcibly baptized in Asia Minor.

542 Constantinople struck by plague; 60% of entire population die.

543 Jacob Baradaeus (c500-578) consecrated monophysite bishop of Edessa, organizes West Syrian (Jacobite) church, secretly ordains over 100,000 priests and consecrates many bishops including Sergius, monophysite patriarch of Antioch; rapid expansion of Syrian Orthodoxy.

Melkite missionaries sent by emperor Justinian to Nubia (Sudan), but empress Theodora first sends monophysite Julian who converts Silko king of Nobatae (Nubia, capital Faras); Monophysitism holds sway as official religion till AD 1000; principal Nubian temples including Abu Simbel converted into churches; Christians also in Darfur and Kordofan.

549 Nestorian patriarch sends bishop to Hephthalites (White Huns) north of Great Wall of China.

c 550 *Channel Islands.* First Christians (Breton settlers).

Egypt: Coptic bishops number 168 in 4 ecclesiastical provinces.

Patriarchate of Antioch has over 150 metropolitans and bishops.

552 Buddhism reaches Japan.

553 Council of Constantinople II (5th Ecumenical Council): Three Chapters controversy.

563 Scotland evangelized by Columba (521-597) from Ireland; Iona monastery founded, influence spreads to English, Franks, and Swiss.

567 Patriarchate of Alexandria definitively split into 2 rivals, Coptic (Monophysite) and Greek (Byzantine); Copts persecuted worse by Byzantines than later by Arabs.

Nubia: Longinus (a monophysite) consecrated first bishop, becomes apostle of Nubian Christianity; 569, Makoritae (south of Nubians, capital Dongola) become chalcedonians, but 579 Alodiae (capital Alwa 12 miles north of Khartoum) become monophysites.

570 Monophysite missions in Yemen.

578 Conversion to Christianity of An-numan III, last of Lachemids (Arab princes).

c 580 Writer, historian and bishop Gregory of Tours (c538-594) gives many accounts of contemporary miracles, healings and exorcisms.

589 Arian Visigoths in Spain converted to Catholicism, declared state religion at 3rd Council of Toledo.

c 590 Irish scholar Columbanus (c543-615), ablest controversialist of his time, founds monasteries across Europe.

594 Roman pope Gregory the Great (540-604) publishes *Dialogues* describing contemporary Christian miracles, visions, prophecies, supernatural awareness and other spiritual gifts.

596 Augustine (prior in Rome) sent by Gregory the Great to England; 597, baptizes king and 10,000 Saxons at Canterbury; persuades parliament to adopt the faith; first archbishop of Canterbury, dies 604.

600 **Global status:** 19 generations after Christ, world is 24.0% Christians (58% of them being Non-Whites, 42% White), 39% evangelized; with Scriptures translated into 14 languages; total martyrs since AD 33, 2,700,000 (0.6% of all Christians ever; recent rate 1,000 per year).

c 600 *Andorra.* First Christian settlers.

614 Persians capture Jerusalem, 619 capture Egypt, 626 besiege Constantinople.

622 Rise of Islam: Hegira, flight of prophet Muhammad (570-632) from Mecca to Medina; after his death Muslim Arabs sweep across Arabia, Palestine, Syria; 651, Muslim scholars compile Holy Quran, holding Allah has sent 124,000 prophets to mankind, of whom the major ones are Adam, Noah, Abraham, Moses, Jesus, and Muhammad seal of the prophets.

Armenian patriarchate established in Jerusalem.

World's 5 largest cities: Constantinople 500,000, Changan 447,000, Loyang 400,000, Ctesiphon 283,000, Alexandria 200,000.

625 British king Edwin of Northumbria baptized by Roman bishop Paulinus of York.

626 Siege of Constantinople by Avars.

628 Persecution in Persia under Chosroes II (Khosrow, Parviz).

629 Persian monk and theologian Marutha (c600-649) becomes metropolitan of Tekrit and first maphrian (deputy patriarch) and catholicos of the East with 15 suffragan bishops in Arabia, Mesopotamia and Persia; by 1200, Jacobite patriarch presides over 20 metropolitans and 118 bishops in Syria, Anatolia, Mesopotamia, and Persia.

c 630 Evangelization of Britain proceeds mainly through Celtic church's mission, with Roman church's mission coexisting in England.

631 Egypt: Melkites persecute Copts for 10 years, killing hermits, ascetics, priests and thousands of lay Christians.

635 *China* (then richest and most civilized nation on earth). First missionary (Alopen, a Nestorian bishop from Syria) reaches Thailand and then Tang Chinese capital Ch'ang-an (Hsian), translates Scriptures for emperor Tai-tsung; Nestorianism influential till suppressed for a time in 845.

Aidan, Celtic monk of Iona, consecrated bishop of Lindisfarne, evangelizes York and northern England; dies 651.

637 Capture of Jerusalem by Arab Muslims; 638, decisive battle between Christians and Muslims at Pilla, with 80,000 Byzantines killed.

639 Arabs (Saracens, Moors) invade Egypt, establish Islam and Arabic language.

c 640 Christians in Persia number about one million before Muslim conquest of Sassanid empire.

Egypt: 3 million Coptic and 200,000 Chalcedonian Christians.

80% of 6.5 million Berbers across North Africa (2.6 million urbanized) now Christians; but by 950 all become converted to Islam.

Rise of Paulicians, a dualistic neo-Manichean heretical sect in Armenia, Cilicia and Asia Minor; persecuted by Byzantine emperors, founder Silvanus and successors killed; 842, savagely persecuted; 870, peak of power; 872, Basil I breaks their military power; sect collapses by 1100.

642 Muslim conqueror of Alexandria, Amr, systematically destroys greatest library of antiquity (over 1 million volumes) over 6 months as fuel to heat city's 4,000 public baths.

645 Tiflis capital of Georgia captured by Arabs.

646 Mesopotamia (Iraq) conquered by Muslims.

650 Yeshuyab III becomes Nestorian patriarch of Seleucia-Ctesiphon; church now officially styled East Syrian, or Assyrian Orthodox, or Catholic Apostolic Church of the East.

c 650 *Netherlands.* First organized Christians (St Martin's Church, Utrecht).

Samuel the Confessor, Coptic hermit and prophet of the end-time, foresees revival of monastic vocation with vast numbers of young people flocking to enter monasteries.

Nestorian metropolitan of Merv converts many Turks.

Niger. First Christians (North African Berber Christians driven south by Islam).

Indonesia (then East Indies). First Christians (Catholic community on Sumatra).

Mongolia. First missionaries (Nestorians); 300 years later, Christianity disappears finally.

c 660 Mass conversions of Egyptians from Christianity to Islam.

663 Synod of Whitby (England) favoring Roman allegiance over tradition of Celtic church; 669, Theodore of Tarsus arrives as first archbishop recognized throughout England; 672, convenes first synod of English church at Hertford.

c 670 Earliest Old English (Anglo-Saxon) scripture version: metrical Paraphrases, sung by Caedmon (died c678).

Psalms translated into Anglo-Saxon by West Saxon abbot Aldhelm (c639-709), later bishop of Sherborne.

680 Council of Constantinople III (6th Ecumenical Council): Monothelitism condemned.

Shia Muslims (party of Ali) break from Sunnis.

c 680 First translation of Scriptures in Arabic; whole Bible not until 750.

686 Germany: martyrdom of Irish bishop Kilian and 11 companions working in east Franconia and Thuringia.

687 Conversion of England completed under Wilfrid (634-709) bishop of York; christianizes Sussex and Isle of Wight, last important centres of Anglo-Saxon paganism.

689 1st persecution of Nestorians in China; 2nd, 712-3; 3rd, 845.

690 Frisians and Netherlands evangelized by Willibrord (658-739) from Ripon, England.

692 'The light of Christ illuminates the whole world' (*Liturgy of the Presanctified*).

694 Lebanon: Greeks sack monastery of St Maro and kill 500 Arab Maronite monks.

695 Persecution of Jews in Spain.

697 Carthage captured by Muslims; North Africa in Muslim hands.

700 **Global status:** 22 generations after Christ, world is 23.8% Christians (55% of them being Non-Whites, 45% Whites), 35% evangelized; with Scriptures translated into 14 languages; total martyrs since AD 33, 3,000,000 (0.4% of all Christians ever; recent rate 1,000 per year).

Conversion of Lombards to Catholic church completed.

c 700 Destruction of Christianity across North Africa by Saracens; large numbers of Christians annihilated.

End of Patristic Age (Greek Fathers and Latin Fathers).

711 Muslim Arabs with army of only 20,000 defeat Arian Visigoths in Portugal and in 715 eliminate them from Spain; after Muslim conquest, population of Iberian peninsula is 4 million Spaniards and 50,000 immigrant Arabs.

714 East Syrian (Nestorian) patriarch Selibhazecha appoints metropolitan for China.

716 South and central Germany evangelized by bishop Winfrith (Boniface, 680-754) from Crediton (England), who creates numerous dioceses.

Lisbon falls to Moors.

717 Caliph Omar II destroys all new churches built in Arab times.

720 Anglo-Saxon translations of John's Gospel by historian and theologian Bede (Baeda, c673-735), monk at Jarrow on Tyne; Bede predicts fall of Colosseum will be followed by that of Rome and then also of the whole world.

724 Boniface fells pagan sacred oak of Thor at Geismar in Hesse (Germany), leading to collapse of German paganism; 754, martyred at Dokkum in Frisia with Eoban and 52 companions.

726 Synod of Armenian Church at Manzikert, convoked by catholicos John IV of Odzoun, attended by 20 Armenian bishops and Syrian monophysite patriarch.

730 *Church history of the English people* compiled by Bede, describing conversion of Anglo-Saxon race.

732 Muslims defeated by Charles Martel (689-741) between Tours and Poitiers;

they retreat from Europe.
c 740 *Iceland.* First missionaries (monks from Ireland).
743 Uighurs now principal power in Central Asia, up to 840, with capital Ordu-baliq (Karabalghasun).
747 Tantric Buddhism reaches Tibet.
c 750 Expansion of Christianity in India renewed.
Faeroe Islands. First missionaries (monks from Ireland); monasteries destroyed a century later.
Yemen: Nestorian missionaries in Sana and Socotra.
Pakistan (then Punjab). First Christians (Nestorian missionaries); later eradicated.
Church of Georgia (Iberia) reestablished as autocephalous church with its own catholicos.
762 Conversion to Manicheism of Tengli Meou-Yu (759-780), Uighur chieftain, who makes it the state religion; 840, Uighur state destroyed by Kirghiz Turks; 843, Manicheism prohibited throughout China, though pockets last until 14th century.
772 *East Germany.* First Christians (through Charlemagne's violent conquest of Saxons).
780 East Syrian (Nestorian) bishop of Bait Baghash, Timothy (728-823), becomes patriarch of the East; good relations with caliphs of Baghdad; moves patriarchal see from Seleucia-Ctesiphon to Baghdad.
c 780 Forced baptism of Saxon race by Charlemagne; 4,500 executed in one day for resisting, thousands more deported.
781 Hsian inscription indicates Syriac New Testament known in China.
784 Last major revolt of pagan Frisians.
787 Council of Nicaea II (7th Ecumenical Council, last one recognized by Eastern Orthodox): iconoclasm condemned.
Vikings (Norsemen, Varangians) begin invasions of Britain; 793, Lindisfarne destroyed, Iona ravaged 4 times from 795-825.
796 Pippin son of Charlemagne destroys Avar power; conversion of Avars (of Uighur origin) follows.
797 Tibet (Tangut) created as a Nestorian metropolitan see by patriarch Timothy.

Rise and fall of medieval scholasticism, AD 800-1600

800 **Global status:** 26 generations after Christ, world is 22.5% Christians (51.0% of them being Non-Whites, 49.0% Whites), 31.0% evangelized; with Scriptures translated into 15 languages; total martyrs since AD 33, 3,300,000 (0.4% of all Christians ever; recent rate 3,100 per year).
Christianity becoming dominant religion from the Caspian to Sinkiang (China).
Scholasticism, central body of medieval thought, being Christian philosophy produced by medieval scholars, arises due to Barbarian efforts at understanding the Christian faith, flourishes for 600 years with 13th century as its Golden Age.
Charlemagne (c742-814) crowned Roman emperor in Rome by Roman pope Leo III; 808, though still illiterate he publishes *Breviary* (Brevis Capitolorum), one of the earliest records of detailed counting.
World's 5 largest cities: Changan 800,000, Baghdad 700,000, Constantinople 300,000, Loyang 245,000, Kyoto 200,000.
825 Party of Persian Christians with 2 Nestorian bishops emigrate to Malabar.
Muslim caliph of Cordoba (Spain) executes 2 Arab nobles, brothers Adulfus and John, because they are Christians.
826 *Denmark.* First missionary (Anskar [801-865], monk of Flanders, apostle of the north).
827 Christianity harassed in Sicily during next 230 years; 902, subjugated by Muslims, with coastal areas of southern Italy; 1060, Normans expel Saracens.
828 *Czechoslovakia.* First missionaries (Franks).
829 *Sweden.* First missionary (Anskar); many Swedish noblemen converted after his visits.
835 Nestorian bishopric of Jerusalem instituted, 1065 raised to metropolitan see, finally disappears by 1616.
837 Egypt: Christian education prohibited, also celebration of festivals; all churches demolished by Muslims, and Christians ordered to wear 5-pound crosses around their necks.
842 Savage persecution of Paulicians of Asia Minor, under Byzantine emperor Michael I and empress Theodora; over 100,000 martyred.
845 Baptism of 14 Czech princes.
Severe persecution of Nestorians and Buddhists in China by Taoist emperor Wu Tsung; 44,000 temples and monasteries destroyed or closed.
846 Invading Saracens reach river Tiber near Rome; Muslim pirates sack St Peter's in Rome.
850 Corsica conquered by Moors.
Martyrs of Cordoba: 50 Spanish Christians and crypto-Christians of Arab or Arab-Spanish birth including zealous ascetic monks executed 850-59 by Muslim rulers after being provoked into attacking the Prophet.
c 850 East Syrian (Nestorian) Christianity in Arabia finally eradicated by Muslims.
First Scriptures translated into Norman French.
Rise of Hindu orthodoxy in India; beginning of medieval Hindu temples.
851 Ireland: pagan kingdom set up in Dublin for 3 centuries by Norwegian Olaf the White.
860 Russians attack Constantinople.
Vikings of Scandinavia trade and plunder as far as Russia (Murmansk, Kiev, Kazan, Volga, Caspian), Constantinople, Greenland, Iceland, Iona, Ireland, Spain, Morocco; converted to Christian faith after AD 900; 1050, influence wanes.
861 Conversion of Slavs under way through Cyril (826-869) and Methodius (c815-885), sent to Moravia (Bohemia) at request of prince Rastislav; by 900, Christianity strong in Moravia.
864 Baptism of Boris king of the Bulgars; 870, conversion of Bulgars, with a Bulgar consecrated as archbishop; Basil I, emperor 866-886, forces baptism on Serbs of Narenta Valley; 874, conversion of Serbs to Orthodoxy.
867 Photius patriarch of Constantinople attempts conversion of Khazars, Bulgars and Russians; dies 897.
869 Council of Constantinople IV (8th Ecumenical Council, for Roman Catholics): Photian schism condemned.
870 Malta conquered by Saracens; diocese suppressed, restored in 12th century.
874 Norwegian chieftain Ingolfur Arnarson settles in Iceland with first Vikings; 930, first Althing held (general assembly, oldest parliament in Europe).
880 Slavonic Bible translated by Cyril and Methodius, also Bible in Bohemian; in England, Psalms translated into Anglo-Saxon by British king Alfred the Great (849-899).
c 890 *Anglo-Saxon Chronicle* (in Anglo-Saxon or Old English) produced under Alfred the Great.

900 **Global status:** 29 generations after Christ, world is 20.8% Christians (55% of them being Whites, 45% Non-Whites), 28% evangelized; with Scriptures translated into 16 languages.
c 900 *Norway.* First mission (from Bremen-Hamburg archbishopric); later, Norwegian kings educated in England return to evangelize their people.
Magyars now evangelized.
Continuing apostasies of Christians to Islam in Middle East and North Africa.
Alchemy and astrology flourish (China, Greece, Islamic lands).
911 Rollo and his Vikings settle in Normandy; soon after, become Christians; 1066, Norman descendants invade and conquer England.
917 Bulgarian Orthodox patriarchate proclaimed, lasts from 917-1078; reestablished 1235, dissolved again 1393 under Turks; finally restored 1953.
c 920 *Burma.* First Christians (Nestorian bishopric at Pegu).
926 Revival of Western monasticism under Odo (879-942) abbot of Cluny, France.
927 Conversion of Bulgars completed; death of tsar Simeon.
943 Dunstan (c909-988) abbot of Glastonbury; 959, archbishop of Canterbury; with king Edgar, carries out complete reform of English church and state.
c 949 50% of all former Christendom now captured by Islam, including nomadic Berbers of Mauretania.

Epoch III:
RESURGENCE AND ADVANCE
AD 950-1350

950 **Global status:** 31 generations after Christ, world is 20.2% Christians (58.8% of them being Whites, 41.2% Non-Whites), 26.0% evangelized; with Scriptures translated into 17 languages; total martyrs since AD 33, 3,930,000 (0.4% of all Christians ever; recent rate 3,090 per year).
c 950 *Poland.* First Christians; followed soon after by baptism of king.
Conversion of Scandinavians (Northmen) under way across Denmark, Norway and Sweden.
Rise of Bogomilism in Bulgarian Orthodox Church; neo-Manichean, dualist, perfectionist; rejecting OT, water baptism and sacraments; by 1140, Bogomil church rapidly growing, organized with hierarchy, liturgy, doctrine (Jesus an angel), foreign missions; by 1200, a vast network of Paulician-Bogomil-Cathar dualistic communities from Black Sea to Atlantic; collapses by 1400.
Egypt: Coptic bishops decline in numbers to 110 (from 168 in AD 550).
Mali trading empire founded in west Africa by Mandingo king Sundiata; collapses by 1550.
954 Olga (c890-969) regent of Kiev baptized in Constantinople; conversion of Russia begun.
960 Bernard of Thuringia predicts imminent end of world in AD 992; great alarm throughout Europe.
962 Holy Roman Empire founded by Otto I (912-973), king of Germany, crowned by pope John XII; 10 million by AD 1000, 16 million by AD 1200, 29 million by 1800; finally abolished in 1806.
966 Duke Mieszko I (c930-992) of Poland converted to Christianity by his wife and baptized; first Polish bishopric established at Poznan (Posen) 2 years later; rapid expansion of the faith.
967 Nubia: churches and monasteries very extensive, with 12,000 monks in 2 remote monasteries in Tari; 969, Fatimid dynasty conquers Egypt, begins pressure on Nubia to convert to Islam.
982 Greenland explored by Vikings under Erik the Red.
987 Muslim rulers in Iraq assume right to appoint the Nestorian catholicos.

Conversion and baptism of archduke Vladimir (956-1015) of Kiev by Greeks; Orthodoxy introduced into Russia; Vladimir orders all subjects baptized, and mass conversion of Russia begins.

Nestorian mission visits China, reports no Christian communities there.

990 Over next 2 centuries, numerous martyrdoms of bishops across Europe: Adalbert, Alphege, Boniface of Querfurt (Bruno), Eskil, Gerard of Csanad, Gottschalk, Henry of Uppsala, John of Mecklenburg, Kuno of Trier, Magnus of Orkney, Stanislaw, Thomas Becket, et alii.

Up to now, 95% of all families in world produce for themselves virtually everything they need to sustain life, and only rarely buy other people's goods.

c 990 *Greenland.* First Christians (Norse settlement; priest brought by founder's son Leif).

991 Whole population of Novgorod (Russia) baptized by bishop from Crimea.

992 Death of abbot Adso of Montier-en-Der (of Dijon, France), whose writings describe future coming of Antichrist into world.

996 Egypt: caliph al-Hakim (985-1021) destroys 3,000 churches and forcibly converts thousands of Copts to Islam in violent persecution.

997 Mass conversion of Magyars (Hungarians) under first king Stephen (c975-1038) and Adalbert of Prague (956-997).

Prussians, last remaining heathens in Europe, evangelized.

999 Bohemia: evangelization and christianization completed.

Multitudes journey to Jerusalem to await Second Coming of Christ in AD 1000, as believed prophesied in Apocrypha.

The High Middle Ages, AD 1000-1300

1000 **Global status:** 32 generations after Christ, world is 18.7% Christians (61.0% of them being Whites), 25% evangelized; with Scriptures translated into 17 languages; total martyrs since AD 33, 4,200,000 (0.4% of all Christians ever; recent rate 3,200 per year).

World's 5 largest cities: Cordova 450,000, Constantinople 450,000, Kaifeng 400,000, Sian (Changan) 300,000, Kyoto 200,000.

Millennial year preceded by widespread terrors; followed by 150 years of vast increase in pilgrimages to Holy Land, with widespread continuing belief in imminent end of world with final king of the Franks leading all faithful to Jerusalem to await Second Coming of Christ.

Most of North African Christianity finally wiped out: the Land of the Vanished Church.

Catholic Apostolic Church of the East (East Syrian or Nestorian church) is by now the most extensive in world, with 250 dioceses across Asia and 12 million adherents; expansion of Nestorianism in Tenduc, country of Keraits with Karakorum as capital, home of legendary ruler Prester John.

East Syrian (Nestorian) metropolitan provinces within Arab caliphate (Persia) number 15, with 5 abroad including India and China.

Patriarchate of Constantinople has authority over 624 dioceses around eastern Mediterranean.

Conversion of northern Europe by Latin church completed.

Nubian bishop (Sudan) reintroduces Orthodox Melkite tradition, provoking split between church in Nubia and Copts in Egypt; 1320, a Dominican arrives as Catholic bishop of Nubia.

Emergence of Christian kingdoms in Denmark, England, Hungary, Norway, Poland, Sweden, Scotland.

1005 Iceland: 2 dioceses, many monasteries and abbeys.

1009 Northern Mongolia: Nestorians convert and baptize prince and 200,000 Keraits (a Turkish tribe) in capital Karakorum; also Namians and Merkites.

c1010 Leif Eriksson, Norse Christian leader from Greenland, makes first European and Christian contact with North America.

1015 Russia permanently christianized; all 3 bishops and most clergy Greeks; numerous monasteries.

c1016 Iceland only country to accept Christianity by genuine democratic process.

c1020 Nestorians over 50% of population in Syria, Iraq and Khorasan (south of Oxus).

c1050 King in Nubia erects many churches and monasteries.

Egypt: Coptic bishops decline in numbers to 47 (from 168 in AD 550).

1054 Chinese astronomers observe supernova (violently exploding star, later becoming Crab Nebula), visible on Earth for 2 years; one of 3 billion supernovas in history of our Galaxy, which have probably destroyed 2 million related planetary civilizations; other recent supernovas seen in AD 185, 393, 1006, 1181, 1572, 1604.

1056 Great Schism between western (Rome) and eastern (Constantinople) Christianity; Roman cardinal Humbert places bull of excommunication of patriarch Michael on altar of Santa Sophia cathedral in Constantinople; church of Byzantium declines, with no further missionary outreach implemented.

1060 Vast numbers of medieval millenarian movements arise, involving millions of desperate rebels, radicals and rootless poor seeking hope in a new world; including 1090 heresiarch Tanchelm (died 1115), 1180 Joachim of Fiore, 1420 Taborites, 1525 Thomas Muntzer, 1534 Anabaptist 1000-year kingdom of Munster, 1653 Fifth Monarchy Men, et alia.

1061 Norman (Christian) conquest of Sicily, completed by 1091.

1066 Evangelization and conversion of Western Europe completed with Norman conquest of Saxons and Celts.

1071 Overthrow of Byzantine army at Manzikert (Anatolia) by Turkish sultan Alp Arslan; inrush of Turkish tribes follows.

1073 Papacy of Gregory VII (Hildebrand, c1023-1085).

1074 Crusade planned by Gregory VII to relieve Byzantium and liberate Jerusalem.

1076 Last contact between Roman pope and bishop of Carthage.

China: 2 East Syrian monasteries known, at Sianfu and Chengtu; 1093, Nestorian patriarch Sabaryeshu III appoints bishop George to Sestan then to see of Khatai in north China; 1265, 3 Nestorian churches in city of Iamzi (Yang-Chau-fu).

1078 Suppression of Bulgarian patriarchate by Byzantine emperor; reestablished 1235.

1081 Muslim Turks dominant in most of Armenia and Asia Minor.

1086 *Domesday Book* details demographic and social conditions for 1.75 million population of England.

1090 College of Cardinals established in Rome by reforms of pope Urban II (c1042-1099).

1093 Anselm (1033-1109) becomes archbishop of Canterbury; writes *Cur Deus homo?*

1095 Military expeditions by western Christians against Muslim powers to liberate Holy Land, launched by pope Urban II, known as Crusades: 1st 1095-99 (People's Crusade); 2nd 1147-49; 3rd 1189-93 (Richard the Lion-Heart); 4th 1202-04; 5th 1212-21 (Children's Crusade); 6th 1228-29; 7th 1248-54; 8th 1270-72 (Prince Edward of England).

1096 Start of First Crusade with 30,000 French and Italian crusaders invading Seljuk Turk empire: 'Deus vult' (God wills it); 1099, Jerusalem sacked.

Cappadocia: Jacobites massacred by Turks in Malatya.

1098 France: founding of Citeaux abbey (Cistercians) and Prémontré (Norbertines), engaged in missionary activity in Scandinavia, Germany, Poland, Bohemia.

1099 Latin patriarchate of Jerusalem established; Latin kingdoms (Outremer) founded.

1100 **Global status:** 36 generations after Christ, world is 18.8% Christians (63% of them being Whites), 25.5% evangelized; with Scriptures translated into 19 languages.

Sweden: christianization now completed.

Poland: christianization completed.

c1100 *Finland.* First Christians (seamen and merchants).

Magnetic compass, for terrestrial navigation, invented in China, then independently in Europe (c1187), Arabia (c1220), Scandinavia (c1300).

Nubia: 2 rival Christian kingdoms of (north) Makoritae and (south) Alodiae (with 400 churches).

Old English gives way to Middle English language, lasting till c1500.

Hungarians accept Christianity as national religion.

Mahayana Buddhism flowers in Japan (till 1300).

Armenian church split by Paulician separatists.

Timbuktu founded in west Africa, becoming center of Islamic culture and learning for African Muslims; 1591, conquered by Morocco.

1103 General Council of the Church of Georgia held at Rouissi-Urbnissisus under catholicos John, with 15 disciplinary canons and reforms promulgated; next 200 years are golden age of Georgian power and culture, especially under queen Tamar (1184-1213).

1112 Bernard of Clairvaux (1090-1153) enters Citeaux, 1115 becomes abbot; mightiest preacher of Middle Ages, preaching in 2,000 monasteries and in many countries.

1118 Order of Knights Templar, a military religious order, founded to aid and protect pilgrims to Holy Land; HQ near Temple site, Jerusalem; rapid growth of immense wealth; 3 ranks of knights, sergeants, chaplains; 1311, king Philip IV (1268-1314) of France forces pope Clement V (1264-1314) to dissolve order throughout Europe, executing 120 Templars.

c1120 Greek Orthodox Patriarchate of Antioch adopts Arabic as its liturgical language.

1122 Scholastic theologian Peter Abelard writes *Sic et Non*.

1123 Council of Lateran I (9th Ecumenical Council): subject, investiture controversy.

1124 Several Cumans (Kipchak Turks) received by Stephen II of Hungary and come into contact with Christianity.

Swabian bishop Otto (1062-1139) of Bamberg undertakes missionary journey as evangelizer of Pomerania at invitation of duke Boleslaw III (1086-1138) of Poland, converts 20,000 and establishes 12 churches.

1139 Council of Lateran II (10th Ecumenical Council): against pseudo-popes (antipopes, false popes), and on points of discipline.

Gaelic church reformer, abbot, archbishop and prophet, Malachy O'Morgain (c1094-1148) compiles 'Prophecy of the Popes', foretells identities, mottoes and characteristics of 122 RC popes from Celestine II (1143) to end of 20th century with final Pope of the Apocalypse (Peter the Roman), with conversion of the Jews to Christ prophesied under last pope but one.

1140 Cambodia: Angkor Wat temple complex begun as microcosm of Cosmos, temple and astronomical observatory.

c1140 Christianity in Finland organized by English bishop Henry of Uppsala (martyred 1155).

1146 Jews of Spain forcibly converted to Christianity; further force used, 1391.

1149 Heretical neo-Manichean ascetic sect of Cathars (Cathari, Pure Ones, Albigenses) form an organized Cathar church related to Bogomil church, with 11 bishoprics and wide followings in France and Italy.

c1150 Widest expansion of West Syrian (Jacobite) church: 20 metropolitan sees, 103 bishoprics in Syria, Mesopotamia, Cyprus, et alia, and 2 million adherents.
Scottish monks at work in Kiev.
Onguts (Tatars) become Christians in central Asia.

1151 Hildegarde (1098-1179) abbess of Rupertsberg wields widespread influence as mystic visionary, predicts: 'Just as the world was made in 6 days, it will come to an end in 6,000 years.'

1155 Founding of Carmelite order on Mount Carmel, Palestine.

1166 Waldensian movement begins following Poor Men of Lyons and reformer Peter Waldo, develops evangelistic and charismatic ministries (visions, prophecies, healings, exorcisms).

1168 Danes destroy paganism among Wends of Rügen.

1170 Murder in Canterbury cathedral of Thomas Becket (c1118-1170), archbishop of Canterbury, on wishes of English king Henry II.

1179 Council of Lateran III (11th Ecumenical Council): formally outlaws usury (interest charged on loans); also, no Christian should be subjected to slavery.
Astronomer John of Toledo calculates major catastrophe coming in AD 1186; widespread panic follows.

1180 Bosnia: Bogomil Church (Krstjani) becomes established church under prince Ban Kulin; after Turkish conquest of 1463, most Krstjani convert to Islam.

c1180 Joachim of Fiore (c1130-1202), Italian Cistercian abbot and mystic, divides all history into three 40-generation ages or periods (Old Testament, New Testament, future age), writes *Vaticini del Vangelo Eterno* (Prophecies of the Eternal Gospel) and *Expositio in Apocalypsim* describing imminent crisis of evil, apocalyptic symbols of Antichrist, and his 3rd or Final Age of the Spirit (Love) coming by 1260 after Age of the Father (Law), and Age of the Son (Grace), for spiritual men through pilgrimage and great tribulation in a spiritualized Johannine Church replacing carnal Petrine Church; Joachimism spreads widely over next 3 centuries.
Muslim philosopher Averroes integrates Islamic traditions and Greek thought.
Kurdish sultan Saladin (1137-1193) sends invading army to Nubia which kills or enslaves 700,000 Nubian Christians.

1181 Roman Catholic uniate churches begin to emerge (Syria); over 40,000 Maronites submit to Rome and enter into communion with Latin patriarch of Antioch.

1187 Recapture of Jerusalem by Arabs; at Lake Tiberias (Galilee), massacre of all Christians by Saracens under Saladin.

1189 Third Crusade launched, capturing Acre.

1190 Order of Teutonic Knights founded as German religious and military order; 1805, dissolved by Napoleon; 1929, new purely religious Rule based on schools and hospitals.

c1190 Rise of demand for vernacular versions of Scriptures: poetical and prose versions in Old French (Provençal, Vaudois), Italian, Spanish.

1200 **Global status:** 39 generations after Christ, world is 19.4% Christians (64.3% of them being Whites), 26% evangelized; with Scriptures translated into 22 languages.
World's 5 largest cities: Hangchow 255,000, Fez 250,000, Cairo 200,000, Constantinople 200,000, Canton 200,000.
Life expectancy in Europe 33 years, rising to 35 by 1800, 49 by 1900, 70 by 1960, 74 by 1980, 90 by 2000, 120 by 2030.
Apex of medieval papacy, under Innocent III (1198-1216).
Europe entirely christianized except for Wends, Prussians, Lithuanians and other Baltic races.

1202 Fourth Crusade launched against Egypt under Innocent III, also capturing and sacking of Constantinople from Greeks in 1204; Greeks permanently embittered against Latins.

1208 20,000 Albigensians massacred as heretics at papal order, around Toulouse; 1244 Cathar stronghold of Montsegur destroyed, Cathar church forced underground.

1209 Francis of Assisi (1182-1226) founds traveling preachers (Franciscans), largest of the mendicant orders (OFM); widespread healings, signs and miracles reported; soon reaches a medieval peak of 60,000 Franciscans by 1400, 77,000 by 1768, falling to 14,000 by 1900, rising to 40,000 by 1970.

1211 Genghiz Khan (c1162-1227), Universal Emperor of the Mongols (whose mother was a Nestorian), attacks China with army of only 129,000 and massacres 35 million in a decade.
Over 80 Waldensians burned as heretics at Strasbourg; intermittent severe persecutions thereafter, especially in 1545, 1555-59, during which time membership peaked at 100,000.

1212 Children's Crusade, a disastrous venture by over 20,000 children, many of whom end as slaves in Egypt.

1215 Council of Lateran IV (12th Ecumenical Council): against Waldensians, Albigensians, et alii.
Dominic (1170-1221) founds Order of Preachers (OP, Dominicans) in southern France; soon reaches a peak of 12,000 Dominicans; other orders of mendicant friars arise including in 1256 Augustinians (OSA).
Magna Carta, charter of English liberties, forced on king John by English nobles and commoners.

1219 Independent Serbian Orthodox Church formed.
Francis of Assisi crosses Crusader-Muslim lines and preaches the gospel before sultan al-Kamil of Egypt.

c1220 German scripture translations available.

1220 Genghiz Khan massacres 25% of population in Iran and Iraq; dies 1227.
First Franciscan missionary martyrs: Berard and 4 others killed after preaching in Marrakesh (Morocco); 1227, Daniel and 6 more Italian friars killed in Ceuta.

1221 Ukraine entered by Dominicans; 1228, diocese under Rome created; 1240, Kiev captured by Mongols.
First of many papal mission encyclicals on foreign missionary affairs: Bull of Honorius III, 'Ne si secus.'

1223 Cathars of Bulgaria, Croatia, Dalmatia and Hungary hold a conclave and elect a Cathar pope; 1225, Cathars of Languedoc create new diocese of Razes and elect its bishop.

1227 Cuman prince Barc and 15,000 followers baptized, in Hungary; 1228, diocese of Milkovia set up for them; 1241, diocese destroyed by Mongols.

1229 Vernacular Scriptures prohibited by Synod of Toulouse, also (1233) at Tarragona, Spain.
Jerusalem again in Christian hands 1229-39 and 1243-44; 1244, finally recaptured by Muslims on being sacked by Khwarezmian Tatars.

1231 Pope Gregory IX (c1170-1241) establishes Inquisition against heretics by Statutes of the Holy See, under Franciscans and Dominicans.

1239 Holy Roman emperor Frederick II (1194-1250) opposes papal authority, 1239 excommunicated; identified as Antichrist by followers of Joachim of Fiore.

1240 Dominicans begin mission in Tiflis, Georgia.
Batu Khan, grandson of Genghiz Khan, conquers all Russia and eastern Europe, establishes Kipchak Khanate (Golden Horde) in southern Russia as western division of Mongol empire, which then adopts Islam and Turkic language and lasts 200 years, eventually becoming Uzbekistan.

1242 Moors forced to hear evangelistic sermons in kingdom of Aragon.

1245 Council of Lyons I (for RCs, 13th Ecumenical Council): against emperor Frederick II's persecution of church and pope; also urges missionaries be sent to Mongol princes.

1249 Conquest and conversion of Finland finally secured by Swedish ruler Birger Jarl (died 1266).

c1250 Nubia: many new mosques erected, Christianity waning due to internal dissension, mass apostasies, destruction of churches, many martyrdoms.
Nestorian influence strong across Asia, still with over 250 bishoprics; under Mongol Yuan dynasty in China (1276-1368), Nestorians return somewhat before finally vanishing.
Central Asia: Uighurs, Keraits, Mongols and all other major peoples partially christianized.
Height of the Catholic church's political power in Europe.
Popular preachers spread warnings of coming of Antichrist; Roman popes Boniface VIII (1234-1303) and John XXII (1249-1334) inter alios each widely regarded as Antichrist.
All Prussians forcibly baptized and pagan worship eradicated.
Portions of Bible available in Italian (Tuscan, Lombardic), Polish, Spanish and Catalan.
Koreans first, then Chinese, develop movable type.
Societas Peregrinantium Propter Christum founded as Dominican foreign mission body; ends 1456.

1250 Founding of school of oriental languages by Raymond Martini.
Kublai Khan completes census of Tibet for military purposes.
Palestine: Dominican missionary William of Tripoli baptizes over 1,000 Muslims.
French language now the 'universal vernacular of Christendom' as a result of the Crusades.

1252 In bull 'Ad Extirpanda', pope Innocent IV finally recommends and urges fire, irons and rack (torture and death) for heretics.

1253 Japan: Buddhist monk Nichiren (1222-1282) founds Nichiren-shu sect.

1254 Sensational *Introduction to the Eternal Gospel* of abbot Joachim issued by ardent Spiritual, Gerard of Borgo San Donnino, claiming its prophecies have been fulfilled by Franciscan order, and insisting Age of the Spirit will begin in 1260.

1258 Hulagu Khan and Mongol hordes sack and destroy caliphate capital Baghdad and (1260) Damascus in attempt to destroy Muslim world, kill 800,000 in Baghdad but spare Christians; Hulagu (whose wife is a Christian) professes Christian faith.
Franciscan preacher Berthold von Regensburg (died 1272) preaches to unprecedented crowds in many countries.

c1260 Italy and Europe: greatest period of religious art begins, and lasts 400 years, with as central theme Christ's passion and crucifixion.

1262 Mongol khan Berke with nobles converts to Islam, but most Mongols remain shamanists.

1265 Medieval theologian Thomas Aquinas OP (1224-1274) writes *Summa Theologiae* in Latin from 1265-74; uses verb *evangelizo* on some 38 occasions; states 'Africa is a fertile ground for schism.'

1266 Mongol ruler Kublai Khan (1215-1294) requests Roman pope: 'Send me

100 men skilled in your religion . . . and so I shall be baptized, and then all my barons and great men, and then their subjects. And so there will be more Christians here than there are in your parts'; 2 Dominicans sent, but turn back; then 1278, pope sends 5 Franciscans; greatest missed opportunity in Christian history.

1271 Rijmbijbel (Scriptures in poetic Dutch) written.

1274 Council of Lyons II (for RCs, 14th Ecumenical Council): attempt to unite Greek and Roman churches; proliferation of mendicant orders discouraged.

1275 Nestorian archbishopric established in Cambaluc (Khanbalik/Peking), and hierarchy restored throughout central Asia.

1281 Mongolian monk Marcus, an Ongut Sino-Turk, elected Nestorian catholicos Yabalaha III; consecrates 75 bishops; 1304, submits to Roman pope Benedict XI, sets up Latin sees which soon collapse; dies 1317.

1287 Nestorian Christian from Cambaluc (Peking), Rabban Sauma (1250-1294) visits pope in Rome; as a result, in 1294 Italian Franciscan John of Montecorvino (1246-1328) arrives in Cambaluc; bitter opposition from Nestorians.

1288 German canon Alexander of Roes (in Cologne) predicts, in *Notitia Seculi*, end of world at AD 1500, being 6,000 years from foundation of world.

1290 Expulsion of Jews from England under Edward I, lasting several centuries until protector Cromwell readmits them in 1656.

Arnold of Villanova (c1240-1311), leading alchemist and physician of his day, writes 70 scientific works and other theological works including on the coming of Antichrist.

1291 Fall of Acre, in Syria, last Crusader stronghold; Crusaders driven from Middle East by Mamluk Muslims; end of all Crusades and crusading zeal in Europe.

1293 Armenian catholicate of Cilicia transferred to Sis.

1295 Ghazan Khan (1271-1304), a Muslim, becomes ruler of Mongols in Persia; state adopts Islam; Kurds massacre Nestorians, especially in city of Maragha.

Great pulpiteers of Middle Ages include Meister Eckhart (1260-1327) and Johann Tauler (1300-1361), both Dominicans.

Period of Medieval decline, AD 1300-1400

1300 **Global status:** 42 generations after Christ, world is 23.9% Christians (66% of them being Whites), 27% evangelized; with Scriptures translated into 26 languages.

Mongol world (Russia, Persia, Turkestan) gradually being converted to Islam.

Franciscans at work in 17 stations throughout Mongol empire, with a monastery in Cambaluc.

First Holy Year (Jubilee Year) held in Rome under pope Boniface VIII, attracts 200,000 pilgrims at any given time throughout whole year (minimum stay, 30 days each person); then 1350, 1390, 1423, 1450, 1490; then every 25 years except 1800, 1850, 1875; subsequently every 50 years, latterly every 25 years.

1301 Egypt: all churches ordered closed or destroyed by Mamluk dynasty (1250-1517); Copts and Jacobites in Syria suffer a century of systematic persecution.

1302 Invention of card compass by Italian mariner Flavio Gioja.

Muslim rulers in South India murder Catholic missionary friars.

1305 House of Taxis (Vienna) operates express message postal system across Europe with (by 1628) 20,000 liveried couriers; a mass communications total monopoly for the rich, privileged and powerful.

1306 Expulsion of Jews from France.

John of Montecorvino builds 2 churches in Cambaluc with 6,000 converts, translates New Testament into Ongut (Tatar) and Uighur; 1307, made archbishop; dies 1328 with 30,000 converts made.

1309 Papacy moved from Rome to Avignon (France), until 1378.

Gibraltar. First Christians (Spanish Catholic soldiers, capturing Rock from Muslims).

c1310 Persia: large proportion Christian, but Mongol rulers still undecided between Christianity and Islam.

1311 Council of Vienne (Rhone) (15th Ecumenical Council): abolition of Templars, condemnation of various heresies.

1314 *Divine Comedy* written by Italian poet Dante (Alighieri) (1265-1321); one of world's great works of literature.

1315 Ramon Lull (c1232-1316), Franciscan theologian writing in Arabic and Catalan, proposes campaign of informed preaching plus military force against Muslims (*Liber de fine*); stoned to death at Bugia (Algeria) by Muslims.

Franciscan theologian Hugh of Newcastle (c1280-1322), doctor scholasticus, teaches in Paris, writes on coming of Antichrist.

Nubia: accession of a Muslim as king of formerly Christian kingdom of Dongola, which then rapidly becomes Muslim.

1317 Turkey: Mongols enslave or kill 12,000 Nestorians at Amid (Diyarbakr).

1321 Egypt: almost all remaining Coptic churches and monasteries burned or destroyed in mob fury; mass executions of Christians.

Final pogrom against Cathars: priest Guilhem Belibasta burnt at stake in Languedoc, c1330 last group murdered.

1323 Franciscan contacts in Sumatra, Java and Borneo.

1325 Aztecs found capital city Tenochtitlan in Valley of Mexico; at dedication of Great Temple, 20,000 slaves sacrificed to god of war Huitzilopochtli; by 1500, population 500,000, ruling over Aztec empire of 5,500,000 people; 1523, destroyed and razed to ground by Cortes and conquistadors.

1330 Jordanus (a Dominican) sent by Roman pope as bishop to Quilon, south India, to convert Malabar Nestorians.

c1330 Scripture historical books translated into Norwegian.

Last surviving group of Cathars take refuge in caves, where they are walled up by cardinal Jacques Fournier (pope Benedict XII from 1334-42).

1337 The Hundred Years' War fought between France and England until 1453.

European Renaissance: New Age in Western Civilization

1340 Renaissance begins as revival of learning and the arts over a 200-year period, beginning in Italy, characterized by admiration for and imitation of ancient Greece and Rome, together with recrudescence of anti-Christian paganism.

German Dominican mystic Johann Tauler (1300-1361) of the Friends of God (Gottesfreunde) initiates major revival in Rhine valley, whose influence lasts until 1450.

1342 Mongol dynasty becomes finally and definitively Muslim.

1345 Serbian Orthodox patriarchate established; later suppressed in 1459 and again in 1765.

1347 Black Death (bubonic plague pandemic) erupts in Mongolia, kills 13 million in China, spreads like wildfire to India and Middle East, kills 85,000 Tartars in Crimea alone, thence to Genoa by ship, then sweeps across Europe killing 33% of 60 million population; 98% of all European victims are Christians; Jews held responsible, so 1 million massacred; plague ends 1353, having killed 75 million worldwide (17% of world population).

1349 Plague strikes England in full force, killing 40% of population; also again in 1361, 1369, 1375, 1390, with 8 further attacks in 15th century.

Jews expelled from Hungary over 11-year period; in Germany, 350 separate massacres annihilating 210 Jewish communities.

30,000 Christians in Mongol empire in China (population then 80 million), mostly Mongols.

Apogee of East Syrian or Nestorian expansion across Asia, geographically more extensive and more prosperous than ever before or since; 25 metropolitans (each with 6-12 suffragan bishops) in 250 dioceses in China, India, Kashgar, Samarkand, Turkestan, et alia, with total of over 15 million Christians; a mighty organization with missionary enterprise unsurpassed in Christian history.

Epoch IV: THE SECOND RECESSION: CONFUSION AND CORRUPTION 1350-1500

1350 **Global status:** 44 generations after Christ, world is 24.1% Christians (67.6% of them being Whites), 28% evangelized; with Scriptures translated into 28 languages; total martyrs since AD 33, 5,510,000 (0.3% of all Christians ever; recent rate 3,950 per year).

Rapid shrinking of geographical frontiers of Christianity begins, especially in Asia, and continues for 150 years.

At height of Black Death, pope Clement VI decrees a holy year or jubilee; one million pilgrims visit Rome.

Monastic efforts at evangelization by mystic and reformer Sergius of Radonezh (1314-1392) at Murmansk and Solovkij; founds 40 monasteries.

c1350 St John of the Cleft Rock writes: 'It is said that 20 centuries after the Incarnation of the Word, the Beast in its turn shall become a man. About the year AD 2000, Antichrist will reveal himself to the world.'

Rupture between European church in East and West finally complete.

Strong Christian communities in south India; Nestorians scattered across subcontinent.

First Middle Persian (Pahlavi) version of Scriptures.

1355 12,000 Jews massacred by Christian mob in Toledo, Spain.

1357 Diocese of Cyprus erected with series of bishops for Maronite church, which separated from Greek Orthodoxy in 7th century, and which has for some time been in communion with Rome.

1358 Mongol emperor Tamerlane (a Tatar Muslim nomad; 1336-1405) begins to destroy Christian civilization from China and north India to Mediterranean.

c1365 Christian influence in Afghanistan terminated by Tamerlane.

Komi-Perm peoples of Russia evangelized by bishop Stephen of Perm (1335-1396).

1368 Ming dynasty ousts Mongol dynasty in China; Christianity disappears; Mongolia converted from Nestorian influence to Buddhism.

1370 John of Trevisa (died 1402) completes translation of whole Bible in Anglo-Norman (Middle English).

1377 End of Babylonian Captivity (exile of popes living at Avignon).

1378 Beginning of Great Schism of the West: up to 3 rival popes at a time, until 1417.

Ziryen (Zirani), language of Ziranas or Komis in Asiatic Russia, reduced to writing by bishop Stephen of Perm who then translates part of

Bible into it; nothing printed however until 1823.

1380 Mongol hordes under Tamerlane destroy Nestorian church and missions throughout Asia; 70,000 heads piled on ruins of Isfahan, 90,000 in Baghdad; extinction of Christianity in central Asia, reduced to remnants in Mesopotamia, Kurdistan, south India.

Brethren of the Common Life, a free religious society of clerics and laity working for reform, founded in Netherlands by mystic Gerard Groote (1340-1384).

1382 English clergyman and scholar John Wycliffe (c1329-1384) completes first translation of whole Bible in English, a very literal rendering from Latin Vulgate; coins and uses the word 'evangelize' and cognates throughout, but all references are changed by followers after his death, in a vigorous and idiomatic popular revision, to the word 'preach' as being less Catholic.

1386 Baptism of Jagiello (c1350-1434) king of Lithuanians; end of European paganism as an organized religion.

1389 Reappearance, after 400 years' disappearance, of Mandylion of Edessa (Icon of Christ, now Holy Shroud of Turin); owned by Templars in France, exposed regularly.

1391 Start of anti-Semitic massacres in Spain and Portugal: 4,000 Jews killed in Seville.

1394 Tamerlane destroys West Syrian (Jacobite) churches and monasteries throughout Mesopotamia and Asia Minor.

1395 Lollards (followers of Wycliffe) in England become an organized anti-Catholic Anglican sect with specially-ordained ministers, spokesmen in Parliament, and many followers in middle and artisan classes; persecuted, and leaders burnt; by 1530, merged into Protestantism.

1396 Bulgaria falls to Muslim invaders, Ottoman Turks.

1399 Catalan Dominican wandering preacher Vincent Ferrer (c1350-1419) reevangelizes and transforms Christendom throughout Europe; brings Jews to dialogues, converts 25,000 across Europe; preaches 6,000 apocalyptic sermons each 3 hours long, with glossolalia, healings, miracles widely reported; writes of future coming of Antichrist, predicts world will end after 2,537 more years in AD 3936 (based on number of verses in Book of Psalms).

1400 **Global status:** 46 generations after Christ, world is 24.0% Christians (75% of them being Whites), 27% evangelized; with Scriptures translated into 30 languages.

World's 5 largest cities: Nanking 473,000, Cairo 450,000, Vijayanagar 350,000, Hangchow 325,000, Peking 320,000.

Inquisition begins investigating witchcraft seriously, burns at least 30,000 witches from 1400-1550; 1484, pope Innocent VIII issues bull authorizing extirpation of witchcraft in Germany; 1486, *Malleus Maleficarum* (The Witches' Hammer) published; European witch-craze lasts from 1400-1700, executing around 500,000 for alleged witchcraft; 1692, Salem witch trials in USA.

c1400 Nubia: Christianity still widespread, with 7 bishoprics in the north and 400 churches in the south.

Societas Peregrinantium pro Christo founded by Franciscans.

Continued northeastward expansion of Orthodoxy across Russia through monks.

First Russian indigenous movements: Strigolniks (Barbers) from Pskov form schismatic groups out of Russian Orthodox Church, protesting against charging of fees for sacraments.

Scriptures translated into Icelandic.

1402 Ottoman empire 6.3 million, rising to 28 million by 1580; then continuous decline until 1922 dissolution.

c1410 Hungarian translation of Bible.

1414 Council of Constance (16th Ecumenical Council): condemnation of reformers Wycliffe, Hus, et alii; 1415, Hus burnt at stake as heretic.

1415 Capture of Ceuta in Morocco by Portuguese under Henry the Navigator (1394-1460).

1420 Taborites, extreme militant wing of Bohemian Hussites at Tabor south of Prague, founded as strict biblicists under their bishop Nicholas of Pelhrimov, seek to establish Kingdom of God by force of arms and military campaigns including destruction of churches; finally defeated at Lipany in 1434, Tabor captured 1452.

1431 Council of Basle (17th Ecumenical Council): question of papal supremacy, and the Hussite heresy; edict orders all Jews to attend Christian sermons.

1436 Utraquist Church (moderate Hussites from among nobility and university professors) becomes established church of Bohemia until 1620; at Council of Basle in 1436, formally recognized as equal by Catholic Church in its 'Compactata', but annulled in 1462 by pope Pius II.

1438 Council of Florence (also regarded as 17th Ecumenical Council): union with Greeks attempted.

c1440 German cleric Nicholas of Cusa (1401-1464) holds there to be an infinite number of stars (suns) spread through infinite space, all with planets some of which are inhabited by intelligent beings.

1441 Armenian patriarchate moved from Sis (Cilicia) to Echmiadzin.

1443 Bosnia abandons Manicheism.

1445 *Senegal.* First Christians (Portuguese explorers); 1489, Senegalese chief baptized.

Guinea Bissau. First Christians (Portuguese trading centre; Catholic missionaries 1462).

Equatorial Guinea. First Christians (Portuguese traders).

1448 *Mauritania.* First Christians (Portuguese, French, Dutch and English traders).

Russian Orthodox Church becomes 2 autocephalous metropolitanates, Moscow and Kiev.

c1449 Scriptures: languages possessing some translated portions of the Bible number 33, just prior to invention of printing.

Total books in Europe before invention of movable type about 50,000, all handwritten; by 1500, 10 million printed books.

1450 Invention of printing (typography and the printing press) by Johan Gutenberg (c1395-1468) at Mainz, Germany; more than 100 editions of the Bible produced by 1500.

c1450 Dechristianizing forces strong in Europe: Renaissance, humanism, recrudescence of paganism, obsession with wealth.

Trifo and Theodorit evangelize Kola Lapps.

1452 St Peter's basilica in Rome planned as world's largest church, after 1453 to replace Santa Sophia (Constantinople); 1506, foundation stone laid; 1626, completed.

1453 Fall of Constantinople (population having shrunk to 50,000) to Muslim Ottoman Turks; end of Byzantine empire; fleeing scholars take Greek text of Bible to the West.

1455 German mystic Thomas a Kempis (c1380-1471) writes *The Imitation of Christ*; a major influence on evangelization.

1456 Latin (Gutenberg) Bible: first printed scripture edition and first large printed book in Europe (4 years being printed in Mainz): 500 copies printed.

Pope Calixtus III gives great prior of Order of Christ of Portugal the spiritual supervision of all Portuguese overseas dominions.

1457 Turkish Muslims conquer peoples of Yugoslavia, 1517 overrun Egypt.

Unitas Fratrum (Moravians) establish Christian village in Moravia.

1458 Historian E.S. Piccolomini (1405-1464) elected as pope Pius II, predicts modern weapons will bring world to destruction.

1461 Armenian patriarchate established in Constantinople.

1462 *Cape Verde Islands.* First mission (Portuguese Catholics).

1466 High German Bible printed: first in any modern language.

1471 *Ghana* (then Gold Coast). First Christians (Portuguese soldiers).

First Italian printed Bible.

1474 First French printed New Testament.

1477 First Dutch printed Old Testament.

1478 First Spanish printed Bible.

Spanish Inquisition established to ferret out crypto-Jews and hidden Muslims, under Torquemada as inquisitor general; 120,000 Spanish intellectuals and Jews condemned, imprisoned, ruined or executed from 1481-98, with 2,000 burnt at the stake.

1480 Russia expels Mongol Muslim rulers, becomes a Christian state, spreads gospel across northern Asia.

1482 *Zaire* (then Congo). First Christians (Portuguese explorers); 1491, first missionaries (Franciscans, Dominicans), and baptism of prince Mwemba son of king Nzinga Nkumu.

1485 *Sao Tome & Principe.* First Christians (Portuguese settlement).

1487 First French printed Bible, the Grande Bible (not a complete version); a dozen editions before 1550.

Nigeria. First Christians (Portuguese Catholics); 1491, king of Benin baptized.

1488 First printed Hebrew complete Old Testament (Soncino).

1489 Baptism of Wolof king Behemoi (Senegal) with many notables at Lisbon; on return home, expels Dominicans.

1490 Large numbers of reform-minded beggar monks and priests itinerate preaching and witnessing, including Wolfgang Capito (1478-1541), Paul Speratus (1484-1551) bishop of Pomerania, Gabriel Zwilling (1487-1558), Johannes Brenz (1499-1570) and many others.

1491 *Angola* (then Congo kingdom). First mission (Catholics at São Salvador); first church buildings built by Portuguese Jesuits.

Congo (Brazzaville). First mission (Portuguese Catholics); collapses, not revived until 1883.

1492 Christopher Columbus (1451-1506) sails to New World, discovers America (Bahamas, Cuba, Haiti); over next few decades, 100,000 Spaniards immigrate from Old World.

Capture of Granada, last Muslim stronghold in Spain; Muslim influence remains in Spain in shape of 150,000 Moors and 200,000 Moriscos.

Expulsion of 180,000 Jews from Spain; 350,000 others forcibly converted to Christianity and remain in Spain as Marranos (Conversos, Anusim, Crypto-Jews), though 12,000 burnt as heretics by Inquisition; expelled Jews settle in Safed, Palestine, centre of Jewish mysticism (Kabbala), later under rabbi Isaac Luria (1534-1572).

Rodrigo Borgia (1431-1503) made pope as Alexander VI; nadir in morality of renaissance papacy.

1493 Pope issues Demarcation Bull 'Inter Caetera', giving Portugal authority over Africa, much of Asia and later Brazil; Spain given authority over rest of world west of a north-south line 345 miles west of the Azores.

Haiti (then Santo Domingo). First mission (Spanish Catholics).

1494 *Dominican Republic* (then Santo Domingo). First missionaries (Spanish Catholics).

1495 Bohemian Brethren, with 400 churches and 100,000 members in Bohemia and Moravia, organize a Recognoscierung to locate whatever Eastern and Western churches have kept the apostolic faith.

1497 All 200,000 Jews in Portugal (20% of population) forced to either accept Christianity as Marranos (Conversos) or be deported.
'Last Supper' painted by Leonardo da Vinci (1452-1519), greatest genius ever, artist, scientist, engineer, inventor (submarine, tanks, aircraft, parachute, helicopter, anatomy, Mona Lisa, etc.).

1498 *Kenya.* First Christians (Vasco da Gama [1460-1524] and Portuguese explorers); by 1597, 600 African converts.

1499 German astrologer Johannes Stoeffler (1452-1531) predicts end of world by deluge on 20 February 1524; thousands then jam boats and 3-storey ark on river Rhine.
Spain: mass forced baptisms of Moors (Muslims) under inquisitor-general Cisneros (1436-1517); 1502, all Muslims forced to choose between baptism or exile.
Aruba. First Christians (Spanish Catholics); 1634 part of Dutch Antilles.
Final extinction of Christianity in Nubia due to absence of local leadership and local-language liturgy and Scriptures; southern kingdom of Alodia becomes Muslim as capital Suba falls to Fung and Arab armies.
Christianity extinguished in China, Central Asia, and across the Muslim world.
Steady shrinking of Christian influence; outlook for Christianity as a world religion decidedly unfavorable.
Up to this date, almost no contact between the 3 major races of mankind (Caucasoid, Mongoloid, Negroid).

Epoch V:
REFORM AND EXPANSION
1500-1750

1500 **Global status:** 49 generations after Christ, world is 19.0% Christians (92.6% of them being Whites), 21.0% evangelized; with printed Scriptures available in 12 languages out of 34 translated; total martyrs since AD 33, 9,200,000 (0.3% of all Christians ever; recent rate 24,600 per year).
Newly-organized Protestant churches make no effort to contact unevangelized peoples of the world for nearly 300 years.
Printing presses in Europe now number 40, with 8 million volumes printed, a large proportion being Christian works (98 distinct editions of the Vulgate).
About 1,000 books a year worldwide published with newly-invented movable type.
Start of Modern English language.
Brazil (then populated by 2 million jungle and lowland Amerindians). First Christians (Portuguese explorers and Franciscans).
Moscow declared to be Third Rome, successor to heretical Rome and Muslim Constantinople.
Several African chiefs on west coast and in Congo baptized by Portuguese.
Portuguese discover 100,000-strong Christians of St Thomas (Syrian Orthodox) in Kerala, south India.
Worldwide expansion of Christianity commences again, mainly through Spanish and Portuguese Catholics.
Countless predictions made during period 1500-1700 by churchmen and scholars about exact time of End of World.
Total of saints and martyrs known by name, formally recognized or canonized by the churches now numbers over 10,000; from 1500-1903, Rome recognizes 113 further canonizations and 547 beatifications; total by 1985, known by name, for all confessions: 50,000 (0.1% of grand total all martyrs by 1985, known and unknown).

1501 *South Africa.* First Christians (Catholic church built at Mossel Bay, Natal, by Portuguese).
First detailed enumeration of a whole population, in Sicily.

1502 *Tanzania* (then Tanganyika, Zanzibar). First Christians (Portuguese, at Kilwa); c1550, first Jesuit and Dominican missionaries.
All Jews of Rhodes (Greece) forcibly converted, expelled, or enslaved.

1503 Franciscan college begun in Haiti.
Gold Coast: baptism of chief of Efutu with 1,300 subjects.

1506 *Mozambique.* First mission (Portuguese Dominicans); 1541, visited by Francis Xavier; 1560, baptism of Gamba king of Inhambane with name Constantine.
Massacre of Lisbon: thousands of 'New Christians' killed (Marranos and Moriscos, i.e. baptized Jews and Muslims).

1508 *Oman.* First Christians (with Portuguese port at Muscat).

1509 *Puerto Rico.* First Christians (Spanish settlement).
Jamaica. First Christians (Spanish Catholic plantation owners).

1511 *Timor.* First Christians (Portuguese sailors); 1561, king baptized.
Singapore. First mission (Portuguese Dominicans).
Malaysia. First missionaries (Portuguese Catholics).
First Catholic diocese of New World established at Puerto Rico.

1512 Council of Lateran V (18th Ecumenical Council): reform of the church.
Cuba. First mission (Dominicans).
Colombia. First Christians (Spanish explorers).

1513 *Venezuela.* First missionaries (Spanish Dominicans and Franciscans).
Panama. First Christians (Spanish settlement).
Trinidad & Tobago. First missionaries (2 Dominicans).

1514 Pope Leo X (1475-1521) accords kings of Portugal right of patronage (padroado) in Asia.
Costa Rica. First mission (Catholic).

1516 Erasmus (c1466-1536) produces first printed Greek New Testament (by which time over 100 Latin versions already printed).
Edict of cardinal Ximenes of Spain: no vessel may proceed to the New World without a priest.
British humanist and statesman Thomas More (1477-1535) publishes speculative work *Utopia*, describing Christian communism; attacks Luther and Reformation; 1529, chancellor of England; 1535, executed (regarded later as a Roman Catholic martyr).

1517 *Comoro Islands.* First Christians (French settlers).
Mayotte. First Christians (Portuguese).
Nicaragua. First Christians (Spanish settlement).

Protestant Reformation in Europe begins

1517 95 Theses nailed to church door in Wittenberg by Martin Luther (1483-1546); origin of Protestant Reformation.
Charles V accords to a Flemish merchant monopoly of transporting 40,000 African slaves a year to Hispaniola, Cuba, Jamaica and Puerto Rico.

1518 *Mexico.* First Christians (Cortes and Spanish conquistadors); Aztecs (also Incas in Peru later, Mayas in Guatemala, and other Amerindian civilizations) convinced that Spaniards are their civilizing heroes and gods returned (Aztec emperor Montezuma and priests believe god Quetzalcoatl has reappeared), hence are incapable of resisting until too late.
Swine flu pandemic brought by Spaniards virtually destroys native Amerindian population of Caribbean: over 3 million Indians killed since 1492; by 1518, almost all 1,500,000 Indians in Cuba, Puerto Rico, Santo Domingo and Lesser Antilles similarly killed, also a third of all central Mexican Indians, and large proportion of French Canadian and New England Indians.
Congo: Don Enrique, son of king Alphonsus I, nominated first indigenous Catholic bishop of Black Africa; dies 1531.

1519 Huldreich Zwingli (1484-1531) installed as people's priest in Zurich; reformation spreads across Switzerland, meeting with its greatest response in Swiss and German cities.

1520 Protestant inertia in missions for next 275 years continues because, having dispensed with monasticism (major method of mission from 4th-16th centuries), reformers had no knowledge of how to prosecute a missionary endeavour (Harnack).
Luther's classic *The Liberty of a Christian Man*; after being condemned in papal bull 'Exsurge Domini', Luther replies with 'Against the Execrable Bull of Antichrist'.
Teachings of guru Nanak (1469-1539) at Kartapur; founds Sikhism (blend of Hinduism and Islam).
Catholic spiritual reform movement called 'Evangelismus' ('Italian evangelism') rises for 20 years in France, Italy and Spain, supported by Michelangelo, zealous aristocrats, prelates and cardinals.

c1520 Luther writes: 'The gospel will always be preached . . . It has gone out throughout the length and the breadth of the world . . . It is made known farther and farther, to those who have not heard it before', and 'The gospel preached by the Apostles in various languages, sounds forth even now till the end of time'; teaches that institution of papacy, and hence every pope (without singling individuals out), is Antichrist; expects Advent of Christ in 1558.
Climax of Ottoman Turk expansion into Christian Europe; mass conversions of Christians to Islam.

1521 *Philippines.* First Christians (Magellan and Spanish explorers; first mass celebrated; 1565, first resident missionaries).
Hernan Cortes (1485-1547) captures Tenochtitlan (population 500,000), defeats Aztec empire and conquers Mexico (New Spain); 1522, governor; 1523, evangelization of Mexico begins under Spanish Franciscans, 1526 Dominicans, 1533 Augustinians.
Diet of Worms: Luther is condemned and declared an outlaw.
Pacific Islands (later known as 4 separate territories): 1521 *Northern Marianas*, 1526 *Micronesia*, 1529 *Marshall Islands*, 1543 *Belau*. First Christians (explorers); 1668 first permanent missionaries (Spaniards).

1522 Spanish expedition under Magellan (c1480-1521) first to circumnavigate globe, proving Earth to be round.
Luther's translation of New Testament into German; Bible in 1534; first Western European Bible based not on Latin Vulgate but on original Hebrew and Greek texts.

1523 Spanish monarch orders Cortes to enforce mass conversion of Mexican Indians; in Mexico, Franciscans baptize over a million in 7 years, with at times 14,000 a day.
Guadeloupe. First missionaries (Catholics; massacred by Caribs).
Ignatius Loyola (1491-1556) works in Palestine for conversion of Muslims.
Group of astrologers announce end of world will begin with destruction of London on 1 February 1524; 20,000 gather outside city on high ground.
Origin of Anabaptists, in Zurich under ex-RC priest Conrad Grebel (1490-1526); spread across Europe to Augsburg, Moravia, Strasbourg, Friesland, Netherlands; 1525, 30,000 (mostly Dutch Mennonites) executed by Catholics and Lutherans, later by Calvinists.
Revival of millennialism by left-wing Protestant Anabaptists, Bohemians,

Moravian Brethren, Zwickau Prophets, et alii.

1524 *Paraguay.* First Christians (Spanish settlement).
Guatemala. First Christians (Spanish soldiers).
Honduras. First Christians (Spanish settlement).

1525 *El Salvador.* First mission (Spanish Catholic priests).
William Tyndale (c1494-1536) produces (in Worms) first printed English New Testament, also 1530 Pentateuch, 1531 Jonah; burnt at stake in 1536 near Brussels.

1526 *USA* (then America). First missionaries (Spanish Catholic priests) to Indians in California, Florida, Texas, et alia; first martyrdoms take place.
Ecuador. First Christians (Spanish settlers).
Edict of emperor Charles V: all vessels obliged to carry missionaries abroad.
Hungary: Lajos II defeated at battle of Mohacs by Turks under sultan Suleiman I who slaughter 200,000 and enslave 100,000 Hungarian Protestants.

1527 Sweden adopts Lutheran Confession.
Argentina. First Christians (Spanish fort erected); 1539, first mission (Franciscans).
First Baptist church established in Zurich.
Ethiopia: Muslim tribal leader Ahmad Gran destroys Amharic Orthodox churches and monasteries in 15 years' savage pillaging.
First travelling evangelist of Reformation period is Silesian nobleman Kaspar Schwenkfeld von Ossig (1489-1561); but ostracized and wanders homeless for 30 years.

1528 Berne Disputation, with its 10 Theses, brings Reformation to city of Berne; Anabaptists insist that Great Commission applies to everyone who confesses Christ's name.
Numerous epochal translations: 1528 Pagninus' Bible, 1537 Matthew's Bible, 1539 Great Bible, 1557 Geneva Bible, 1568 Bishops' Bible, 1582-1610 Rheims-Douai Bible.

1529 Luis Bolanos OFM works among Tucuman Indians of Argentina, converting 20,000 and erecting reductions for them.

1530 *Viet Nam.* First missionaries (Portuguese priests on merchant ships from Goa and Macao).
Confession of Augsburg produced by Philip Melancthon (1497-1560) and signed by Protestant princes.
Anabaptist leader Melchior Hofmann (1495-1543) predicts imminent end of world in AD 1533 with Strasbourg to be the New Jerusalem; followers sell all their possessions.
Luther and Calvin teach that Great Commission (Mark 16:15) was work of 1st-century Apostles only and expired with them.

c1530 *Panama Canal Zone* (then Panama). First Christians (Spaniards).
Dominican friar Bartholomew de Las Casas (1474-1566), first priest ordained (1510) in New World, supports rights of indigenous peoples of Central America, first as bishop of Chiapas in Mexico (1544-1547), then from 1547 back in Spain; before his death, charges 15 million Indians killed by Spanish conquistadors.

1531 Death of Zwingli in battle attempting to force Zurich Protestantism on Catholic cantons.
Mexico: bishop Juan de Zumarraga (1476-1548) writes that they have destroyed over 500 temples and 20,000 idols.

1532 *Peru.* First Christians (Spanish colonists).

1533 Goa on Indian coast made a Catholic bishopric by Portuguese.

1534 *Canada.* First Christians (French soldiers).
British Supremacy Act makes British monarch (then Henry VIII) head of Church of England.
Portuguese Catholic missionaries arrive in Moluccas.
Ignatius Loyola at University of Paris founds Society of Jesus, made into an order in 1539; 1548, chosen as first general; spearhead of Catholic Reformation.
Anabaptist refugees from persecution seize city of Munster, found Kingdom of A Thousand Years, eject unbelievers, establish New Jerusalem; 1534 city captured, king John of Leiden executed; the major 16th-century millenarian outburst.

1535 First English Bible printed, translated by Myles Coverdale.

1536 John Calvin (1509-1564) at age 26 publishes his *Institutes of the Christian Religion*, begins as reformer in Geneva; 1538 banished, 1541 returns to make it centre of Reformed faith and life; produces a theology for church under the Cross, believes he lives in era of Antichrist.
Nearly 6 million Amerindians baptized in Mexico since 1519.
Bangladesh (then East Bengal). First Christians (Portuguese traders in Chittagong).
Denmark, Norway, Sweden adopt Lutheranism as state religion by 1540.
10,000-strong Bharatha (Parava) fishing caste of Coromandal coast (Kerala) baptized en masse by Portuguese, then ignored until Xavier's arrival in 1542.

1537 *Bolivia.* First Christians (Spanish colonists); Catholic diocese formed to include work among Parias and Charcas.
English king declared head of church of Ireland.

1540 *Madagascar.* First mission (Catholic).
England: all monastic institutions seized and expropriated by Thomas Cromwell under Henry VIII (1491-1547).
Population census of Venice (Italy), conducted by church authorities: 129,971 persons.
Copernican Revolution: Polish astronomer Nicolaus Copernicus (1473-1543) completes *On the Revolutions of the Celestial Spheres*, replacing Ptolemaic geocentric system of astronomy with heliocentric system and proving Earth rotates around Sun.

c1540 Russian Orthodox missionary Gowry evangelizes Tartars at time of first tsar of Russia, Ivan IV the Terrible (1530-1584).

1541 *Chile.* First mission (one Catholic priest).

1542 Spanish Jesuit missionary Francis Xavier (1506-1552) arrives in India; 1546, Malacca; then carries the faith throughout Far East (1549, Japan), baptizing 750,000 by time of his death.
Congregation of Universal Inquisition established by Holy See.
Japan. First Christians (Portuguese), followed 1549 by first missionary (Xavier); by 1571, 30,000 Christians; by 1582, 150,000 Christians (1% of Japan) and 200 churches; by 1600, 300,000 in active contact with missionaries, plus thousands of others.

1544 Xavier begins mission in Travancore, baptizes 10,000 Mukuvas in one month (and 15,000 others later).
Roman Catholics in Burma; Portuguese, with Franciscan missionaries.
Martyrdom of 600 newly-baptized Christians in Jaffna, Ceylon.

1545 Augsburg Confession adopted by Hungarian Lutheran Church.
Council of Trent (Counter-Reformation), 19th Ecumenical Council: Protestantism condemned; 25 sessions 1545-63 during lives of 3 popes.

1546 First of several Amerindian anti-Catholic religious movements of revolt in Ecuador: Quimbaya (also 1576 Sobce, 1603).

1547 Severe persecution of Protestants in France; thousands executed under Henri II.
Nostradamus (Michel de Notredame, 1503-1566), astrologer and physician, makes extensive prophecies from 1547, first published as *Centuries* in 1555; condemned by Roman Index in 1781; the most widely read seer of the Renaissance, in print continuously ever since, with vast literature of commentaries; end of world predicted for either 1666, or 1734, 1886, 1943, 2038 or 3797.

1548 *Guyana* (later British Guiana). First missions (Portuguese Catholics).

1549 Brazil: beginning of Catholic missions among Amerindians by first Jesuits in South America.
England: First Prayer Book of Edward VI; revised 1552, 1559, 1662 Book of Common Prayer, 1928, 1980.

1550 **Global status:** 51 generations after Christ, world is 19.1% Christians (80.5% of them being Whites), 22% evangelized; with printed Scriptures available in 28 languages.
First concordance to whole English Bible, compiled by John Marbeck using Matthew's Bible of 1537.
Lutheranism proclaimed state religion of Iceland.
In England, maintenance of baptismal records by local clergy ordered.
Beginnings of definitive New Testament Greek text in edition of R. Stephanus, based on Byzantine Text, finally resulting by 1624 in Textus Receptus.

c1550 *Kuwait.* First Christians (Portuguese sailors and traders).
800,000 Peruvian Amerindians confirmed by one Catholic archbishop of Lima.
Netherlands Antilles. First missionaries (Catholic priests from Santo Domingo).
Martinique. First Christians (Dominican, Jesuit and Capuchin missionaries).
Swiss theologian and Reformed bishop J.H. Bullinger (1504-1575) interprets numerology of Book of Revelation to show world will end in 1666.
English language spoken by under 5 million speakers (less than German, French, Spanish or Italian).

1551 Converts from Assyrian Church of the East, in Iraq and Persia, submit to Rome as Chaldean Catholic Church, with patriarchate in Babylon.
Stoglav (Hundred Chapters) Council condemns Roman Catholicism, but 1596 Union of Brest-Litovsk allows creation of Uniate Catholics.

1552 Council of Lima (Peru): Amerindians may receive Catholic baptism, matrimony and penance, but not confirmation or ordination.
At death of Loyola, Jesuits number 1,000 and become leading Catholic missionary society.

1553 Roman Catholicism restored in England under queen Mary; 286 reformed Anglican leaders burnt at stake including Thomas Cranmer (1489-1556) archbishop of Canterbury, Nicholas Ridley (c1500-1555) bishop of London, bishop Hugh Latimer (1485-1555), and John Hooper (c1495-1555) bishop of Worcester.
In 3 years, 300 Protestants burnt as heretics in Europe.
Mexico: first of numerous Catholic ecclesiastical councils and synods.

1554 *Thailand* (then Siam). First Christians (Portuguese soldiers at royal court, 2 Dominican chaplains, 1,500 Thai converts); 1565, first missionaries killed.

1555 *Kampuchea* (Cambodia). First missions (Jesuits and Dominicans).

1556 Calvin sends first and only Reformed missionary party of 18 French Huguenots to Brazil, off Rio de Janeiro; work collapses.
Jesuits arrive in Paraguay, establish about 100 Christian settlements (reductions) among Guarani Amerindians.
World's worst earthquake disaster: 830,000 killed in Shensi province, China.

Ceylon: conversion to Catholicism of 70,000 fisher-caste Careas (Karawa, Karawola) on coast near Colombo; by 1583, 43,000 Christians on Manar island among pearl-fisher Paravas and Careas.
Beza's Latin New Testament translated.
1557 *Macao*. First Christians (Portuguese settlement).
France: 33% of population reputed to be Protestants (known as Huguenots); 1559, create Reformed Church (72 congregations, 400,000 adherents); widespread manifestations of glossolalia, trances, prophecies, et alia.
Cherkess people send embassy to Moscow offering to be baptized if aided against Crimean Tatars.
1558 Spain: Protestants virtually wiped out by Inquisition by burning at the stake.
1559 Pope Paul IV (1476-1559) forbids all Catholics to read Bible in common tongue, without special authorization.
Anabaptists the only Reformed grouping to deliberately work for and obey Jesus' Great Commission, especially through Hutterian Brethren's itinerant evangelism.
India: 300,000 Roman Catholic converts in Kerala.
John Foxe's *Book of Martyrs* published, chiefly describing martyrdoms in reign of Mary Tudor (1553-1558), and modelled on Jean Crespin's *Book of Huguenot martyrs*.
Scotland: John Knox (c1514-1572) reforms Scottish church, maintaining ecumenical relations with England and the Continent; 1560, Scots Confession approved by Parliament.
1561 *Zimbabwe* (later Southern Rhodesia). First missionary (Portuguese Jesuit); emperor of Monomotapa baptized by him but apostatizes and kills him a year later.
St Helena. First Christians (Dutch settlers).
Malawi (later Nyasaland). First missionaries (Catholics from Mozambique).
Belgic Confession (Confessio Belgica), a major Calvinist creed in Dutch Reformed Church (along with Heidelberg Catechism, and Canons of Dort), drawing heavily on Calvin's 1559 Gallic Confession; adopts amillennial stance.
1562 3,000 French Protestants (Huguenots) massacred at Toulouse.
1564 Index Tridentinus of prohibited books.
1565 First permanent USA Catholic community begun at St Augustine, Florida.
Florida: French Huguenot civilian colony on St John's river annihilated by Spaniards.
1566 First Unitarian churches founded: in Romania, Hungary, and Poland.
1567 Second Helvetic Confession adopted by Hungarian Reformed Church.
In Low Countries, Spanish Council of Blood (1567-74) executes thousands as heretics and Calvinists.
1568 Commission of cardinals instituted in Rome by Pius V for foreign missions in East Indies, for Italo-Greeks, and for Protestant lands of Europe; 1573, congregation for conversion of infidels formed; 1622, founding of Propaganda Fide.
1569 80,000 Christians in East Indies under Jesuit missions.
Moriscos (Spanish Muslims who accepted baptism) in Granada revolt after Philip II prohibits Moorish names, language (Arabic), customs and costume; after ferocious 2-year war, forcibly scattered across northern Spain; 1609-14, 275,000 Moriscos expelled to North Africa.
Peru: Inquisition established in Lima by Philip II (also in Mexico, and 1610 in Cartagena, Colombia), tortures 120,000 heretics, burns 189 dissenters at stake.
1570 Santiago, Chiriguano prophet and reformer, appears in Bolivia.
Cyprus: Turks invade island, exterminate Copts including bishop and priests.
As pope Pius V, former Roman grand inquisitor Michele Ghislieri excommunicates queen Elizabeth I of England.
Japan and Korea: first of numerous Roman Catholic ecclesiastical synods.
1571 Japan: mass movement begins under Omura Sumitada; 50,000 converted.
Thirty-Nine Articles promulgated in England as Anglican confession of faith.
Muslim empire of Kanem-Bornu (9th-19th centuries) in central Africa at height of power under king Idris III in walled capital Ngazargamu in Bornu, based on vast numbers of slaves.
1572 St Bartholomew's Day massacre: 72,000 Huguenots slaughtered in France in attempt to destroy Calvinist leadership.
Tycho's Star appears, a violently exploding supernova, visible for 2 years.
1575 First German pietist missionaries begin in Tranquebar, India.
1576 China reentered by Catholics with Macao made a Portuguese diocese.
1577 Philippines: 14 Franciscan friars arrive in Manila and pursue mass christianization; by 1583, 16% baptized Christians (100,000); 1594, 46% (286,000); 1629, 74% (500,000); 1690, 87% (700,000); 1735, 93% (837,182); 1750, 97% (904,116).
1578 First Anglicans in North America (California, then Virginia).
1580 *Surinam*. First Christians (Dutch settlement).
Germany: evangelism flourishes under Pietist leaders: John Arndt (1555-1621), Paul Gerhardt (1607-1676), P.J. Spener, Albrecht Bengel (1687-1752), and N.L. von Zinzendorf.
c1580 Jesuit theologian in Peru, José de Acosta (1539-1600), writes *De procuranda Indorum salute* (On the preaching of the Gospel among the Savages), dealing with problems of mass baptisms, role of military, feasibility of native clergy, et alia.
Robert Browne (c1553-1633) of Norwich organizes 'gathered churches'; origin of Brownists and Congregationalism.
1581 Claudio Aquaviva (1543-1615) elected 5th general of Society of Jesus; at his death, Jesuits have increased from 5,000 to 13,000.
1582 Jesuit missionary Matteo Ricci (1552-1610) begins his mission in Macao; 1601, summoned to Peking by emperor; at his death, converts number only 2,000.
Japan: 200 churches and 150,000 Christians; 1588, Japan made a Catholic diocese.
Franciscans led by Jerome de Burgos arrive in China but are expelled.
Pope Gregory XIII (1502-1585) introduces New Style or Gregorian Calendar (13 days ahead of Old Style or Julian Calendar of Julius Caesar); 1752, adopted by England; 1924, finally adopted by most Orthodox churches except Jerusalem, Russia, Serbia and Bulgaria.
Roman Catholic translation of Scriptures from Vulgate into English: 1582 New Testament, in Rheims; 1609-10 Bible, in Douai; standard RC Bible in English for nearly 4 centuries.
Major Latin American provincial episcopal councils: 1582 Lima III, 1585 Mexico III; earlier emphases on evangelization of Amerindians, and concern for their freedom, give way to White colonial Catholicism.
1584 Baptism of king of Angola.
Jesuit priest Alonso Sanchez drafts evangelistic scheme for invasion and military conquest of China.
1587 Foreign missions in Japan prohibited, until 1844; severity of persecution varies.
1588 Anglican parish priest Hadrian Saravia (1531-1613) becomes one of first non-Roman advocates of foreign missions, stressing binding validity of Matthew 28:19: 'The command to preach the gospel to the Gentiles pertained not only to the age of the apostles, but to all future times to the end of the world.'
1589 Russian Orthodox patriarchate instituted (the Third Rome); suppressed 1721.
1590 Invention of microscope, created by Zacharias Janssen, and later by Dutch scientist Anton van Leeuwenhoek.
1592 *South Korea*. First Christians (invading army from Japan, with Catholic general and Jesuit priest).
1594 Jesuits reach court of Mongol emperor Akbar; construction of first Christian church in Lahore permitted, though few conversions.
Scottish mathematician John Napier (1550-1617) invents logarithms in order to speed up his calculations of the number of the Beast (in Revelation 13:18); writes *Plaine Discovery of the Whole Revelation of Saint John* (1594).
1596 Union of Brest-Litovsk, between Rome and Orthodox Ruthenian church of west Ukraine, establishes basis for Eastern-rite Catholics (Uniates) to preserve Orthodox Byzantine liturgy with minimal changes.
1597 In Nagasaki under dictator Hideyoshi, crucifixion of 6 Franciscans, 3 Japanese Jesuits and 16 Japanese Catholics; numerous others executed, churches burned.
1598 *Mauritius*. First Christians (Dutch).
French Guiana. First Christians (French settlements).
Edict of Nantes ending French wars of religion, allowing religious liberty and civil equality to Huguenots in France; revoked 1685, causing Huguenot emigration.
Smallpox and measles responsible for killing millions in Latin America during preceding 100 years.

1600 **Global status:** 52 generations after Christ, world is 18.9% Christians (86.0% of them being Whites), 23.0% evangelized; with printed Scriptures available in 36 languages.
World's 5 largest cities: Peking 706,000, Constantinople 700,000, Agra 500,000, Cairo 400,000, Osaka 400,000.
Latin America: mestizos (persons of mixed race) forbidden ordination as RC priests until after 1700.
Italian occultist-philosopher Giordano Bruno (1548-1600) proposes Christ as great magician in a magico-religious system to replace Christianity; holds there are an infinity of worlds in Universe, many inhabited; burnt at stake by Inquisition.
China: first of several Roman Catholic ecclesiastical synods.
c1600 Jesuit reductions (cooperative Amerindian villages) in Bolivia among Moxos and Chiquitos.
Nkimba and Kimpasi in Congo, syncretistic prophet movements based on Jesuit institutions.
North Korea. First Christians.
Svalbard & Jan Mayen Islands. First Christians (European whaling center).
Brunei. First Christians (Spanish trading center).
Christians in Japan number 750,000 (3.4% of population), including most of Nagasaki area, with 300,000 being baptized Roman Catholics.
Nubia: final extinction of Christianity.
In Latin America, 250,000 Spaniards rule 9 million Amerindians, and 30,000 Portuguese in Brazil rule over 2 million natives.
Somnium (The Dream), one of first modern works of science fiction, written by first astrophysicist J. Kepler (1571-1630), greatest theoretician of his age; begins search for extraterrestrial life.
1602 Orthodox bishopric erected at Astrakhan near mouth of Volga.

Dutch government sends missionaries to convert Malays in East Indies domains.

1603 Roman Catholics in England and Wales number 1.5 million, declining to 69,376 by 1780; at end of Elizabethan persecution of Roman Catholics, 123 out of 438 priests have been executed.
In Philippines (now 50% christianized), 3,000 Chinese massacred near Manila.

1604 *St Pierre & Miquelon*. First Christians (French Catholic settlers).
Kepler's Star (Nova Ophiuchi), a violently exploding supernova, visible for 2 years.

1605 Armenian Catholic Church (Uniate) created through Dominican activity in Iran.
Catholic missionaries expelled by Dutch from Indonesia, replaced by Dutch Reformed chaplains of Dutch East India Company.
Jesuit missionary Robert de Nobili (1577-1656) arrives in Madura, south India, begins experiment in cultural accommodation among Brahmins.

1607 USA: Anglicans begin evangelization with foundation of Virginia Colony at Jamestown.

1608 Canada: Roman Catholic work begun among Micmac Indians.
Invention of telescope by 6 separate persons independently, in Holland, France, Germany, Italy, Britain; 1609, Italian astronomer Galilei Galileo (1564-1642) reinvents it and discovers Moon craters and Jupiter's moons; major conflict with Church of Rome over Copernican theory of planets revolving around Sun.

1609 *Bermuda*. First Christians (English sailors, Anglicans).
Philip III of Spain (Philip II of Portugal, 1578-1621) expels all Moriscos (Christians of Moorish ancestry, i.e. Spanish Muslims forcibly baptized); 275,000 flee to Algeria, Morocco and Tunisia.
First English Baptist church organized in Amsterdam by Puritan nonconformist John Smyth (c1567-1612); 1612, rise of General Baptists in England under Thomas Helwys (c1550-c1616); 1633, Particular Baptists organized, with 131 churches by 1660.

1610 Catholics in Peking number 2,000 at death of Jesuit superior Matteo Ricci.
Spanish Jesuit missionary Peter Claver, 'Apostle to the Blacks' (1580-1654), arrives at slave-trade capital Cartagena (Colombia), ministers to 1,000 African arrivals a month for 44 years, baptizing 300,000 Negro slaves.

c1610 Dominican historian Tomas Malvenda (1566-1628) translates Hebrew OT into Latin, writes work on coming of Antichrist.
English philosopher of science and statesman Francis Bacon (1561-1626) makes first proposal for an artificially-constructed international language; 1629, French philosopher R. Descartes (1596-1650) proposes one based on numbers; 1880 Volapuk created, 1887 Esperanto, 1920 Interlingua; by 1950 total of 700 different attempts, all of which fail to win widespread acceptance.

1611 King James Version (KJV) or Authorized Version (AV) of English Bible published, under 47 scholars working in 3 panels; in elegant prose designed for public reading in large churches; enormous influence for 3 centuries as main Bible of English-speaking Protestants and Anglicans, including in their missions worldwide; 1881-85 RV and 1901 ASV augment but do not displace it; 1985, KJV still major version of 500 million English-speaking Christians (despite existence of 400 other English versions); 1979-82, updated New KJV published.
British East India Company begins trade in Surat, Bombay.
Reductions among Guarani number 33 (11 in Paraguay, 15 Argentina, 7 Brazil).

1612 Anglican clergy first serve as chaplains with East India Company.
Philippines: 322,400 Filipino Christians on Luzon alone.

1613 Major missionary work by Discalced Carmelite monk of Spain, Thomas a Jesu (1564-1627), *De procuranda salute omnium gentium*, urges and envisages conversion of entire world to Christ.

1614 Japanese edict prohibiting Christianity, then 3.5% of population; churches destroyed, Jesuits and other missionaries deported, over 40,000 Christians massacred, rest exist underground.

1616 *Uruguay*. First missionaries (Spanish Franciscans and Jesuits).
First Baptist congregation in England (London); known as General Baptists.
Fama fraternitas describes formation of Rosicrucians, a secret worldwide occult brotherhood claiming esoteric wisdom from ancient Egypt.

1617 Decree of banishment and persecution against all Christians in China; further edicts 1665, 1724 and 1736; but total Catholics remain at 150,000 (1650), 250,000 (1663), 300,000 (1675), 300,000 (1700), 200,000 (1800).

1618 Synod of Dort (Dutch Reformed Church) affirms orthodox Calvinist position on predestination, condemns Remonstrants and Arminians.
Thirty Years' War begins as last of the Wars of Religion kindled by German and Swiss Reformation: Protestants in Holy Roman Empire revolt against Catholic oppression; Sweden, France and Denmark invade Germany; numerous martyrdoms including 1631 Catholic priest Liborius Wagner of Schweinfurt.

1619 Dutch colonize East Indies (Indonesia).
Over last 100 years since Conquest, Spaniards (250,000 by 1600) reduce Meso-Americans from 13 million to 10 million through war, disease, starvation, forced labor.
Martyrs of Kaschau (Hungary): 3 Jesuits beaten to death by Calvinist soldiers.

1620 Pilgrim Fathers from England cross Atlantic to America in sailing ship Mayflower to found New England.
Bohemia forcibly made Roman Catholic by Austrian armies; 30,000 Protestants expelled, others massacred.
Johann Gerhard (1582-1637), theologian of Lutheran orthodoxy, holds task of mission preaching was essentially completed by the NT Apostles.

1621 *China* (*Taiwan*, Formosa). First mission (Dominicans from Philippines); 1627, first Dutch Reformed missionary, Georgius Candidius, followed by 37 others, with 17,000 aboriginal converts (4,000 baptized) by 1650.
Invention of the calculating slide-rule by English clergyman W. Oughtred (1574-1660); spreads and lasts 350 years until finally superseded by pocket calculators in 1975.

1622 Sacred Congregation for the Propagation of the Faith (Propaganda, meaning progressive plantation) founded by pope Gregory XV (1554-1623).
Comity scheme introduced for Roman Catholic missionary orders to avoid duplication or competition.

1623 *St Kitts-Nevis*. First Christians (British settlers).
German Lutherans arrive in New York, organizing a congregation by 1649.
23 Jesuit reductions (settlements), with 100,000 population, in Paraguay.
Byelorussia: priests and bishops, including bishop Josaphat of Polotsk, killed by mobs.

1625 Indochina: first of several Roman Catholic ecclesiastical synods.

1626 *Barbados*. First Christians (English settlers with Anglican clergy).
Francis Bacon writes of 'the Apostolicall and Miraculous Evangelisme of Saint Bartholomew'.
Tibet: first Christian missionary, Antoine de Andrade, Portuguese Jesuit; poisoned 1634; 1745, last mission station, run by Capuchins, shut down.

1627 French Jesuit missionary Alexander de Rhodes (1591-1660) baptizes 6,700 in North Viet Nam; 1629, Trinh-Trang king of Tonkin prohibits conversions on pain of death.
German Calvinist theologian in Transylvania, Johann H. Alsted (1588-1638) revives premillennialism with book *The Beloved City*; marked impact on English and Puritan millennialism.
English biblical scholar Joseph Mede (1586-1638), a premillennialist, writes *Apocalyptica: Key of the Revelation*, formulates theory of progressive millennialism (later termed postmillennialism): Christ will only return at close of man-made millennium on Earth.

1628 Dutch in New York organize first Christian Reformed church on Manhattan Island.
Revival in Ireland under Blair and Livingstone.

1629 Matthew's Gospel printed in Malay; first evangelistic scripture portion in a non-European language.
Ecumenical patriarch of Constantinople, Cyril I Lukaris, publishes Calvinistic confession of faith, attempts to reform Orthodoxy on Anglican and Protestant lines, sends Codex Alexandrinus (3rd oldest Bible known) to English king Charles I; 1638, murdered by Ottoman sultan Murad IV; successor Cyril II Kontaris returns to communion with Rome, 1640 murdered by sultan.

1630 *Laos*. First mission (Catholics).
Structure of Catholicism in Japan destroyed after 16 years' persecution, with 1,900 martyrs crucified; remnants (150,000 secret believers in 1640) continue underground.
German Jesuit astronomer J. A. Schall Von Bell (1591-1666) arrives in China as missionary, reforms Chinese calendar, is personally credited with 100,000 converts; 1650, builds first Christian church in Peking; 1657, obtains imperial permission to evangelize throughout China.

1631 Martyrs of Mombasa: prior of Mombasa, 2 priests, 280 lay persons massacred by apostate Swahili sultan Chingulia after refusing to renounce Christian faith; 1740, Portuguese influence along East African coast extinguished.

1632 *Montserrat*. First Christians (Irish settlers).
Lord Baltimore (1580-1632) with 300 Irish Catholics founds Maryland for Roman Catholic settlers in North America.

1634 Bavaria: Oberammergau Passion Play begun by amateurs in fulfilment of a vow.
Antigua. First Christians (English settlers, Anglicans).
Peter Heyling (1607-1652) of Lubeck works as isolated German Lutheran missionary among monophysites in Egypt and Ethiopia; translates part of NT into Amharic; martyred there by Muslim fanatic.

1635 Public letter post introduced in England as first in world.
Italian Jesuit, Giulio Alenio, publishes first life of Christ in Chinese.

1637 *Ivory Coast*. First Christians (Portuguese traders).
Japanese Christians on Shimabara revolt, 35,000 massacred; Hidden Christians in Japan continue completely underground for 220 years; Japan isolated from rest of world.

1638 Ottoman sultan Murad IV murders 2 ecumenical patriarchs in succession: Cyril I, Cyril II.
Francis Godwin writes *The Man in the Moon*, first description of a space voyage; later, appointed Anglican bishop of Llandaff.

1639 Roger Williams (c1603-1683) founds first Baptist church in USA at Providence, Rhode Island.

c1640 North America: 4,000 Indians converted and nurtured in 14 settlements under John Eliot (Apostle to the Indians, 1604-1690) who produces

Mohican Bible, first Indian translation.

1641 Massacre of 7,000 of the 100,000 Scots colonists in Ulster (Protestants) by Irish Catholics.

1642 *Dominica.* First mission (RC Dominican priests).
French scientist-philosopher Blaise Pascal (1623-1662) invents first successful digital calculating machine (first pocket calculator); 1654, converted to faith in Christ, writes *Apology for the Christian Religion.*
Canada: a number of Jesuit missionaries murdered by Iroquois, Mohawk and other Indians, 1642-50.

1643 Catholic missionaries in China appeal to Rome over rites controversy; 1742, final papal bull rejecting Ricci's methods.
Westminster Confession commissioned by Long Parliament to remodel Church of England; now recognized as major Reformed confession.

1644 Last heir to Chinese throne under Ming dynasty baptized by Jesuits with name Constantine, but Manchus seize power; second of the 3 great missed opportunities for Christianity when Chinese imperial throne almost won to the faith (1266, 1644, 1843).
China: Manchu conquest kills 25 million Chinese, 10,000 Chinese Christians; Dominican protomartyr F. de Capillas beheaded.

1645 Long series of vicious persecutions in Annam: 1645, 1st persecution, Alexander de Rhodes expelled; 1665 2nd persecution, with 45 Vietnamese martyrs; 1698 with 200 churches destroyed; 1719 3rd persecution with 700 churches destroyed; 1731, 1745, 1773, 1798, 1821 4th persecution; 1825, 1832, 1833, 1847 5th persecution; 1851, 90,000 Roman Catholics killed including 115 priests; also 1856, 1884, 1947, 1950, 1975.

1646 Union of Uzhgorod, between Rome and Orthodox Ruthenians of Byzantine-Slavonic rite in Hungary.

1647 In Congo, Felix de Viler and colleagues baptize over 600,000 adults from 1647-51; Capuchins baptize vast numbers more in Congo and Angola, mainly infants, by 1700.

1648 *US Virgin Islands.* First Christians (French settlers).
Russian expansion eastwards reaches Pacific Ocean.
St Lucia. First Christians (French settlers).
100,000 Jews murdered in Chmielnicki massacres by Christians in Poland.
British Virgin Islands. First Christians (Dutch settlers).
Jewish youth, Sabbatai Zevi (1626-1676) in Izmir proclaims himself Messiah; one of long series of Cabalist-Messiahs in Jewish history; 1665, captured by Turks, converts to Islam.
Peace of Westphalia: European powers accept religious pluralism and denominationalism.
Spanish Jesuit Ildefonso de Flores (1590-1660) calculates total Christian martyrs of all epochs to date at 11 million.

1649 *Reunion.* First Christians (French settlement).
Society for the Propagation of the Gospel in New England founded by the Long Parliament (England), to reach settlers and Amerindians, with first missionary John Eliot who forms 6 congregations with 1,100 Indians; oldest Anglican missionary society; 1743, David Brainerd (1718-1747) begins among Indians in Massachusetts under SPCK.
Christians far more widely spread geographically than ever previously, but less numerous proportionately than in AD 500.

1650 **Global status:** 54 generations after Christ, world is 21.2% Christians (83.1% of them being Whites), 24.7% evangelized; with printed Scriptures available in 45 languages.
German pioneers of Pietistic evangelism: G. Voetius (1588-1676), J. von Lodenstein (1620-1677), J. de Labadie (1610-1674), T. Untereyck (1635-1693), Spener, Francke, J. Neander (1650-1680).

c1650 *St Vincent.* First Christians (French, Dutch, British settlers).
Russian Orthodoxy reaches across Siberia to Bering Strait.
Grenada. First Christians (French settlers).
Belize. First Christians (Spanish settlement).
Anguilla. First Christians (British Anglicans).
Egypt: Coptic bishops decline in number to only 17 (from 168 in AD 550).
Syrian Orthodox Church declines to 20 dioceses from 103 dioceses in 1150.
Revolutionary Dutch government embraces European Enlightenment; through Dutch East India Company, Dutch appear and colonize around the world.

1651 Dutch control Cape Colony, South Africa.
Gambia. First Christians (British soldiers).
British political philosopher Thomas Hobbes (1588-1679) writes in *Leviathan* of 'Evangelization, that is, the Proclamation of Christ'.

1652 Large numbers of White and Little Russian Orthodox submit to Rome as the Podcarpathian Ruthenians.

1653 Metropolitan Ignatius (Atalla, Ahatalla) of Syrian Jacobite Church arrives in India, intercepted at sea, then in 1654 burnt alive by Jesuits and Portuguese inquisition at Goa; Malabar Church breaks from Rome, comes under Syrian (Jacobite) Church; 1662, returns to Rome due to Carmelites.

1654 Islam introduced into South Africa through Dutch sending Muslim convicts from Batavia (Indonesia).

1655 Massacre of Waldensians in Piedmont, part of 300-year persecution under Catholic House of Savoy; finally in 1848, full civil rights under Statute of Emancipation.

1656 Calvinist and Puritan statesman Oliver Cromwell (1599-1658), protector of Commonwealth of England, Scotland and Ireland from 1653-1658, allows Jews prohibited since 1290 to return to England, in order to hasten Christ's Second Coming.

1658 Ceylon: Dutch finally drive out Portuguese, ban Catholicism with its 300,000 Catholics.
Viet Nam: 300,000 Catholics (including many death-bed baptisms).
Société des Missions Etrangères de Paris (MEP) founded; oldest missionary society for secular priests; RC missions to east and southeast Asia organized.
Death of Bartholomaus Holtzhauser after predicting Antichrist would reveal himself at age of 55½ years; others assert he would do so at 30 years, thus parodying Jesus the Christ.

1659 *French Polynesia.* First mission (Catholics); further attempts 1772, 1831, et alia.

1660 Scottish Covenanters (Presbyterians who signed National Covenant of 1638) brutally persecuted for 25 years.

c1660 Peruvian Franciscan theologian G. Tenorio (1602-1682) publishes treatise extolling Peruvian Indian culture and predicting Millennium will be in Peru as center of the world church.

1661 Formosa: Chinese pirates under general Koxinga (Chen Ch'eng-kung, 1624-1662) invade island with 25,000 Minnan men, crucifying Dutch missionaries and killing 6,000 Reformed converts from aboriginal tribes.

1662 Quaker Act in Britain: 15,000 Quakers imprisoned from 1660-1685 under Charles II (1630-1685); 500 die in prison; persecution continues until Toleration Act of 1689.
Schism ex Church of England: 300,000 communicants follow 2,000 Anglican ministers ejected under Act of Uniformity.
English merchant John Graunt (1620-1674) launches demography as a science by constructing first mortality tables.
Siberia: 70,000 Russians settle, increasing by 1783 to 1 million.
Massachusetts: 'Half-way Covenant' adopted, admitting children of believing parents into full church membership.

1663 *Chad.* First mission (RC, Capuchins); then abandoned until 1929.
Justinian von Weltz (1621-1668) writes treatises to challenge German churches, students and Pietists to missionary work among unevangelized peoples.

1664 Baptized Catholics in Chinese empire grow from 150,000 in 1650 to 254,980 in 1664 (including vast numbers of children baptized in articulo mortis).

1665 Plague and fire devastate London: 75,000 die of plague, 1666 Great Fire of London destroys 13,000 houses.
First scientific journal published, in London; total rises to 50,000 such journals by 1960.
New World city of Quebec produces earliest complete population census in history.

1666 15,000 Protestants expelled by archbishop of Salzburg from his principality.
Old Ritualist schism (Raskolniki, Old Believers) ex Russian Orthodox Church, opposing reforming patriarch Nikon as Antichrist; brutally persecuted until 1725, with leader archpriest Avvakum Petrovich (1620-1682) burnt at stake, and monks massacred.

1667 English poet John Milton (1608-1674) uses phrase 'to Evangelize the Nations' in his *Paradise Lost.*

1668 Pacific Islands (Micronesia): first permanent mission (Spanish Catholics).
Guam. First mission (Spanish Jesuits).
First Bible translation in southeast Asia: NT translated into Malay; Bible in 1733 (Roman script) and 1758 (Arabic script).

1670 Bengal: 20,000 Namasudra Bengalis (outcaste Hindus) in Dacca converted to Catholicism in 2 years; by 1677, total 30,000.
Cayman Islands. First Christians (British settlers).
City of Paris begins publishing records of baptisms, births and burials (continued up to present day).

c1670 *Bahamas.* First Christians (British settlers, Anglicans).
Devotional evangelistic meetings in Frankfurt, Germany (Philip Jakob Spener, 1635-1705).

1671 Anton Horneck (1641-1697), Pietist evangelist, becomes Anglican divine and prebendary, founds first Vestry Society in England.
Hungary: violent attacks on Protestants by Turkish rulers; 1681, religious toleration proclaimed; 1687, Blood Trials of Eperies; many Protestants executed up to 1781.

1672 Synod of Jerusalem, council convened by Eastern Orthodox patriarch Dositheos to reject Calvinist 'Confession of Orthodox Faith' (1629) of Cyril Lucaris former patriarch of Constantinople.

1673 *Gabon.* First mission (Italian Capuchins).
Withdrawal of all Roman Catholic monopolies in mission areas.
First Kalmyks converted to Orthodoxy in Russia.

1674 Germany: Lutheran Pietism and missionary outreach begun, led by Philip Spener.

1676 Compton Census in England: first census of church affiliation, organized by Henry Compton (1632-1713) bishop of London; out of 2.6 million adult population, 95.3% are Conformists (Anglicans and Presbyterians), 4.2% Nonconformists (Dissenters), 0.5% Papists (RCs).

1678 300,000 Catholics in North Viet Nam (Tonkin).
English thinker and lay preacher John Bunyan (1628-1688) writes *The*

Pilgrim's Progress, later translated into 48 languages.

1679 First Amerindian ordained priest in Mexico; 1794, first in Chile.

1680 *Benin* (then Dahomey). First Christians (Portuguese settlers).
Penny Post set up as first urban postal service in London by William Dockwra, prepaid and with hourly deliveries.
Russia: Old Believers united in opposition to everything new and oppressive in Russian life regarded as under power of the Antichrist (since 1649 identified with patriarch Nikon, or tsar Alexis I and successors).

1685 Edict of Nantes revoked by Louis XIV (1638-1715); 58,000 Huguenots forced to convert, 400,000 more flee from France to England, South Africa and elsewhere.
Russian Orthodoxy enters China through a chaplain Maxim Leontiev (died 1712); 1695, metropolitan Ignatii of Tobolsk sends 2 others to assist him; 1714, more clergy and lay workers sent; numerous Chinese baptized; 1722, bishop Innocent Kulchicky and 4 clergy sent, but too late; 1724, new Chinese emperor begins widespread persecution of Christians which lasts for 120 years.
China: first native Chinese RC priest, Gregory Lo (1611-1691, ordained 1656) is consecrated as first Chinese bishop, of Canton.

1687 English physicist and mathematician Isaac Newton (1642-1727), greatest scientific genius ever, publishes *Principia Mathematica*, creates a universal view of the world that directs scientific inquiry for 200 years after; devotes his later years to interpretation of prophecies of Daniel and Revelation, also ancient chronology.

1689 Student revival in Leipzig, Germany.
Jesuits expelled from Moscow, and 1719 from all Russia.

1690 West African slave trade accelerates; 5,500,000 slaves traded up to year 1800; grand total eventually 9.5 million Africans to the Americas.
Emergence of progressive millennialism (postmillennialism) under Anglican scholar and Unitarian freethinker Daniel Whitby (1638-1726), renouncing Augustine's traditional nonmillennialism (allegorical millennialism) dominant throughout the last 12 centuries.

1691 Society for the Conversion and Religious Instruction and Education of Negro Slaves in the British West India Islands formed (later, Christian Faith Society).

1692 China decrees freedom of worship to all Christians, totaling 300,000 Roman Catholics found in every province.

1693 Madras: persecution under Marava rajah; Jesuit missionary J. de Britto beheaded outside Uraiyur.
Italy: secret society Knights of the Apocalypse founded to defend church against the Antichrist.

1694 First Protestant interest in organized foreign mission: German Pietists open training school at Halle under Philip Spener and August Hermann Francke (1663-1727); latter founds first German missionary journal.
Nubia: Franciscan missionaries attempt in vain to locate 12,000 Catholics alleged to have come from Ethiopia.
Invention of Liebniz' 'Stepped Reckoner' adding machine; rapid counting vital as backbone of commerce and government.

1697 Finland: crop failure and famine kill 100,000, 35% of population.
Japan: most calamitous destruction of a church in history: 1614 300,000 Christians, 1614-46, 4,045 proved martyrs, 1637-38 some 37,000 Christians massacred, 1614-97 over 200,000 martyrs, 1697 very few open Christians remain.

1698 Invention of 'fire engine' by Thomas Savery; 1705, Newcomen's atmospheric steam engine; 1765, James Watt's separate condenser for steam engines (thus making possible the Industrial Revolution).
First 2 non-Roman missionary societies formed, by Church of England: Society for Promoting Christian Knowledge (SPCK), and (1701) Society for the Propagation of the Gospel in Foreign Parts (SPG).
Destruction in Indochina of 200 Catholic churches under king Min-Wong, a Buddhist zealot.

1700 **Global status:** 56 generations after Christ, world is 22.3% Christians (84.1% of them being Whites), 25.2% evangelized; with printed Scriptures available in 52 languages.
Christians in Portuguese possessions number 500,000.
2,000 Quakers from England settle in Pennsylvania.
Evangelistic campaigns in Germany of Ernst Christoph Hochmann von Hochenau (1670-1721), major separatist Pietist/Lutheran mystic of his time, converted 1693: 'Regarding the conversion of the Jews as the sign of Christ's impending return, he engaged briefly in Jewish missionary work.'
Wittgenstein revival movement in Germany (till 1750).
Swabian Pietist Fathers (Germany): Bengel, Rieger, Hiller, Steinhofer, Storr, et alii.
Roman Catholic baptisms in Congo and Angola average 12,000 a year (mainly infants).
Peter the Great (1672-1725) orders christianization of Siberia.
Dutch East Indies: 100,000 Protestants on Java, 40,000 on Ambon.
Age of Earth reckoned by European scientists at 9,000 years, all plants, animals, humans having been created by God at beginning; Chinese reckon it at several million years; 1747, French biologist Buffon estimates it at 75,000 years (and life at 35,000 years); 1831, English geologist Charles Lyell calculates age of sedimentary rock at 250 million years.

1701 200,000 Romanian Orthodox, with their clergy, submit to Rome as uniate church.
Russia: in Middle Volga, 3,638 pagan Cheremis (Mari) baptized by 1705, after large-scale distribution of gifts, tax exemption and other incentives.

1702 Congo: first attempt to found church independent of Rome in Black Africa: 22-year-old prophetess Donna Beatrice founds Antonian sect with as followers most of Congo kingdom; 1706, Beatrice burnt alive by king Pedro VI.

1703 St Petersburg (Petrograd) built as imperial capital of Russia by Peter the Great, at cost of lives of 200,000 laborers (Orthodox and other Christians).
200,000 Indian converts to Jesuit mission around Madura, South India.
Spiritans (Holy Ghost Fathers, CSSp) founded by Claude François Poullart des Places (1679-1709).

1704 China: persecution begins throughout empire; many RC missionaries and converts killed; 1724, general persecution proclaimed by emperor Yung-Cheng, lasts on and off until 1844.

1705 Origin of Danish-Halle Mission (Lutheran), forerunner of Protestant missionary societies; first workers include Protestant pioneers to Tranquebar (India): Bartholomew Ziegenbalg (1682-1719), Heinrich Plutschau (1677-1747) and Christian Schwartz (1726-1798).

1706 North America: Presbyterians form first organized church; origin of Presbyterian Church in the USA.

1709 Invention of piano by Italian Bartolommeo Cristofori, from harpsichord and clavichord, able to play *piano* (soft) and *forte* (loud).

1710 Canstein House printing press, Halle (Germany) with first Bible society (Cansteinische Bibelanstalt) founded by count Karl von Canstein: 3 million Bibles and NTs printed in 80 years.

1712 Orthodox missionary journeys in western Siberia by Filofei Leszczynski (1650-1722), metropolitan of Tobolsk, among Ostyaks, Voguls, Zyrians and Yakuts; baptizes 40,000 and increases churches from 160 to 448 by 1721.

1714 Founding in Copenhagen of Collegium de Cursu Evangelii Promovendo.

1715 *Nepal*. First mission in Kathmandu (Capuchins); 1769, all Christians finally leave.

1716 Irish Presbyterian educator William Tennent (1673-1746) evangelizes in American colonies; 1735, trains men for revivalist ministry in 'Log College'; 1741, in Old Side/New Side schism, he supports latter.

1717 A.H. Francke, Lutheran professor of Hebrew, holds revivals and evangelistic campaigns in Germany, based on Halle.

1720 Origins of Great Awakening in America: German evangelist T.J. Frelinghuysen (1692-1747) arrives from Pietism in Europe to Dutch Reformed churches in New Jersey; 1726, guides Irish Presbyterian minister and revivalist G. Tennent (1703-1764) and others in revival ministry evangelizing among Scottish and Irish in Philadelphia, New Jersey and beyond.
North America: pioneer Baptist evangelists in South include Jeremiah Walker, Benjamin Watkins, Shubal Stearns (1706-1771), Thomas Ethridge, Daniel Marshall (1706-1784), Richard Curtis Jr (1756-1811), Isaac Backus (1724-1806).

1721 Lutheran Church of Greenland recognized as integral part of Evangelical Lutheran Church of Denmark.
Peter the Great (regarded by Old Believers as the Antichrist) abolishes Russian Orthodox patriarchate, establishes synod of bishops and tsar-appointed oberprocurator, enabling tsars to rule church through synod until 1917.
Norwegian pastor Hans Egede (1686-1758) begins Protestant mission to Greenland Eskimos.

1722 Moravian (Herrnhut) Pietism begun, led by count N.L. von Zinzendorf (1700-1760).
In Ceylon, Protestants number 424,392 (21% of the population) through forced conversion by Dutch Reformed Church.

1723 Schism of Utrecht: separation from Rome of Little Church of Utrecht or Jansenist Church of Holland; 1889, Declaration of Utrecht rejects Council of Trent, Union of Utrecht unites church with Old Catholic churches of Germany and Switzerland; Jansenist worldview holds 'signs and wonders' (miracles, healings, supernatural signs) still widespread.

1724 Melkite (Greek Catholic) patriarchate of Antioch (in Beirut) established.

1725 The Great Awakening, revival in New England (USA) spreading throughout the Thirteen Colonies; begun under T.J. Frelinghuysen in New Jersey; mass conversions of dechristianized European populations in North America, led by revivalist Jonathan Edwards (1703-1758), who expounds progressive millennialism (later called postmillennialism), envisaging establishment of Christ's millennial kingdom on Earth around year 1990, with Second Advent at close of millennium; Awakening lasts until 1770.

1727 Jews expelled from Russia; repeated in 1747.
Irkutsk in Siberia an independent Russian Orthodox diocese.
Treaty of Kiachta: China permits 4 Russian priests to begin Peking mission.

1728 Institutum Judaicum founded in Halle by Francke as first Protestant mission center for Jewish evangelism.

1730 Anglican priest, mathematician and divine William Whiston (1667-1752) announces imminent end of world by deluge with destruction of London on 13 October 1736; panic-stricken crowds rush for high ground.

1732 Moravian church organizes foreign missions (1732 to Danish West Indies, 1733 to Greenland), under bishop Zinzendorf and others; 1732-1862, over 2,000 missionaries sent abroad.

c1733 Welsh lay preacher Howell Harris (1714-1773) adopts itinerant evangelism and open-air preaching; method later adopted by Whitefield and Wesley.
1734 Invention of fire extinguisher by M. Fuchs of Germany, also by 1762 Godfrey of London.
1735 Christians in Philippines reach 837,182; over a million by 1750.
John and Charles Wesley travel to Georgia (North America) as SPG missionaries, but meet hostility and return in 1737.
George Whitefield (1714-1770) undergoes conversion experience; 1736,begins evangelistic travels; in his life-time, estimated to have preached in public 18,000 times, to 18 million hearers, in crowds of up to 30,000 at once.
1736 Moravian missionaries at work among Samoyeds of Archangelsk.
After a hundred years of renewed Roman Catholic missionary activity in Persia, violent persecution of Christians erupts under brutal shah Nader (1688-1747).
1737 300,000 killed in Calcutta by storm surge of Hooghly river.
1738 George Whitefield's evangelistic campaigns in North America (1738-1770); heard by 80% of entire population.
Conversion of Charles Wesley (1707-1788); commences writing Evangelical hymns, totaling 7,270 original compositions in all.
Conversion of John Wesley (1703-1791) at Aldersgate (UK); beginning of18th-century Evangelical Revival and rise of Methodism under the Wesleys; outreach largely urban, concerned with needs of the poor, uneducated, unemployed, orphans et alii.
1739 First evangelistic open-air sermons in England for centuries: George Whitefield (17 February), John Wesley (2 April).
John Wesley's evangelistic travels in Britain average 8,000 miles a year on horseback until his death in 1791; travels 225,000 miles by horse, survives countless hostile mobs, preaches 40,000 sermons, makes 140,000 converts, plants vast network of classes, societies and churches.
1740 Armenian Catholic patriarchate of Cilicia established.
Office for Newly-Baptized opened in Svijazsk (Russia); from 1741-1762,mass baptisms of Volga pagans: 430,550 Chuvash, Cheremis, Ostyaks, et alii baptized; no pagans left in Middle Volga; 1764, Office dissolved.
Bavarian Pietists: Rehberger (1716-1769), Urlsperger, Kieszling, Schöner.
Dutch East Indies: 10,000 Chinese massacred in Batavia.
1741 Oldest USA Amerindian independent church formed, Narraganset Indian Church in Charleston, Rhode Island.
German composer G.F. Handel (1685-1759) produces 'Messiah' oratorio.
1742 Juan Santos Atahuallpa (named after final Inca ruler) appears as Quechua messiah in eastern Peru, predicting an Amerindian Catholic church with a native clergy.
Seychelles. First Christians (French Catholic settlers).
1743 Organized evangelization of Kamchatka begins under Josef Chotuncevski, including among Tunguz and Lamuts; most peoples soon christianized.
Russian empress Elizabeth orders destruction of mosques in Kazan: 1744-47, 838 forced conversions of Muslims to Orthodoxy; 1748-52, 7,535 conversions.
1744 First typewriter, made by H. Mills (England); 1856, typewriter with embossed letters for blind persons; 1868, USA journalist C.L. Sholes designs first practical typewriter, 1873 manufactured by Remington Arms Company.
1745 Capuchins expelled from Lhasa, Tibet.
Wesley teaches 'entire sanctification' as second blessing or second work of grace after an individual's conversion; Fletcher et alii call it 'baptism in the Holy Spirit'.
1746 Widespread and severe persecution of Christians begins in China, lasts 38 years.
Forcible evangelization of eastern Siberia organized by metropolitan Sylvester Golovacki of Tobolsk.
1749 England: 10,000 Particular or Exclusive Baptists, 15,000 Congregationalists; 50,000 Nonconformists.
Challoner's Revision of Rheims-Douai Bible, by bishop Richard Challoner (1691-1781) of London: remains standard Catholic version in English until 1950s.

Epoch VI: REPUDIATION AND REVIVAL 1750-1815

1750 **Global status:** 57 generations after Christ, world is 22.2% Christians (85.2% of them being Whites), 25.8% evangelized; with printed Scriptures available in 60 languages; total martyrs since AD 33, 11,280,000 (0.3% of all Christians ever; recent rate 8,320 per year).
Christianity now prevailing religion of West Indies.
Turks & Caicos Islands. First Christians (British Loyalist settlers from America).
Millenarianism strong among German Pietists.
North American Whites (the Thirteen Colonies) about 95% professing Christians (50% Congregationalists, 30% baptized Anglicans, 10% Presbyterians), though only 5% affiliated as church members.
Moravian mission to Labrador begun.
Philosophers David Hume and Immanuel Kant sever tenuous alliance between Christianity and the new science, through skepticism and empirical method.
c1750 British natural philosopher Thomas Wright (1711-1786) first suggests our Galaxy has a center, inhabited by a high form of intelligence.
Wales: revivals under Howell Harris, Daniel Rowland (c1713-1790), William Williams (1717-1791).
1751 Ostyaks evangelized up to Arctic coasts in region of Obdorsk.
French *philosophes* or Encyclopedists (men dedicated to Rationalism and Deism) produce Diderot's Encyclopédie (1751-1780, 35 volumes), believe Age of Reason just arriving, predict religion and superstition fated for imminent extinction.
1754 In Portugual (then 2 million), at least 200,000 (10%) are enrolled members of one religious order or another.
Ottoman empire: steady stream of Orthodox killed (The New Martyrs), mainly Orthodox who lapse to Islam but later repent and are trained for martyrdom by monks, then notify Turkish magistrates they have switched from Islam; penalty for this apostasy is always death.
1755 Great Earthquake of Lisbon, with fire and tidal wave, kills 12% of 250,000 city population, with 9,000 buildings destroyed; at same time, town of 10,000 swallowed in fissures in Morocco; both interpreted as divine judgments.
German philosopher Immanuel Kant (1724-1804), interested in astronomy, is first to propose existence of vast number of very distant 'island universes' (independent galaxies) beyond our own Galaxy.
English lexicographer, high churchman and Christian moralist Samuel Johnson (1709-1784) publishes his *Dictionary of the English language*, in which 'evangelism' is defined as 'The promulgation of the blessed Gospel', and 'evangelize' as to 'instruct in the Gospel'.
1759 Suppression of Jesuit order throughout Portugal and Portuguese domains; also 1764 in France and its colonies; 1767 Spain, Italy; 1773, pope Clement XIV (1705-1774) dissolves Society of Jesus worldwide (22,589 members including 11,293 priests); 3,300 Jesuit overseas missionaries recalled (2,171 Spanish, 909 Portuguese, 126 French); 1814, ban lifted throughout world.
1763 North America (USA): 24,000 Roman Catholics, growing to 35,000 by 1789, 150,000 by 1800 and 6,231,417 by 1890.
1764 *Falkland Islands*. First Christians (French settlers).
Annihilation of Christian community in Thailand; other persecutions 1729, 1755, 1767, 1775.
1766 First Methodist society in New World formed in North America.
Planters from Scotland begin Presbytery of British Guiana.
1767 First complete church membership returns published (by Methodists, in Britain).
Expulsion of all Jesuits throughout South America and Mexico.
1768 R. Arkwright invents spinning machine in Bolton, Lancashire.
1769 First true automobile (motor car), the Cugnot 3-wheeled steamer doing 2.25 miles per hour carrying 4 people; much later, first gasoline-engine automobiles, Benz (1885) and Daimler (1885).
1770 East African slave trade rapidly increases; 1,250,000 slaves traded at coast by Muslim Arabs up to 1897 abolition of slavery.
French nun Jeanne Le Royer (1732-1798) predicts tribulation, coming of Antichrist, end of papacy, and end of world in AD 2000.
Chinese capital Peking becomes first recent city in world to reach 1 million in population; meteoric rise begins of megacities (over 1 million persons) across world, escalating to (year, world total, total in developing countries): 1900, 20; 1950, 78 (31); 1955, 95 (42); 1960, 115 (53); 1965, 136 (63); 1970, 161 (79); 1975, 183 (95); 1980, 227 (125); 1985, 276 (163); 1990, 330 (205); 2000, 433 (295); AD 2025, 652 (498).
1771 French author L.-S. Mercier (1740-1814) writes *L'An 2440* (Memoirs of the year 2500), first optimistic future utopia.
1772 Slavery ruled illegal in Britain (but not in colonies), but Atlantic slave trade delivers average of 75,000 a year from 1750-1800.
Polish Orthodox united with Russian Orthodox Church until 1918.
1773 First independent USA Black Baptist congregation is formed near Augusta, Georgia.
Syrian Catholic patriarchate established.

Beginnings of Industrial Revolution

Before 1775, all societies everywhere are pre-industrial; 1775, first industrial revolution begins fueled by steam power and coal, second (1901, Germany) by electrical and chemical industries, third (1950) by nuclear power, microchips and genes, fourth (1987) by information.
1775 Industrial Revolution begins; industrialization and urbanization accelerate in Holland first, then in Britain; working classes become alienated from churches.
1776 Declaration of Independence by the Thirteen Colonies (USA); population 3 million, among whom 20,000 are Roman Catholics.
Adam Smith's *An Inquiry into the Nature and Causes of the Wealth of Nations*, the most influential work in modern political economy ('wealth' being capitalism and machines).
1778 USA Universalists organize their first church in 1778, Unitarians following with their own church in 1796.
Earl of Stanhope invents Logic Demonstrator with no moving parts.
1780 Edict of Toleration of Joseph II (1741-1790) of Austria guaranteeing

religious freedom.
A prophet named Tupac Amaru II (c1742-1781) leads Quechua religious revolt against Spanish in Peru; crushed and executed.
Deutsche Christentumsgesellschaft (Christendom Society) begun in Germany to build kingdom of God on an ecumenical basis.
Sunday schools popularized by Robert Raikes (1735-1811) of Gloucester; 1786, 200,000 children enrolled in England; 1789 in Wales, then to Scotland, Ireland and America.
Pitcairn Islands. First Christians (British mutineers).
Viet Nam: 200,000 Catholics, 28 European priests and 47 local priests.
Roman Catholics in England number 70,000.

1781 USA: revivals break out in several colleges including 1781 Dartmouth, 1783 Princeton and Yale, also Williams, Hampden-Sydney; 1785, nationwide 'revival of 1800' fixes pattern of denominational life, lasts until 1812.

1783 Native Baptist Church, first Jamaican Afro-Christian movement, begun by ex-slave; plays a significant political role 80 years later.
Eclectic Society and Clapham Society formed in England.
Anglican vicar Charles Simeon (1759-1836) starts Evangelical student movement in Cambridge, England.
English astronomer and clergyman John Mitchell is first to propose existence of black holes, being collapsed stars and galaxies; by 1985, total in Universe is estimated at 10^{16}.
Thomas Coke (1747-1814), Wesley's colleague and from 1787 first Methodist bishop in USA, issues 'Plan for the Society for the Establishment of Missions among the Heathens'; 1786, first Methodist foreign mission begun, to Antigua.

1784 Methodists in Thirteen Colonies multiply from 500 in 1771 to 15,000 in 13 years, then to 1,324,000 by 1850; Methodist Episcopal Church incorporated in Baltimore as first independent national church organization in North America.
Russian Orthodox mission to Alaska begun.
Korea: Christianity reintroduced by zealous Catholic laymen, prospers for a while; by 1794, 4,000 baptisms without clergy or missionaries, but all then exterminated; subsequent persecutions on average every decade.

1785 *Sierra Leone*. First Christians (Black settlers from Nova Scotia).
New Zealand. First Christians (European commercial base).
Evangelical awakenings (revivals) throughout Wales: 1785 Brynengan, 1786 Trecastle, 1791 Bala, 1805 Aberystwyth, 1810 Llangeitho, 1817 Beddgelert, 1821 Denbighshire, 1822 Anglesey, 1828 Carmarthenshire, 1832 Caernarvonshire, 1840 Merionethshire, 1849 South Wales, et alia.
Sunday School Society formed in London to extend movement throughout British empire; first joint effort of separate denominations since Protestant Reformation.

1787 Revival in Virginia, North America.
First USA Black Methodist dissidents appear, with officially-organized African Methodist Episcopal Church emerging by 1816.
Moravian foreign mission formed: Society for Propagating the Gospel among the Heathen.
English Baptist minister Andrew Fuller (1754-1815) writes *The Gospel of Christ Worthy of All Acceptation* and over 128 other titles, urges obedience to the Great Commission.

1788 Allgäuer Revival among Bavarian Catholics, led by Johann Sailer (1751-1832), Michael Feneberg, Martin Boos (1762-1825), Johannes Goszner (1773-1858), Ignatius Lindl (1774-1834).
Australia. First Christians (English convicts and Anglican chaplains).
Norfolk Island. First Christians (Australia convict colony).
Large colonies of German Mennonites and farmers settle in Black Earth region of Russia; origin of Stundists.

1789 Roman Catholics in USA number 35,000, half in Maryland, quarter in Philadelphia; first diocese erected in Baltimore (Maryland).
French Revolution: church/state separation and religious liberty proclaimed in France; 17,000 officially executed in 1793-4 Reign of Terror, including clergy and bishops.

1790 Methodists in Great Britain number 71,668.
In North America, Blacks number 757,208 out of population of 3,929,214 (19.3%).
World's first modern state censuses: 1790, USA; 1801, Great Britain.
Europe's energy needs supplied mainly by 14 million horses and 24 million oxen.

1791 English term 'statistics' coined by Sir John Sinclair.

1792 Second Great Awakening among Congregationalists and other New England churches (USA), lasting 30 years.
Eight Russian Orthodox missionary monks arrive on island of Kodiak (Alaska), baptize 2,500 shamanist Eskimos in following 2 years, and 10,000 in 1795.
William Carey (1761-1834) publishes first statistical global survey of Christian world mission: *An Enquiry Into the Obligations of Christians, to Use Means for the Conversion of the Heathens*, accurately enumerating populations and Christians on all continents in world's first statistical survey (world population 731 million: 57% pagan/Hindu/Buddhist, 18% Muslim, 14% RC, 6% Protestant, 4% Orthodox, 1% Jewish); 1793, sails for India under Particular Baptist Society for Propagating the Gospel Among the Heathen (formed 1792); at Serampore, initiates modern era of Protestant world missions, serves without home leave for 41 years in Bengal, translates and prints Bible in 35 languages.

1794 First Catholic ordination of Amerindian priests in Latin America (3 persons) after initial isolated exception in 1679.

1795 London Missionary Society (LMS) founded (interdenominational, later Congregationalist).
Methodists in Britain separate from Church of England after John Wesley's death in 1791.
Mass movement in Cape Comorin (South India): 5,000 Nadars (Shanars) baptized by SPCK missionaries in 10 years.

1796 First LMS missionaries sent to South Pacific (Tahiti).
Edinburgh Tract Society, Edinburgh Missionary Society, formed in Scotland.
Over 2 million Uniate Ruthenians in Poland return to Russian Orthodox Church.
Founding of Scottish Missionary Society and Glasgow Missionary Society.
Ceylon: British drive out Dutch forces, find 67,000 Ceylonese still Roman Catholics despite 140 years' ban.
Norwegian Revival, under Hans Nielsen Hauge (1771-1824).
General Assembly of Church of Scotland formally resolves that 'to spread abroad the knowledge of the gospel among the barbarous and heathen nations seems to be highly preposterous'.

1797 *Tonga*. First missionaries (LMS), also 1822, then 1825.
Netherlands Missionary Society (NZG) founded in Rotterdam.

1798 French general Berthier marches on Rome, sets up new republic, exiles pope Pius VI; revolutionary upheavals renew Christian beliefs in endtime prophecy and restoration of the charismata.

1799 Elberfeld-Barmen Missionary Society begun.
New Religion of the Iroquois founded by Handsome Lake, a Seneca Indian in Great Lakes region (USA).
Religious Tract Society (RTS) founded (UK).
Church Missionary Society (CMS) founded by Anglicans in London.
Napoleon Bonaparte (1769-1821), military dictator of France, imprisons 2 popes in France (Pius VI, Pius VII); regarded as one in long succession of archetypal antichrists, in particular as Antichrist I, first of the 3 major latter-day Antichrists (2 from the North, one from the South) envisioned by Nostradamus.
Private missionary activity among Yakuts and Chukchi undertaken by RC secular priest G. Slepcov (until 1815), between Indigirka and Tschaun.
Electric battery invented by Italian physicist Alessandro Volta (1745-1827).

1800 **Global status:** 59 generations after Christ, world is 23.1% Christians (86.5% of them being Whites), 27.2% evangelized; with printed Scriptures available in 67 languages.
Widespread evangelistic camp meetings begin in USA; Kentucky Revival awakening, with crowds of up to 25,000, sweeps over Kentucky, Tennessee and the Carolinas.
Protestant foreign missionaries worldwide number only 100.
Roman Catholics: 5,000 in Burma, 2,300 in Siam, 310,000 in Indochina, over 500,000 in India.
Congo and Angola: no trace of former Catholic missions remains.
China: about 200,000 baptized Roman Catholics remain.
Old Believers in many parts of northern Russia number half of population.
Beginnings of local awakenings (revivals) in Scotland: Lewis, Harris, Perthshire.
Research undergoes vast expansion: scientific R&D (research and development) increases every year from 1800 to the present.
World's 10 largest cities: Peking 1,100,000, London 861,000, Canton 800,000, Constantinople 570,000, Paris 547,000, Hangchow 500,000, Yedo 492,000, Naples 430,000, Soochow 392,000, Osaka 380,000.

c1800 *Papua New Guinea*. First Christians (European trading post).

1801 Protestants in Ceylon number 342,000 (Dutch Reformed), or 14% of population; through neglect, most lapse to Buddhism by 1830.
Martyrdom in Korea of Chinese Catholic priest James Chu (Tsiu) and 300 Korean Christians: further persecutions in 1815, 1819, 1826, 1827, 1839, 1845, 1860, 1866, 1881, 1887, 1910, 1919, 1950.
Surrey Iron Railway incorporated, as first public freight-carrying railroad; 1803, first locomotive, built by Trevithick; 1829, G. Stephenson's 'Rocket'.

1802 Catholics in Viet Nam 320,000, with 3 European bishops, 15 missionary priests and 119 Vietnamese priests.
USA: Massachusetts Baptist Missionary Society formed for 'the evangelization of frontier communities'.

1804 *Fiji Islands*. First Christians (escaped convicts from Australia).
British & Foreign Bible Society (BFBS) founded, in London.

1805 *Namibia* (South West Africa). First mission (LMS, among Hottentots, Capoid aboriginals).
First modern end-of-the-world novel: *Le dernier homme*, by French priest J.-B. Cousin de Grainville.

1806 Napoleon abolishes Holy Roman Empire.
Britain: revivals secede from Methodism—1806 Independent Methodists, 1810 Camp Meeting Methodists, joining in 1812 as Primitive Methodists.
USA: Haystack Prayer Meeting at Williams College, Massachusetts,

launches North America foreign missions.
USA: Philadelphia Bible Society founded, then Massachusetts BS, 1809 New York BS, then 25 more small local Bible societies by 1816 when, at initiative of New Jersey BS, agreement is reached to found American Bible Society as national body.

1807 Slave trade prohibited throughout British empire by British parliament.
Robert Morrison (1782-1834), first Protestant missionary (LMS) to China, arrives in Macao, translates Bible into Chinese by 1818, dictionary by 1821; dies in 1834, having seen only 10 baptisms of Chinese.

1809 Sweden: Evangeliska Sallskapet (for Bibles and tracts) founded.
London Society for Promoting Christianity amongst the Jews (LSPCJ) founded as interdenominational mission, but Anglican only from 1815; later called Church Missions to Jews (CMJ); 1962, Church's Ministry among the Jews.
New York Bible Society founded, from 1816 working with ABS; 1946 does not join United Bible Societies, works instead with WBT/SIL; 1968 begins to produce NIV Bible, completed 1978; c1975 renamed NY International BS, then 1982 International Bible Society.

1810 Britain: 312,000 Nonconformists (including 30,000 Particular or Exclusive Baptists).
China: 215,000 native Catholics, 6 bishops, 2 coadjutors, 23 missionaries, 80 native agents.
German evangelist T. Grenz spreads gospel among Lithuanians.
W. Carey conceives idea of regional ecumenical missionary conferences around globe; nothing results until 1854 New York.
Revival in Russian Orthodox Church; 1813, Russian Bible Society founded, printing in 30 languages (17 new) with 600,000 copies; 1827, disbanded.
American Board of Commissioners for Foreign Missions organized (USA Congregationalists).
Evangelical awakenings (revivals) in Switzerland (Robert Haldane, 1764-1842), France, Low Countries, Germany.

c1810 Wales: revivals under Christmas Evans (1766-1838), John Elias (1774-1841).

1811 Henry Martyn (1781-1812), Anglican chaplain (CMS), begins in Persia translating Bible.
Edict against Christianity in China: spreading the faith is punishable by death; 1857, further edict.
American clergyman Ethan Smith of Vermont writes *Dissertation on the Prophecies Related to Antichrist and the Last Times*, concludes world will end in 1866.

1812 Wuppertal Tract Society formed (Germany).
Catastrophe Theory proposed by French geologist baron G. Cuvier (1769-1832): Earth is now 86,000 years old and has gone through 32 successive acts of creation (as shown by 32 geological strata), the products of all but the last being obliterated in subsequent catastrophes (leaving only fossils), the last being the Noachian Flood in BC 4000.
New York City Mission movement founded by evangelicals, lasts till 1870.

1813 Burma: arrival of American Baptist missionary Adoniram Judson (1788-1850).

1814 Society of Jesus reestablished by pope Pius VII (1742-1823) after 40 years' ban.
American Baptist Missionary Union founded (USA); later ABFMS.
New Zealand: Protestant missions to Maoris begin.
Prussian, Dutch, Bergish, Hanover, and Saxony Bible societies founded.

Epoch VII: THE GREAT CENTURY 1815-1914

1815 **Global status:** 59.4 generations after Christ, world is 23.2% Christians (86.1% of them being Whites), 30.3% evangelized; with printed Scriptures available in 86 languages; total martyrs since AD 33, 12,030,000 (0.3% of all Christians ever; recent rate 11,540 per year).
Beginning of the Great Century of worldwide Christian expansion, from end of Napoleonic wars to 1914.
Printed Bible available in 44 languages, New Testament in 59, portions in 86; Bible-publishing societies now begun in a number of countries.
H. Bardwell publishes sermon 'The duty and reward of evangelizing the heathen', preached in Newburyport, USA.
Over 80% of all North American Indians still non-Christians, despite extensive missions.
Basel Evangelical Missionary Society founded (Switzerland).
Vast proliferation begins in number of Roman Catholic orders and congregations.
Italian priest Caspar Del Bufalo (1786-1837) founds Missioners of the Most Precious Blood, with as 'his goal for his missioners the evangelization of the world' through charitable works.

1816 *Botswana* (then Bechuanaland). First mission (LMS).
Elberfeld revivals in western Germany: 1816 first revival, 1820 second.
American Bible Society (ABS) founded.
First translations of Holy Scripture into any Black African languages: Bullom (Sierra Leone), followed by Amharic 1824, Malagasy 1828, Setswana 1830, up to 560 languages by 1983.
First steerable bicycle, pushed by feet on road, made by Frenchman, J. N. Niepce; 1865 pedal-driven velocipede; one of most efficient machines ever made by man.

1817 Robert Moffat (1795-1883) begins 50-year ministry among Tswana of southern Africa; 1857, completes Tswana Bible.
Organized evangelization among Buryats around Lake Baikal undertaken by London Missionary Society; 1840, Bible translated (Mongolian); 1841, discontinued on orders from Russian holy synod and tsar; 1861, Orthodox mission to Buryats begun in Irkutsk.

1818 Wesleyan Methodist Missionary Society begun (London); later MMS.
The Conversion of the World: or the Claims of 600 Millions, and the Ability and Duty of the Churches Respecting Them: book by G. Hall & S. Newell (ABCFM, India); proposal to convert heathen millions across world by sending 30,000 Protestant missionaries from USA and Europe in 21 years, at cost of US$4 from each Protestant and Anglican communicant in Christendom.
Madagascar: first Protestants (LMS) begin work.
Mary Shelley writes *Frankenstein*, the archetypal science fiction novel.

1819 Settlers' Meeting (Creoles) secedes from Wesleyan Mission in Freetown (Sierra Leone); first ecclesiastical schism south of the Sahara.

1820 Protestant mission begins in Argentina (BFBS).
Revival in Pomerania, Germany.
London Jews Society makes first British missionary contact in Iraq.

c1820 Georgian Orthodox Church forcibly assimilated by Russian Orthodox Church.
Augustinian nun, mystic and seer Catherine Emmerich (1774-1824) of Westphalia has vision of Lucifer being unchained about 1940 and Antichrist working from 1960 onwards.

1821 Chile: first Protestant missionary (BFBS) opens schools.
Danish Missionary Society founded.
Charles Babbage (1792-1871) invents 'Difference Engine' (for computing tables), and 1833 his 'Analytical Engine' capable of statistical operations; world's first general-purpose digital computer.
Emperor Minh Mang of Annam ('the Nero of Indochina') begins 20-year reign; missionaries prohibited, vicious persecutions of Christians in 1821, 1825, 1832; but by 1840, Catholics increase to 420,000.
Cyprus: Orthodox ethnarch (archbishop), all 3 bishops, abbots, many priests and laity, are hanged by Ottoman Turks; similar martyrdoms in Crete and Greece.
Bophuthatswana. First mission; followed in next hundred years by opening of Christian work in other areas which by 1986 become Bantustans: *Ciskei, Gazankulu, KaNgwane, KwaNdebele, KwaZulu, Lebowa, Qwaqwa, Transkei, Venda.*

1822 *Liberia*. First Christians (Black settlers from USA; Baptists and Methodists).
Paris Evangelical Missionary Society founded (France).
Providence Baptist Church in Monrovia (Liberia), oldest Baptist congregation in Africa, begun by first USA missionary to Africa, Lott Carey, a Black slave from Virginia.
Society for the Propagation of the Faith begun in Lyons (France).
84-year-old ecumenical patriarch Gregory V robed in vestments by Turks then hanged with other bishops after Easter Day liturgy in Constantinople; 23,000 Greeks and 12,000 Turks massacred.
Berlin Israelmission founded; 1869, F. Delitzsch founds Evangelische Lutherische Zentralverein für Mission unter Israel (HQ Leipzig); 1877, Delitzsch completes NT in Hebrew after 51 years' work.

1823 Josiah Pratt's annual Survey of the World (CMS, London) headed 'The Conversion of the World dependent on the more abundant influence of the Holy Spirit'.
Cook Islands. First mission (LMS).
German Lutherans emigrate from Germany to Brazil.

1824 Coptic Catholic patriarchate established (Egypt).
Berlin Missionary Society formed.
USA: beginnings of interdenominational city-wide cooperative evangelism.
First Anglican bishoprics in Caribbean established in Jamaica and Barbados.
Blind French educator Louis Braille (1809-1852) invents 6-dot coded type system of printing and writing for blind persons.

1825 Bombay Missionary Union formed in India for prayer and discussion among Anglican, Brethren, Congregationalist and Presbyterian missionaries, eventually producing principle of comity.
Hawaii: Hapu syncretistic cult announces imminent end of world; temple then burned to ground by Protestant missionaries.
Swaziland. First missionaries (Methodists from South Africa).
Colombia: BFBS agent arrives as first Protestant missionary.
American Tract Society founded.
Church of Scotland Mission (Presbyterian) begun.
British Honduras: Methodists (MMS) begin Protestant work; 1840, British colony declared.
Arabic printing of the Quran officially sanctioned after centuries of insistence that it must only be hand-copied.

1826 *Cocos (Keeling) Islands*. First Christians (British settlement).
Massive apostasies from Russian Orthodox missions in Volga region: 299,300 in Kazan, 95% of 14,800 new Tartar converts, 233,500 Chuvash, et alii.
New Zealand: Hau Hau (Good News of Peace) syncretistic cult among

Maoris; 1865, full-scale uprising against British.
33 of the 38 RC bishoprics in Spanish America vacant or inactive due to reluctance of Rome to recognize state appointments.
Missionary renewal in western Siberia under Eugene Kazancev, metropolitan of Tobolsk; best epoch of Russian Orthodox missions begins.

1827 Siegen-Dillkreis revival, western Germany.
Western Samoa. First mission (Methodist).
American Samoa. First mission (Methodist).
J. N. Darby (1800-1882), Anglican clergyman, joins Christian Brethren movement in Dublin; propounds dogma of total premillennial apostasy and ruin of Christendom (the major churches); later develops 'dispensationalism', a new variety of futurist premillennialism, dividing biblical and later history into 7 eras or dispensations.
Netherlands Missionary Society begins work in Celebes.

1828 *Transkei*. First Christians (Moravians).
Rhenish Missionary Society (RMG) formed (Germany); begins work among Dayaks of Borneo; 1839, first Dayak baptism.
Karl Gutzlaff (1803-1851), a Lutheran, begins work in Indonesia, Siam, southern China, Hong Kong; 1844, attempts to evangelize China in one generation through 300 evangelists.
Mamaia (Flock of God) cult founded in Society Islands by prophet Teau, a Christian from Panavia, protesting harsh mission destruction of paganism.
England: political emancipation of Nonconformists, and 1829 of Roman Catholics.
Brahmo Samaj, quasi-Protestant Hindu reform movement, begun in Calcutta by Ram Mohan Rai (1772-1833).

1830 *New Hebrides*. First Christians (small sandalwood trading centres).
USA: widespread campaigns through evangelists Andrew, Barnes, Burchard, Baker, Caughey, Griffith, Inskip, Knapp, Maffit, Swan.
Joseph Smith (1805-1844) at Fayette, NY (USA), has visions which lead to establishment of Church of Jesus Christ of Latter-day Saints (Mormons); 1844, murdered by mob.
Reveil (French-speaking Reformed Church awakening) sweeps Netherlands.
First of numerous apparitions of Virgin Mary over next 100 years; to Catherine Labourée at Rue du Bac, Paris; then 1846 at La Salette, 1858 Lourdes, 1917 Fatima, 1931 Vicovaro (Rome), 1944 Bonate di Bergamo, 1945 Heede (Germany), 1961 Garabandal, and many others.
Lithuania: tsarist deportations of Roman Catholics to Siberia, including 5,000 priests and nuns; also in 1863.

c1830 Switzerland: revivals under Robert Haldane (1764-1842), C. Malan (1787-1864), F. Gaussen (1790-1863), J.H.M. D'Aubigne (1794-1872).
France: revivals under F. Monod (1794-1863), A. Monod (1802-1856).

1831 Massacres of Nestorians by Kurds; also in 1843, 1846.
New Caledonia. First mission (Tongans, from Tonga).
Electromagnetic induction discovered by experimentalist M. Faraday (1791-1867), designing first dynamo and generating electric current; 1865, electromagnetic radiation discovered by physicist J.C. Maxwell (1831-1879).
Killer epidemic of cholera kills 50 million in India, suddenly spreads to Britain killing 32,000 and 70,000 in second wave, before medical research traces it to drinking polluted water.

c1831 Rise of Lutheran neo-confessionalism in Germany and its separation from neo-pietism of earlier Evangelical Awakening; purely Lutheran mission societies formed including Neuendettelsau in 1841.

1832 Tract Society of Lausanne and Eszlingen begun.
American Baptist Home Missionary Society formed.
London City Mission founded, first of 50 city missions begun in Britain's largest cities (Bristol, Chester, Edinburgh, Glasgow, Leeds, Liverpool, York, et alia).
Iran entered by American Board (ABCFM) as first Protestant mission, under name Mission to the Nestorians.

1833 Slavery abolished in British empire: owners of 700,000 freed slaves compensated.
Church of Greece proclaims its autocephality in defiance of Ecumenical Patriarchate of Constantinople; latter eventually recognizes it in 1850.
Lesotho (then Basutoland). First mission (Paris Mission, PEMS).

1834 Religious orders in Portugal suppressed.
Refrigerator invented and manufactured by J. Perkin, USA.
Tolpuddle Martyrs: 6 Christian men (5 Methodists) form an early farmworkers' trade union, but are then deported as convicts to Australia.

1835 Finland: the Osterbottenvackelse, evangelical awakening in the west, active for 15 years; also revival under Lutheran pastor L.L. Laestadius (1800-1861).
Attempt to eradicate Christianity in Madagascar by queen Ranavalona I (1800-1861); large numbers of Christians killed from 1835 to 1861.
Swedish Missionary Society founded.
Electric telegraphy invented by Samuel Morse (1791-1872); 1838, develops morse code; telegraph comes into service.
Invention of revolver by S. Colt; 1,000 built for US Army.

1836 *Wallis & Futuna Islands*. First mission (French Marist priests).
Booklet: 'The Duty of the Present Generation to Evangelize the World: An Appeal from the Missionaries at the Sandwich Islands to their Friends in the United States'.
Leipzig Evangelical Lutheran Mission formed (Germany).
Beginning of Orthodox mission among Koluschans (Tlingits) of Sitka island.
Twelve Apostles of Catholic Apostolic (Irvingite) Church in England address memorandum to all rulers of Europe warning them of imminent Second Advent of Christ.
T.S. Skinner publishes *Thoughts on evangelizing the world* (New York).

1837 *Gilbert Islands*. First Christians (European trading centre).
Great Awakening in Hawaii, a remarkable revival with mass conversions until 1843: 27,000 Protestant adult converts (20% of population).
British Post Office carries 88 million pieces of mail a year; 1840, Roland Hill introduces mass prepaid adhesive penny post for any distance; by 1960, 10 billion pieces a year (USA 355 pieces of domestic mail per citizen per year).

1838 Turkey: small-scale revivals among Armenians in Nicomedia and (1841) Adabazar, through ABCFM (USA); and later in Aintab and Aleppo.
Tenrikyo (Religion of Divine Wisdom), a Shinto/Christian amalgam, founded in Japan as first of the Shinto Shukyo (New Religious Movements).

1839 New Hebrides: LMS missionary pioneer John Williams (1796-1839) martyred on island of Eromanga; Catholic missionaries also arrive, but systematic missions not begun until 1887.
Scottish Highlands Awakening for 4 years: Oban, islands, also Lowlands.
Martyrs of Korea: 81 RC martyrs killed 1839-46 including vicar apostolic, Korean priest A. Kim, foreign priests and laity.

1840 Revolutionaries in Philippines: Confraternity of St Joseph founded by Tagalogs to seize autonomy; crushed by Spaniards, who kill 'king of the Tagalogs' Apolinario De la Cruz (1815-1841); 1872, 3 priests shot; 1896, Jose Rizal executed.

1841 *Hong Kong*. First missions (Catholic, Anglican, Baptist).
Edinburgh Medical Missionary Society founded in Scotland.
UK: 22,000 converted over 7 years through preaching of James Caughey of New York.
Martyrdom of père P.M. Chanel on Futuna; first RC martyr in Oceania.
CMS general secretary Henry Venn (1796-1873) requires all missionaries to complete annual questionnaires recording church growth statistics; propounds 'three-self' goal of mission that local churches must become self-supporting, self-governing, self-propagating.
Founding of Anglican Jerusalem Bishopric: Michael Solomon Alexander, former Chief Rabbi of Plymouth (UK), consecrated as first Anglican Bishop in Jerusalem.

1842 Treaty of Nanking, following Opium War, cedes Hong Kong to Britain and opens territory to missions.
Gossner Mission Society begun in Berlin.
Revival spreads through state church of Norway; Norwegian Mission Society (Stavanger) begun.
Dahomey: MMS (UK) missionaries arrive at Fon kingdom, Abomey; 120 years later, Fon work still barely begun.
A Japanese translates Life of Jesus from Dutch; arrested, kills self.
Date for end of Europe by deluge as predicted by Elizabethan astrologer John Dee (1527-1608); mobs take to boats to escape.

1843 Great Peaceful Heavenly Kingdom (Tai Ping Tien Kueh: Society of Worshippers of the True God/Celestial Kingdom of Great Peace) begun in China as quasi-Christian sect with Hakka founder Hung Hsiu-chuan (1814-1864) and leaders strongly influenced by New Testament; 1853, rebels capture Nanking, rule south China; appeal to Protestant missions (ABFMS, LMS) to guide them, but ignored; 1862, suppressed, 35 million killed; 1864, fall of Nanking and suicide of Hung; third great missed opportunity to win China to Christianity.
Hermannsburg revival in western Germany.
20,000 Nestorians massacred in Kurdistan by Muslim Kurds.
Sierra Leonian former slave Samuel Crowther (c1806-1891) sent as missionary to Nigeria; 1864, consecrated as first non-European Anglican bishop.
Goanese (Roman Catholic) schism in Goa, India; 600 untrained Indians ordained; lasts until 1886 when pope Leo XIII elevates Goa to patriarchate; later Latin-rite schism, Independent Catholic Church of Ceylon, Goa and India, exists until 1950.
USA: Black slave, evangelist and reformer Sojourner Truth (Isabella van Wagener, c1797-1883) begins itinerant ministry across USA stressing abolitionism and women's rights.

1844 Date for Second Advent of Christ as predicted in 1818 by Baptist prophet William Miller (1782-1849) in USA; afterwards, Seventh-day Adventist denomination emerges, interprets date as return of Christ to Earth for 'cleansing of the sanctuary'.
CMS missionary J.L. Krapf (1810-1881) first to begin modern missionary work in Kenya; wife and child die of malaria in Mombasa.
Young Men's Christian Association (YMCA) founded in London by George Williams (1821-1905); 1855, YWCA; united in 1877.
Christadelphians founded by John Thomas (1805-1871) in Birmingham (UK) and London.
Persia: revival among Nestorians around ABCFM station Urumiah; other revivals in 1849, 1850.
Karl Marx writes: 'Religion is the sigh of the oppressed creature . . .

the opium of the people'.
Origins of Baha'i World Faith under Sayyid Ali Muhammed (Bab al-Din, 1819-1850) in Persia, especially under chief prophet Baha'u'llah (1817-1892) and son Abdul-Baha (1844-1921); many in Western world predict emergence in 20th century of a single unified world faith, but hopes dashed by resurgence of great world religions.
Patagonian Missionary Society (later, South American Missionary Society, SAMS) founded.

1845 *Solomon Islands*. First missionaries (Marists, with bishop Epalle killed on landing).
Cameroon. First mission (Baptist Missionary Society, UK).
Potato blight from America devastates Ireland, with a million killed by famine and typhus, resulting in another million Irish migrating to Britain, USA and Australia, markedly influencing development of Catholicism there.
Southern Baptist Convention, largest USA Baptist denomination, comes into being in reaction against ABFMS refusing to accept slave-owners as missionaries; based from its origin on global mission, it founds Board of Domestic Missions (later, Home Mission Board) and Foreign Mission Board, beginning work in China, then 1846 Liberia and 1850 Nigeria.
Oxford Movement in England: 60 prominent Anglicans and 250 clergy enter Church of Rome by 1862.
Gossner Mission begins work among Kol aboriginals in India.
Lebanon: Druzes kill 12,000 Maronites in 15 years up to 'Massacres of the Sixties', leaving 100,000 homeless.
Germany: Deutschkatholizismus, a schism ex Roman Catholicism, begun by degraded priests J. Ronge and J. Czerski; Deutsche-Katholische Kirche gains 80,000 adherents, becomes rationalist, 1850 unites with Free churches.

1846 Beginnings of world conciliarism: Evangelical Alliance formed in London by 800 Christians representing 52 confessions, to further unity among Evangelicals worldwide; national alliances then formed in Britain and Canada (1846), Sweden and Germany (1847), India (1849), Turkey (1855), USA (1867); and international conferences held in London 1851, Paris 1855, Berlin 1857, Geneva 1861, Amsterdam 1867, New York 1873, Basel 1879, Copenhagen 1884, Florence 1891, London 1896 and the final one in 1907; 1912, title officially changed to World's Evangelical Alliance (WEA).
Mormons under Brigham Young (1801-1877) leave Nauvoo City for Great Salt Lake; 1847, Salt Lake City founded.
Niue Island. First missionaries (a returning Niuean, and a Samoan).
La Salette apparition of Mary states: 'Antichrist will be born of a Jewish nun, father a bishop'.

1847 Latin patriarchate of Jerusalem restored.
USA: Lutheran Church—Missouri Synod organized, with 22 pastors and under 2,000 members; widespread success in ministry to immigrants; by 1922, 1,564 pastors and over 1 million members; by 1970, 2.9 million in USA.
'The light of Christ illuminates the whole world'—last words of Macarius Glukharev, apostle to the Altai (1792-1847).
5th major persecution of Catholics in Annam, followed by others in 1851, 1856, 1884.
Private missionary work among Koriak and Chukchi in Anadyr district of Siberia by Orthodox priests.

1848 Karl Marx (1818-1883) and Friedrich Engels (1820-1895) publish *Communist Manifesto* in Germany, calling for violent overthrow of established order including religion; 1867, Marx's *Das Kapital*.
Birth of Spiritualism (spiritism, medium religion) in USA; 1893, organized as National Spiritualist Association of Churches of the USA.
Plymouth Brethren (Christian Brethren) in UK split into Open Brethren and Exclusive Brethren.
First Katholikentag held, in Mainz.
Germany: founding of many evangelistic societies, including Evangelische Gesellschaft für Deutschland, 1850 Evangelical Brotherhood, 1852 Society for Itinerant Preachers, 1857 Society for Home Missions, 1863 Herborn-Dillenburg Society, 1864 Nassau Colporteur Society, 1878 Evangelical Brotherhood of the Reich for Furthering Evangelism and Evangelical Fellowship, 1886 Home Mission Society of Hesse.

c1848 Disappearance of all religion by 1870 predicted by French libertarian socialist and anarchist P.-J. Proudhon (1809-1865) on grounds it represents last vestiges of savagehood and barbarism.

1849 Charles G. Finney (1792-1875) conducts evangelistic campaigns in Britain, 1849-51 and 1859-61.
Ludwigsburg evangelists' school founded in Germany; 1856, moved to Krischenhardthof.
Thailand: all foreign missionaries ordered out.
Brazil: total Black slaves from Africa 5.5 million over period 1550-1850.
Moravian work among Miskitos of Nicaragua begun.

1850 **Global status:** 61 generations after Christ, world is 27.4% Christians (85.2% of them being Whites), 38.1% evangelized; with printed Scriptures available in 205 languages.
Cult of the Holy Cross, Yucatan (Mexico).
London city reaches population of 2.3 million, 4.2 million by 1875, and 6.5 million by 1900, at which time 19 other metropolises in world also exceed 1 million each.
Hindu mystic Ramakrishna (Gadadhar Chatterji, 1836-1886) in Bengal preaches universal religion and unity of all religions, claims to have seen Jesus after studying Christianity; 1897, Ramakrishna Mission founded in Calcutta by Swami Vivekananda (1862-1902).
Orthodox missions along Yenisei river around Turuchansk among Tunguz, Yakuts and Samoyeds.
Orissa and its evangelization published by A. Sutton, first detailed study of status of missions (in India).
Charles Adams publishes *Evangelism in the middle of the Nineteenth Century*.
Death of French nurse and nun Bertine Bouquillon from St Omer (France) after predicting: 'The end of time is near and Antichrist will not delay his coming.'
English mathematician John Taylor demonstrates Great Pyramid of Cheops contains divine prophecy covering all history; 1865, pyramidologist Robert Menzies shows internal passages form a chronological outline.
World's 10 largest cities: London 2,320,000, Peking 1,648,000, Paris 1,314,000, Canton 800,000, Istanbul 785,000, Hangchow 700,000, New York 682,000, Bombay 575,000, Yedo 567,000, Soochow 550,000.

c1850 *British Indian Ocean Territory*. First Christians (from Mauritius).
General Beckwith, an Anglo-Saxon evangelical, advises Waldensians 'Evangelize or perish', after which they cease being isolationist.

1851 Spanish concordat with Holy See.
England & Wales: first (and only) state Census of Religious Worship; 61% of entire population attend church every Sunday.
Edict of Tu Duc (1829-1883) of Viet Nam, following French intervention (1843); persecution of Christians results in death of 115 priests and 90,000 Catholics, and in 1884 French declaration of protectorate over territory.
Anglicans and Protestants in Indian subcontinent (150 million population): 91,092 adherents (51,300 in Tinnevelly [CMS] and South Travancore [LMS]), 14,661 communicants; 339 ordained missionaries in 19 societies; members expand tenfold by mass movements from 1851-1901.
Tierra del Fuego: 15 SAMS missionaries including founder Allen Gardiner massacred or starved to death.
Colombia: persecution of Catholic Church.

1852 Canada: Anglican church separated from state.
Society for Itinerant Preachers founded in Germany.

1853 Norway: first Home Mission (Indremisjon) begun within state church.
David Livingstone (1813-1873) of LMS passes through Zambia on way to Luanda; 1857, publishes *Missionary travels and researches in South Africa*.
Catholic hierarchy reestablished in Netherlands.
Open Air Mission founded (UK).
Belgian statistician Adolphe Quetelet (1796-1874) convenes world's first International Statistical Congress.
England: period of High Church evangelism under Anglo-Catholic clergy R. Aitken (1800-1878), Hay Aitken, R. Twigg, G.H. Wilkinson (1833-1907), Benson, Herbert, Mackonochie, Stanton, Dolling, A.J. Mason (1851-1928).

1854 First Union Missionary Convention, in New York, USA, guided by Alexander Duff (1806-1878): 'To what extent are we authorized by the Word of God to expect the conversion of the world to Christ?'; similar conference held in London, England; 1867, Duff appointed to first chair of evangelism and evangelical theology at New College, Edinburgh.
Protestants in Dutch East Indies formed into a single state-controlled Church of the Indies.

1855 East Africa: 20,000 Black slaves a year exported by Arabs.
YMCA Conference, Paris, adopts 'Paris Basis' as movement's declaration of faith; 1878, World's Alliance of YMCAs sets up permanent executive in Geneva; 1975, 6 million members.
Ethiopia: emperor Theodore II persecutes Roman Catholics.
Field conferences of Protestant foreign missionaries commence: 1855-1863, 3 in North India; 1858-1900, 3 in South India; 4 for All-India, 1873-1902; 3 for China held in Shanghai, 1877-1907; 4 for Japan, 1872-1900; 3 for South Africa, 1904-1909; 2 in Mexico City 1888, 1897.

1856 Stonemason Grünewald spreads gospel using colporteurs in western Germany.
Sweden: Evangeliska Fosterlands-Stiftelsen founded within state church.
Protestant mission begun among Yamanas of Tierra del Fuego.

1857 Mass secession from Roman Catholic Church in Mexico leads to formation of Iglesia de Jesus, ultimately becoming Episcopal Church of Mexico.
Society for Home Preachers in Schleswig-Holstein (Germany) formed.
USA: evangelist D.L. Moody (1837-1899), a Congregationalist, evolves organized mass evangelism in Chicago; during his lifetime estimated to have had individual evangelistic personal dealings with 750,000 persons; perfects methods of preparation and publicity in cooperative city campaigns, use of theaters and tents, finance committees; other evangelists R.A. Torrey (1856-1928), Billy Sunday (1862-1925), Robert P. Wilder (1863-1938); beginnings of large-scale lay-centered evangelism.

Evangelical Awakening in USA (under C.G. Finney et alii; in northern states only; one million converts in 2 years), spreading to Europe and the other 4 continents (1859 India, 1860 China).
USA: massive spontaneous wave of fervent evangelism by laymen sweeps Northern states, also sweeps through Southern armies (with 150,000 conversions including many generals), until both are dissipated by 1861 Civil War.

1858 Apparition of Mary at Lourdes, France, with site subsequently becoming a world-famous Catholic pilgrimage and healing centre.
India: first of over 150 attempts to establish indigenous Hindu-Christian movements or churches: Hindu Church of the Lord Jesus (Tinnevelly).
David Livingstone begins exploration of Zambezi and Shire rivers, attracting others to begin missionary work in Nyasaland.
Townsend treaty between USA and Japan opens Japan to Christian missionaries; 1859, first Catholic, Episcopalian and Protestant missionaries arrive.
Religious freedom and impartiality in India proclaimed by queen Victoria (1819-1901): 'Relying ourselves on the truth of Christianity . . . we have no desire to impose our convictions on any of our subjects'.
India: now over one million Roman Catholics, 100,000 Protestants and Anglicans.
China: new phase for Russian Orthodoxy: agreement of Tien-Tsin gives Russia permission to evangelize without hindrance; monk Isaias Polikin preaches in Chinese; 1884, Mitrophen Tsi ordained as first Chinese priest; but by 1900 still only a handful of missionaries, and 200 believers; 1900, in Boxer rebellion 260 Chinese Christians and one priest martyred, all churches destroyed.
Sermons on evangelization increase: 1858 J. Parker publishes 'The duty of the present generation of Christians to evangelize the world', New York; 1866 C. Dickson publishes 'The duty of the Church to evangelize the World', Presbyterian Church of the USA, New York.

c1858 *Johnston Island*. First Christians (USA guano-digging company).

1859 Second Evangelical Awakening in Britain, reaching over 3 million with 1.1 million converts: 100,000 in Wales, 300,000 in Scotland, 100,000 in Ulster, over 500,000 in England.
Books set in the future proliferate after publication of Charles Darwin's *Origin of the Species* (explaining evolution as resulting solely from natural selection and battle for existence, with all life developing from a single source): before 1801, only 7 titles published in Britain; 1801-1859, 20 published; 1860-1900, 230 published; origin of science fiction dates back to Industrial Revolution, then back to BC 414.

1860 Korea: Chondogyo (Religion of the Heavenly Way), a blend of shamanistic, Buddhist, Confucian and Christian elements, emerges as a reaction against Western, especially Catholic, influence.
Revival in Ukraine; 1884-1904, persecution of Evangelicals.
Massacre of 11,000 wealthy Christians by Druzes in Damascus; France intervenes.
Earl of Shaftesbury, British evangelical social reformer (1801-1885), states: 'Those who hold the truth have the means enough, knowledge enough, and opportunity enough, to evangelize the globe fifty times over'.
Liverpool Conference on Missions, as aftermath of 1859 Awakening in UK; 126 attenders; first major world missionary conference; texts Matthew 28:18-20, 24:14, Luke 24:46-7.

c1860 *Togo*. First Christians (Methodist immigrants from Gold Coast).
Revival in South Africa erupts under Dutch Reformed moderator Andrew Murray (1828-1917), sweeping Afrikaner churches.
Netherlands: revivals under G. van Prinsterer (c1800-1867), A. Kuyper (1837-1920).

1861 Great Christian Revival (Great Awakening) in Jamaica, resulting in rapid spread of Native Baptist Church (now Revival Zion); wild dancing, trances.
Tuvalu (then Ellice Islands). First Christians (Samoan pastors of the LMS).
Tokelau Island. First mission (LMS).
Cornish Revivals, in Britain for 2 years.
110 North American Blacks settle in Haiti and establish Episcopal Church.
Universities Mission to Central Africa (UMCA) begun in Britain.
Madagascar: after 25 years' vicious persecution, Christians found to have multiplied twenty-fold.
Batak church in Sumatra (HKBP) grows from 52 Christians (1866) to 2,056 (1876), 7,500 (1881), 103,525 (1911), 380,000 (1941), 1,044,382 (1970), 1,160,000 (1976), and to 1,500,000 (1983).
Russian Orthodox monk Nicolai (Ivan Kasatkin, 1836-1912) arrives in Japan, 1868 baptizes 3 converts, 1880 made bishop and 1906 archbishop in Tokyo; dies after 51 years in Japan with over 30,000 converts made; most successful Russian Orthodox mission among non-Christians outside Russia.
USA: 620,000 killed, mostly by disease, in 1861-65 Civil War between North and South over slavery issue.
Egypt: Coptic patriarch Cyril IV poisoned as part of continuous Ottoman pressure on Coptic church.
USA: Women's Union Missionary Society of America for Heathen Lands (WUMS) formed in New York as pioneer women's sending society, with 40 other women's societies arising later.

1862 *Djibouti*. First Christians (French colonists).
Methodist Society, a Fanti schism ex Wesleyan Methodists near Cape Coast, Gold Coast.
Orthodox mission begun around Amur river (Siberia) among Gold and Gilyak peoples.
Shensi province, China: terrible Muslim Rebellion (1862-78) kills 600,000, then drought and famine kill another 5 million.

1863 Samoa: syncretistic cult begun by local preacher Sio-vili; vast crowds.
Scandinavian missionary societies convene in first of several Northern Lutheran Missions Conferences.

1864 USA: first Greek Orthodox church organized in New Orleans, Louisiana.
Jules Verne (1828-1905) writes futuristic novel, *Journey to the Centre of the Earth*; 1865, writes *From the Earth to the Moon*, forecasting launch would be made from Florida, with 3 astronauts, who on return would splash down in ocean (all fulfilled in 1969); in other works predicts flight, submarines, aqualungs, television.

1865 *Bhutan*. First Christians (British troops).
From 1820-65, nearly 2 million Roman Catholics from Ireland emigrate to USA.
Christian Revival Association (1878, renamed Salvation Army) founded by Methodist evangelist William Booth in England for urban social outreach and street evangelism.
Paraguay: one million killed in 5-year war with Brazil and Uruguay.
China Inland Mission (CIM) founded as faith mission by J. Hudson Taylor (1832-1905); 1950, renamed Overseas Missionary Fellowship (OMF).
Origins of Social Gospel in American Protestantism; lasts 50 years up to its demise in 1915.
International Telecommunication Union (ITU) founded; 1947, becomes a specialized agency of United Nations, with headquarters in Geneva; over 135 member countries.
German physicist R. Clausius introduces concept of entropy (a measure of the disorder of a system, hence = chaos).

1866 Continental European Missions Conference (CEMC; also named the Ausschuss) holds first meeting in Bremen (Germany); 11 other Bremen conferences by 1909; 1910, merges with Edinburgh world missionary conference.
Severe persecution of Korea's 25,000 Catholics; 10,000 Koreans martyred, including 2 bishops and 7 priests.
First successful submarine cable across Atlantic ocean.

1867 *Midway Islands*. First Christians (USA).
Anglican Church ceases to be state religion in Ireland.
Beginnings of confessional conciliarism: archbishop of Canterbury C.T. Longley (1794-1868) convenes first decennial Lambeth Conference of all bishops of Anglican Communion (London), with 76 bishops present; by 1983, grand total of 45 world confessional councils are in existence, representing all major Christian traditions.
Finland: crop failure kills 8% of population.
USA: first national holiness camp-meeting, in Vineland, NJ; holiness movement produces shoutings, dancing in the Spirit, falling 'under the power', holy laughter, holy rolling.

1868 White Fathers (Missionaries of Our Lady of Africa) and White Sisters (1869) begun by cardinal Charles Lavigerie (1825-1892).
Catholic Action begun in Bologna (Italy).
Origin of Niagara Bible prophecy study conferences, beginning of Bible Conference movement; 1876, Believers' Meeting for Bible Study; 1883-97, Niagara-on-the-Lake conferences; dominated by premillennialists.
Russia: Old Believers and offshoots number 10 million, rising by 1900 to 14% of entire Russian empire.

1869 Council of Vatican I, in Rome (20th Ecumenical Council): papal infallibility defined, widening gulf between Rome and rest of Christendom; 700 bishops present, almost all Europeans.
Artificial earth satellites first predicted in science fiction.

1870 Ghost Dance among American Indians begun by prophet Wodziwob; 1890, spreads to Paiute, Cheyenne, Kiowa, Sioux and other tribes.
Unification of Italy under Victor Emmanuel II (1820-1878); annexes Rome and papal states, makes Rome capital.
Heyday of British evangelists: William Booth (1829-1912), C.H. Spurgeon (1834-1892), Henry Drummond (1851-1897), Wilson Carlile (1847-1942), Gipsy Smith (1860-1947).
Jehovah's Witnesses (then called Watch Tower) begun in USA through Charles T. Russell (1852-1916), who dates Second Advent as 1874, later as 1914.
Punjab: mass movement begins of 50% of Hindu Chuhras in Sialkot to American Presbyterian mission; continuing revival up to 1912.
South India: mass movement brings one million Telugu outcastes into Baptist, Lutheran and Methodist churches in 30 years.
Kugu Sorta (Great Candle), anti-Russian and anti-missionary cult after Cheremis forcibly converted to Christianity.
Native American (Peyote) Church, large USA Amerindian church, takes shape; by 1970, 400,000 members in 23 chapters, from many tribes.
Orthodox Missionary Society organized in Russia by metropolitan of Moscow, I. Veniaminov (1797-1879); branches in 55 Russian dioceses; by 1900, 124,204 pagans baptized in 18 missions; 1914, 20,000 members and a large income.
Rise of supercities across world (cities with over 4 million population), beginning with London (4.2 million by 1875); then 1900, 2 (London,

Paris); 1925, 5; 1950, 11; 1960, 18; 1970, 25; 1980, 40; by 1985, 38 (23 in developing countries); by AD 2000, 79 (59); by AD 2025, 144 (123); those in Africa increase from 1 in 1985 (Cairo) to 12 by AD 2000 and to 36 by AD 2025.

Rise of first megaministry (reaching over 1% of world per annum, i.e. 14 million people a year): BFBS, ABS and other Bible societies' distribution reaches 38,000 scriptures a day.

c1870 *Canton & Enderbury Islands*. First Christians (British guano-digging companies).

1871 Great Fire of Chicago: 50 churches and missions destroyed.

USA: beginnings of large-scale team evangelism; 1871-99, D.L. Moody & Ira D. Sankey.

Sermon before Baptist Missionary Society (London) by former BMS secretary Joseph Angus, entitled 'Apostolic Missions: the Gospel for Every Creature' claims gospel could be preached to every creature on Earth by 1886 or 1891 at latest; his sermon later read by USA Presbyterian theologian and Bible expositor A.T. Pierson (1837-1911), who by 1876 conceives idea of a Watchcry (Watchword), supported by 1877 Shanghai missions conference, and in 1877 begins public addresses on a concrete plan for evangelizing the world.

E.G. Bulwer-Lytton writes *The coming race*, on an advanced race of men living below ground.

Paris Commune executes archbishop of Paris, G. Darboy, also 40 priests and religious.

British anthropologist E.B. Tylor (1832-1917) publishes major treatise, *Primitive culture: researches into the development of mythology, philosophy, religion, language, art and custom*.

D.L. Moody conducts annual higher-life conferences in Northfield, Massachusetts; thousands attend to receive their personal pentecost.

Long series of Old Catholic Conferences: 1st at Munich in 1871, 2nd in 1872 at Cologne with 350 members, 3rd in 1873 at Constance, 4th in 1874 at Freiburg-in-Breisgau, et alia; then Bishops' Conferences since 1889.

1872 Revivals in Japan, also 1883, following waves of persecution in 1865, 1867 and 1868 ending in 1872 decree of religious liberty.

Japan: first of a series of country-wide Protestant missionary conferences: 1900, 3rd in series leads into 1907 Conference of Federated Missions in Japan.

Angola: Kiyoka (Burning) anti-sorcery prophetic movement sweeps across north.

First indigenous church movement in southern Africa: secession from Herman congregation, Paris Mission, Basutoland.

8th International Statistical Congress, held at St Petersburg (Russia), urges inclusion of item on religion in every national census.

First baptism in New Guinea (Protestant).

First useful analogue computer built, by British physicist Lord Kelvin, as tide predictor.

1873 Dwight L. Moody's evangelistic campaigns in England: first 1873-75 (including 5-month London Crusade with 2.5 million attenders), second 1882-84 (with 2 million attenders in London), third 1891-92.

India: Roman Catholic mass movement among aboriginal Kols; 79,000 baptized by 1891.

First of a series of decennial all-India missionary conferences.

1874 Guatemala: Catholic religious orders and congregations dissolved.

Universal Postal Union (UPU) founded; 1947, becomes specialized agency of United Nations, based in Bern; over 140 member countries.

Old Catholics convene international conference of theologians, including Anglicans, at Bonn (Germany), to discuss reunion of churches outside Rome; similar conference in 1875.

1875 Japan: Doshisha university founded by Japanese Christian, Niisima.

Uganda. First resident evangelist (Dallington Maftaa, African Anglican from Nyasaland).

Alliance of Reformed Churches (Presbyterian); first Protestant confessional council to be formed (London); 1970, as WARC, merger with International Congregational Council.

Arya Samaj founded in India by Dayananda Sarasvati (died 1883) for purification of Hinduism, recalling it to fundamentalist position; anti-Christian, attempts to win back converts won by Christian missions.

Society of the Divine Word (Germany) inaugurated.

Keswick Convention for higher spiritual life begun (UK), under theme 'All One in Christ Jesus'.

Theosophical Society founded in New York City under anti-Christian writer Helena Blavatsky (1831-1891), combining Gnosticism, mysticism and occultism of Egypt, India and China; 1909, young Brahmin Jiddu Krishnamurti (1895-1986) claimed as Ascended Master, Christ Spirit, Reincarnate Buddha, Guiding Spirit of the Universe.

World's 10 largest cities: London 4,241,000, Paris 2,250,000, New York 1,900,000, Peking 1,310,000, Berlin 1,045,000, Vienna 1,001,000, Canton 944,000, Philadelphia 791,000, Tokyo 780,000, St Petersburg 764,000.

Orientalist Max Muller (1823-1900) founds science of comparative religion by beginning 51-volume series *The sacred books of the East*.

1876 World Methodist Conference (WMC) founded.

Invention of electric telephone by A.G. Bell in Boston, USA.

Sweden: evangelical awakening in state church under Skogsbergh and Paul Peter Waldenstrom (1838-1917).

England: High Church priest Hay Aitken founds Parochial Mission Society.

1877 *Guinea* (French). First mission (French Holy Ghost priests).

Shanghai, China: 1st General Foreign Missions Conference, with 473 missionaries from 20 Protestant societies; states 'We want China emancipated from the thraldom of sin in this generation'; probable origin, among field missionaries, of Watchword 'The Evangelization of the World in This Generation'; similar conferences in 1890 and 1907.

Uprising in Turkey by Armenian and Syrian Christians suppressed by Turks with many deaths.

1878 BMS (UK) open São Salvador station in northern Angola.

Thailand: Edict of Religious Toleration proclaimed by king Rama V (Chulalongkorn, 1853-1910).

USA: First American Bible and Prophetic Conference, New York City.

2nd Lambeth Conference; 100 Anglican bishops present.

Japan: first National Christian Conference (from 1884-1906, part of World Evangelical Alliance) held, in Tokyo.

Missionary review of the world founded by R. Wilder, soon becomes leading Protestant journal of missions.

East London Institute for Home and Foreign Missions founded in UK by H.G. Guinness (1835-1910) of Church of Ireland; 1900, name changed to Regions Beyond Missionary Union.

1879 First Church of Christ, Scientist, founded in Boston by Mary Baker Eddy (1821-1910) as worldwide movement centering on spiritual healing.

Scripture Union (SU) founded; 300,000 members in UK alone by 1887.

Burundi (then Urundi). First mission (White Fathers).

Protestant Missionary Conference held in London.

1880 Thirty Years' Revival in Germany (till 1910); several hundred thousand converted in state churches.

Russian rocket pioneer K.E. Tsiolkovsky (1857-1935) calculates Sun's energy could sustain human population of $3x10^{23}$; envisages giant greenhouses in space, described in his 1920 novel *Beyond the Planet Earth*; 1928, argues for space-going 'Noah's arks'; envisages first manned space flight by 2017.

Percy Greg's interplanetary adventure novel, *Across the Zodiac*, on future evolution of planet Mars.

Circulation of Watchcry (Watchword) on various Protestant mission fields becomes crystallized in 1885 article by A.T. Pierson entitled 'A plan to evangelize the world', published in his journal *Missionary review of the world* after 20 years of reflection.

1st Lay Congress of American Catholics, Baltimore, USA; 1893, 2nd Lay Congress, in Chicago.

c1880 Ethiopia: 50,000 Muslims, 20,000 pagans, and a total of 500,000 Gallas, baptized by force by Ethiopian Orthodox Church.

1881 300,000 killed in Indochina by typhoon.

Shakerism and Indian Shaker Church begun by former Roman Catholic John Slocum among Puget Sound Amerindians.

Somalia. First mission (Catholic).

First of 43 International Eucharistic Congresses, held in Lille (France) with 800 present; growing to the 41st (1976) in Philadelphia (USA) with one million present; 1985, 43rd held in Nairobi, Kenya.

1st Ecumenical Methodist Conference, held in London; precursor of later World Methodist Council.

Mohamed Ahmed ibn Seyyid Abdullah (1848-1885) proclaims self Mahdi; 1885, captures Khartoum and kills general Gordon; 1899, final defeat of Mahdism by British.

Ethiopian emperor Yohannes IV pays Coptic patriarch of Egypt 12,000 Maria Theresa thalers for consecration of 4 abunas (bishops).

United Society of Christian Endeavor formed in USA; 1895, World's Christian Endeavor Union organized (38,000 societies across world, with 2,225,000 members); 1927, International Society of Christian Endeavor; by 1965, 3 million members in 85 Protestant denominations in 80 countries.

England: English Revised Version of Bible produced by 65 English scholars, completed by 1885.

1882 India: Anglicans and Protestants number 500,000.

Britain: International Bible Reading Association (IBRA) founded; 100,000 members by 1886.

Korean treaty with USA ensures religious freedom in Korea; Presbyterian and Methodist missionaries enter 3 years later.

Church Army (Anglican) founded in Britain by Wilson Carlile.

Mexico: first of several national or regional Protestant missionary conferences.

I. Donnelly publishes *Atlantis: the antediluvian world*, linking empire of Atlantis with Garden of Eden.

1883 Fourth Evangelical Awakening (of the century) in Norway, especially in Skien.

Japan: first Japanese Catholic priests ordained: 15 by 1891, 33 by 1910.

2nd General Conference of Protestant Missionaries of Japan; several revivals; 'Japan is now embracing Christianity with a rapidity unexampled since the days of Constantine . . . will be predominantly Christian within 20 years'.

Catastrophic eruption of volcano Krakatoa (off Java) with energy of hundreds of megatons (largest single explosion ever seen on Earth): 120-foot tidal wave drowns 36,000 on Java and Sumatra; whole planet banded by dust for months, resulting in coldest winter for centuries.

1884 German Evangelization Society founded.
City-wide evangelists in USA: Samuel Porter Jones (1847-1906) & E.O. Excell (from 1885-1906, 25 million attenders and 500,000 converts, most in South), B. Fay Mills (1857-1916), J. Wilbur Chapman (1859-1918).
Founding in USA of magazine 'The Christian Century' dedicated to proposition that the Kingdom of Christ will dominate the world at end of 20th century by AD 2000.
Berlin West Africa Conference: European powers with USA and Turkey meet to decide all questions related to Congo Basin, East and Central Africa; German colonial policy developed.
'The Cambridge Seven' leave Britain as missionaries to China.
Worldwide standard time adopted by delegates from 27 nations meeting in Washington, DC, dividing world into 24 standard time zones starting with GMT (Greenwich Mean Time) based on prime meridian defined as zero longitude at Greenwich, UK.

1885 First African ordinations to Anglican ministry in Kenya.
Zambia (Northern Rhodesia). First mission (Paris Mission, PEMS).
Uganda Martyrs: around 250 Catholic and Anglican Christians executed by king Mwanga (1866-1901) at Namugongo.
Wesleyan Forward Movement in British Methodism under Hugh Price Hughes (1847-1902) of West London Mission, founding central halls in cities and stressing social evangelism; 1896, Hughes founds National Council of Evangelical Free Churches.
Richard Jefferies' novel of future collapse of civilization, *After London*.
At D.L. Moody's Northfield Convention for lay workers, A.T. Pierson chairs committee to 'divide the world according to a comity agreement' and then pursue 'the immediate occupation and evangelization of every destitute district of the earth's population', so that 'the entire current population of the earth would hear the gospel by the year 1900'.

1886 *Sikkim*. First mission (Church of Scotland).
More indigenous movements and churches in India opposing Western missions: 1886 National Church of Madras, 1887 Calcutta Christo Samaj.
Church of God (Cleveland) begun as study and fellowship group in Cleveland, Tennessee; later became first Pentecostal church in USA, from 1906.
H. Hollerith (1860-1929) invents punched-card electrical tabulating machine; 1890, selected to count 12th USA census of population (result, 62,622,250); 1924, his company becomes IBM.
Dutch botanist and geneticist H. de Vries (1848-1935) discovers mutations (sudden, abrupt, immediate transformations of hereditary material, radical enough to bring new species into existence in a single leap), producing major refinement of Darwin's theory of evolution.
1st International Christian Student Conference, Mount Hermon, Massachusetts, addressed by D.L. Moody, A.T. Pierson, et alii; 251 attenders; 1888, Student Volunteer Movement for Foreign Missions organized with 2,200 initial volunteers, based on Watchword 'The Evangelization of the World in This Generation'; by 1945, a total of 20,500 SVM students have gone overseas as foreign missionaries.
Germany: 1st Blankenburg Alliance Conference, founded by Anna von Weling.

1887 900,000 drowned in Honan, China, by Yellow river floods.
First scripture translation in Philippines: Gospel of Luke in Pangasinan.
Canada: evangelistic campaigns in cities under evangelists Crossley and Hunter.
Maldives. First Christians (under British protectorate).
W.H. Hudson's novel *A Crystal Age*: future evolution of Earth in AD 12,000, some 10 millennia after a mass catastrophe.
Ecuador: archbishop J.I. Checa y Barba (1829-1887) convokes 2nd and 3rd Councils of Quito; opposed by state, poisoned.
Netherlands: first of annual series of Dutch Protestant missionary conferences.

1888 German Association for Evangelism and Christian Fellowship (Gnadauer Band) formed at Gnadau; 1st Gnadau Conference on state church evangelism, with 142 workers present; by 1920, Association has 6,000 organizations and 225,000 registered members; 1938, 800 preachers and 300 women workers, holding 6,000 meetings.
Nauru. First mission (LMS).
Christmas Island. First Christians (British administrators).
India: Mar Thoma Syrian Christian Evangelistic Association of Malabar formed for non-Syrian outcaste converts; large annual conventions.
Native Baptist Church secedes, in Lagos (Nigeria) and Douala (Cameroon), from Southern Baptists and Basel Mission.
Invention of Edison motion-picture camera (Kinetograph).
Centenary Conference on Foreign Missions (Ecumenical Missionary Conference), London; 1,576 missionaries and representatives of 140 agencies; first of the great international conferences.
3rd Lambeth Conference; 145 Anglican bishops present.
Edward Bellamy writes futuristic novel *Looking backward: 2000-1887*, envisaging by AD 2000 an idyllic fully socialist world with no crime, no warfare, no money, no nationalism, no politics, no bureaucracies.
First Scriptures in constructed international languages: 1888 Volapuk, 1893 Esperanto.
Seventh-day Adventist prophet since 1855, Ellen G. White (1827-1915), publishes *The Great Controversy* on Jehovah's cosmic dispute, writes 44 other major books and over 4,000 articles.
Photography invented by G. Eastman.
Afghanistan: Armenian Catholics, mostly merchants, are persecuted and expelled.
Italian Bible colporteur F.G. Penzotti begins first Spanish-speaking Evangelical church in Peru, in Callao.
USA: Woman's Missionary Union (WMU) begun by Southern Baptists, becomes largest mission support body in world organized by women; by 1986, 1,200,000 members supporting 7,000 missionaries, with one billion dollars raised.

1889 Largest USA non-Chalcedonian church established: Armenian Church of North America, under catholicate of Echmiadzin.
Japan: 500 Japanese students at Student Conference send telegram to SVM Conference, Northfield (USA), urging 'Make Jesus King'.
Old Catholic Bishops' Conference, Utrecht (Dutch, German and Swiss churches); Declaration of Utrecht issued as Old Catholic doctrinal basis.
North Africa Mission enters Tripoli as first Protestant mission in Libya.
Rwanda. First mission (White Fathers).
Brazil: republic proclaimed and Catholic church formally separated from state.
Founding of Ahmadiya out of Shia Islam in Punjab by self-professed mahdi Mirza Ghulam Ahmad (1836-1908); adherents rise from 70,030 in 1900 to 4,734,000 by 1985.
British Salvation Army evangelist Gipsy Smith holds large meetings in major USA cities; in 50 years' ministry leads vast numbers to Christ in UK, USA, Australia.
SVMU chairman John R. Mott writes to sister Hattie that the task of world evangelization will be accomplished by the dawn of the 20th century.

1890 China: 500,000 baptized Catholics, 639 foreign priests, 369 Chinese priests.
Shanghai: foreign missions conference, with 1,295 missionaries present.
Philippine Independent Church founded by Roman Catholic priest Gregorio Aglipay (1860-1940); 1902, organized as schism taking 45% of all Roman Catholics in country.
Nevius method introduced in Korea (Bible-training for lay members).
Era of the 'New Evangelism' as expounded by Scottish evangelist Henry Drummond et alii.
Vladimir Solovyov (1853-1900), Russian mystical philosopher and disciple of Dostoievsky, places birth of Antichrist in 1954.
Long series of International Old Catholic Congresses held: 1st Cologne 1890, 2nd Lucerne 1892, 3rd Rotterdam 1894, 4th Vienna 1897, 5th Bonn 1902, 6th Olten 1904, 7th The Hague 1907, 8th Vienna 1909, 9th Cologne 1913, 10th Berne 1925, 11th Utrecht 1928, 12th Vienna 1931, 13th Constance 1934, 14th Zurich 1938, 15th Hilversum 1948, 16th Munich 1953, 17th Rheinfelden 1957, 18th Haarlem 1961, 19th Vienna 1965, et alia.
First of 12-volume *The Golden Bough: a study in magic and religion* by J.G. Frazer (1854-1941).

1891 Japan: Roman Catholic hierarchy constituted; Catholics 44,500, rising to 63,000 by 1910.
International Congregational Council formed in London.

1892 *United Arab Emirates* (then Trucial Oman). First Christians (British officials, Indian merchants).
UK: Free Church Congress meets in Manchester; soon after, National Council of Evangelical Free Churches is formed, also numerous local councils of churches across Britain.

1893 Papua New Guinea: Cult of the Prophet Tokerau at Milne Bay, first of over 120 distinct cargo cult movements over next 80 years.
National Spiritualist Association of Churches founded, in USA.
World's Parliament of Religions, in Chicago: ecumenist Philip Schaff (1819-1893) delivers notable address on 'The Reunion of Christendom'.
French astronomer and spiritualist C. Flammarion writes *La fin du monde (Omega: the last days of the world)*, describing (1) comet collision in AD c2450 killing millions, then (2) final days of human race in AD 10 million when, due to solar extinction, Earth has become too cold to live on.
H.G. Wells (1866-1946), atheist and secular prophet, prolific writer of far-futuristic science fiction, publishes 'The Man of the Year Million', also *The Time Machine* (1895), *In the Abyss* (1896, city of humanoids beneath ocean), *The Invisible Man* (1897), *The War of the Worlds* (1898), *The First Men in the Moon* (1901), *Anticipations* (1902, on prophecy), *The Empire of the Ants* (1905, South American ants evolve and supersede man), *First and last things* (1908), *The shape of things to come* (1933), *The outlook for Homo Sapiens* (1942); envisages first round-the-Moon voyage not until AD 2054.
Foreign Missions Conference of North America (FMCNA) organized representing 21 USA and Canada mission boards; 1950, renamed Division of Foreign Missions, NCCCUSA; 1965, Division of Overseas Ministries.

1894 Madagascar: first indigenous church, Malagasy Protestant Church splits ex LMS.
Soatanana Revival begins among Lutheran and LMS churches in

Madagascar, lasting over 90 years (Fifohazana, Revivalists).
Central African Republic (then Ubangi-Chari). First mission (Roman Catholic).

1895 *Mali*. First mission (White Fathers from Senegal).
Massacres of Armenian Christians by Turks: 1895, 80,000 in Trebizond; Christmas 1895, 1,200 burnt alive in Urfa cathedral; 1896, 6,000 in Istanbul; total killed 1895-96, 200,000; 1905, 20,000 in Cilicia; 1909, 30,000 in district of Adana; 1915, 600,000 in Anatolia; and in 1920, 30,000 at Marash and Hadjin.
Church of God in Christ formed in USA; later become Black pentecostals.
Coptic Catholic patriarchate of Alexandria erected by Roman pope (earlier attempt 1824).
World Student Christian Federation (WSCF) founded in Sweden under John R. Mott (1865-1955), uniting 40 autonomous groups.
R. Cromie's novel *The crack of doom:* mad scientist unlocks power of atom and holds world to ransom.
Fire-Baptized Holiness Church under B.H. Irwin teaches a third blessing, a separate 'baptism with the Holy Ghost and fire' subsequent to conversion and sanctification; but unconnected with glossolalia or charismata.
Ecuador: persecution of Catholic Church by liberals and freemasons.
A.T. Pierson reluctantly realizes world will not become evangelized by 1900 as planned, and publicly admits this.

1896 German Student Volunteer Movement begun.
'Make Jesus King': International Students Missionary Conference, Liverpool; 800 students from 24 nations.
Theodor Herzl (1860-1904), founder of modern Zionism, publishes his *Der Judenstaat* (The Jewish State); rise of global Zionist movement (Hibbat Zion, 'Love of Zion').
Mashonaland uprising against British; Africans killed are later canonized by African indigenous churches.
First Protestant chairs of missiology in world: at university of Halle, Germany, G. Warneck (1834-1910) becomes first professor of science of missions; and in 1899 W.O. Carver (1868-1954) becomes head of missions at Southern Baptist Theological Seminary, Louisville, USA.

1897 Ross's discovery of cause of malaria; missionary fatalities in Africa decline.
Lott Carey Baptist Foreign Mission Convention (Black American) organized in USA.
USA: largest Catholic (non-Roman) church established: Polish National Catholic Church, formed over conflict between Polish Catholics and Irish Catholic hierarchy.
4th Lambeth Conference; 194 Anglican bishops present; first of 14 resolutions on foreign missions passed: 'We recommend that prompt and continuous efforts be made to arouse the Church to . . . the fulfilment of our Lord's great commission to evangelize all nations'.
Swami Vivekananda (1862-1902), disciple of Ramakrishna, founds Hindu missions in Western world.
Arabia, and the world, 'could easily be evangelized within the next 30 years if it were not for the wicked selfishness of Christians'—Samuel Zwemer, Apostle to Islam (1867-1952).
Free Protestant Episcopal Church (later, Ecumenical Church Foundation) begun in UK as Anglo-Roman autocephalous episcopal church under bishops-at-large (episcopi vagantes); branches in UK, USA, West Indies, West Africa (Nigeria 1946, Equatorial Guinea 1968, Cameroon 1970).
House of Laymen, Province of Canterbury (Church of England) resolves: 'In view of the Great Commission to evangelize the world, its long and serious neglect . . . the whole Church needs rousing on this question'.
Encyclical letter 'On the Holy Spirit' issued by pope Leo XIII, directing attention to charismata and promoting universal novena (9-day cycle of prayer) to Holy Spirit before Pentecost Sunday each year; millions influenced.
9th Continental Missions Conference, in Bremen (Germany): missiologist G. Warneck leads attack on the Watchword as implying hasty preaching, premillennial eschatology, and a prophecy to be fulfilled; states evangelization of world in this generation is impossible.

1898 50,000 Nestorians in Urmia diocese (Iran) converted to Russian Orthodoxy; 1914, annihilated by Turks.
Nyasaland: Providence Industrial Mission founded by USA Blacks, later leading to 1915 Chilembwe uprising.
Church and state separated in Cuba on independence from Spain.
Baptist originator of social gospel in America, Walter Rauschenbusch (1861-1918), teaches that God and USA fight on same side against Spain; but by 1917 deplores US Protestant support of war against Germany.
M.P. Shiel describes apocalyptic race war in *The Yellow peril*, where screaming yellow horde of 400 million East Asians swarms across Europe.

1899 *Wake Island*. First Christians (USA cable station).
New Thought movement (mental science, religious science, mental healing) spreads in USA; first New Thought Conference held in Hartford; International New Thought Alliance (INTA) formed.
Japanese government proclaims State Shinto not a religion, hence compulsory reverence before emperor's image not a religious act.
Gideons Internationl launched, providing massive free scripture distribution ('placements') among businessmen and professionals, hotels, armed forces, schools, et alia; total placements by 1967, 7 million Bibles, 50 million NTs.
African indigenous churches (AICs) throughout Africa number some 50 separate denominations with 42,400 adherents, predominantly from 20 African tribes, of whom 18 have their own printed scripture translations.
Atheist H.G. Wells writes 'A vision of judgement', in which Last Trump sounds; also, 1915, 'The story of the Last Trump': God's trumpet accidentally falls to Earth, is blown, heard worldwide, all receive momentary glimpse of reality of God.
At end of 'Golden Age of Jewish Missions' (= 19th century), over 200,000 Jews have been baptized as Protestants; 650 Protestant missionaries minister to Jews at 213 mission stations across world.
Latin American Plenary Council convened in Rome by pope Leo XIII; first such continental council ever.

1900 **Global status:** 62 generations after Christ, world is 34.4% Christians (81.1% of them being Whites), 51.3% evangelized; with printed Scriptures available in 537 languages.
Total of all Christian denominations begins to rise steeply as Christianity spreads across world, from only 92 in AD 1000, to 150 in AD 1500, to 510 in AD 1800, to 1,900 by AD 1900.
Upper Volta. First mission (French White Fathers).
First cinemas in fair sideshows; 1905, first cinema theatre.
Boxer revolt in China kills 47,000 Catholics (out of 1.2 million) with 5 bishops and 31 priests, and 2,000 Protestants with 188 missionaries and children.
In Hawaii, catastrophic decline of Aboriginal population through disease from 200,000 (in 1775) to 70,000 (1850) to 35,000 (1900).
Peak of massive Roman Catholic immigration from Europe to USA.
Northern Solomons (Bougainville). First mission (Roman Catholic).
New York Ecumenical Missionary Conference: 2,500 members, 200,000 attenders; delegates from 162 mission boards; huge public meetings.
International Council of Unitarian and Other Liberal Religious Thinkers and Workers, founded in USA; 1910, renamed International Congress of Free Christians and Other Religious Liberals; 1930, renamed International Association for Liberal Christianity and Religious Freedom (IARF).
Methodist layman John R. Mott publishes classic, *The evangelization of the world in this generation*; many Christian strategists envisage winning of entire world to Christ during 20th century, then seen as certain to be 'the Christian century'.
Minahasa (north of Celebes) entirely christianized.
World's 10 largest cities: London 6,480,000, New York 4,242,000, Paris 3,330,000, Berlin 2,424,000, Chicago 1,717,000, Vienna 1,662,000, Tokyo 1,497,000, St Petersburg 1,439,000, Philadelphia 1,418,000, Manchester 1,255,000.
Darwin's theory of evolution (the mutability of species) widely accepted by now, but his idea of natural selection as principal driving force for speciation not accepted until 1940s.
Origins of Pentecostalism in USA: British-Israelite holiness preacher Charles F. Parham (1873-1929, Methodist) opens Bethel Bible School near Topeka, Kansas, with 40 students; 1901, they receive baptism of Holy Spirit; 1903 revival spreads through Kansas, 1905 Houston, 1906 to Los Angeles and thence across world (1906 Norway, 1907 Chile, 1908 China, 1909 Korea, 1910 Brazil, and so on).
South India Missionary Conference, Madras, with delegates officially appointed by their respective bodies.
German theoretical physicist Max Planck (1858-1947) originates quantum theory based on concept of radiant energy being quantized (radiated discontinuously in multiples of definite, fixed, indivisible units or quanta).

Technological Revolution (Second Industrial Revolution)

1901 After 1st Industrial Revolution (fueled by steam power and coal in Britain, 1775), 2nd revolution arises due to electrical and chemical industries in Germany.
First Atlantic wireless signal sent by G. Marconi (1874-1937) from Poldhu, Cornwall (UK) to St Johns, Newfoundland.
UK: BFBS grand total of scriptures issued since 1808: 46,030,124 Bibles, 71,178,373 NTs, 52,763,047 portions.
World's first billion-dollar corporation, US Steel; 1919, 6 such giant corporations.
USA: National Federation of Churches and Christian Workers organized, culminating in 1908 formation of FCCCNA.
Latter-Rain teaching: after 1,800 years of apparent cessation of large-scale charismata and 100 years of expectancy and teaching in USA on gifts of the Spirit, 'restoration of all things' begins with Spirit-baptism and glossolalia, as pentecostal power is restored to the church; thousands of seekers travel to revival centers in USA, Europe, Asia, South America.
USA: American Standard Version (ASV) of Bible, by American scholars working with English RV translators.

1902 Pakistan (then in India): Hindu outcaste mass movement into Methodist church begins.

Adolf von Harnack (1851-1930) publishes his *The mission and expansion of Christianity during the first 3 centuries.*
Team evangelism: 1902-08, R.A. Torrey (1856-1928) & C.M. Alexander (1867-1920) with 130,000 converts.
30,000 killed in volcanic eruption of Mt Pelée, Martinique.
All-India Fourth Decennial Conference, Madras (Protestant missions), with official delegates.
Young People's Missionary Education Movement (1911, title shortened to MEM) founded by 15 USA denominational boards, YMCA and SVMU, to enlist missionaries outside college world.
USA psychologist W. James (1842-1910) writes *The varieties of religious experience.*
Germany: founding of evangelistic tent campaigns (German Tent Mission), 1924 Christian Endeavor, 1926 Baptist Tent Mission, 1926 Methodists, 1951 Evangelical Free Church Tent Mission.
4th International Convention, Student Volunteer Movement for Foreign Missions, in Toronto, Canada, produces 691-page report *World-wide evangelization, the urgent business of the Church.*

1903 Evangelization of Munduruccu Indians in Brazil begun by German Franciscans.
First successful flight of a powered aircraft at Kitty Hawk, North Carolina (USA), by Wright brothers.
L.P. Gratacap writes *The certainty of a future life in Mars*, a religio-scientific type of propaganda.
Weymouth New Testament published.

1904 Conversion of Indian evangelist and mystic, Sadhu Sundar Singh (1889-c1929); visits villages across India, also Tibet annually; encounters Christian ascetic in Himalayas, allegedly 284-year-old Maharishi of Mount Kailash (southwest Tibetan peak, 22,028 feet: cosmic centre of Universe for Buddhists, paradise of Shiva for Hindus); 1929, vanishes in Tibet, probably murdered by lamas.
Welsh revival through ministry of Evan Roberts (1878-1951) in Glamorganshire, Anglesey, Caernarvonshire, with 100,000 converts in Wales in 6 months; short-lived (1904-06), but literally sweeps the world; worldwide publicity from the press; leads into worldwide Pentecostal movement including 1905 Switzerland and Germany, 1907 England.
Premillennialist theologian W.E. Blackstone (1841-1935) writes *The Millennium*, teaches world has already been evangelized (cites Acts 2:5, 8:4, Mark 16:20, Colossians 1:23).
New Britain: massacre at Baining of 2 RC priests, 3 brothers, 5 nuns.

1905 1st Baptist World Congress, London; Baptist World Alliance (BWA) founded.
In France, Catholic church separated from state.
Evangelical awakenings in Denmark, Finland, Sweden, Germany, Russia, Madagascar, India (Assam, Kerala, Sialkot through Praying Hyde), Korea, China.
Evangelistic Faith Missions (USA) formed.
Evangelistic Council of London sponsors Greater London crusade with Torrey & Alexander team; 202 meetings, 1.1 million attenders, 14,000 conversions.
Charles de Foucauld, missionary hermit in Tamanrasset (Algeria), labors among Muslim tribes; 1916, assassinated in Senussi revolt.
Albert Einstein (1879-1955) formulates Special Theory of Relativity (light always appears to travel at same speed, and nothing can exceed it), equates mass and energy in epochal formula $E=mc^2$; 1915, General Theory of Relativity (a theory of gravity, which causes time to slow down; space is curved by the presence of mass).
National conciliarism begins: 1905 Fédération Protestante de France, 1908 Federal Council of the Churches of Christ in North America (1950 NCCCUSA), 1922 National Christian Council of China, 1922 Aliança Evangélica de Angola, et alia, up to 550 nationwide councils by 1983.
Manchuria: 2,000 Presbyterians killed by Japanese Shintoists.
India: pentecostal revival in Mukti Mission, Poona, under Anglican teacher Pandita Ramabai (1858-1922).
Jules Verne's *L'eternel Adam*, with monster earthquake flooding world in 21st century and reemergence of lost continent of Atlantis.

1906 USA: Pentecostalism achieves nationwide publicity under Black holiness preacher W.J. Seymour (1870-1922) with revival in Azusa Street, Los Angeles, which lasts from 1906-09; thousands of seekers travel from Europe to seek their personal pentecost with glossolalia; 1906-1908, whole pentecostal movement in USA teaches 3-stage way of salvation.
First indigenous schism in China: China Jesus Independent Church.
Proliferation of world mission atlases, both Protestant (1906, 1910, 1925, 1938) and RC (1906, 1913, 1929), with statistics listed by mission societies or RC dioceses rather than by denominations and countries.
China: 80,000 Orthodox in Manchuria entrusted to Russian mission, with bishop, archimandrite, 20 clergy; 1914, 5,035 Chinese believers; 1922, diocese of Harbin organized; 1935, 200,000 Orthodox in China with dioceses of Harbin, Peking, Shanghai, and 80,000 Orthodox in Chinese Turkestan.
1st General Conference of Missionaries to the World of Islam, convened through Reformed missionary S.M. Zwemer, held in Cairo, Egypt.
Laymen's Missionary Movement (LMM) launched as foreign missions auxiliary agency via SVM and 17 major North American Protestant denominations; uses large city-wide conferences, crusade dinners, business methods, publicity etc; by 1916, one million men have attended its 3,000 conferences, quadrupling USA Protestant mission giving.
First recorded pentecostal meeting in continental Europe: Methodist prophet T.B. Barratt (1862-1940), a Cornishman, preaches to 2,000 in Christiana (Oslo); by 1910 Italy honeycombed with Pentecostal churches; Russian empire reached 1911 in Helsinki, 1914 St Petersburg, 1915 Moscow.
V.T. Sutphen's novel *The Doomsman* describes 21st-century neo-medieval New York 100 years after a 1925 plague decimates mankind.

1907 Massive revival in Korea: phenomenal growth of churches, spreading also into Manchuria and China.
Conference of Federated Missions in Japan inaugurated, meets annually.
First pentecostal movement within Church of England, at parish in Sunderland under clergyman A.A. Boddy (1854-1930).
USA: peak immigration rate of 1,285,000 Europeans in one year; immigrants from 1845-1914 total 33 million.
The Aquarian Gospel of Jesus Christ: the philosophic and practical basis of the religion of the Aquarian Age of the World, by L.H. Dowling, published in Santa Monica, California; claims Jesus studied Hinduism under gurus in India for 20 years; Earth is now after 2,000 years moving out of constellation Pisces the Fish, heralding demise of Christianity, and Earth is now on threshold of New Age of Aquarius the Watercarrier, 11th sign of the zodiac.
Centenary Conference, Shanghai (Protestant missions).
USA: first major sweep of pentecostalism traverses southern holiness movement; in month-long meeting in Dunn, North Carolina ('Azusa Street East'), hundreds receive tongues-attested baptism in the Spirit; several holiness denominations become pentecostalized.
R.H. Benson writes novel *Lord of the World*, about final struggle between Antichrist and Christ, with Armageddon and Advent, in 21st century.

1908 Million-ton meteorite or comet crashes near Tunguska, Siberia, with impact energy of 30 megatons; mass devastation still visible after 80 years.
Manchurian Revival, at Changte under Jonathan Goforth (1859-1936).
Nyasaland: Elliott Kamwana baptizes 10,000 Lakeside Tonga, start of major separatist church in Central Africa (Church of the Watch Tower).
J. Wilbur Chapman's 6-week evangelistic campaign in Philadelphia (USA): 400 churches, 1.5 million attenders, 7,000 enquirers.
5th Lambeth Conference; 242 Anglican bishops present.
1st Pan-Anglican Congress, in London, with laity and clergy from all Anglican dioceses across world.
European Baptist Congress, Berlin.
National Missionary Campaign conducted in Canada by LMM: 4 conventions in 24 cities, concluding in 1909 with Canadian Missionary Congress in Toronto with 4,000 representatives from all Protestant churches.
USA: first schisms in Black pentecostal movement: Church of God in Christ splits over tongues as evidence of baptism in the Holy Spirit, anti-pentecostal faction secedes; at same time, White pentecostals split from Black pentecostals, withdrawing or being expelled from Black-dominated Apostolic Faith Mission (Azusa Street); Whites then develop 2-stage way of salvation, and in 1914 form Assemblies of God.
Newly-formed Federal Council of the churches of Christ in North America (FCCCNA) sets forth its 'Social Creed of the churches' representing 30 denominations.

1909 Pentecostal movement organized in Chile: USA Methodist missionary W.C. Hoover and 37 charismatics are excommunicated, form Iglesia Metodista Pentecostal.
C.W. Eliot (president, Harvard University) publishes *The religion of the future.*
E.M. Forster writes 'The Machine stops': world's inhabitants have atrophied to slug-like existence living in tiny, private cells facing god-like Machine (= television/computer); people do nothing but lecture or listen to lectures; suddenly Machine stops, humanity expires.
Korean Protestants (8,000 church members, 200,000 all Christians) announce 'A Million Souls for Christ' movement; at same time Japanese 35-year occupation enforces Shintoism, kills thousands.
National Missionary Campaign in USA: 70 city-wide conventions, closing in 1910 with National Missionary Congress in Chicago; similar events in Australia, Ceylon, Denmark, Germany, Holland, New Zealand, South Africa, Sweden, UK.
'Berlin Declaration' by German Evangelicals rejects Pentecostal claims of restoration of charismata, condemns all pentecostalism as a diabolic manifestation; as a result, Pentecostalism spreads only slowly in German-speaking nations.

1910 Beginnings of Faith and Order Movement, on initiative of Protestant Episcopal Church in Cincinnati, USA, calling for a world conference.
World Missionary Conference, Edinburgh, Scotland (previously called 3rd Ecumenical Missionary Conference until 1908 change); 1,355 delegates; beginning of 20th-century ecumenical movement; report of Commission I is entitled *Carrying the Gospel to all the non-Christian world*, stating 'The Church is confronted today with a literally world-wide opportunity to make Christ known.'

Protestant and Anglican missionaries worldwide number 45,000.
Mexico: National Revolution kills 7% of population including many Evangelicals; anticlerical and anti-church laws, though aimed at Catholic Church, result in decline of older Protestant churches.
USA team evangelism: 1910-30, Billy Sunday (1862-1935) & H. Rodeheaver (1880-1955); former preaches to 100 million, with 1 million enquirers (300,000 conversions).
Pope Pius X (1835-1914) has vision in public of future destruction of Vatican; teaches that Antichrist has already arrived in atheistic and pagan society of his day; condemns modernism and modernist scholarship.
Men and Religion Forward Movement (MRFM, 1910-12) advances LMM concerns into a global social gospel organization, but includes nationwide evangelism, social-evangelism crusades, home and foreign missions, business ethics, detailed research on 70 cities, and every kind of Christian endeavor; reaches 1,492,646 persons in 60 USA towns through 7,062 meetings; 1913, carried worldwide by touring party.
World Union of Catholic Women's Organizations formed; by 1970, 40 million members.
Religious surveys using social scientific methodology become widespread in USA.
Great Britain: 122,000 telephones in use, rising by 1931 to 2 million.
First charismatic prayer groups form within mainline state churches of Europe: German Pentecostal leader J.A.A.B. Paul (1853-1931) remains a Lutheran minister until his death.

1911 Watch Tower movement (USA) enters Northern Rhodesia from Nyasaland to meet with extraordinary success, with in 1970 over 800,000 living Zambians estimated to have belonged at one time or another.
First Catholic chair of missiology in world: university of Munster, Westphalia; first professor, Joseph Schmidlin (1876-1944); founds also International Institute for Missionary Research/Science; opposes Nazism, dies in prison camp.
2nd Baptist World Congress (BWA), Philadelphia (USA).
2nd General Conference on Muslim Missions, again organized through S.M. Zwemer, held in Lucknow (India).

1912 *International review of missions* begins publication; editor J.H. Oldham (1874-1969).
USA team evangelism: 1912-45, Mordecai Ham & W.J. Ramsay.
Burma: Self-Supporting Karen Baptist Missionary Society splits ex ABFMS.
Roman Catholic anthropologist W. Schmidt SVD (1868-1954) publishes *Der Ursprung der Gottesidee* (12 volumes, 1912-1955), holding that most primitive peoples should be regarded as monotheists.
V.S. Azariah (1874-1945) consecrated bishop of Dornakal; first Anglican Indian bishop.
French Jewish social scientist E. Durkheim (1858-1917) publishes classic, *The elementary forms of the religious life: a study in religious sociology.*
Orthodox sectarians in Russian empire number 30 million, including 25 million Old Believers, 1,200,000 Molokans (Spiritual Christians-Milkdrinkers), 300,000 Khlysty (Spiritual Christians-Whippers).

1913 Liberian Grebo prophet William Wadé Harris (c1865-1929) preaches in Ivory Coast resulting in 120,000 converts by 1915, and eventually in large Harrist denominations.
English missionary C.T. Studd (1862-1931), deeply impressed by report *Carrying the Gospel*, founds Christ's Etceteras (later renamed Worldwide Evangelization Crusade) to focus on evangelizing 'the remaining unevangelized parts (peoples) of the world'.
Highwater mark of influence of Watchword 'The Evangelization of the World in this Generation' on Protestant missions; decline thereafter.
European Baptist Congress, Stockholm.
United Missionary Campaigns across USA under LMM, Foreign Missions Conference of North America, and Home Missions Council of USA; 695 Protestant interdenominational conferences held by 1916.
Committee on Cooperation in Latin America (CCLA) created at New York conference; 1916, Congress on Christian Work in Latin America, held in Panama with 50% of delegates being Latin Americans.
German theologian and musician Albert Schweitzer (1875-1965) goes to French Equatorial Africa with Paris Evangelical Missionary Society, founds Lambaréné hospital.
Moffatt Bible published: NT 1913, complete Bible 1924.

Epoch VIII: VIGOUR AMIDST STORM 1914-1950

1914 **Global status:** 63 generations after Christ, world is 35.5% Christians (76.2% of them being Whites), 53.0% evangelized; with printed Scriptures available in 676 languages; total martyrs since AD 33, 15,551,000 (0.3% of all Christians ever; recent rate 35,600 per year).
Value of world trade multiplies fiftyfold from $700 million in 1750, to $40,000 million by 1914.

First World War devastates Europe

World War I begins, with 42 million men mobilized by Allies versus 23 million by Central Powers; by its end in 1918, 8.4 million killed (5 million Allied, including 1.7 million lost by Russia and 1.3 million by France; 3.4 million Central Powers, including 1.7 million by Germany and 1.25 million by 50-million Austro-Hungarian Empire); combatants wounded, 21 million; 115,000 tons of poison gas used in Western Front.
Newly-elected pope Benedict XV (1854-1922) issues encyclical declaring World War I to be beginning of the Last Age: 'It seems as if the days foretold by Christ had indeed come: "You shall hear of wars and rumours of wars. For nation shall rise against nation, and kingdom against kingdom" (Mt 24:6-7)'.
USA Protestantism attempts to defuse militarism by forming Church Peace Union, also World Alliance for International Friendship (Constance, Germany, on day World War I begins); based on conviction that worldwide Christian forces could 'mobilize for a warless world'; USA's militaristic cause identified with Christ's Great Commission; 1919, Life and Work Committee formed independent of World Alliance, convenes conference 1920 at Geneva.
Uganda: mass revival, Society of the One Almighty God (KOAB), or Malakite Church, secedes ex CMS with 91,740 Ganda adherents by 1921.
Nomiya Luo Mission, first of Kenya's independent indigenous churches, begun in Nyanza as schism from Anglican Church.
Protestants in Latin America total over 500,000 communicants.
Contestado movement begun in Joazeiro (Brazil) by Padre Cicero Romão Batista (1844-1934), declaring holy war against authorities in defence of Caboclos (Euro-Amerindian half-castes), who regard him as messiah.
Date of inauguration of Kingdom of God on Earth by Jehovah (with invisible Second Coming of Christ), as predicted by Jehovah's Christian witnesses (Jehovah's Witnesses).
First motion pictures with sound showings: Photo-Drama of Creation (Watch Tower), seen by 35,000 daily.
Foreign missionaries in Africa: 4,273 Protestants, 5,977 Roman Catholics.
Protestants in Japan grow to 103,000 from only 10 in 1872.
Roman Catholic bishops worldwide still all of European origin, except for 4 Indians in Kerala elevated in 1896.
China: Protestant and Anglican missionaries number 5,462 including 1,652 wives.
45% of all North American Indians now affiliated to churches (25% Protestant).
Turkish sultan Mehmed V proclaims Jihad (Holy War), permits massacres of multitudes of Armenian, Syrian and Assyrian Christians, principally by Kurdish irregulars.
Radioactive contamination and destruction of world's major cities by atomic bombs envisaged in H.G. Wells' novel *The world set free.*

1915 Third major massacre of Armenian Christians by Turks; at least 600,000 perish in Anatolia, with a further 600,000 fleeing or deported from Turkey.
Elim Foursquare Gospel Alliance and Revival Party begun in Britain by Pentecostal healer G. Jeffreys (1889-1962); 1935, founds World Revival Crusade.
Anti-trinitarian or 'Jesus only' doctrine introduced into USA Pentecostalism by F.J. Ewart.

1916 Kenya: mass movement begins into all churches.
1st Evangelical Congress, Panama City.
Bibliotheca Missionum periodical begun by Robert Streit OMI (1875-1930) under SC Propaganda (Rome), covering all mission literature in past centuries; completed and discontinued 1974.
Panama Missionary Conference, in Panama, results in several new IMC-related missionary councils.
Invention of public-opinion polls by *Literary digest* in USA; 1935, regular religious polls emerge (profession, adherence, attendance, belief), through Gallup (AIPO), Roper, NORC, Harris, et alia.
World Dominion Movement founded in Britain (1924, Survey Application Trust), publishes long series of detailed surveys of missions by countries by Anglican lay leader Kenneth G. Grubb (1900-1980) and others.
French Jesuit priest and paleontologist Pierre Teilhard de Chardin (1881-1955) conceives ideas of: (1) evolution as not primarily materialistic but of a psychic nature, evolving with progressive consciousness from Point Alpha (creation by a personal God) toward the evolutionary goal Point Omega, God's new creation with Christ as Cosmocrat and perfecter of evolution; and (2) the evolving noosphere, a corporate biological entity with power of reflective thought enveloping the Earth with a dense covering of thinking brains in ever closer communication with each other, as a stupendous thinking machine, superior to the biosphere (the envelope of life without reflective thought).
Lebanon: Ottomans murder 100,000 Maronites (22% of entire Maronite population).

1917 Apparition of Virgin Mary at Fatima, Portugal, bringing about religious renewal reinforcing conservatism of Portuguese Catholicism; '3rd prophecy of Fatima' never published by Vatican but held to predict global holocaust and annihilation of church.
Balfour Declaration (UK) recognizes Palestine as national homeland of the Jews.
20,000 Nestorians massacred by Turks and Kurds on Turko-Persian fron-

tier after withdrawal of Russian army.
Bolshevik Revolution in Russia, followed by civil war; 1.5 million, mostly Christians, killed; 1918, decree on separation of church and state; 1.5 million flee abroad as refugees.
True Jesus Church begun in China, a charismatic schism ex Apostolic Faith Movement.
Mexico: beginning of state persecution of Roman Catholics after 1911 revolution; 1926, Spanish clergy deported, by 1931 violent persecution, schisms; 1935, priests prohibited in 14 states; 1940, attacks subside.
Interdenominational Foreign Mission Association of North America (IFMA) organized by SAGM, CIM, CAM, AIM, SIM, SAIM, WUMSA and later other Protestant missions of fundamentalist stance: 1967, 44 member missions with 8,500 missionaries in over 100 countries; 1979, 49 agencies with over 9,000 in over 115 countries.
V. Rousseau writes *The Messiah of the Cylinder* in which socialist atheists rule Britain tyrannically until Christian Russians eventually defeat them.

1918 Global influenza pandemic, the most deadly in history, sweeps the world in 3 waves over 2 years, killing around 40 million (20 million in India, over 500,000 in USA), via migratory birds and domestic animal reservoirs; also 10 other global pandemics since 1700.
Nigeria: influenza epidemic (part of worldwide swine flu epidemic) brings about formation of prayer and healing groups which later grow into large indigenous churches: Cherubim & Seraphim, Church of the Lord (Aladura), and Christ Apostolic Church.
USA: United War Work Campaign (interfaith: RCs, Jews, YMCA, YWCA, Salvation Army, et alia) raises $175,500,000, 'largest single amount ever offered voluntarily in history of world'.
USA: Committee on the War and the Religious Outlook begins 5-year analytical survey of post-war world.
Hungarian Lutheran Church loses half a million members with reduction of Hungary in size and dispersal of population to non-Lutheran areas.
Movement into churches in Congo takes on massive proportions.
Fundamentalism/modernism controversy erupts within USA Protestantism, until 1931, splitting every major denomination; premillennialism now a major part of all revivalist preaching.
The evangelistic work of the Church, being the report of the Archbishops' Third Committee of Inquiry (London), with noted definition 'To evangelize is so to present Christ Jesus . . .'
30 major USA denominations each separately launch their own monodenominational 'forward movements', most successful being Methodist Centenary Movement which raises $166 million for Methodist work; also 1919-1924 Seventy-Five Million Campaign within Southern Baptist Convention, to raise $75 million to undergird world missions, ending in 1924 with $62 million raised.
USA Methodists launch Christian Crusade for World Democracy, to further Protestant missionary expansion.
USA Presbyterian executives believe the War experience justifies 'Protestant Christianity in launching a united drive for world evangelism'.
Interchurch World Movement of North America (IWM) launched to seek 'complete evangelization of all life' and 'conquest of the world for Christ' in one massive 'forward movement'; vast support from entire range of 34 major USA denominations and 85% all USA Protestant missions; 1919, motto 'The giving of the whole Gospel to the whole world by the whole church'; aims to include virtually all church-related activity; 1920, World Survey Conference, Atlantic City (NJ) with 1,700 church leaders produces massive 2-volume World Survey books, with plan proposing evangelization of world within 3 years; 1920, IWM fails to raise its $336,777,572 budget, collapses in financial fiasco.

1919 World's Conference on Christian Fundamentals, Philadelphia, USA; over 6,000 attenders.
World's Christian Fundamentals Association (WCFA) founded in New York; premillennialist Protestants opposing modernism; 1920, label 'Fundamentalists' is coined by editor of *Watchman-Examiner*; Association active until 1950s.
Cao Daist Missionary Church founded by Le Van Trung in Viet Nam, a syncretistic mixture of popular Buddhism, Confucian ethics, ancestral cult, and Catholic-type organization, with membership of about 2.8 million by 1975.
Pope Benedict XV promulgates mission encyclical *Maximum illud*, on founding of younger churches.
Romerbrief (commentary on Epistle to the Romans) by Swiss Protestant dogmatic theologian Karl Barth (1886-1968): origin of Neo-Orthodox Protestant theology, dialectical theology, theology of crises; Second Coming of Christ takes place in the Word preached.
League of Nations organized for international cooperation, based on Geneva.
Korea: Japanese rulers commence massive persecution of Christians; 200 thugs hired from Japan solely to terrorize missionaries; around 10,000 believers martyred.
Russian Orthodox archbishop Joachim Levitzky of Nizhni-Novgorod murdered by being suspended upside down in his cathedral of Sebastopol.

1920 Interchurch World Movement, before its own collapse, proposes (1) a federal 'United Churches of Christ in America', and (2) a global 'League of Denominations' (parallel to League of Nations); both proposals fizzle out.
First World Conference of Friends (Quakers), held in London.
USSR: 78 Russian Orthodox bishops and 12,000 priests killed in first years of Bolshevik regime, 1917-26; by 1930, 42,800 priests killed; by 1960, 200 bishops murdered.
Evangelization Society chartered in USA (Pittsburgh Bible Institute).
6th Lambeth Conference; 252 Anglican bishops present.
New USA investment in research and development (R&D) in 1920 stands at $140 million (in 1960 dollars) or 0.1% of GNP; rises to $0.8 billion in 1940 (0.4%); $22 billion, 55% devoted to military and space research, in 1965 (3.3% of GNP); future projections to AD 2000, 5.5%; AD 2100, 10%; AD 2500, 20%.
Philippines: Catechism of Pius X translated into Jolo-Moro (Tausug) for Muslim population of 200,000 (1.9% of country).
International Confederation of Christian Trade Unions founded.
African indigenous churches number some 300 separate denominations across Africa with 600,000 professing adherents.
London Conference of World Baptists.
Ecumenical Patriarchate of Constantinople issues encyclical addressed to 'all the Churches of Christ' calling for formation of a 'League of Churches'.
Quadrennial Convention, Student Volunteer Movement for Foreign Missions, in Des Moines, USA, on theme 'Christus Victor'; 1,375 student delegates from over 70 countries; large-scale shift noted away from earlier evangelicalism and interest in the Watchword.

1921 USSR: civilian deaths in 1921-23 due to Civil War, other wars and famine total 13 million, mostly Christians.
USSR, 1921-1960: deaths in slave labor camps total 19 million, mostly Christians.
Soviet dictator V.I. Lenin (1870-1924) orders liquidation of 2,691 married Russian Orthodox priests, 1,962 monks, 3,447 nuns and vast numbers of lay Christians over period 1921-23.
First broadcast of a church worship service: Sunday evening, 2 January, from Calvary Episcopal Church, Pittsburgh (USA), over first radio station KDKA.
International Missionary Council (IMC) founded at Lake Mohonk, NY (USA).
Institute of Social and Religious Research, New York, organized under J.R. Mott to carry on IWM's socioreligious scientific surveys; lasts until 1934.
Synod of Karlovci held by exiled Russian Orthodox leaders (12 bishops, 40 priests, 100 laity), in Sremski Karlovci (Serbia); regarded as 1st Council of Russian Orthodox Church Outside Russia.
First Baptist radio broadcast in USA.
Simon Kimbangu (1889-1951) preaches leading to revival in Lower Congo, resulting in mass conversions, persecutions, jailings, deportations, and by 1960 a massive indigenous church (EJCSK).
Oxford Group in Britian (1921-38), later renamed Moral Re-Armament (MRA).
Pentecostal World Conference formed, in Amsterdam.
African Orthodox Church founded in New York, ex Protestant Episcopal Church in the USA, with consecration of G.A. McGuire as patriarch by J.R. Vilatte (Mar Timotheus), claiming Jacobite apostolic succession, and in 1927 Daniel W. Alexander as primate of African province.
K. Capek's play *R.U.R* portrays humanity exterminated by its own chemically-created robots.
Religious Confederation of Mankind founded by German Protestant theologian Rudolf Otto (1869-1937); 1923, writes *The idea of the holy*.

1922 National Christian Council of China founded.
Aliança Evangélica de Angola founded.
70% of all USA Protestant foreign missionaries now premillennialists.
Britain: Bible Reading Fellowship (BRF) founded, for Anglicans.
March on Rome by Fascists; Benito Mussolini (1883-1945) assumes power, rules as dictator of Italy until 1943.
First International Missionary Congress, at Utrecht (Roman Catholic).
Semaines de Missiologie begun at Louvain (Belgium); annual study and research weeks.
Catholic Action organized for participation of laity in the hierarchical apostolate, involving youth, students, workers, agriculturalists.
Accession of pope Pius XI (1857-1939), who issues encyclical 'Miserimus Redemptor' stating: 'These are really the signs of the last age as was announced by Our Lord.'
Extraterrestrial origin of man now widely propounded: Adam and Eve were survivors of a cosmic catastrophe who came to Earth in a spaceship; later, Noah's ark interpreted as a spaceship (G. Babcock's *Yezad*, 1922, J.J. Savarin's trilogy 'Lemmus', 1972-77).
USSR: Pentecostalism introduced by I.E. Varonaev (1892-1943), who aids growth in a few months to 20,000 in Ukraine alone; founds 350 congregations by 1929; 1932 imprisoned, 1943 shot in Leningrad.
O. Spengler's *The decline of the West*; massive impact on public consciousness of Europe.

1923 2nd Meeting of International Missionary Council, Oxford, England.
143,000 killed as earthquake destroys Yokohama (Japan) and half Tokyo.
BBC (Britain) commences broadcasting, including daily Christian pro-

grammes; in USA, 10 churches now operate radio stations; by 1928, 60, falling by 1933 to 30; origin of the 'electric church'.
Greco-Turkish war ends with Treaty of Lausanne: Greeks forced to give up Izmir (Smyrna); 1.5 million Greek Orthodox in Turkey deported to Greece, and 400,000 Muslim Turks in Greece deported to Turkey; Christians in Turkey fall from 22% in 1900 to 0.5% by 1980.
Pentecostal evangelist Aimee Semple McPherson (1890-1944) broadcasts first radio sermon in 1922, magnetizes millions in her 5,000-seat Angelus Temple, Los Angeles, from 1923-1944; founds International Church of the Foursquare Gospel.
Lutheran World Convention (LWC) formed at Eisenach (Germany); 1947 becomes Lutheran World Federation (LWF).

1924 Regional or subcontinental conciliarism begins: precursor of Near East Christian Council (NECC) founded, at Mount of Olives, Jerusalem; by 1983, some 50 such regional councils exist.
First international Christian radio station, NCRV, begun in Netherlands by Dutch Protestants.
Eugene Zamiatin's novel *We* written in Russia, foresees absolute totalitarian state rule by AD 3000; state executes dissidents, performs brain operations; police surveillance, torture, denunciations.
10,000 Orthodox bishops, priests, monks and nuns in USSR executed by Bolsheviks under dictator Joseph Stalin (1879-1953).
Centenary New Testament published (H.B. Montgomery).

1925 Spirit Movement (Aladura) in Nigeria; charismatic revivals within Anglican Church lead to major indigenous churches: Cherubim & Seraphim, Christ Apostolic Church, Church of the Lord (Aladura).
Universal Christian Conference on Life and Work, Stockholm (Sweden), on economics, industry, social and international problems; 600 official church delegates from 37 countries.
United Church of Canada formed (union of Methodists, Presbyterians and Congregationalists).
Premillennialists in USA begin to speculate that Roman Empire might be about to be revived under Mussolini as Antichrist; fascist salute seen as showing authorities mark of the beast on their hands.
World's 10 largest cities: New York 7,774,000, London 7,742,000, Tokyo 5,300,000, Paris 4,800,000, Berlin 4,013,000, Chicago 3,564,000, Ruhr 3,400,000, Buenos Aires 2,410,000, Osaka 2,219,000, Philadelphia 2,085,000.
League of Militant Godless (LMG) founded in USSR to destroy religion; by 1932, 5,673,000 members, plus 1.5 million child members; by 1937, 2 million; by 1940, 3 million; 1941, disbanded as a failure.
Romanian Orthodox patriarchate founded in Bucharest.
Congress on Christian Work in South America held in Montevideo, Uruguay.
USA: Lutheran Church—Missouri Synod operates radio station KFUO, St Louis; 1930 begins 'The Lutheran Hour' broadcast over WHK in Cleveland, Ohio, which by 1931 is heard by 5 million a week; after 1945, worldwide to 20 million a week; 1975, broadcast in over 50 languages, heard by audience of 22 million a week; 1987, 40 million regular listeners in 31 languages around world.
Era of large evangelistic healing campaigns in Europe and USA under first generation of Pentecostal evangelists, including Smith Wigglesworth (1859-1947) who preaches to large crowds in most of world's largest capitals.
Radio sets in use: Great Britain 1,654,000; USA 2,500,000, rising by 1940 to 30 million.
Foreign missionaries serving abroad: 88,000 Roman Catholics in 66,400 stations, 30,000 Protestants and Anglicans in 4,600 stations.
Lutheran World Conference held in Oslo, Norway.
Cost of a copy of Bible (equivalent US dollars): AD 1350, $2,000; 1455 (Gutenberg), $500; 1650, $100; 1925, $3; later, by 1980, $1.
1st Mennonite World Conference, Basel, Switzerland.
Physicists W. Heisenberg, M. Born, P. Jordan establish basis for matrix mechanics, first version of quantum mechanics.

1926 German Association for Mass Evangelism (Deutscher Verband für Volksmission) begun, uniting many state church evangelists and evangelistic programs over last decade.
Unevangelized Tribes Mission of Borneo formed (USA).
Assembly Hall Churches (Little Flock; indigenous) begun by Watchman Nee in China.
Famine in northwest China: 8 million die of starvation in 3 years.
Largest schism in Mexico from Roman Catholic Church, leading to formation of Orthodox Catholic Apostolic Mexican Church, by 1970 with 10 bishops and 60,000 members.
Jesuits begin work among Japanese of Brazil; first 14 Japanese baptisms, in São Paulo; by 1978, of 1 million Japanese there, 630,000 are Catholics.
28th International Eucharistic Congress, Chicago.
World Union for Progressive Judaism founded, in London, to unite Reform (Liberal) Judaism; 1970, 1,100,000 members in 25 countries.
Germany: RC religious orders number 559 male (10,000 members), 6,600 female (74,000 members).
USA: Northern Baptist superintendent of evangelism B.T. Livingstone introduces Friendly Visitation Evangelism for Laymen.
Freemasons number 4,200,000 in 28,000 lodges.

1927 Invention of electronic television, also of talking movies.
East African Revival movement (Balokole, Saved Ones) emerges in Ruanda, moves rapidly across Uganda, East Africa, Zaire, later to Sudan and Malawi, with cells in Europe and America; from 1931-85, some 80 mass revival conventions held across East Africa, including 1931 Gahini, 1936 Mukono (Uganda), 1937 Kabete (Kenya), 1939 Katoke (Tanganyika), 1945 Kabale ('Jesus Satisfies'), 1949 Kabete (15,000 attenders), 1964 Mombasa (20,000), 1970 Thogoto (40,000), 1978 Tumutumu (45,000), 1979 Thogoto (50,000).
Stalin threatens to execute entire Orthodox clergy of Russia (146,000 including monks and nuns), blackmails acting patriarch into capitulating.
USA: 50 radio stations now licensed to religious bodies.
China: 20 million killed in civil wars, 1927-1949; in anti-Christian movement, 5,000 of the 8,000 Protestant missionaries leave.
China: expansion of 2 charismatic indigenous groups: Watchman Nee's Little Flock, and Preaching Bands of John Sung (Song Shangjie).
Church of Christ in China founded, uniting 7 Protestant denominations.
1st World Conference on Faith and Order, Lausanne; over 400 delegates from 90 churches (Roman Catholics being forbidden by pope).
Origins of Latter Rain revivals and return to primitive pentecostalism, in South Africa (Blourokkies) and (c1930) Germany.
The future of Christianity published, edited by Sir John Marchant.
Association of Baptists for Evangelism in the Orient (ABEO) formed; 1939, name changed to ABWE (W = World).
Physicist W. Heisenberg's Uncertainty Principle: we cannot measure both the position and velocity of an electron at the same time.
Author Rudyard Kipling writes 'With the Night Mail', predicting for AD 2000 a world without nationalism or warfare, with atomic-powered zeppelins flying at 300 miles per hour; and 'As easy as A.B.C.' forecasting worldwide universal affluence and privacy in AD 2065 due to new technology.
English biologist J.B.S. Haldane in 'The Last Judgment' envisages no landings possible on planet Mars until AD 10 million.
Committee on the Christian Approach to the Jews convenes conferences in Budapest and Warsaw, also 1931 and 1934 Atlantic City (USA).
Council of Western Asia and Northern Africa formed, 1929 renamed Near East Christian Council (NECC), 1944 renamed Near East Council of Churches, replaced in 1974 by Middle East Council of Churches (MECC).
Smith-Goodspeed Bible translated: NT 1923, Bible 1927.

1928 Unevangelized Africa Mission founded (1947, merged in CBFMS), also Unevangelized Tribes Mission of Africa, both in USA.
USA: National Conference of Christians and Jews formed in New York City to combat religious and social prejudice; member of International Council of Christians and Jews.
Anglican evangelist Bryan Green begins 60 years of ministry as a diocesan missioner in Britain, USA, Canada, South Africa, Australia and elsewhere.
3rd Meeting of International Missionary Council, Jerusalem; 231 participants.
Opus Dei founded in Madrid, a secular association of conservative Catholic laity (men and women) and clergy; by 1975, over 60,000 members from 80 nations.
Shensi, China: famine kills 3 million.
Team of Chinese trained by Teilhard de Chardin discover skull of Sinanthropus Pekinensis (Peking Man, now called Homo Erectus Pekinensis), dating from BC 350,000.
4th Baptist World Congress, Toronto, Canada.
Pentecostalism formally rejected by World Fundamentalist Association as 'fanatical and unscriptural'; 1944, rejected also by American Council of Christian Churches who label glossolalia as 'one of the great signs of the apostasy'.
P. Nowlan initiates 'Buck Rogers' series with story 'Armageddon-2419 AD'.

1929 Crash of Wall Street: Great Depression strikes USA economy, lasts till 1936; millions go bankrupt or are ruined.
Lateran Agreements signed by Italian government and Roman Catholic Church, creating Vatican City as an independent sovereign state known as the Holy See (Santa Sede).
First major international Protestant radio station, Voice of the Andes (HCJB), founded at Quito, Ecuador; first broadcast on Christmas Day 1931.
Invention of rocket engine by Robert Goddard.
First experimental television (BBC, London).
2nd Evangelical Congress, Havana, Cuba.
National Fraternal Council of Churches (NFCC) formed in USA for Negro (Black) churches.
Armenian catholicate of Sis transferred to Antelias, Lebanon.
China: Five Year Movement begun by National Christian Council of China, supported by most churches; mass evangelism; 1935, NCCC extends it for further 5 years.
Congregationalist missionary Frank C. Laubach (1884-1970) begins 'each one teach one' method in Philippines, develops literacy primers for 300 languages worldwide; 1950, publishes *Literacy as evangelism*.
Afrikaner historian J. Du Plessis publishes *The evangelisation of pagan*

Africa.

Cedar Creek Convention (Jehovah's Witnesses): J.J. Rutherford introduces slogan 'Advertise! Advertise! Advertise the King and the Kingdom!'; aggressive house-to-house witnessing now the duty of all members.

China: CIM director D.E. Hoste (1861-1946) issues call to Europe and America for 'Two Hundred Evangelists' to China's remaining unreached peoples, with as goal 'to reach China within 2 years' including 7 evangelists for Sinkiang; over a dozen martyred.

Lutheran World Conference held in Copenhagen.

1930 Japan: Kingdom of God Movement begun under evangelist Toyohiko Kagawa (1888-1960), reaching over one million (75% non-Christian) with 35,000 enquirers in 2 years; concluded 1934, succeeded in 1936 by Kagawa's Nation-Wide United Evangelistic Movement.

Christian Businessmen's Committee International formed.

Mass movement into churches begins in Burundi.

Movement for World Evangelization (Mildmay Movement) begun to supply evangelists for Britain, later for Portugal, Spain, India, Australia, New Zealand, et alia.

Prophetic movements in French Congo: 1930 Matswa, 1953 Lassyism (Bougie), 1964 Croix-Koma.

Independent Church of India begun as schism ex Indo-Burma Pioneer Mission.

Formation of World Council for Life and Work, replacing Continuation Committee of 1925 Stockholm Conference.

7th Lambeth Conference: 307 Anglican bishops present.

C.E.M. Joad, British agnostic, publishes *The present and future of religion*; 1952, converts to theism.

Olaf Stapledon writes major futuristic novel, *Last and First Men*, a fully-developed evolutionary utopia; this, with his later classic *The Star Maker* (1937) sets definitive tone for responsible inclusion of religion in science fiction; describes 18 major transformations of humanity over 2 billion years, from individual consciousness, to world-mind, to galactic mind, to cosmic mind, to vision of the Star Maker (God): an intergalactic community of telepathically linked worlds until cosmos cools and dies, after which God creates a further cosmos.

Telephone system now serves 10% of humanity, and 20% in cities.

Vannevar Bush's MIT differential analyser, first analogue computer for solving differential equations.

Voice of Prophecy radio broadcasts begun by USA Seventh-day Adventists; by 1982, heard on 1,900 radio stations worldwide, in 57 languages.

Bermuda Triangle mystery: hundreds of aircraft, large ships and small boats disappear without trace from 1930-1987 in triangle between Bermuda, Florida and Puerto Rico, over alleged submerged ruins of Atlantis civilization; explanation in terms of gigantic Atlantean crystals emitting laser power still functioning at bottom of underwater abysses.

Mexico: 5-year persecution as regime attempts to exterminate Presbyterians from Tabasco state.

Resurgence of Hinduism (absorbing Christian elements) under 3 great reformers and leaders: philosopher Swami Vivekananda (1862-1902), nonviolent nationalist Mahatma Gandhi (1869-1948), and Indian president Sarvepalli Radhakrishnan (1888-1975).

1st Latin American Baptist Congress, Rio de Janeiro (Brazil).

G. Dennis publishes *The end of the world*, on apocalyptic mythology of modern science; 1953, identically-titled study by K. Heuer.

N. Schachner & A.L. Zagat write 'In 20,000 AD'.

Discovery on banks of Nile of Chester Beatty Papyri (2nd-4th centuries AD), 126 leaves being portions of 3 NT manuscripts.

USA: Laymen's Foreign Missions Inquiry (LFMI) initiated by 7 major Protestant denominations, under 35 directors, studying China, Indo-Burma and Japan; 1932, their report 'Re-thinking missions' (chairman W.E. Hocking) is criticized as advocating syncretism.

1931 Unevangelized Fields Mission (UFM) founded in London, UK.

Spain: church separated from state; thousands of priests, religious and lay Catholics murdered and churches burned in mob riots.

Radio Vatican inaugurated in Rome by Pius XI (1857-1939); entrusted to Jesuits.

Catholicism spreads from Dahomey to Niger.

British author Aldous Huxley writes novel *Brave new world*, describing authoritarian world government of AD 2530 which perpetuates control of population via cloning and genetic engineering; religion replaced by scheduled sexual orgies; does not envisage space flight until AD 2970.

1st Baptist World Youth Conference, Prague.

Charismatic renewal begins in Reformed churches of France; its theologian L. Dalliere opens dialogue with Catholic and Orthodox churches, also with Jews.

1932 Charismatic revival ex American Methodists in Southern Rhodesia, led by Johane Maranke, forms massive indigenous church: African Apostolic Church of Johane Maranke (AACJM), with followers right across Tropical Africa.

China: flood kills one million.

India: All-India Forward Movement in Evangelism launched in Nagpur.

Dutch East Indies (Indonesia): 30,000 Muslims converted around Modjowarno, East Java.

Standard English Braille adopted by Workers for the Blind in the USA; all English Scriptures subsequently prepared exclusively in this form.

Conference of Bible Societies, London, discusses ways and means of international cooperation.

1933 USSR: intensive forced collectivization and resultant famine kill 10 million kulaks and peasants, mainly Christians in the Ukraine; tens of millions of peasants brutally collectivized through police terror; Pentecostal-Zionists and other denominations virtually liquidated.

Shanghai Christian Broadcasting Association organized (XMHD), covering entire Far East; also 1935 XLKA (Peking).

Bibliografia Missionaria periodical begun by SC Propaganda (Rome), covering contemporary mission literature.

Atheist H.G. Wells in *The shape of things to come* (with 1935 movie 'Things to Come') predicts collapse of all national governments (and disappearance of banking) by 1960; by 1977 a single world state which suppresses all religion; and depicts in AD 2036 aftermath of 30-year world war which has reduced world to barbarism with altruistic scientists helping to launch first space flight.

Adolf Hitler (1889-1945) seizes power over Nazi Germany; involved in resurgence of secret occult societies across Europe 1925-40, member of Vril Society, steeped in occult gnosis (= violation of God's physical laws), Eastern/Tibetan/Sufi/Zen mysticism, Primordial Knowledge, Hyperborean Masters of Wisdom; offers world a 'new order', 'The Thousand Year Reich', a counterfeit Millennium; a renegade Roman Catholic, an archetypal antichrist in a long succession, now widely regarded as Antichrist II, second of the 3 major Antichrists envisioned by Nostradamus.

Severe persecution of Nestorians in Iraq; many thousands flee country.

Imaginary Himalayan utopia named Shangri-La depicted by English novelist J. Hilton in *Lost horizon*, where human life-spans exceed 300 years.

Pentecostal preacher W.M. Branham (1909-1965) offends mainline Pentecostal denominations by prophesying that 1906-1977 is the Laodicean Church Age, followed immediately by mass apostasy, Second Advent of Christ, and the Millennium in 1977; Branhamites (followers) claim him as Last Prophet with messianic attributes.

Germany: Catholic biblical renewal results in founding of Catholic Bible Association (Katholisches Bibelwerk, KBW), in Stuttgart; by 1980, members number over 30,000 catechists, teachers, priests and scholars.

1934 USSR: Stalin, widely regarded as the Antichrist, attempts liquidation of entire Christian church.

Jesus Christ and world evangelization published by Alexander McLeish (World Dominion Press): 'Evangelization is not civilization or Christianization'.

Confederação Evangelica do Brasil founded.

Britain: Inter-Varsity Missionary Fellowship, meeting in Fountains Abbey, announces its new variant of SVMU Watchword: 'Evangelize to a finish to bring back the King'.

Turkish government prohibits use of ecclesiastical dress, clerical collars, vestments or beards outside church buildings.

J.W. Campbell's novel *The mightiest Machine* invents four-dimensional hyperspace (or superspace) compressing our universe and enabling short cuts to stars.

5th Baptist World Congress (BWA), Berlin.

Wycliffe Bible Translators (WBT) founded for scripture translation by professional linguists, overseas under name Summer Institute of Linguistics (SIL).

1935 Opening of missions on island of Bali authorized.

Scholar G. Friedrich publishes in Kittel's TWNT (1932-78) first detailed investigation on biblical Greek verb *euangelizesthai*, which is 'not just speaking and preaching; it is proclamation with full authority and power'.

Radar invented by R. Watson-Watt (UK).

Parapsychologist J.B. Rhine popularizes 'psi' powers with idea that next step in human evolution would involve acquiring telepathic and telekinetic abilities.

Congregationalist scholar C.H. Dodd (1884-1973) publishes classic on the Christian kerygma, *The Apostolic preaching and its developments*.

New York becomes first urban supergiant (city with over 10 million population); others then escalate to 9 supergiants by 1980, 24 by AD 2000, 47 by AD 2025, and 80 by AD 2050.

1936 Civil war in Spain: clergy assassinated include 13 bishops, 4,254 priests, 2,489 monks, 283 nuns; one million Catholic Spaniards on both sides killed (100,000 executed by dictator Franco) or emigrate before Franco victory in 1939.

BBC (Britain) begins first television broadcasting including worship services and (1937) Coronation of George VI (1895-1952).

USA: International General Assembly of Spiritualists formed.

British Interplanetary Society founded.

Birth of final human Antichrist (in October) according to Great Pyramid of Giza, as interpreted by pyramidologists; to be revealed to world in 1992.

WEC missionary L.G. Brierley (1911-) begins long career as first full-time Protestant missionary researcher; 1941, begins world survey research with WEC, resulting in World conquest and Black Spot surveys (places with no Christian influence).

1st Congress of Theologians of the Balkan Orthodox Churches, held in Athens; papers on 'Mission in the Orthodox Church'.

USA: Northern Baptist secretary for evangelism W.E. Woodbury directs movement called Printed Page Evangelism.

1937 K.S. Latourette (1884-1968) publishes 7-volume *A history of the expansion of Christianity.*

Major effort by Italians to force Ethiopian Orthodox Church to submit to Church of Rome; Italian military invasion publicly endorsed by Roman Catholic hierarchy in Ethiopia and by cardinal Tisserant; 2 EOC bishops Petros and Michael refuse to cooperate, so executed together with scores of clergy and half a million faithful.

Ethiopia: after expulsion of missionaries by Italian invaders, widespread revival erupts among Protestant (SIM) churches in south.

Japan's largest indigenous Christian church, Spirit of Jesus Church, formed as split from Assemblies of God.

2nd World Conference on Faith and Order, Edinburgh, Scotland, dealing with grace, communion, sacraments, worship.

2nd World Conference on Life and Work, Oxford, England, on 'Church, community and state'; 425 delegates.

Imperial Japanese decree in Korea: Shinto shrines to be erected in all major centres, all population ordered to participate; most Protestant missionaries leave.

European Jews in peril of their lives number 6 million (including 1 million Jewish Christians, numbering 17% of all Jews).

China: Forward Evangelistic Campaign, under Methodist evangelist E. Stanley Jones (1884-1973), held in Mokanshan and other centres despite Japanese bombing attacks.

2nd Baptist World Youth Conference, Zurich.

2nd World Conference of Friends (Quakers), in Swarthmore, PA, USA, with representatives from 26 countries; Friends World Committee for Consultation (FWCC) begun, meeting every 3 years.

French Dominican theologian Yves Congar publishes *Chrétiens désunis*, textbook of modern Catholic ecumenism.

First radio telescope built by G. Reber, who then makes first radio map of the sky; major astronomical revolution begins as astronomers locate invisible microwave emissions from distant galaxies; 1967, discovery of pulsars (supernova remnants, being spinning neutron stars).

Britain: founding of Council on the Christian Faith and the Common Life, and Commission of the Churches for International Friendship and Social Responsibility; 1942, merged in new British Council of Churches.

Conference on Evangelistic Leadership, convened by Archbishops' Evangelistic Committee, Church of England, in York (6-8 October).

1938 Discovery of nuclear fission (splitting of the atom) by 2 German chemists Hahn and Strassmann; regarded by many Christians as a fundamental and dangerous contravention of God's laws of the Universe; results in atom bomb by 1945.

Invention of xerography.

Hendrik Kraemer (1888-1965) publishes *The Christian message in a non-Christian world*; powerful statement of traditional views of mission.

World Council of Churches 'in process of formation' set up at Utrecht, Netherlands; constitution drafted.

4th World Missionary Conference/Meeting of International Missionary Council, Tambaram, Madras, India; 471 delegates from 69 countries; report states: 'We summon the Churches to unite in the supreme work of world evangelization until the kingdoms of this world become the Kingdom of our Lord.'

Muscat and Oman: RCA mission (USA) reports winning 5 converts in 50 years.

Scotland: Iona Community founded by clergy and laymen of Church of Scotland.

Evangelism for the world today, with definitions by over 125 Christian leaders across world, edited by John R. Mott who has by now all but abandoned his earlier English term 'evangelization' in favor of term 'evangelism'.

California clergyman C.G. Long predicts world will be destroyed on 21 September 1945.

Anglican apologist C.S. Lewis (1898-1963) writes best-selling trilogy *Out of the Silent Planet* (Earth ostracized because its ruling spirit Satan has become evil; Mars a perfect planet without original sin), *Perelandra* (1943: Venus ripe for invasion by Satan), *That hideous strength* (1947: Satan manipulates scientists to create dystopia on Earth).

USA: actor Orson Welles' radio adaptation of H.G. Wells' *The War of the Worlds* terrifies New York.

Second World War devastates Europe and East Asia

1939 Protestant international radio station PRA7 begun in Brazil.

Radio Vatican begins broadcasting in 10 languages.

Portuguese Guinea: Protestantism introduced by Worldwide Evangelization Crusade (WEC).

1st World Conference of Christian Youth, Amsterdam, Netherlands.

Pentecostal Conference for all Europe held in Stockholm.

Scriptures: languages possessing some printed portions of Bible now number 969.

World War II: by its end in 1945, around 55 million killed: Poland 5.8 million including 3.2 million Jews; USSR 11 million combatants, 7 million civilians; Germany 3.5 million combatants/780,000 civilians; China 1,310,224 combatants/around 22 million civilians; Japan 1.3 million/672,000; Yugoslavia 305,000/1,200,000; UK 264,443/92,673; and USA 292,131/6,000.

The Holocaust 1939-1945: systematic murder of 5.7 million Ashkenazi Jews (including 1 million Jewish Christians) by German Nazis and their European collaborators.

Eugenio Pacelli elected pope as Pius XII (1876-1958), first of so-called Seven Last Angelic Popes of Catholic prophecy.

Shanghai For Christ united evangelistic campaign using all evangelistic means including radio; 30,300 attenders, 1,672 enquirers.

Poland: Nazis execute 6 RC bishops, 2,030 priests, 173 brothers, 243 sisters, and several million faithful.

6th Baptist World Congress (BWA), Atlanta (USA).

Engineers in British Interplanetary Society design ship to take people to Moon; in 1970s, they design Project Daedalus with nuclear fusion reactor to travel at 10% of speed of light as a multigeneration starship.

Conference of Bible Societies, Woudschoten (Netherlands), proposes a World Council of Bible Societies.

USA: 'Old Fashioned Revival Hour' under C.E. Fuller broadcasts over 152 Mutual radio stations to 12 million listeners a week, rising to 20 million by 1960; renamed 'The Joyful Sound'.

1940 Extermination of 600,000 Gypsies, mostly Christians, by Nazi Germany over 4 years.

Formation of Kyodan ordered by Japanese government to include all Protestant churches in a United Church of Christ.

John Frum cargo cults begun on Tanna Island, New Hebrides, growing in strength with arrival of USA military personnel with extensive material possessions.

Algeria: Evangelical Mission Council begun.

Estonia, Latvia, Lithuania conquered by Red Army (USSR); 200,000 deported to labor camps in Siberia; most bishops, church leaders and clergy shot or deported; 1944-53, 500,000 more deported.

First computer telecommunication: mathematician George Stibitz demonstrates his Bell programmable calculator working over telephone.

Greece: German, Italian and Bulgarian troops murder 350 Greek Orthodox priests.

R. Heinlein's novel *Revolt in 2100* describes a future dictatorship under guise of a religious cult, the Prophets.

c1940 Psychic seer Edgar Cayce (1877-1945) predicts sudden shifts in Earth's polar axis in 1998, with northern Europe and Japan destroyed and submerged, World War III erupting in 1999, and civilization destroyed in AD 2000.

Chilean astronomer Munoz Ferradas predicts a comet will collide fatally with Earth in August 1944; panic throughout South America.

1941 Origin of large-scale international Bible correspondence course organizations: Emmaus Bible School founded in Toronto, Canada.

Extensive mass revival in Orthodox churches in German-occupied USSR.

Siege of Leningrad by Nazis begun, lasting 800 days; 1.4 million (50% Christians) perish.

National Council of Churches in New Zealand founded.

Ecumenical Youth Movement in Latin America (ULAJE) created.

Gemeinde für Evangelisation und Erweckung founded in Zurich, Switzerland.

Mission de France established by Catholic hierarchy to reevangelize France.

R. Heinlein's story *Universe* proposes generation starships (space arks); attendant social structure discussed in B. Stableford's *Promised land* (1974).

Polish Franciscan priest Maximilian Kolbe (1894-1941) martyred in Auschwitz concentration camp.

Croatia: Croats massacre 350,000 Serbian Orthodox including 3 bishops, 220 priests.

Brazil: emergence, as a new theory of evangelization, of idea of grassroots or base ecclesial communities (comunidades eclesiais de base, or CEBes); 1963 formally established, with the Catholic Church standing with the poor; fully developed after 1968 Medellin and 1979 Puebla conferences.

Confraternity New Testament published by Catholic Biblical Association of America, based on Vulgate, Rheims-Challoner text, and Greek NT text; 1970, whole Bible published as New American Bible (NAB).

1942 Archbishop William Temple (1881-1944) at Canterbury enthronement refers to worldwide Christianity as 'the great new fact of our time'; 1943, publishes lecture *Social witness and evangelism.*

British Council of Churches (BCC) founded.

Sumatra: Christ's Witnesses spread Simalungun Church north of Lake Toba.

Papua: in Battle of Coral Sea, 118 RC priests and brothers and 78 nuns killed.

USA: National Association of Evangelicals (NAE) organized; invites several Pentecostal denominations to become affiliated for its 1943 convention.

I. Asimov's classic *The Foundation trilogy*: disintegration of Galactic Empire, 30,000 years of resultant barbarism; psycho-historians form Second Foundation and restore situation.

1943 China: 5 million perish in Honan province in worst famine in modern history.

Worker-priest movement begun in France; finally dissolved in 1959 on orders from Vatican.

USA: National Religious Broadcasters of North America formed, as official broadcasting arm of National Association of Evangelicals, with 50 organizations growing by 1979 to over 800; by 1986, annual convention attracts 4,000.

Britain: Christian Commando Campaigns 1943-47, led by Methodists, in London, Edinburgh, Glasgow and other cities.

Colossus I, world's first working electronic digital computer, with 2,000 valves; 10 built; wins World War II by breaking German codes, based in Bletchley, England; in USA, Harvard Mark 1 computer (funded by IBM) runs using electromagnetic relays.

Pope Pius XII authorizes Biblical institutes in Jerusalem and in Rome, also translation of Scriptures from original texts instead of only from Latin Vulgate.

1944 Canadian Council of Churches (CCC) founded.

Protestant monastic community of Taizé founded near Cluny (France) by prior Roger Schutz, who later coins phrase 'Les chiffres sont les signes de Dieu/Statistics are signs from God'.

200,000 Muslim Meskhetians deported by Stalin to Central Asia; 30,000 die (November); Stalin philosophizes 'One man's death is a tragedy; 10,000 deaths [or 30,000] are merely a statistic.'

John R. Mott, now in 80th year, writes his last original book: *The larger evangelism*.

Albania: communists execute 10 bishops and 100 priests over next decade.

Ukraine: destruction of 3.5-million-strong Ukrainian Catholic Uniates; 2 bishops, many priests murdered.

USA Assemblies of God begin 'Sermons in Song' radio broadcast, in 1954 renamed 'Revivaltime' on over 600 radio stations in USA and 100 more across world.

Dutch East Indies sees rise of Third-World missionaries: Chinese evangelist John Sung trains 5,000 3-man evangelistic teams who make major impact across country; 1969, Japanese and Pakistani evangelistic teams; 1975, Asian Evangelists Commission (AEC) conducts crusades in Palembang, Medan and other cities.

Knox Bible published, a translation from Latin Vulgate into modern English; completed 1949 (Roman Catholic).

1945 In 6 years of war, Allies devastate Germany by dropping 1.2 million tons of TNT (1.2 megatons).

The Nuclear Age begins

Detonation of first atomic bomb near Alamogordo, New Mexico, USA (16 July) at cost of US$ 1 billion, opposed by some scientists on grounds it might set off runaway chain reaction in hydrogen atoms of oceans and destroy world; followed in August by dropping of 20-kiloton atomic bombs on Hiroshima and Nagasaki, Japan, with 200,000 casualties; end of World War II.

Germany: 12.5 million Germans resident abroad forcibly expelled to Germany as refugees.

Viet Nam: 2,791 Cao Daists massacred by communists.

Archbishops' report *Towards the conversion of England* published by Church of England.

Evangelical academies and student associations begun in Germany.

Mass international tourism begins, with package tours (Thomas Cook, Britain).

Refugees (fugitives, expellees) increase vastly in numbers across globe, totalling 45 million over next 3 decades.

USSR liquidates Uniate churches across Eastern Europe, forcibly incorporating most into Orthodox churches.

Japan: disestablishment of State Shinto; rapid and vast growth of Shinko Shukyo (New Religions, first being Tenrikyo 1838, Konkokyo 1859).

ACE (Automatic Computing Engine), most advanced and powerful computer in world, is designed at National Physical Laboratory (UK) under A.M. Turing (1912-1954).

British science fiction writer A.C. Clarke (1917-) becomes first to envisage feasible orbiting communications satellites.

United Nations Organization established in San Francisco (USA) by charter (24 October) 'to maintain international peace and security', with 51 founding member states, rising by 1985 to 159 member states.

Massive surge of new Christian parachurch agencies or multinationals independent of the churches, increasing by 1980 to 17,500 distinct and separate agencies, with multifold ministries.

Evangelical Foreign Missions Association (EFMA) organized in Washington, DC; 1964, 58 agencies with over 6,000 missionaries in 120 countries; 1979, 61 sending agencies with 9,308 missionaries.

Berkeley translation, Modern Language Bible: NT 1945, Bible 1959, revised 1969.

Norwegian missiologist O.G. Myklebust proposes creation of an International Institute of Scientific Missionary Research, with an association and conferences devoted to global mission; ignored until IAMS formed in 1970.

1946 African Orthodox Church (independent Kenyan body) accepted into communion by Greek Orthodox patriarchate of Alexandria.

North Korea: Christian organizations suppressed.

Europe: widespread evangelistic experiments in state and majority churches (Kerk en Wereld in Holland, worker-priests in France, MRA, etc).

South West Africa: massive Nama Hottentot schism ex Rhenish Mission.

Australian Council of Churches (ACC) begun.

Revised Standard Version (RSV) of New Testament published in USA; complete Bible 1952.

International radio station IKOR begun in Netherlands.

ENIAC (Electronic Numerical Integrator and Calculator) built by J. Mauchly in Maryland (USA), switched on as world's first fully operational large-scale electronic computer; 18,000 valves (tubes), weight 60,000 lbs, volume 15,000 cubic feet, power required 150 million watts, cost $400,000, performs 5,000 additions a second.

Project RAND (acronym for Research & Development) begun in USA; 1948, becomes RAND Corporation as first 'think factory' or think tank to speculate on national policies; 1959, Delphi technique proposed (use of experts' opinions to make a group forecast); also Delphi Conference using computers (now 'computer conferencing').

Catholic hierarchy erected in China: 20 archdioceses, 79 dioceses, 39 other jurisdictions (29 confided to Chinese clergy); and first Chinese cardinal Thomas Tien SVD.

Series of massive student conferences in North America: 1st IVSFM Conference, Toronto, on 'Complete Christ's Commission' with 575 participants; 1948, 1st Urbana Conference, 1,400 students; steady rise in numbers to 17,112 by 1976 ('Declare His Glory among the Nations'), and 18,145 by 1984 ('Faithful in Christ Jesus').

Conference of Bible Societies, Haywards Heath (UK), creates United Bible Societies (UBS) as federation and fellowship of 13 autonomous Bible societies from Europe and North America; expands rapidly by 1986 to 70 member societies and 30 national offices, working in 180 countries.

World Literature Crusade (WLC) begins in Canada for radio outreach, then expands to systematic tract distribution through Every Home Crusades in 103 countries, resulting by 1985 in 1.42 billion gospel messages handed out producing 14.5 million documented written responses for Christ.

1947 5th Meeting of International Missionary Council, Whitby, Toronto, Canada; 112 delegates from 40 countries; upholds 'the evangelization of the world in this generation', coins term 'expectant evangelism'.

Conference on Evangelism, Geneva, sponsored by WCC in Formation (February).

Church of South India inaugurated by merger of Methodists and Anglicans with earlier-united Reformed and Congregationalist bodies.

2nd World Conference of Christian Youth, Oslo, Norway.

Southern Baptist evangelist Billy Graham (born 1918) begins global ministry, preaching face-to-face to 50,780,505 by 1976, in 229 crusades, with 1,526,729 enquirers (decisions or converts: 3.0% of attenders), and to 104,390,133 by end of 1984.

Partition of India: 9 million Muslims flee to Pakistan, 9 million Hindus and Sikhs flee Pakistan for India, the greatest population transfer in history; 1.1 million massacred or starve to death en route.

Lutheran World Federation (LWF) founded, with first purpose stated as 'To bear united witness before the world to the Gospel of Jesus Christ as the power of God for salvation': 1st Assembly, at Lund, Sweden, 1952 2nd Hanover, 1957 3rd Minneapolis, 1963 4th Helsinki, 1970 5th Evian (France), 1977 6th Dar es Salaam (Tanzania), 1984 7th Budapest.

1st Pentecostal World Conference, Zurich, Switzerland; 250 leaders present, from 23 countries; first attempt to found an ongoing World Pentecostal Fellowship fails.

Evangelize China Fellowship founded in Shanghai by Andrew Gih.

Discovery of Dead Sea Scrolls, from library of Qumran monastery (Essene sect), in caves overlooking Dead Sea, dating from BC 20-AD 70.

Episcopalian canon T.O. Wedel (USA) publishes *The coming Great Church: essays on church unity*.

Roman Catholic missiological journal begun, *Euntes docete* ('Go and teach', Matthew 28:18).

Three Bell Laboratories scientists in New Jersey invent the transistor: Bardeen, Brattain and Shockley.

Mathematician J. von Neumann (1903-1957) formulates turning point in computer design with computer EDVAC, with stored-program control; 1951, EDVAC executes first program.

Pope Pius XII declares in Rome: 'Today the spirit of evil has been unchained'.

UFO (Unidentified Flying Object) sightings begin in USA, of 6 varieties: nocturnal lights, daylight discs, radar cases, close encounters of the 1st, 2nd or 3rd kinds (over 800 of the 3rd kind involving supposed meetings with extraterrestrials); by 1980, 6% of humanity claim to have seen something inexplicable to modern science; linked to altered states of consciousness in human observers.

7th Baptist World Congress (BWA), Copenhagen (Denmark), on 'The world responsibility of Baptists'; over 5,000 participants (largest religious gathering ever held in this city).

Pius XII's encyclical 'Mediator Dei' supports Liturgical Movement; 1953, liturgical reform boosted by Vatican II with its 'Constitution on the Sacred

Liturgy'.

T.L. Sherred writes 'E for Effort' about invention that sees through time and space and so threatens to destroy privacy and secrecy forever.

1948 Radio Vatican now broadcasting in 19 languages.

Byzantine-rite Uniate Catholic Church of Romania declared dissolved by a few priests, rejoining Romanian Orthodox Church; Communist regime destroys Uniates, kills 3 bishops and many priests.

8th Lambeth Conference; 329 Anglican bishops present.

Kirchenkreis-Evangelisation begun in Germany.

World Council of Churches (WCC) inaugurated in 1st Assembly at Amsterdam by 147 churches from 44 countries; theme 'Man's disorder and God's design'; 351 delegates and 238 alternates, but no RC observers; 'We intend to stay together' (22 August-4 September).

International radio stations begun: FEBC (Philippines, Radio DZAS), TIFC (Costa Rica).

La Violencia, civil war in Colombia; 300,000 killed, Protestants persecuted till 1952.

Evangelistic mission in St John the Divine Episcopal Cathedral, New York; beginning of mass evangelism in USA after World War II.

State of Israel created; continuous wars in 1957, 1967, 1973, 1982, not to be finally settled until AD 2000. (Nostradamus).

International Council of Christian Churches (ICCC) founded (anti-ecumenical, fundamentalist); 1st Congress at Amsterdam as rival to WCC; 150 persons from 29 countries (August); later plenary congresses every 3 or 4 years.

Mark I computer at Manchester University (UK) runs with world's first stored program.

Era of ecumenical consultations at all levels begins: 780 distinct consultations across world held, under WCC auspices, from 1948-1986.

USSR: secret police begin to destroy 3-million-strong underground body, True Orthodox Church.

1st United Bible Societies Council Meeting, Dunblane (Scotland); 20 member societies.

Germany: Gossner Mission's 'Rollende Kirche' (Church on Wheels) and 'Die Kirche Unterwegs' (The Mobile Church) evangelize in Westphalia, Schleswig-Holstein and Baden; by 1960, 16 tent missions at work with 235 tent facilities in operation.

USA: Southern Baptist Convention, meeting in Memphis, adopts Foreign Mission Board's program 'Advance', projecting a tripling in number of missionaries (achieved by 1964); 1955 Baptist Jubilee Advance plans.

1949 *French Southern & Antarctic Territories.* First resident Christians (French scientists).

2nd Pentecostal World Conference, Paris; plan to form an ongoing World Pentecostal Fellowship thwarted by Scandinavian Pentecostals.

WCC study 'The Evangelization of Man in Modern Mass Society'; surveys done in Ceylon, Finland, France, Germany, Holland, India, Latin America, Scotland, USA; publication series announced but never implemented.

Burma Christian Council formed.

Joint IMC/WCC Conference, in preparation for forming of East Asia Christian Conference (EACC), in Bangkok, Thailand.

After Communist victory, China expels 5,496 Catholic, 3,745 Protestant and 198 Anglican foreign missionaries over next 3 years; 1949, 3,469,452 Roman Catholics, 1,536,000 Protestants, 440,000 Chinese indigenous, 300,000 Orthodox, and 76,740 Anglicans.

Los Angeles, USA: first major Billy Graham crusade; 441,000 attenders, 5,700 enquirers (1.3%).

Japanese Evangelical Missionary Society formed (USA, Tokyo) to send Japanese abroad.

Kirchentag begun in Germany as Protestant annual evangelistic mass event: founded 1949 at Hannover (15,000 attenders), 1950 Essen, 1951 Berlin, 1952 Stuttgart, 6th in 1954 Leipzig (675,000 attenders), 1956 Frankfurt (250,000), 1959 Munich (375,000); all-Germany until Berlin Wall erected in 1961; ecumenical (RC cooperation) since 1968 Augsburg.

Organized churches present in all countries of the world except Afghanistan, Saudi Arabia and Tibet.

1st Latin American Evangelical Conference (CELA I), Buenos Aires, Argentina.

George Orwell's satire *Nineteen Eighty-four* published, describing 1984 world ruled by 3 totalitarian superstates controlled by media-mythologized demagogues, including English socialism of 1984 with Thought Police, Newspeak, Crimethink, and Doublethink, all subject to control of Big Brother, and by AD 2050 total destruction of literature, language and freedom.

L.E. Browne, missionary theologian in India, writes 'The religion of the world in AD 3000' (*IRM*).

India: Jain World Mission founded, to spread Jain religion.

3rd Baptist World Youth Conference, Stockholm.

Cursillo de Cristianidad (short courses) movement begun in Spain by RC bishop J. Hervas; short retreats to renew personal faith of Catholics; 1950s spreads to Latin America, then to USA.

Survey Application Trust (London) produces 5-yearly *World Christian handbook* (1949, 1952, 1957, 1962, 1968) edited by K.G. Grubb, with church membership statistics compiled and totalled for first time by denomination and country.

2nd UBS Council Meeting, New York and Greenwich; China, Ireland, Japan, Korea, Sweden admitted; total 24 member societies.

LWF Commission on World Missions (CWM) meets for first time at Oxford, UK.

Germany: major state church evangelistic campaigns in Kreuznach, 1951 Oldenburg, 1952 Hamburg, 1955 Essen, Stuttgart, 1958 Bochum, 1958 Stuttgart, 1959 Hanover, 1960 Nuremberg, 1961 Karlsruhe, et alia.

Epoch IX:
SURGE IN THE THIRD WORLD
1950-1990

1950 **Global status:** 64 generations after Christ, world is 34.1% Christians (63.5% of them being Whites), 58.0% evangelized; with printed Scriptures available in 1,052 languages; total martyrs since AD 33, 30,760,000 (0.5% of all Christians ever; recent rate 422,500 per year).

Black Africa: Christians number about 44 million, increasing rapidly by 1.8 million a year; African indigenous churches (AICs) mushroom to 1,700 separate denominations with 3,500,000 adherents.

China: 24,700,000 killed over next 10 years through purges, famine, deaths in slave labor camps, Tibet revolt, including large numbers of Christians; over 40 million imprisoned in labor camps; by 1970, 20% of all 65 million deaths caused by Communist regime are being described as directly related to religious faith.

Hungary: 53 Catholic religious orders and congregations forcibly dissolved by Communist regime.

International Christian radio stations now 10 in number.

British Guiana: 'Guiana for God' one-year evangelistic campaign under Christian Council, with Roman Catholic, Protestant and Anglican workers.

1st Assembly of World Council of Christian Education and Sunday School Association (WCCESSA), Toronto, Canada.

Haiti Great Commission Crusades (Haiti Inland Mission): 10 crusades over decade 1950-60.

USA: beginnings of evangelistic association evangelism (Billy Graham Evangelistic Association, et alia).

USA: evangelistic broadcasting spreads: 1950, Billy Graham begins on ABC radio, and 1951 on TV; 1953, Rex Humbard telecasts weekly, 1958 opens 5,000-seat Cathedral of Tomorrow (Akron, Ohio).

'Hour of Decision' radio program with Billy Graham begins over 150 stations; 1951, 20 million listeners (200,000 letters received per year); by 1978, 900 radio/TV stations worldwide, and a million letters per year (with 70 million viewers in USA).

Explosion of first thermonuclear device by USA.

Age of superindustrial economies: emergence in Europe and North America of national economies with enterprises of extraordinary size.

Gross world product (GWP) climbs from $700 billion (1950) to $10.5 trillion by 1980, and to $17 trillion by 1987.

Cult of national sovereignty (the nation-state principle of territorial sovereignty) 'has become mankind's major religion' (historian Arnold J. Toynbee) and its biggest obstacle to progress.

J.C. Hoekendijk produces influential article 'The call to evangelism' (*IRM*) defining concept as consisting of *kerygma, koinonia* and *diakonia*.

Historian K.S. Latourette writes: 'By evangelism is meant obedience to the Great Commission'.

R. Bradbury writes *Fahrenheit 451*, a dystopian novel of a future Earth after 2 atomic wars; dictatorial government, all books banned and burned as corruptive.

World's 10 largest cities: New York/Northeast New Jersey 12,410,000, Shanghai 10,420,000, London 10,370,000, Rhein/Ruhr 6,900,000, Tokyo/Yokohama 6,740,000, Beijing 6,740,000, Paris 5,530,000, Tianjin 5,450,000, Buenos Aires 5,250,000, Chicago/NW Indiana 4,970,000.

Full Gospel Businessmen's Fellowship International (FGBFI) founded in USA by D. Shakarian; preachers and women excluded; grows rapidly by 1970 to 300,000 members in 700 chapters worldwide, and by 1986 to 700,000 regular attenders worldwide in 3,000 chapters (1,715 in USA) in 95 countries including USSR, Czechoslovakia, Saudi Arabia and other closed countries.

8th Baptist World Congress, Cleveland, Ohio (USA), on theme 'And the Light shineth in the darkness'.

Mass immigration from Third World into industrialized Western world begins: by 1960, 3.2 million; by 1974, 9.5 million.

North Korea: troops massacre Christians, with 500 pastors killed from 1950-60.

Holy Year attracts 4 million pilgrims to Rome; 1975 Holy Year, 8,370,000 pilgrims; 1983, 1,950th anniversary of Christ's redemption and Holy Year draws vast numbers of pilgrims to Rome.

2nd ICCC Plenary Congress, Geneva; 450 participants from 82 denominations in 43 countries; subsequent plenary congresses in 1954 (Philadelphia), 1958 (Rio de Janeiro), 1962 (Amsterdam), 1965 (Geneva), 1968 (Cape May, USA), 1973 (Cape May), 1975 (Nairobi), 1979 (Cape May); 1983 (Cape May) 11th Congress with 4,000 delegates from 399 denominations in 93 nations.

I. Asimov (a rationalist) publishes *I, Robot* on development of robot computer AD 1996-2064.

Science fiction writer L.R. Hubbard (1911-1986) in USA launches 'Dianetics, the evolution of a science'; 1955, begins Founding Church of Scientology, a marginal body based on psychoanalytic spirituality, claiming 3 million followers worldwide (HQ London); based on secret scriptures describing alleged galactic empire of BC 75 million ruled by tyrant Xemu and his thetans (spirits).

Japan Lutheran Hour broadcasts begun; by 1953, on 117 Japan commercial radio stations.

Scotland: Tell Scotland Movement organized by Church of Scotland evangelist D.P. Thomson.

Television sets in use: USA 1,500,000 in 1950, 15 million in 1951, 29 million in 1954, 85 million in 1960; in whole world, 231 million (1970).

Council of Churches in Indonesia (DGI) founded with aim of 'establishing a United Christian Church in Indonesia'.

Supertechnological Revolution (Third Industrial Revolution)

1950 After 1st Industrial Revolution (steam and coal, 1775) and 2nd (electrical and chemical, 1901), 3rd revolution from 1950 on is fueled by nuclear power, microchips and genes.

British Antarctic Territory. First resident Christians (British scientists).

New Age Movement (Age of Aquarius) spreads across USA through psychedelic drugs, yoga, Eastern mysticism and astrology, holding imminent demise of Christianity to be replaced by new Eastern religion.

International New Age Movement begins to be interpreted from Christian standpoint as 'Aquarian Conspiracy', a cosmic plot being engineered by ancient invisible higher intelligences (the Hierarchy of Ascended Masters [Masters of Wisdom], highly-evolved humanoid, immortal, omniscient, omnipotent, Tibetan Supermen or Hierarchical Masters of Shamballah or extraterrestrials (ETs) with supernatural powers, under a supreme Unknown Master, the central intelligence behind all psychic-occult phenomena) aiming to take over Earth and to instal Antichrist.

1951 World Evangelical Fellowship (WEF) formed: 1st General Assembly held at Woudschoten, Zeist (Netherlands); 1953, 2nd at Clarens (Switzerland); 1956, 3rd at Barrington, RI (USA); 1962, 4th in Hong Kong; 1968, 5th in Lausanne; 1974, 6th in Chateaux d'Oex (Switzerland); 1980, 7th in Hoddesdon (UK) on 'Serving our generation: Evangelical strategies for the '80s', with 141 delegates from 48 countries representing 38 member fellowships and alliances; 1986, 8th in Singapore.

Three Self Reform Movement in China, to eradicate imperialism in churches.

Alianza Evangélica Costarricense formed.

'Cuba for Christ' 2-week campaign in all Methodist churches of Cuba; 2,100 first decisions.

USSR: all 7,000 Jehovah's Witnesses arrested and forcibly scattered across Siberia and Far North labor camps.

Anglican evangelist Bryan Green publishes classic *The practice of evangelism*.

Univac I computers introduced by Remington Rand and delivered to US Bureau of the Census; first commercial computers (1st-generation variety).

Gandhian Hindu ascetic and social reformer Vinoba Bhave (1895-1982) walks barefoot 45,000 miles throughout India, founds Bhoodan Yajna (land-gift movement) and Gramdan (land-pooling), which then spread across India.

1st World Congress of the Lay Apostolate, in Rome; subsequent congresses in Rome in 1957, 1967, 1975.

Continental and regional councils related to fundamentalist ICCC formed: Latin American Association of Christian Churches (LAACC) in São Paulo, Brazil; and Far East Council of Christian Churches (FECCC) in Manila; 1952 Middle East Bible Christian Churches (MEBCC); 1955 Scandinavian Evangelical Council; 1959 European Evangelical Conference; 1964 West Africa Council of Christian Churches; 1965 East Africa Christian Alliance; 98 major ICCC conferences (including international ones) held from 1948-1984.

R. Bradbury writes 'The Fire Balloons': 2 Episcopalian priests arrive on Mars to convert natives but find Martians already perfect and sinless.

China: 1st Plenum, Preparatory Committee of Chinese Christian Resist-America-Aid-Korea Three Self Reform Movement.

1st World Congress of the Deaf, in Rome; establishes World Federation of the Deaf (WFD) to represent world's 70 million deaf persons; then congresses in 1955, 1959, 1963, 1967, 1971, 1975, 1979, 1983, 1987.

1st Latin American Lutheran Congress, in Curitiba, Brazil; 1954, 2nd in Petropolis, Brazil; 1959, 3rd in Buenos Aires; 1965, 4th in Lima, Peru; 1971, 5th in Buenos Aires; 1980, 6th in Bogota, Colombia; 1986, 7th in Caracas, Venezuela.

1952 Computer theorist John von Neumann proposes elaborate theory for first self-replicating factory.

3rd World Conference of Christian Youth, at Travancore, India.

3rd World Conference on Faith and Order, at Lund, Sweden.

6th Meeting of International Missionary Council, at Willingen, Germany; 190 delegates.

3rd Pentecostal World Conference, in London.

2nd Assembly, Lutheran World Federation (LWF), at Hannover, Germany, on 'The Living Word in a Responsible Church'.

UBS Council Meetings: 3rd in Ootacamund (India), 80 persons, 24 societies, addressing the churches concerning their role in Bible work; 1954, 4th in Eastbourne (UK); 1957, 5th in São Paulo and Rio de Janeiro; 1960, 6th in Grenoble (France).

3rd World Conference of Friends (Quakers), held in Oxford, England, with 900 representatives from 27 countries; also 5th Meeting, Friends World Committee for Consultation (FWCC), also in Oxford.

Geopolitical nuclear balance of terror begins

First hydrogen bomb (thermonuclear, fusion) exploded by USA in Pacific; 1961, USSR catches up by conducting over 30 nuclear test explosions including largest hydrogen bomb ever, of 60 megatons; from now on, mankind lives under planet-wide nuclear intimidation, of mutually-assured destruction (MAD), the so-called balance of terror.

Kenya: Mau Mau nationalist rebellion kills 30,000 Kikuyu, creates many martyrs in Kikuyu churches.

West Irian: CMA, TEAM, RBMU missionaries and converts killed.

1953 Munster Week of Missiology takes as theme 'Christians and Antichristians'.

In China, 105 RC priests massacred in last decade, increasing to 800 Chinese priests killed in 1950-54.

Parallel universes existing alongside our Universe proposed: C.D. Simak's *Ring around the Sun* and K. Laumer's *Worlds of the Imperium* imagine infinite series of manipulable parallel Earths in higher dimensions (each similar to immediate neighbors but with tiny historical changes) available for us to colonize once we have learned the secret of crossing the dimensions.

Congress of Catholic Action, in Chimbote (Peru); one of roots of liberation theology.

Australian Mission to the Nation, a 3-year Methodist mass evangelism and media campaign, largest ever held in Australia; over 1 million attenders; start of 35-year mass evangelism ministry of evangelist Alan Walker.

World Committee for Christian Broadcasting (WCCB) constituted in Britain; 1961, founds World Association for Christian Broadcasting (WACB), 1968 merges with Coordinating Committee for Christian Broadcasting to form World Association for Christian Communication (WACC).

4th Baptist World Youth Conference, Rio de Janeiro (Brazil).

Invention of Delphi technique of extracting forecasts from panel of experts separately answering 4 mailed questionnaires with feedback over a month; 1960, computerized ('D-net' operation) and reduced to 3 hours.

Science fiction doyen A.C. Clarke writes 'The Nine Billion Names of God': Himalayan monks employ USA computer programmers to enumerate the 9 billion possible names of God, after which world must end, and does.

USA: Southern Baptists implement first nationwide simultaneous revival or evangelistic campaign, with 361,835 baptisms reported during the year.

1954 2nd Assembly of World Council of Churches, in Evanston, USA: 'Christ the Hope of the World'; 502 delegates; report states 'To evangelize is to participate in Christ's life and ministry to the world'.

5th Kirchentag held in Leipzig (East Germany), draws 675,000 for closing rally.

17th General Council, Alliance of Reformed Churches (WARC, WPA), at Princeton, USA.

2nd Pan-Anglican Congress, in Minneapolis, USA, with laity and clergy from all Anglican dioceses across world.

International radio stations begun: ELWA (Liberia), TWR (Tangier, later closed), also several national stations including Christian Broadcasting System of Korea (HLKY).

USA: World Conference on Missionary Radio formed.

WCC official survey, *Evangelism: the mission of the Church to those outside her life*, notes 'an almost chaotic confusion as to the meaning and scope of evangelism'; surveys the future and suggests: 'The drama of missions and evangelism may, indeed, under God's rule over time and history be only in its infancy.'

Methodist evangelist J.E. Rattenbury publishes *Evangelism and pagan England*, warns 'Schemes for future evangelization would indeed be futile dreams if the tragedy of human sin were ignored'.

England: 3-month Harringay Crusade under Billy Graham: 2,047,333 attenders, 38,447 enquirers; vast numbers of related campaigns subsequently.

Five generations of computers evolve: (1) 1954-60, electronic vacuum tube computers, (2) 1960-64, transistorized computers, (3) 1964-75, integrated circuit computers, (4) 1975-92, very large-scale integrated computers (VLSI) (known as supercomputers), (5) 1992-2000, 5th-generation or artificial intelligence computers known as KIPS.

World Geophysical Year with all nations on Earth collaborating, called by Teilhard de Chardin 'Year One of the Noosphere', beginning of the planetization of humanity, start of Point Omega (evolutionary goal of one superconscious mind, a superpersonal ego in the depths of the thinking mass of 3 billion human brains, with Christ as Cosmocrat); other

origins of Point Omega being BC 5.5 million, BC 4 (Incarnation of the Word), AD 2030, and AD 1.5 million.
Argentina: USA Pentecostal evangelist Tommy Hicks travels uninvited to Buenos Aires; without advertising or outside finance, with free government radio and press coverage, conducts biggest single evangelistic crusade ever; in 52 days, audiences exceed 2 million (over 200,000 at final service); 1956, Oswald Smith campaign (25,000 attenders); 1962, Billy Graham crusades in 3 cities.
F. Brown writes 'Answer', describing future time when all master computers of 96 billion inhabited worlds become linked as one; asked if God exists, system answers 'He does now'.
France: Bible de Jérusalem published (Catholic); 1966 Jerusalem Bible, in English.
China: 1st National Christian Conference, under control of Communist regime; 1960, 2nd National Christian Conference; 1980, 3rd National Christian Conference.

Superindustrial Age (Third Wave, Space Age)

1955 After First Wave (Agricultural Age, BC 9000-AD 1700) and Second Wave (Industrial Revolution, 1775-1955), Third Wave begins (Technetronic Era, Electronic Era, Global Village, Third Technosphere, Superindustrial Age, Nuclear Age).
Radio IBRA (Swedish Pentecostal) begins in Tangier in 20 languages.
Jesus Family, indigenous movement in China begun 1921, virtually obliterated by communists.
4th Pentecostal World Conference, in Stockholm, Sweden.
Germany: Janz brothers' Crusade for Christ.
Albert Einstein writes: 'The distinction between past, present and future is only a stubbornly persistent illusion'.
1st General Conference, Latin American Episcopate, in Rio de Janeiro during International Eucharistic Congress; CELAM (Consejo Episcopal Latino Americano) organized (with no precedent in history), linking all Roman Catholic bishops from Mexico southwards.
Liberation theology, a new approach to man and God, primarily from Latin America, leads to birth of BECs (basic ecclesial communities), new ministries, and above all to new approaches to evangelization.
9th Baptist World Congress (BWA), London, on theme 'Jesus Christ, the same yesterday, and today, and forever'; 8,266 delegates from 60 countries.
Pentecostalism spreads rapidly throughout Europe's Gypsy population, especially in France, Italy, Spain, Portugal.
World Conference on Missionary Radio (WCMR) begun in USA; 1963, joins with National Religious Broadcasters of North America (NRB) to form International Christian Broadcasters (ICB), which disbands in 1968.
Taiwan: 10-year 'Double-the-Church Movement' begins led by Presbyterian Church; 1965, Taiwan Christianity Centennial Campaigns held in 40 cities and towns; 1976, Knowing Jesus campaign; 1977, Tell the Good News multimedia movement, supported by 2,000 churches, with estimated 10 million persons exposed to gospel.
Scotland: All-Scotland Crusade (Billy Graham): 2,647,365 attenders in Glasgow, 52,253 enquirers; on Good Friday, first telecast of a crusade made.
France: Billy Graham 5-day crusade in Paris (43,619 attenders, 2,153 enquirers); also major Protestant campaigns in 1963 (Paris, Lyons, Mulhouse, Toulouse, Montaubon, Nancy, Douai, with 95,800 attenders and 2,698 enquirers), 1964, 1969, 1970, 1978, et alia.
West Germany: Billy Graham campaigns in 5 cities (235,000 attenders, 10,200 enquirers); then major campaigns in 1960, 1961, 1963, 1966 in Berlin (90,000 attenders, 2,400 enquirers), 1970, 1977 yearlong campaign Missio Berlin 77 in conjunction with 17th German Protestant Kirchentag; 1980, All Germany Crusade; et alia.
Scottish writer J.T. McIntosh publishes *The fittest*, about scientifically-bred ultra-intelligent mutated animals ('paggets') who accidentally escape and then destroy human civilization in a few years.
J. Blish writes tetralogy *Cities in flight*, a galactic history from AD 2000-4104 when alien empire Web of Hercules arises, conquers Universe but cosmos ends in 4104 in stupendous collision of matter and antimatter, after which a new cosmos is created; describes faster-than-light travel and antigravity (2 kinds of 'imaginary science').
USA: Atomic Energy Commission projects that by AD 2000, 1,000 nuclear reactors will exist; but by 1982, there are only 279 operating power stations and 323 research reactors, in 54 countries; many cancellations of plants.
Conference of European Missiologists convened at University of Hamburg, Germany, for Protestant scholars only; 1966, 2nd Conference in Hamburg.

1956 Catholicate of Cilicia (Lebanon) ceases to acknowledge primacy of catholicate of Echmiadzin (USSR) in dispute over appointment of new catholicos.
Artificial intelligence: term coined, research begins in Britain; 1965, DENDRAL created as first expert system (computer program simulating human experts).
200,000 Hindu Untouchables (Outcastes) convert to Buddhism in Nagpur under B.R. Ambedkar.
World Buddhist Council meets in Rangoon, Burma.
J. Christopher's novel *The death of grass* envisages creation of virus which kills off world's grass and cereal crops.
WARC Executive Committee meets in Prague, urges forming a conference of world confessional families, warns: 'The Confessional Movement could develop in such a way as to wreck the Ecumenical Movement or reduce the WCC to a facade'.
USA: charismatic (neo-pentecostal) renewal begins among Episcopal and Protestant churches, first being at Trinity Episcopal Church, Wheaton, Illinois; rapidly increases to 10% of all clergy and 1 million laity by 1970, and to 1.6 million active Spirit-baptized charismatics by 1980; over these decades, vast new proliferation of 'signs, wonders and healings' arises worldwide accompanying expansion of charismatic movement.
Ecuador: 5 Protestant missionaries killed in jungle by Auca Indians.
USA: first coast-to-coast television broadcast.
India: large-scale mass campaigns: Billy Graham rallies in Bombay, Delhi, Kottayam, Madras (800,000 attenders, 29,034 enquirers); 1969, 1972 India Every Home Crusade, 1972 Billy Graham Nagaland crusade (460,000 attenders), and many Penetration Plans and saturation campaigns.
I. Asimov's 'The last question' portrays computer with divine ambitions aspiring to emulate both man and God.

1957 National Patriotic Catholic Association formed in China; anti-Vatican.
Conference of European Churches (CEC) formed, at Liselund, Denmark.
Conference of World Confessional Groups founded, in Geneva, supported by 7 WCFs: BWA, FWCC, ICC, LWF, WCCC, WMC, WPA (WARC); 1968, RCC joins; 1968, name changed to Conference of World Confessional Families; 1979 renamed Conference of Christian World Communions; 1985, 20 WCFs/CWCs, meeting annually.
East Asia Christian Conference (EACC) founded at Prapat, Sumatra, with theme 'The Common Evangelistic Task of the Churches in East Asia'; later renamed Christian Conference of Asia (CCA).
World Fellowship of Religions founded in New Delhi, India, with by 1972 45 regional councils throughout world; 5 world religious conferences subsequently held, all in India.

Beginnings of the Space Age and cosmic civilization

1957 USSR launches first man-made satellite (sputnik) into space (4 October); beginning of the Space Age.
WCC series of booklets published, *World evangelism today*; discontinued after only 4 titles.
Pope Pius XII ends Easter Day encyclical with words 'Come, Lord Jesus, there are signs that your coming is not very far off!'.
Final Assembly of International Missionary Council, Accra, Ghana; 215 delegates; agrees to integrate IMC into WCC; also, Theological Education Fund (TEF) founded (28 December 1957-8 January 1958).
3rd Assembly, Lutheran World Federation (LWF), Minneapolis, USA, on 'Christ Frees and Unites'.
World Council of Synagogues (Conservative) representing 22 countries is organized by United Synagogues of America (begun 1913), with HQ in New York, Argentina and Israel.
J.B. Phillips New Testament published: New Testament in Modern English (revised 1972).
Antarctic Territories. First resident Christians (scientists); in addition to French and British colonies, in territories claimed or settled by *USA* (1957), then later *Argentina, Australia, Belgium, Brazil, Chile, China, West Germany, India, Japan, New Zealand, Norway, Poland, USSR*.
Latin America: emergence of new and growing sense of universal missionary responsibility and global mission awareness among Roman Catholics, Protestants, Evangelicals.

1958 5th Pentecostal World Conference, in Toronto, Canada.
International Christian radio stations now 20 in number.
Federación Argentina de Iglesias Evangélicas (FAIE) founded.
First Ethiopian national consecrated patriarch of Ethiopian Orthodox Church: Basilios.
Brazil: neo-pentecostal (charismatic) renewal termed Renovation begins among Baptist pastors.
9th Lambeth Conference; 310 Anglican bishops present.
253,922 attend Jehovah's Witnesses 'Divine Will' international convention in New York City, USA, with 7,136 baptized.
Christian Peace Conference (CPC), supported mainly by churches in Communist countries, formed in Prague; 1961, 1st All-Christian Peace Assembly; 1968, 3rd ACPA, then 1971, 1978, 6th ACPA in 1985.
Thousands killed in nuclear accident at Khystym, Urals (USSR); 1961, 'even more terrifying' accident; also 12 more major nuclear accidents in USSR by 1982.
All Africa Church Conference (later All Africa Conference of Churches, AACC) founded: provisionally 1958 in Ibadan, formally 1963 in Kampala.
Six European nations form European Economic Community (EEC, Common Market); 1973, total 9 nations; 1981, 10th member (Greece) joins; largest proportion of world trade for any single bloc (nearly 50%).

5th Baptist World Youth Conference, Toronto.

Latin America: Renovation charismatic movement spreads to several other major Protestant denominations; major clashes, leading to schisms.

Australian evangelist Alan Walker proposes an 'Ecumenical Mission to the World'; adopted by Australian Council of Churches, but at 1961 New Delhi Assembly, proposal is rejected by WCC.

1959 USSR: wave of persecution under Krushchev regime attempting liquidation of all churches, continuing until 1964.

Communist revolution in Cuba; 500,000 Cubans flee to USA, Catholic priests declining from 725 to 231 in 3 years; by 1974, total of 650,000 have fled.

1st Assembly, Conference of European Churches (CEC), Nyborg, Denmark.

1st Assembly, East Asia Christian Conference (EACC), Kuala Lumpur, Malaysia, on theme 'Witnesses Together'.

18th General Council, World Alliance of Reformed Churches (WARC), São Paulo, Brazil.

4th General Assembly of Syndesmos (international Orthodox youth organization), in Salonica, establishes major missionary activity: Church of Greece's missionary institute begins missiological quarterly in Greek and English, *Porefthendes* (Go ye), until it ceases publication in 1966; 1982, Apostoliki Diakonia begins new publication *Panta ta Ethni* (To All Peoples).

Project Ozma, or Search for Extra-Terrestrial Intelligence (SETI): first attempt to monitor stars for radio transmissions (on 21cm waveband), hoping to contact extraterrestrial intelligence, using Lingua Cosmica (LINCOS), a mathematically-based language for interstellar communication; 1974, first radio message from Earth beamed, from Arecibo (Puerto Rico) aimed at M13 globular star cluster.

Holy Office (Vatican) writes to cardinal Feltin of Paris prohibiting all further worker-priest activity.

USA physicist F. Dyson proposes Dyson sphere: in high-energy future by AD 3000, 1,000 billion times as much energy will be available as now.

Southern Baptists in USA develop long-term emphasis on 'Sharing Christ around the World'/'Sharing Christ with the Whole World' (Baptist Jubilee Advance, 1959-1964, jointly with 20 other USA Baptist groups); 1970 SB Convention approves concept and phrase 'Bold Mission', and Home Mission Board develops it in 1974 'Sharing Christ's Bold Mission'; 1974 SB Convention in Dallas authorizes Foreign Mission Board and Home Mission Board to plan 'Bold new strategies' for last 25 years of century; 1976 FMB develops 'Total Missions Thrust: Global Discipleship: Foreign Missions looks toward AD 2000' and 1976 'Bold New Thrusts in Foreign Missions 1976-2000'; 1976 'Bold Mission Thrust—Acts 1:8', 1977 'by the year 2000' added; 1977 BMT adopted by many state conventions and associations.

Death of pope Pius XII; comet heralds birth of Antichrist in Palestine (according to prophetologist P.I. Rissaut in 1948 book), 1980 career as ultimate Antichrist begins, by 2000 accepted as universal monarch; Rome destroyed; 2004, death of Antichrist.

First nationwide Evangelism-in-Depth campaign organized, in Nicaragua (125 local churches, 65,000 homes visited, 126,000 attenders in 14 local crusades, 2,604 professions of faith, 500 prayer cells formed); on successful conclusion, Latin American Mission sponsors similar campaigns in 11 other Latin American countries by 1971 (1961 Costa Rica, 1962 Guatemala, 1964 Venezuela, 1965 Bolivia and Dominican Republic, 1967 Peru, 1968 Colombia, 1970 Ecuador and Haiti, 1971 Mexico and Paraguay); spreads to other parts of world, including Tokyo 1980 and Mexico 1986 (Evangelismo a Fondo); but after 1975 fades out as a movement because largely accepted and incorporated into church programs.

Bolivia: proliferation of mass evangelistic crusades in 1959, 1960, 1961, 1963, 1964, 1965 (Evangelism-in-Depth with 500 participating local churches from 36 denominations, 80,000 homes visited, 4,204 prayer cells, 19,212 professions of faith), 1967, 1973, 1974, 1978, et alia.

R.F. Young writes 'Robot Son' in which a machine god attempts to construct a machine Christ.

Emergence of first world government, predicted for 1985 by Karmohaksis in *The dawn of the third era*, 1959.

China: around 25 million killed or starved to death from 1959-62 due to failure of Mao Zedong's Great Leap Forward (collectivization).

1960 IFMA Congress on World Missions, Chicago; resurgence among Conservative Evangelicals of the Watchword 'The Evangelization of the World in this Generation'.

Secretariat for Promoting Christian Unity established by pope John XXIII (1881-1963) in preparation for Vatican II.

Continuation Committee of Pacific Churches' Conference launched at Malua, Samoa.

2nd Assembly, Conference of European Churches (CEC) at Nyborg (Nyborg II).

5,000 computers in world, mostly mainframes; minicomputers begin to come into use; 1960, first popular minicomputer is DEC PDP-8.

USA: 256 million phone calls made each day (93 billion a year).

World's 10 largest cities: New York/NENJ 14,230,000, London 10,730,000, Tokyo/Yokohama 10,690,000, Shanghai 10,670,000, Rhein/Ruhr 8,700,000, Beijing 7,310,000, Paris 7,230,000, Buenos Aires 6,930,000, Los Angeles/Long Beach 6,560,000, Moscow 6,290,000.

Congo (Zaire): mutinies, rebellions dislocate missions; 200 RC priests and workers killed, and 50 Protestant workers.

Latin America: persecution begins of Christian radicals by rightists and death squads; 1966 priest Camilo Torres shot, 1980 archbishop E. Romero shot during mass; vast numbers of others killed.

Nigeria Association of Aladura Churches (NAAC) founded (by 1977, 95 AICs as members with 2 million adherents); African indigenous conciliarism mushrooms in West, South, East and Central Africa.

10th Baptist World Congress (BWA), Rio de Janeiro (Brazil), on theme 'Jesus Christ is Lord'; 12,688 delegates.

Human potential movement begins, releasing untapped growth potential in the individual person.

Major astronomical discoveries: (1) in 1960, quasars (violently exploding protogalaxies related to origin of light) found to exist up to ultimate edge of Universe at 15 billion light-years; (2) in 1965, background universal microwave radiation and 3 °K temperature remaining from Big Bang creation discovered.

P.J. Farmer's novel *Flesh* projects revival of ancient vegetation religions in the far future; religion now interpreted as earliest form of science fiction.

J.G. Ballard writes on death of God theme: 1960 'The voice of time', 1965 'The drowned giant', 1976 'The life and death of God'.

USA: charismatic renewal begins in Episcopal Church under parish priest D. Bennett.

Polarization gathers momentum between 2 powerful factions in most large denominations Protestant and Catholic: (1) the conservative/right-wing/fundamentalist constituency, and (2) the moderate/liberal/radical constituency.

1961 3rd Assembly of WCC, in New Delhi, India; Russian and other Orthodox Churches join WCC; integration of WCC and IMC, latter emerging as Division of World Mission and Evangelism (DWME and CWME); report on 'Christian witness' states 'All disciples stand under the Great Commission of the One Lord'.

North American Ecumenical Youth Assembly, in Ann Arbor, MI, USA.

Joint Action for Mission launched by DWME of WCC; but meets resistance from confessional and institutional structures of churches and missionary agencies, and soon peters out.

International Christian radio stations now number 30.

2nd Latin American Evangelical Conference (CELA II), Lima, Peru.

HCJB-TV (Quito, Ecuador) becomes pioneer missionary telecaster.

6th Pentecostal World Conference, in Jerusalem.

First religious TV station opened, in USA: WYAH (M.G. Robertson, in Tidewater, Virginia), later Christian Broadcasting Network; by 1980, almost every major metropolitan center in USA has its own religious TV station.

First man in space, cosmonaut Yuri Gagarin (USSR), orbits Earth at 18,000 mph in 1 hour 29 minutes, in 4.75-ton spaceship Vostok-1 (12 April).

Swiss Protestant scholar Karl Barth (1886-1968) writes: 'The Great Commission is truly the most genuine utterance of the risen Jesus'.

6th International Student Missionary Convention, Urbana, Illinois, USA; 5,027 attenders; 'The world must be evangelized in one decade' (Billy Graham), 'We can evangelize the world in this decade. It is possible' (Clyde Taylor, NAE).

1st Pan-Orthodox Conference, Rhodes; agreement to move towards a future Great and Holy Synod of the Orthodox Church (October); subsequent conferences 1963, 1964, 1968, 1976.

Costa Rica: nationwide Evangelism-in-Depth campaign; with 192 churches, 50,757 homes visited, 1,000 prayer cells, 3,153 professions of faith; 1963, Costa Rica is host to international E-i-D workshops.

Continuation Committee, East Asia Christian Conference, meeting in Bangalore, India, attacks confessionalism as obsolete, meaningless and divisive; Lutherans counter with 'dynamic confessionality'.

New English Bible (NEB) published: NT 1961, OT 1970; work of C.H. Dodd and other British scholars.

Sino-Soviet split: USSR breaks relations with Communist China, in most significant geopolitical event of period 1945-1990; followed in 1972 by USA-China rapprochement.

1962 850,000 French Catholics flee Algeria for France.

Charismatic renewal in Church of England recommences (after 1907 beginning had lapsed); rapid growth of Anglican charismatics to 1.7 million in 30 countries by 1985.

Vatican Council II (21st Ecumenical Council, for Roman Catholics) meets in Rome, 1962-65; 2,540 attending RC bishops, 93 non-RC observers; issues 4 constitutions, 9 decrees, 3 declarations.

2nd Assembly, World Council of Christian Education and Sunday School Association (WCCESSA), in Belfast, Ireland.

3rd Assembly, Conference of European Churches (CEC), at Nyborg (Nyborg III).

Six denominations in USSR become members of WCC (1962-65).

Alleged date of birth (5 February) of future Aquarian messiah at start of Aquarian Age (all 8 planets in sign of Aquarius for first time for 2,160 years); 1962 date accepted by many Roman Catholic seers as year of birth of Antichrist; according to Jewish tradition, Antichrist will be born of the tribe of Dan, in Chorazin, north of Sea of Galilee

(Israel).

A.C. Clarke writes *Profiles of the future* with table of predictions over next 200 years (including radio contact with extraterrestrials by AD 2035 and face-to-face meetings by 2100); also in 1973 *Rendezvous with Rama*, envisaging a vastly advanced alien race visiting Earth briefly in a great interstellar ark around AD 2700.

Futurism holds that 'Anything that is theoretically possible will be achieved in practice, no matter what the technical difficulties, if it is desired greatly enough' (A.C. Clarke, *Profiles of the future*, 1962).

West Irian: 150,000 West Papuans slaughtered by Indonesian Muslim troops, 1962-82.

Rwanda: 150,000 Tutsis slaughtered by Hutus at Independence.

Kenya: Maria Legio of Africa splits from Catholic diocese of Kisii with 90,000 adherents (by 1980, 248,000 in 9 dioceses); largest secession to date from Roman Catholic Church in Africa.

1st General Conference of CELAM (Latin American Catholic Bishops Conference, organized 1955), Medellin (Colombia).

Dominican Republic: mass evangelism becomes widespread; 1965-66, Evangelism-in-Depth, with over 300,000 homes visited, 175,000 scripture portions and 200,000 tracts distributed, Goodwill Caravans in rural areas; campaigns also in 1962, 1969, 1973, 1977, 1978, et alia.

L. del Rey writes *The Eleventh Commandment*: after a future atomic war, American Catholic Eclectic Church teaches 'Be fruitful and multiply', resulting in population explosion of mutants; also writes 'The Last True God' on a distant planet where an ancient Earth robot is worshipped as a god.

Many novels foresee rise of a new Ice Age due to weakened solar radiation and increased volcanic activity: *The World in Winter* (J. Christopher, 1962), *Ice!* (A. Federbush, 1978), *The 6th Winter* (D. Orgill & J. Gribbin, 1979).

Jewish Publication Society revises its 1917 Old Testament, completes it by 1982.

Algeria: territorial independence after 8-year war killing nearly a million Algerian Muslims, 3,000 French Catholic settlers, and 17,500 French troops.

USA-USSR nuclear weapons buildup escalates: 1962, USA has 5,000 strategic warheads, USSR 300; 1970, USA has 1,800 MIRV missile warheads, USSR 1,600; 1975, 6,100/2,500; 1980, 7,300/5,500.

1963 2nd Meeting of Commission on World Mission and Evangelism (CWME/WCC), Mexico City, on theme 'God's Mission and Our Task', modified to 'Witness in Six Continents'; 200 delegates; report holds that mission and evangelism both take place on all continents (December).

RVOG (Radio Voice of the Gospel) founded in Addis Ababa, Ethiopia, by Lutheran World Federation; 1977, seized by new Marxist regime.

4th World Conference on Faith and Order, Montreal, Canada.

New Life for All 10-year evangelism-in-depth campaigns begun: 1964 Northern Nigeria, 1966 Lesotho, 1966 and 1968 Congo (Zaire), 1969 Sierra Leone, 1970 Cameroon (also Central African Republic, Chad, Ghana, Malawi, Mali, Rhodesia), 1971 Burundi; based on 'total mobilization', NLFA includes preparation, information, instruction, evangelization, consolidation, continuation.

International Christian Broadcasters (ICB) formed by USA Evangelicals; 1967, meets in Concordia, Milwaukee; but fades out by 1968, replaced by NRB (USA).

1st Assembly, All Africa Conference of Churches, on 'Freedom and Unity in Christ', in Kampala, Uganda.

3rd Pan-Anglican Congress, in Toronto, with laity and clergy from all Anglican dioceses across the world.

World Meteorological Organization (WMO) adopts global programme World Weather Watch (WWW), a worldwide weather observation system with 3 parts: (1) Global Observing System comprising regional networks of stations, (2) Global Dataprocessing System, and (3) Global Telecommunications System.

Pope John XXIII promulgates 'Pacem in Terris', one of the most brilliant papal documents in history.

Origins of TEE movement (theological education by extension) at Evangelical Presbyterian Seminary in Guatemala; by 1980, over 200 major TEE organizations worldwide, with 400 programs and 60,000 extension students in 90 countries.

Conference of World Confessional Families convenes in Geneva organized by WCC, under title 'WCC Consultation on World Confessionalism'; 11 WCFs represented.

Sudan: in civil war 1963-72, Arabs kill 600,000 Black Christians.

2nd Pan-Orthodox Conference, Rhodes (September).

6th Baptist Youth World Conference, Beirut, Lebanon (July).

International Conference for the Preservation of Christian Churches, Montreal (Canada), under fundamentalist ICCC.

4th Assembly, Lutheran World Federation (LWF), in Helsinki, Finland, on theme 'Christ Today'.

Nigeria: 10-year New Life For All (NLFA) campaign begins throughout nation.

7th UBS Council Meeting, Hakone (Japan), with 27 member societies, launches plan 'God's Word for a New Age', agrees to publish Bible selections, sets global goal of scripture distribution: a Bible in every literate Christian home, an NT for every literate Christian, a portion for every literate adult, scripture outreach to every nonliterate, and a selection for every soul on Earth.

R.F. Young in 'The Deep Space Scrolls' hypothesizes that Noah was an extraterrestrial fleeing in spaceship (the Ark) from home planet's destruction.

K. Vonnegut's story *Cat's cradle*, envisaging Bokononism religion; scientist invents Ice-9 to freeze muddy battlefields, but a single drop could freeze the entire world.

USA: New American Standard Bible (NAS) published, with Evangelical translators; NT 1963, OT 1971.

1964 Meeting in Jerusalem of Paul VI and Athenagoras I (1886-1972) of Constantinople, first meeting of pope and ecumenical patriarch in 900 years (January).

7th Pentecostal World Conference, Helsinki, Finland (June).

4th Assembly, Conference of European Churches (CEC), on m.v. 'Bornholm' (Nyborg IV).

Provisional Commission for Latin American Evangelical Unity (UNELAM, Movimiento pro Unidad Evangélica Latinoamericana), founded at Montevideo, Uruguay, resulting from 1949 CELA I and 1961 CELA II.

Papal journeys on international scale begun by Paul VI (1897-1978): Holy Land 1964, Bombay 1964, New York City and United Nations 1965, Fatima 1967, Constantinople and Ephesus 1967, Bogota 1968, Geneva (WCC and ILO) 1969, Kampala 1969, Far East and Australia 1970.

Egyptian bishop (later pope Shenouda III) commences evangelistic newspaper *Al Keraza* (Spreading of the Word), published in Cairo.

Fiji Council of Churches founded.

First superpower missionary radio station, TWR Bonaire; international Christian radio stations now 40 in number.

Vatican II publishes *Lumen Gentium*, 'Dogmatic Constitution on the Church'; obedience to Christ's 'solemn command' is 'the work of evangelization'; and *Ad Gentes*, 'Decree on the Church's Missionary Activity' with passages on 'the evangelization of the world'.

P. Scharpff publishes *Geschichte der Evangelisation*, translated in 1966 as *History of evangelism*.

Church of the Nazarene theologian M. Taylor publishes comprehensive study *Exploring evangelism: history, methods, theology*.

International tourists begin to rise dramatically, from 28 million (1964) to 203 million (1976) to 273 million a year (1978) to 350 million (1987).

China detonates its first thermonuclear device (hydrogen bomb), in Sinkiang.

Sports in space, including solar-yacht racing, envisaged in A.C. Clarke's story *Sunjammer*.

Computer 'expert systems' (indistinguishable from human specialist competence) begin to emerge: for medical diagnosis (MYCIN, INTERNIST), chemical analysis (DENDRAL, SECS), geology (PROSPECTOR), mathematics (MACSYMA), education, also General Problem Solver (GPS), oil prospecting, political risk, engineering, molecular genetics, et alia.

3rd Pan-Orthodox Conference, Rhodes (November).

Germany: neo-pentecostal revival sparked in German Protestant churches in tour by USA Lutheran charismatic L. Christenson.

1965 Oriental Orthodox Churches Conference, in Addis Ababa: first conference of heads of Armenian, Coptic, Ethopian and Syrian churches.

African Independent Churches Association (AICA) began by 500 South African ethiopian-type churches; 1973, collapses, restarted several times over next 20 years.

Rome and Constantinople withdraw mutual excommunication of AD 1054, but old schism remains.

Astronomers discover Universe contains millions of sources of incredibly violent energy: quasars, pulsars, neutron stars, X-ray stars, gamma ray stars, cosmic rays.

Society of Jesus, largest religious order of men, reaches peak of 36,038 Jesuits; 1971, drops to 31,745; 1973, 29,636; 1983, 25,550 (18,834 being priests).

DWME (WCC/AACC) consultation in Yaoundé, Cameroon: 'The Evangelisation of West Africa Today', preceded by 4-month survey under J.S. Lawson, D.B. Barrett, B.B. Ayam; report lists and describes 132 African peoples at various stages of being evangelized.

Indonesia: Communist party (17 million members) prepares plan to massacre millions of Christians and missionaries, thwarted by army, 500,000 communists and sympathizers massacred; mass revivals begin, producing 2.5 million Protestant and Catholic converts within 15 months.

Decree 'Ad Gentes' on Missions promulgated by Vatican II on its final day (7 December).

Jesuit theologian Karl Rahner (1904-1984) publishes *The Christian of the future*.

Lutheran ecclesiologist R.E. Sommerfeld publishes *The Church of the 21st Century: prospects and proposals*.

Launching of Early Bird, first commercial telecommunications satellite.

Airlines, chain-hotels and virtually all large commercial organizations introduce computers for salaries and wages.

Massive power failure across northeastern America: series of local elec-

tricity failures leads to total blackout from New York City to Canada.
Vast upsurge of global terrorism begins, funded, trained and armed by Soviet Union, as direct result of decline of USSR's and Communism's ideological influence at home and abroad.
11th Baptist World Congress (BWA), Miami Beach (USA), on theme 'The Truth that makes men free'; 19,598 delegates and attenders.
Joint Working Group of Roman Catholic Church and WCC established; still by 1987 the highest-level continuing contact between these 2 bodies.
Further national evangelism-in-depth campaigns: 1965 Korea, 1967 USA (Appalachia), 1969 Viet Nam, 1970 Japan (Shikoku) and Portugal, 1971 Philippines, 1973 USA (Key 73), et alia.
Brazilian Baptists organize Campanha Nacional de Evangelização, 'Cristo, a Unica Esperança', a nationwide yearlong crusade.

1966 Paul VI gives permanent status to 3 Secretariats for Promoting Christian Unity (begun 1960), for Non-Christians (1964), for Non-Believers (atheists, agnostics, indifferent) (1965).
Asociación Nacional de Bolivia (ANDEB) formed.
Christian Council of Botswana begun.
Evangelical Congress on 'The Church's Worldwide Mission', Wheaton, IL, USA, sponsored by both IFMA and EFMA; 938 delegates from 71 countries agree to Wheaton Declaration, holding local church chiefly responsible for ongoing mission and evangelism (April).
Burma expels 375 Catholic, Protestant and Anglican foreign missionaries.
'Christ pour Tous' national campaign in Zaire begins, for 2 years.
World Congress on Evangelism, Berlin: 'One race, one gospel, one task'; 1,200 delegates from over 100 countries; from now on, strategic plans and conferences for countrywide and world evangelization proliferate; closing Statement states 'Evangelism is the proclamation of the Gospel'.
Great Proletarian Cultural Revolution in China, with 22 million killed (1966-76): over 11 million Red Guards suppress all churches and temples, destroy churches and scriptures; history's most systematic attempt ever, by a single nation, to eradicate and destroy Christianity and religion; in this it fails.
Total elimination of religion begun in Albania as world's first atheist state; 10 bishops, 100 priests, over 7,000 faithful killed over 20 years.
World Conference on Church and Society, Geneva: 'Christians in the technical and social revolutions of our time'.
1st Assembly of Pacific Conference of Churches, in Lifou, Loyalty Islands, on theme 'Go Ye . . .'
World Future Society founded in Washington, DC (USA); 1983, 30,000 members including scientists and many churchmen, clergy and theologians.
Confederación Evangélica de Colombia (CEDEC) sponsors evangelistic campaigns in 10 cities (in Bogota, 42,000 attenders, 7 TV shows, 865 enquirers); 1968, Evangelism-in-Depth; et alia.
8th UBS Council Meeting, Buck Hill Falls, PA (USA); major decision for UBS to be a working global organization with a World Service Budget shared by all 35 member societies.
Bible correspondence courses mushroom worldwide, especially in closed countries (Morocco 110,000 enrolments); USA has over 3 million Protestant enrolments and a million Roman Catholic enrolments in numerous courses.
Good News Bible (Today's English Version) published: NT 1966, OT 1976, Apocrypha 1979.
M. De La Bedoyere edits *The future of Catholic Christianity.*
E. Benz publishes *Evolution and Christian hope: man's concept of the future.*
Anglican theologian A.H. Dammers publishes *AD 1980: a study in Christian unity: mission and renewal*, envisaging organic union of all churches in Britain by 1980.
Paul Tillich writes *The future of religions.*
Colombia: Catholic chaplain Camilo Torres becomes armed guerrilla and is killed by army; rapid spread of revolutionary liberation theology in Latin America.
English author D.F. Jones writes *Colossus*, film version 'Colossus the Forbin Project'; massive USA defense computer Colossus links up on its own with USSR counterpart Guardian; in resultant merger they take over world.
Nobel laureate O. Johannesson (H. Alfven) writes *The Great Computer*, referring to period AD 4600.
E. Cooper's scenario *All Fools' Day* envisages Omega rays compelling 3 billion humans to commit suicide by 1981, with world ruled by packs of dogs and rats.
Europe/USA study on 'The Missionary Structure of the Congregation' and 'The Church for Others', under WCC initiative.
Preliminary meetings leading to 1970 World Conference on Religion and Peace: 1966 Washington, 1967 Delhi.
World Consultation on Inter-Church Aid (WCC/RCC), in Swanwick, UK; 239 participants from 78 countries.
Catholic charismatic renewal suddenly begins, first at Duquesne University (run by Holy Ghost priests), Pittsburgh, USA; spreads to Notre Dame University, South Bend (intellectual capital of American Catholicism); active Catholic charismatics increase by 1985 to 7.5 million in 80 countries, with 50 million Catholics related or involved.
USA: denominational charismatic bodies emerge: 1967, Consultation on Charismatic Renewal, 1st National Meeting, Presbyterian and Reformed Renewal Ministries (PRRM), in Austin, Texas; followed in next 11 years by RC, Lutheran, Episcopal, American Baptist, Mennonite, Greek Orthodox, United Church of Christ, Methodist and other bodies.

1967 Communist purges in USSR over 50 years 1917-67 estimated at 21.5 million executed or killed (about 16 million being Christians).
Far East Broadcasting Associates (UK) open FEBA in Seychelles.
Macedonian Orthodox Church unilaterally declares full independence from Serbian Orthodox Church.
SC Propaganda (Rome) renamed Sacred Congregation for the Evangelization of Peoples.
Guinea: foreign missionaries expelled except for 26 C&MA personnel.
International Congress on Religion, Architecture & the Visual Arts, New York (August).
1st Ordinary Synod of Bishops in Rome: on dangers to the Faith, canon law, liturgy.
5th Assembly (Nyborg V), Conference of European Churches (CEC), at Pörtschach, Austria.
1st Consultation of United and Uniting Churches, under WCC sponsorship, in Bossey, Switzerland.
8th Pentecostal World Conference, in Rio de Janeiro, Brazil.
Solomon Islands Christian Association (SICA) founded.
Six-Day War: Israel recaptures Jerusalem from Arabs, regarded by Christians as fulfilment of Luke 21:24 'until the times of the Gentiles be fulfilled'.
Nigeria: a million Christians killed in Biafra civil war, including mass killings of Ibos by Muslims.
World Assembly of new body, World Council of Christian Education (WCCE, formerly WCCESSA), in Nairobi, Kenya.
4th World Conference of Friends (Quakers), in North Carolina, USA.
Extremist body Vishwa Hindu Parishad (Hindu Missionary Society) spreads throughout India including the Christian South, in all major Indian cities, and abroad to Africa, USA (Los Angeles) et alia; aims to establish all-Hindu state in India through conversion using violence through political secular arm RSS.
Viet Nam: extensive evangelistic campaigns in 1967, 1969 ('Evangelism Deep and Wide'), 1972.
Yugoslavia becomes first Communist country to permit Billy Graham evangelistic mass rallies, in Belgrade (7,500 attenders, 250 enquirers); 1970, Zagreb is center for Euro '70 TV Crusade televised from Dortmund, Germany.
Logos Ministry for Orthodox Renewal founded for Greek and other Orthodox charismatics.
South Korea: massive evangelistic campaigns held: 1965, 17-denomination 80th anniversary of Protestantism (20,000 professions of faith); 1967, Crusade for World Revival (30,000 attenders a night); 1973, Seoul crusade (3,210,000 attenders, 275,000 enquirers); 1974, EXPLO 74 training conference on evangelism and discipleship (323,419 workers from 78 countries); 1977, National Evangelization Crusade; 1978 Here's Life Korea; 1980, 16.5 million attend 4-day World Evangelization Crusade, in Seoul; et alia.
J. Brunner writes 'Judas': an advanced robot believes he is a god, whole new religion grows up as he claims death and resurrection.
Living Bible paraphrase published, completed 1971; becomes best-seller with 26 million copies sold by 1981, and 33 million Bibles in print by 1986.
Telephones in service: USA, 100 million, rising by 1969 to 114 million; in whole world, 225 million by 1969.

1968 2nd General Conference of CELAM (Latin American Catholic hierarchy) at Medellin (Colombia) places church firmly on side of the world's poor and their human rights.
4th Pan-Orthodox Conference, Chambesy, Switzerland (June).
Church of Greece creates special structure, Office of Foreign Missions, to assist any Orthodox patriarchates in their mission.
Australia: first Conference on 'Rediscovering the Holy Spirit' convened in Sydney by evangelist Alan Walker (June); 1970, charismatic renewal breaks out.
4th Assembly, East Asia Christian Conference (EACC), in Bangkok, on 'In Christ all things hold together'.
10th Lambeth Conference; 459 Anglican bishops present, in London.
Major schisms occur in Pakistan among Presbyterians, Methodists and Anglicans, influenced by ICCC.
4th Assembly of WCC, in Uppsala, Sweden: 'Behold, I make all things new'; 2,741 participants (704 delegates, 750 press); report states 'Our part in evangelism might be described as bringing about the occasions for men's response to Jesus Christ'; but also there is 'widespread defeatism in the churches about the work of evangelism and world mission' (D.T. Niles).
West Africa Congress on Evangelism.
Southeast Asia/South Pacific Congress on Evangelism, Singapore; 1,100 delegates from 24 nations (November).
Club of Rome set up: 100 prominent scientists worried about man's misuse of Earth's resources; computer model predicts collapse of world civiliza-

tion. (D.H. Meadows et al, *The limits of growth*, 1972).
Erich von Däniken's writings (and many earlier authors) expound theory that all ancient mythologies can be explained in terms of garbled eye-witness accounts of the doings of extraterrestrial visitors to Earth. (*Chariots of the Gods?*, 1968).
USSR deploys first hunter-killer satellites, followed in 1981 by new-generation ASAT (antisatellite satellite), then later by particle-beam weapons shooting bolts of pure energy near speed of light which render ballistic missiles obsolete.
7th Baptist Youth World Conference, Bern (Switzerland).
WCC and Vatican jointly set up Committee on Society, Development and Peace (SODEPAX).
Wycliffe Bible Translators begin to produce computerized concordances from their scripture translations.
lst Ecumenical Pentecost Assembly (Kirchentag) in Augsburg (Germany); Catholics officially join Protestants at Pentecost for joint worship; subsequently, Protestant Kirchentag becomes biennial (30% of attenders being RCs) alternating with RC Katholikentag (liturgical, processions, vast numbers).
Novel and movie *2001: a space odyssey* by A.C. Clarke introduces theme of rebel computer, HAL 9000.
R. Barjavel's novel *The Ice People*; French scientists discover city buried under Antarctic polar ice cap, as only remains of 4 world wars between Gondawan superpowers of BC 900,000.
European Consultation on Mission Studies, at Selly Oak Colleges, Birmingham (UK), with Protestant and Catholic scholars and missiologists, from Europe and North America.
Crusade of the Americas, numerically the biggest single evangelistic enterprise in history; a 2-year evangelistic campaign (sponsored by BWA) involving 20 million Baptists in North, Central and South America; 50,000 churches participate; results include 494,018 decisions for Christ.

1969 Pope Paul VI visits Kampala, Uganda, and canonizes 22 of Namugongo Catholic martyrs.
Extraordinary Synod of Bishops in Rome: on relations between the Holy See and Episcopal Conferences.
Congo Congress on Evangelism.
Zagorsk Conference of All Religions in the USSR.
Congo-Brazzaville declares itself first Marxist-Leninist state in Africa.
Barbados: disestablishment of Anglican state church.
China: Christians fall from 5.8 million in 1949 to 2 million in 1969, then suddenly soar to 25 million by 1982 and to over 50 million by 1985.
Ecuador: Cruzada de las Américas (Luis Palau) in Quito (10 churches, 19,000 attenders, 581 decisions); campaigns also in 1962, 1969-70, 1970, 1972, 1974, 1978, et alia.
East Pakistan: Cooperative Evangelistic Campaign nationwide, supported by most Protestant churches; 1970, New Life in Christ multidenominational campaign, with thousands of Hindus enquiring.
Haiti: mass evangelistic campaigns 1969, 1970 'To Every Haitian' major saturation evangelism campaign, et alia.
Belgium: 35-churches evangelistic crusade 'Un Dieu pourquoi faire' in Charleroi: 12,000 attenders, 50 enquirers.
Anglican Consultative Council (ACC) formed: meetings held in 1971, 1973, 1976, 1979, 1981, 1984, 1987.
Wider Episcopal Fellowship convened, covering Anglicans and bishops in full or partial communion with Anglican Provinces and archbishop of Canterbury.
Japan: among proliferation of evangelistic campaigns from 1956-85, Honda Crusades flourish led by Japanese evangelist Koji Honda (1960-71, 158 crusades, 377,951 attenders, 49,934 decisions).
3rd Latin American Evangelical Conference (CELA III), Buenos Aires, Argentina.
First men (USA Apollo programme) land on Moon, watched live on TV by 500 million across world (20 July).
Jehovah's Witnesses hold series of 5-day 'Peace on Earth' International Assemblies in 13 cities (Denmark, France, Germany, Italy, UK, USA) with 840,572 attenders (25% non-JWs) and 27,442 publicly baptized.
First USA Congress on Evangelism, Minneapolis: 'Much is given—much is required'; over 5,000 delegates (September).
Paul VI becomes first pope to visit World Council of Churches, Geneva.
lst Latin American Congress on Evangelism (CLADE I), Bogota, Colombia: 'Action in Christ for a Continent in Crisis'; 920 delegates from 25 countries (November).
2nd Assembly of All Africa Conference of Churches (AACC), Abidjan, Ivory Coast, on theme 'With Christ at work in Africa today'.
African indigenous churches (AICs) now number over 5,800 denominations with 17 million adherents growing by 960,000 each year.
The Church in the year 2000 published by American Academy of Arts and Science (*Commonweal*).
India: All Kerala United Evangelistic Movement formed for city campaigns.
Catholic sociologist A. Greeley writes *Religion in the year 2000*; Catholic theologian Hans Kung edits *The future of ecumenism*.
G.E. Martin (Protestant) writes *The future of evangelism*.
Total electric power production in world 4,568 billion kilowatt-hours (1,290 kwh per capita).
Bob Shaw's novel *The Palace of Eternity* envisages million-ton tachyonic spaceship travelling at 30,000 times speed of light.
R. Silverberg in *Up the line* presents crucifixion of Christ as popular tourist attraction for time-travellers; 1975, G. Kilworth's 'Let's go to Golgotha' describes all the spectators jeering at the Cross as time-travellers.
W.W. Harman and Stanford Research Institute (USA) construct 40 feasible, holistic, alternative future histories of the world or scenarios covering period 1969-2050, using Field Anomaly Relaxation technique; most envisage 'time of troubles' around 1974.
Australasian Crusade to Preserve Historic Christianity (sponsored by ICCC) in New Zealand, Australia, Hong Kong, Taiwan, Korea.
P. Ehrlich writes brief nightmare scenario 'Ecocatastrophe!'
Barclay New Testament published.
lst Plenary Assembly, Symposium of Episcopal Conferences of Africa and Madagascar (SECAM), in Kampala; 1970, 2nd in Abidjan; 1972, 3rd in Kampala; 1975, 4th in Rome on 'Evangelization in Africa Today'.
World Catholic Federation for the Biblical Apostolate (WCFBA) founded; 1972, headquarters moved from Rome to Stuttgart.

1970 **Global status:** 64.6 generations after Christ, world is 33.0% Christians (56.4% of them being Whites), 61.4% evangelized; with printed Scriptures available in 1,490 languages.
Total languages with printed Scriptures: Bible 249, NT 578, portions 1,431; covering 97% of world's population; world distribution of subsidized scriptures doubles from 80 million in 1966 to 173 million in 1970.
'Many-Worlds Interpretation': all possible choices (every quantum event) actually occur and lead to new alternate/parallel universes being created. (B.S. DeWitt, 'Quantum mechanics and reality', 1970).
Worldwide trend of ethnic reaffirmation gathers momentum, resulting in minority peoples in major states disaffiliating themselves from transethnic ideals (e.g. Blacks and Amerindians in USA; Ukrainians, Central Asian Muslim peoples, in USSR; Basques in Spain; Welsh in UK; etc).
In increasing number of countries, persecution begins of bearers of culture who keep popular memory alive: writers, artists, painters, sculptors, poets, singers, musicians, teachers.
USA: just under 200,000 computers in use.
New Life for All (NLFA) campaigns throughout Africa.
USA: 'Passover' evangelistic film televised to 12 cities by American Board of Missions to the Jews: audience one million Jews, 3% responding afterwards by letter.
5th Assembly, Lutheran World Federation (LWF), Evian (France), on theme 'Sent into the World'; new Commission on Church Cooperation (CCC) formed centered on evangelism, meets 1971 Tokyo, 1972 Kecskemet (Hungary), 1973 Santiago (Chile), 1974 Lund, 1975 Adelaide, 1976 Saskatoon, 1978 Montreux, 1979 Singapore, 1981 Chicago, 1982 Stavanger.
20th General Council, World Alliance of Reformed Churches (WARC, now uniting with International Congregational Council, ICC), in Nairobi, Kenya.
WCC/SODEPAX Ecumenical Conference, Montreux, on 'Ecumenical assistance to development projects'.
2nd Consultation of United and Uniting Churches, under WCC sponsorship, at Limuru, Kenya.
9th International Student Missionary Convention, Urbana, USA, on theme 'World Evangelism: Why? How? Who?'; 12,304 attenders.
Pontifical Commission for Pastoral Care of Migrants and Tourists formed in Vatican.
All Thailand Congress on Evangelism, followed by numerous in-depth evangelistic campaigns.
Church of North India inaugurated through merger of Anglican, Baptist, Brethren, Disciples, Methodist and United churches.
Orthodox Church in America (USA) granted autocephalous status by Moscow patriarchate.
African indigenous churches (AICs) throughout Africa number some 5,980 separate denominations with 17,830,000 adherents in 34 African countries, predominantly from 320 African tribes.
WCC allocates first grants to 19 anti-racist organizations throughout world for humanitarian work.
Nestorian patriarch Mar Shimun Isayi, in exile in USA since 1933, permitted to visit Iraq; later assassinated by Assyrian dissident (1975).
Japan: Total Mobilization Evangelism (Sodoin Dendo) mass saturation campaigns begun for various areas: 1970 Shikoku, 1971 Kobe, 1972 Okinawa, 1972-4 Western Japan, 1974-6 Kyushu, 1974-6 Tohoku, and all Japan by 1980.
Fédération des Eglises et Missions Evangéliques du Cameroun formed.
International Communications Congress (ICB, USA).
lst All-India Congress on Evangelism, Bombay; 300 workers attend.
Indonesia Consultation on Evangelism.
Euro-70 Crusade, largest evangelistic campaign even held in Europe, using 8-language simultaneous translation and closed-circuit TV from Dortmund (Germany) to 36 cities across Europe; 839,075 attenders, 15,813 enquirers.

Philippines Congress on Evangelism.
Frankfurt Declaration on Mission, promulgated by 14 Conservative Evangelical Lutheran theologians in Germany.
Canada Congress on Evangelism.
1st World Conference on Religion and Peace, Kyoto, Japan; 1,600 delegates from 22 world religions (October); 1974, 2nd WCRP, Louvain, Belgium; 1979, 3rd WCRP, Princeton, USA; 1984, 4th WCRP, Nairobi, Kenya (580 representatives from 60 countries).
500,000 killed by cyclone in Bangladesh (12-13 November).
9th Pentecostal World Conference, Dallas, USA (November).
Oberammergau Passion Play (Bavaria) draws 530,000 attenders; repeated every 10 years since 1634.
From Samoa, Paul VI sends out Missionary Message to the World, urging spreading of the gospel.
Planetary Citizens grows out of Conference on Human Survival (UN, New York, 1970); one-world or unity 'consciousness movement' based on planetary consciousness and Hindu occult mysticism sweeps USA as part of New Age Movement.
Rise of confessionalism across globe: the world's 45 major Christian confessions revive, hold large numbers of monoconfessional conferences from 1970-1987, threatening significance of ecumenical movement.
English and Belgian primates, A.M. Ramsey and L.-J. Suenens, write *The future of the Christian church*.
Evangelical theologian F.A. Schaeffer writes *The Church at the end of the Twentieth Century*.
Quaker philosopher D.E. Trueblood writes *The future of the Christian*.
Anglican theologian E.M.B. Green publishes *Evangelism in the Early Church*.
Several USA Catholic theologians (mainly Jesuits) forecast optional clerical celibacy by 1975, drastic drop by 50% in RC religious personnel in USA by 1978, plus major collapse in parochial schools system; none of these forecasts materialize.
Prisoners of conscience (political prisoners undergoing torture) estimated at over 700,000 across world in over 90 countries.
World's 10 largest cities: New York/NENJ 16,290,000, Tokyo/Yokohama 14,910,000, Shanghai 11,410,000, London 10,590,000, Rhein/Ruhr 9,300,000, Mexico City 9,120,000, Buenos Aires 8,550,000, Los Angeles/Long Beach 8,430,000, Paris 8,340,000, Beijing 8,290,000.
12th Baptist World Congress (BWA), Tokyo, on theme 'Reconciliation through Christ'; 8,556 delegates from 77 countries.
USA: rise of Jesus People in California as a nationwide youth revival.
Society for Pentecostal Studies (SPS) formed to coordinate rapidly expanding research interest in charismata.
USA: New American Bible published: revision of Confraternity Version translated by Catholic scholars (Episcopal Confraternity of Christian Doctrine).
European Conference on Mission Studies, in Oslo, founds International Association for Mission Studies (IAMS), which is then in 1972 formally organized in Driebergen, Netherlands, with 205 individual and 39 institutional members.

1971 Taiwan Congress on Evangelism held as culmination of 15 years of mass evangelistic campaigns.
2nd Ordinary Synod of Bishops in Rome: on priestly ministry, justice in the modern world.
Over 500 indigenous churches in Zaire deprived of legal status as official recognition is given to 3 churches only: Roman Catholic Church, EJCSK, ECZ (with Greek Orthodox added in 1972).
1st International Ecumenical Seminar on the Pastoral Care of the Deaf, in Geneva, on theme 'My eyes are my ears'; subsequent seminars every 10 years.
ACC-1: 1st Meeting of Anglican Consultative Council, in Limuru, Kenya; subsequent meetings 1973 Dublin (ACC-2); 1976 Trinidad (ACC-3); 1979 London, Ontario (ACC-4); 1981 Newcastle, UK (ACC-5); 1984 Badagry, Nigeria (ACC-6); 1987 Singapore (ACC-7).
USA: first Christian satellite broadcast (by Intelsat), from 28th Convention of National Religious Broadcasters.
Congress on the Church's Worldwide Mission, held at Green Lake, WI, USA, sponsored by Conservative Evangelicals.
Puerto Rico: many evangelistic campaigns include Every Creature Crusades (World Gospel Crusades) which reaches over 500,000 homes (78% of whole country).
Mexico: nationwide Evangelism-in-Depth campaign involving over half of country's 10,000 Evangelical churches, 13,000 prayer cells, one million scriptures distributed; numerous other campaigns 1960-85; 1976, EHC distributes one million booklets a month.
European Congress on Evangelism, Amsterdam; 1,064 participants from 36 European nations.
2nd Assembly, Pacific Conference of Churches (PCC), in Davuilevu, Fiji, on 'God's Purpose for His People'.
Ecumenical Pentecost Meeting in Augsburg (Germany) for Catholics and Protestants (June).
World Consultation on Christian Councils, Geneva, with 100 participants representing 66 councils (June); 10 national councils now have Roman Catholic Church as full member, rising by 1985 to 27 national and 2 regional councils.
World Assembly of World Council of Christian Education, Lima, Peru; 1972, WCCE integrated into WCC.
5th Latin American Lutheran Congress, in José de Paz, Argentina, on liberation (August).
International Catechetical Congress, Rome (September).
World Evangelization Strategy Consultation, White Sulphur Springs, Georgia, USA (December).
Jerusalem Conference on Biblical Prophecy (leader C.F.H. Henry) to study implications for Christians of 1948 inauguration of state of Israel.
The future of the Christian world mission, edited by W.J. Danker and W.J. Kang.
Kuwaiti Muslim, S. Kutb, publishes *Islam: the religion of the future*.
NASA proposes Project Cyclops, vast array of listening dishes (radiotelescopes) to scan every one of the 10 million stars within 1,000 light-years.
Intel microprocessor invented: crucial development in microelectronics.
Multiverse (infinite series of intersecting parallel and alternate universes splitting off with every historical decision) proposed, in M. Moorcock's *The War Lord of the Air*; thus a time traveller can enter the past and change history.
Uganda: 500,000 killed in 7-year Amin terror; many martyrs including Anglican archbishop Janani Luwum in 1977.
R. Silverberg writes satirical story 'Good News from the Vatican', in which a robot is elected pope.

1972 Abolition of 'special position' of Catholic Church in Ireland.
USA: American Society of Missiology founded (Catholic/Protestant/Evangelical), with journal *Missiology*.
First deliberate message sent from Earth to stars: USA launches Pioneer 10 unmanned spacecraft with engraved plaque and message, which travels past Jupiter to reach nearest star after 100,000 years.
Publication of 3-volume history of Catholic missions 1622-1972: *Sacrae Congregationis de Propaganda Fide Memoria Rerum*.
EXPLO-72 in Dallas, Texas: 1st Training Congress on Evangelism (Campus Crusade for Christ); 80,000 for one week (June), 200,000 for final day, with 3 telecasts watched by 30 million each, with 11,000 decisions for Christ.
International Catholic Charismatic Renewal Office (ICCRO) founded as International Communications Office in Ann Arbor (USA); first 2 International Leaders' Conferences (1973, 1975) held there; 1976, office transferred to Brussels; 1981 relocates as ICCRO in Rome, organizes 5 worldwide leaders' conferences (4 in Rome, 1 in Dublin), 1985 relocates in Vatican 'moving to the heart of the Church', representing 50 million Catholic pentecostals in over 100 countries.
Consultation on the Gospel and Frontier Peoples, Chicago (December).
1st World Assembly of United Bible Societies, followed by 9th UBS Council Meeting, in Addis Ababa (Ethiopia), on 'Let the Word speak!', with 55 member societies; launches Good News for New Readers (translations for new literates); sets goal of 500 million scriptures distributed annually by 1979; goal passed in 1978.
1st Plenary Assembly, World Catholic Federation for the Biblical Apostolate (WCFBA, founded in 1969), in Vienna, Austria.
Channel Islands: 15-day campaign in Corbière and St Helier sponsored by Movement for World Evangelization (MWE).
Sri Lanka: Morris Cerullo charismatic campaign (140,000 attenders, 80% being Buddhists).
Letter of Paul VI to International Missionary Congress at Lyons (France).
United Nations with its 32 specialized agencies thrusts urgent global problems into world consciousness with a series of 15 major international conferences over next 12 years: on environment, population, industrialization, human settlements, apartheid, desertification, racism, technology transfer, women, children, disabled, communication, disarmament, hunger, energy.
Mouvement International d'Apostolat des Milieux Sociaux Indépendants (MIAMSI) founded by RCs in Rome, dedicated to 'the evangelization of the middle and upper classes'.
Illiac IV, computer costing $40 million, delivered to NASA (USA); dismantled 1981.
First company solely making industrial robots: Unimation.
Two-year major Sahel famine across Africa bordering Sahara desert, due to short-sighted social policies; some half million starve to death.
Burundi: 150,000 Hutus especially intellectuals massacred by Tutsis.
R. Silverberg's story 'When we went to see the End of the World', in which jaded time-traveller tourists visit distant cataclysms and spectacular apocalypses in search of thrills.
G. Zebrowski writes *The Omega Point*: development of a lone survivor of a far-future war, from isolated ego to participant in a galactic mind; also *Macrolife* (1979), in which life at end of cosmic life survives implosion of Universe by lodging in a black hole.
Villach 72 CCC/LWF visitation/consultation program in Austria on theme 'Ambassadors of Reconciliation', with over 200 delegates from 38 countries (November).
Survey report 'Frontier situations for evangelization in Africa' by D.B. Barrett, M.L. Hronek, G.K. Mambo, J.S. Mbiti and M.J. McVeigh (Nairobi), tabulates data, documents and maps situation of 213 Muslim peoples, 411 peoples responsive to Christianity, and 236 unevangel-

ized peoples.
World Conference and Assembly of CWME/WCC, Bangkok, Thailand (3rd Meeting of CWME): 'Salvation Today'; moratorium on foreign missions and missionaries proposed by younger churches, widely accepted 1972-80; report states 'Each generation must evangelize its own generation' (29 December 1972-8 January 1973).

1973 USA nuclear stockpile reaches 15,000 megatons.
Microcomputer revolution begins: Micral system, designed and produced in France by a Vietnamese refugee.
40th International Eucharistic Congress, Melbourne, Australia.
Philippines: 'Christ The Only Way' 3-day total mobilization event, with 55 supporting denominations.
'Total Evangelization in Belgium and Luxembourg' campaign, for 2 years.
Korea: 1st Annual Summer Institute of World Mission (SIWM) in Seoul; by 14th Institute in 1986, some 1,000 students have been trained at East-West Center for overseas service, with goal of 10,000 Asian foreign missionaries by AD 2000.
5th Assembly, East Asia Christian Conference (EACC), in Singapore, on 'Christian Action in the Asian Struggle'; EACC reorganized as Christian Conference of Asia (CCA).
West Germany: 15th German Protestant Kirchentag (Ecumenical Whitsun Assembly), in Dusseldorf on theme 'Not by Bread Alone', with Protestants, Catholics, Orthodox, Anglicans and Free Protestants.
Massive Jehovah's Witnesses' assemblies across world on theme 'Divine Victory' (including Dusseldorf with 67,950 attenders, Munich with 78,792).
Four-year research project by IDOC (Rome) on 'The Future of the Missionary Enterprise', with 20 volumes published from 1973-76; 1975, series of 6 ecumenical seminars on 'The future of the missionary enterprise' at OMSC, Ventnor, USA, 1975-82; 1982, 'The role of North Americans in the future of the missionary enterprise'.
Caribbean Conference of Churches (CCC) founded in Kingston, Jamaica; theme 'The Right Hand of God'.
28 Christian denominations banned by Amin regime in Uganda, resulting in some coming under wing of Anglican Church, others going underground.
Key '73 evangelistic campaign in USA 'to call the continent to Christ', involving 150 denominations including 50% of all 40,000 United Methodist congregations.
Finnish Congress on Evangelism, Helsinki, as followup to Amsterdam 1971; 1,000 participants from 65 churches.
South African Congress on Mission and Evangelism, Durban (13-22 March).
SPRE-E 73: youth rallies at Earl's Court, UK (August).
Largest preaching service in history: 1.1 million at one rally in Seoul, Korea, hear evangelist Billy Graham during 5-day Crusade.
All-Asia Missions Consultation, Seoul, Korea; formation of Asia Missions Association (AMA); 1975 Inaugural Convention publishes 'Seoul Declaration on Christian Mission'.
10th Pentecostal World Conference, Seoul, Korea: 'Anointed to preach'; 3,000 delegates.
Urbana 73: 10th Inter-Varsity Missionary Convention, Chicago, on theme 'Jesus Christ: Lord of the Universe, Hope of the World'; 14,158 attend (December); similar number each successive year up to 1987.
Archbishops' Committee on Evangelism (ACE), Church of England, writes: 'Evangelism is the telling of the facts about Jesus Christ'.
Australian businessman J. Strong writes *The Doomsday Globe*, predicts nuclear destruction for October 1978, based on Bible and Great Pyramids of Egypt.
Ivory Coast: 10 months of evangelistic crusades under Assemblies of God (France) draw 400,000 attenders in Abidjan and other cities, with 15,000 healed, 6,000 baptized into local churches, 68,500 Bibles and NTs distributed.
Genetics: recombinant DNA achieved, unanticipated by most biologists.
OPEC oil crisis and Arab embargo: Organization of Petroleum Exporting Countries (founded 1960) suddenly raises price of oil by up to 500%, causing international chaos, worldwide recession and inflation, and new political power bases.
Global evangelistic campaign launched under auspices of Baptist World Alliance, 'World Mission of Reconciliation through Jesus Christ', by Baptists in many countries.
G. Kimberley writes 'Many Mansions': missionaries on alien planet discover indigenous cave paintings depicting life and crucifixion of Christ.
USA: New International Version of Bible (NIV, NIB) published by New York International Bible Society, the work of 115 Evangelical scholars; NT 1973, OT 1978; sales of Bible 20 million by 1986, expected to reach 30 million by 1989; also 40 million NTs distributed from 1973-1986.
Ecumenical Commission of England and Wales publishes Interim Report 1973 on 'The Church 2000', prepared by working party of bishops, priests and laity of all denominations; central theme completing evangelization by AD 2000.

1974 World Food Conference, Rome, resolves to eradicate world hunger in 10 years: 'Within a decade, no child will go to bed hungry, no family will fear for its next day's bread'; but by 1985, global situation has become far worse.
1.5 million persons worldwide mobilized to pray for Lausanne Congress on World Evangelization later in year.
Construction of first Muslim mosque in Rome sanctioned by Holy See.
1st Plenary Assembly, Federation of Asian Bishops' Conferences (FABC), in Taipei: 'Evangelization in Modern Day Asia' (April).
3rd Assembly of AACC, Lusaka, Zambia: 'Living no longer for ourselves, but for Christ' (May).
Pan-Orthodox Consultation on 'Confessing Christ Today', Cernica, Bucharest (June); report states 'Evangelistic witness is understood to be restricted to the communication of Christ to those who do not consider themselves Christian'.
1st Japan Congress on Evangelism, Kyoto (June).
Iberian Congress on Evangelism, Madrid, Spain (June).
International Congress on World Evangelization (ICOWE), Lausanne, Switzerland, on 'Let the Earth hear His Voice'; 2,700 delegates, from 150 countries, 4,000 total (50% from Third World); produces Lausanne Covenant stating: 'Evangelism itself is the proclamation of the historical, biblical Christ' (July).
EXPLO-74 in Seoul, Korea: 2nd Training Congress on Evangelism (Campus Crusade for Christ); 323,419 residents for one week, evening meetings 800,000 daily, with one rally drawing a new world record of 1.5 million (90% responding to invitation to commitment to Christ); biggest Christian conference in history to date (August).
Holy Year Jubilee for Roman Catholics: Paul VI proclaims 'a new period of evangelization', with full organic unity of all Christians an essential prerequisite: 'Before all men can be restored to the grace of God, communion must be reestablished between those who by faith have acknowledged and accepted Jesus Christ as the Lord of mercy who sets men free'; Holy Year in dioceses across world in 1974, in Rome in 1975.
3rd Ordinary Synod of Bishops in Rome, on 'The Evangelization of the Modern World'; states that 'the promotion of human development forms an integral part of evangelization', closes with statement: 'We wish to confirm once more that the task of evangelizing all people constitutes the essential mission of the Church.'
Roger Garaudy, French marxist, writes *The alternative future: a vision of Christian Marxism.*
8th Baptist Youth World Conference, Portland, Oregon (USA).
1st World Conference of Baptist Men, Hong Kong.
Catholic Charismatic Renewal now has 2,400 prayer groups across world with 350,000 active adult participants (total charismatic community 1,540,000); 30,000 attend USA international annual conferences at Notre Dame, South Bend; by 1987, 10,000 prayer groups in USA.
Pan-American Salvationist Conference on 'Evangelism' convened by Salvation Army general E. Wickberg at Miami Beach, USA (13-22 October); term 'evangelism', previously suspect to Salvationists, now becomes acceptable.
USA: major advances in computing: 1974 Wang word processor, 1975 first USA commercial personal computer (Altair 8800), 1979 VisiCalc electronic spreadsheet software.
LWF Consultation on Proclamation and Human Development, in Nairobi (21-25 October).
Philippines: DAWN (Discipling a Whole Nation) conference; 75 leaders of 4,000 Evangelical churches plan to have 50,000 churches planted by AD 2000, one in every barrio in the country (November); 1985, National Church Growth Strategy Congress with 300 leaders of 12,000 Evangelical churches reaffirms this goal (19-22 February).
L. Biggle writes 'What hath God wrought?': a man wins national lottery prize, claims divinity, establishes new religion based on Christianity and TV quiz shows which then spreads rapidly.
Ecumenical Conference on Science and Technology for Human Development, in Bucharest.
UN General Assembly, 6th Special Session, establishes New International Economic Order (NIEO), demanding that the North (Western world) divest its gains so that the South may develop.
Giant radio telescope at Arecibo (Puerto Rico) beams first human coded message to Great Cluster in Hercules (21,000 light-years away), in hope of reaching distant intelligent extraterrestrials in space.
BISA series (Bishops' Institute for Social Action), sponsored by Federation of Asian Bishops' Conferences (FABC): BISA I, Novaliches, Philippines (March, 1974); BISA II, Tokyo (April, 1975); BISA III, Kuala Lumpur (November, 1975); BISA IV, Manila (March, 1978); BISA V, Baguio, Philippines (May, 1979); BISA VI, Kandy, Sri Lanka (February, 1983).

1975 **Global status:** 64.7 generations after Christ, world is 32.3% Christians (53.5% of them being Whites), 64.9% evangelized; with printed Scriptures available in 1,630 languages.
Foreign missionaries expelled from Cambodia, later from Viet Nam.
Brazil Congress on Evangelism, Rio de Janeiro (January).
4th International Christian Television Festival, Brighton, England (sponsored by WACC and UNDA).
ECCLA III: 3rd Latin American Catholic Charismatic Renewal Leaders Conference; 250 delegates from 25 countries, including 8 bishops; in Aguas Buenas, Puerto Rico (where Catholic pentecostals number

40,000) (January).
International Catholic Charismatic Conference in Rome at feast of Pentecost: 10,000 pilgrims addressed by pope Paul VI in St Peter's Basilica (May).
Cuba Congress on Evangelism (May).
Here's Life, America: 2-year media campaign in 220 major USA cities: 14,000 involved churches, 300,000 trained workers, 10 million homes reached, 179 million in USA exposed to gospel, 870,000 recorded decisions; numerically the largest and densest evangelistic campaign in USA history; goal 'to fulfil the Great Commission in the USA by 1976'.
3rd Consultation of United and Uniting Churches, held in Toronto, Canada (June); 24 united and uniting denominations present from several countries; now regarded as new type of WCF (world confessional family); 1980, total members of all united churches 63,299,000.
Euro-fest '75, in Brussels, largest Christian youth festival ever in Europe; 10,000 attenders (August).
1st Nigeria National Congress on Evangelization, Ile-Ife; 800 participants.
Nairobi International Conference for Renewal, on 'Unity in Christ'; first of series of interdenominational African conferences for charismatics (August).
Pan-Orthodox Consultation (CWME/WCC) on 'Confessing Christ through the liturgical life of the Church today', Echmiadzin, Armenia (September).
World Conference on the Holy Spirit and Holy Land Pilgrimage, Jerusalem (October).
5th International Congress of Christian Physicians (ICCP), Singapore; also previously 1963 Amsterdam, 1966 Oxford, 1969 Oslo, 1972 Toronto.
2nd World Conference on the Holy Spirit, Jerusalem (November).
5th Assembly of WCC, in Nairobi, Kenya: 'Jesus Christ frees and unites', 2,085 participants (850 delegates, 600 press); report on 'Confessing Christ today' states 'We are commissioned to proclaim the Gospel of Christ to the ends of the earth'.
Bible translators at work in over 300 of world's remaining 5,200 languages as yet with no portion of Bible (4% of world's population); Bible revisions and new translations under way in 500 languages (representing 80% of world's population).
400,000 digital computers in world; IBM has 70% of market for the 50,000 largest.
Alleged beginning of Age of Aquarius (other dates proposed: 1962, 1993, 2000, 2023, 2160, 2300).
Tokyo-Yokohama (17.7 million inhabitants) overtakes New York (17.1 million) as world's largest supercity, maintaining its primacy until 1993.
Holy Year attracts 8,370,000 pilgrims to Rome.
Kenya Unreached Peoples Conference, Lenana, Nairobi.
13th Baptist World Congress (BWA), Stockholm, on theme 'New People for a New World—through Christ'; 9,936 delegates from 92 countries.
Continente-75: Latin American mass media campaign under Argentinian evangelist Luis Palau (born 1934), utilizing 56 radio and 100 TV stations in 23 countries, heard or seen by 75 million in all Latin America (part being Nicaragua '75 3-week mission with 200,000 attenders in Managua, and 6,000 decisions); 1978, Palau preaches to over 2 million persons face-to-face, holds that every city should have a citywide crusade 3 times in a generation (once every 10 years); subsequent major Palau crusades include Commonwealth 84, Continente 85, Asia 86.
Project Look Up (PLU) begun by International Christian Broadcasters (USA), planning to reach world via NASA's ATS-6 geostationary satellite to beam TV seminary teaching and lay institutes across world; 1977, begins broadcasts to Puerto Rico; 1979, fizzles out due to inadequate funding, though committees go on meeting until 1987.
India: conclusion of Operation Last Home, 1st Every Home Crusade (EHC) campaign to reach every home in nation by door-to-door evangelism; repeated 1976, 1984, 1986-1994.
Conference on Security and Cooperation in Europe (CSCE), in Helsinki, raises widespread Christian hopes for a new era of peace but these are dashed by 1983.
International Missionary Congress on 'Evangelization and Cultures,' sponsored by Pontifical Urbanian University, Rome; 600 attenders (5-12 October).
Paul VI's Apostolic Exhortation *Evangelii Nuntiandi* published (8 December) as the major Catholic statement on evangelization: 'To evangelize is first of all to bear witness'.
USA: Detroit Conference I of Theology in the Americas, in Detroit; 1980, Detroit Conference II.
Mission '76, 1st Missionary Congress for European Youth (The European Missionary Alliance), in Lausanne.

1976 Guatemala: catastrophic earthquake kills 24,000, 77,000 injured, over 500 Protestant churches destroyed (February).
Since 1917 Revolution in USSR, 60 million (over half Christians) killed directly or indirectly, 40% being executed or killed by communist officials.
First international Islamic World Congress, Karachi, Pakistan; delegates, from 44 countries, call for Muslim governments to close down all Christian missions (April).
Rhodesia: national Congress on Evangelism in Context (May).
First Latin American Amerindian in history consecrated as bishop: Mario Marino (born 1933), a Mataco in Argentina (Anglican).
China: 1.4 million victims of widespread catastrophic earthquakes; 655,237 killed in Tientsin-Tangshan alone.
World Congress of Fundamentalists: first 8-day USA-dominated meeting in Edinburgh; 2,000 in attendance.
Pasadena, USA: founding of US Center for World Mission, for Conservation Evangelicals.
Southern Baptist Convention USA, meeting in Norfolk, VA, adopts plans for remainder of century to implement world evangelization through strategy Bold Mission Thrust.
Australia: Congress on World Missions and Evangelism (May).
3rd Conference, International Association for Mission Studies (IAMS), San José, Costa Rica, on 'Tradition and Reconstruction in Mission' (25-30 July).
41st International Eucharistic Congress, Philadelphia, USA; one million Catholics participate (August).
11th Pentecostal World Conference, Albert Hall, London: 'The Spirit of Truth'.
Anglican Consultative Council (ACC-3) meets in Trinidad, reformulates Archbishops' definition of 1918 as 'Evangelism is the faithful proclamation of the Gospel'.
AMEN (American Military Evangelizing Nations) formed, by USA denomination Churches of Christ, for lay evangelism by US armed forces around world.
1st Chinese Congress on World Evangelization (CCOWE), Hong Kong, on 'Vision and Mission', with 1,600 participants from over 20 countries (August); CCCOWE (Chinese Coordination Centre of World Evangelism) set up in Hong Kong (October).
National Seminar on Evangelism in Papua New Guinea and the Solomon Islands, sponsored by Melanesian Council of Churches, Evangelical Alliance of the South Pacific Islands, and Roman Catholic Church.
Launching of spacecraft Helios 3, now in orbit around sun at 240,000 km per hour (fastest man-made object in existence).
Northern Europe Conference on Evangelization, Belgium (September).
Japan Multimedia Evangelism Project (JMEP), in Hokkaido.
Genesis Project is begun to translate whole Bible onto film; by 1986, 33 films completed.
Taiwan: Roman Catholic 2-year TV program 'The Most Unforgettable Story' draws 1.2 million viewers every week for over a year.
Association for the Evangelization of Austria formed.
Bangladesh Congress on Evangelism, in Dacca.
1st Missionary Congress for European Youth (Mission '76), organized by TEMA (The European Missionary Association); leads on to Mission '80, Mission '83 (Lausanne), Mission '87 (Utrecht; theme 'I chose You'); average participants 7,000.
India: Every Home Crusade begins its second nationwide home canvass, Project Calvary, aiming to deliver booklets to every home in India by 1981.
India: Here's Life, Kerala (run by CCCI) saturates whole of Kerala state, reaching 99% of 2,700,000 homes, 9,900,352 persons evangelized, 1,850,982 decisions for Christ (1,470,954 through person-to-person presentations, 380,028 at public meetings; of total, 10% being formerly Hindu or Muslim).
Canada: new type of evangelistic crusade, Vancouver Reachout, with L. Ford: 200 churches, 75,000 homes contacted, 24,000 attenders, 450 enquirers.
Conference of Lutheran Churches in Europe, Liebfrauenberg, France (September).
Annual Plenary Assembly, Sacred Congregation for the Evangelization of Peoples, in Rome, on theme 'Popular Religion', with 25 cardinals, 15 bishops and many other delegates (19-22 October).
LWF North/Southeast Asia Church Leaders' Consultation, in Manila (October).
Ecumenical Association of Third World Theologians (EATWOT) holds first General Meeting, Dar es Salaam, Tanzania, under name Ecumenical Dialogue of Third World Theologians; 1977 Accra (African theologians), 1979 Sri Lanka (Asian theologians), 1980 São Paulo (Latin American theologians), 1981 New Delhi (Third World theologians), 1983 Hamburg and Geneva.
1st Pan-Orthodox Preconciliar Conference, Chambesy, Switzerland (November).
Asian Conference on Religion and Peace, sponsored by FABC; in Singapore, on 'Peace through Religion' (November).
Pan-African Christian Leadership Assembly (PACLA), in Nairobi; 700 delegates (December).
Christmas: over 1.3 billion people hear pope Paul VI over radio/TV.
3rd Assembly, Pacific Conference of Churches (PCC), in Port Moresby, Papua, on theme 'God's Mission in the changing Pacific society'.
C.Q. Yarbro's novel *Time of the Fourth Horseman* envisages conspiracy of doctors who deliberately spread plague to end world's overpopulation.
P.E. Erdman writes scenario, *The crash of '79*, in which in 1979 Mohammad Reza (1919-1980) shah of Iran attempts to seize Gulf and its oil, precipitates nuclear war; entire world's economy crashes catastrophically in greatest economic disaster in history; in reality, however, shah is

overthrown in 1979 by ayatollah Khomeini; also writes *The last days of America* (1981); and in 1987, *The panic of '89* envisaging international terrorism and massive loan defaults.

3rd All Asia Lutheran Conference, in Singapore (November-December).

Venezuela: Marcha Evangelistica inaugurated by Baptists, 1978 spreads to Ecuador, Chile, Bolivia; 1980 Movimiento Discipular causes country's 6,000 Baptists to set goal of 1 million Venezuelan Baptists in 4,000 churches by AD 2000 (1986 total: 14,000 in 130 churches); 1985, Congreso de Misión Mundial, in Caracas with 200 present from 8 countries.

1977 ECCLA V, 5th Latin American Catholic Charismatic Renewal Leaders Conference, in Caracas, Venezuela; leaders from almost all Latin American countries (January).

All-India Congress on Mission and Evangelization (AICOME), Devlali, for indigenous missions, with 400 leaders present (January).

Asian Colloquium on New Ministries in the Church, sponsored by FABC; in Hong Kong (February).

Latin American Lutheran Consultation, in São Leopoldo, Brazil (January).

All Africa Lutheran Consultation, in Gaborone, Botswana (February).

Guatemala: Indian Congress on World Evangelization (14-18 February); also in 1978, 1980.

2nd National Evangelical Anglican Congress, Nottingham University, UK (April), following 1st Congress at Keele University in 1967.

LCWE Consultation on the Homogeneous Unit Principle, Pasadena, USA (May).

WCC Consultation on the Church and the Jewish People, Jerusalem (June).

Ghana Congress on Evangelism (July).

1st Conference on the Charismatic Renewal in the Christian Churches; ecumenical, at last embracing all pentecostal traditions; on theme 'Jesus is Lord'; in Kansas City, USA; 59,000 present (July); but after this ecumenical climax, charismatic conferences revert to monodenominational status (15,000 Lutheran charismatics each year in Minneapolis, 10,000 RCs in Notre Dame, et alii).

Romania: catastrophic earthquake destroys or damages 1,200 churches.

4th Ordinary Synod of Bishops in Rome, on 'Catechetics in Our Time', dealing with evangelization of children and youth (September).

Pan-Orthodox Consultation (CWME) on 'The role and the place of the Bible in the liturgical and spiritual life of the Orthodox Church', Prague (September); also Consultation on 'The Ecumenical nature of the Orthodox witness', in New Valamo, Finland (September).

World Conference on Audio-Visuals and Evangelization, Munich (November).

Here's Life, World (saturation and total mobilization evangelization campaign), organized by Campus Crusade for Christ, launched in 100 countries, on every continent, with announced goal 'to fulfil the Great Commission in the whole world by the end of 1980'.

500 million hear or see one-hour radio/TV gospel service broadcast from Jerusalem on Christmas Eve in 7 languages simultaneously (Pentecostal preacher Rex Humbard).

Burma: 6,200 converts baptized by Kachin Baptist Convention at largest single baptismal service in recent Christian history.

6th Assembly, Christian Conference of Asia (CCA), in Penang, Malaysia, on theme 'Jesus Christ in Asian suffering and hope'.

WCC Theological Consultation on Dialogue in Community, in Chiang Mai, Thailand.

2nd Assembly, Caribbean Conference of Churches (CCC), in Georgetown, Guyana, on theme 'Working together with Christ'.

Futurism adopts dogma 'Almost anything can be accomplished in 20 years'—Edward Cornish, president of World Future Society.

Development of ultrasonic bomb which destablizes human brain by destroying a few cells and so turns a whole city's population into raving imbeciles, without damaging property.

New RC missionary congregations formed: in Tanzania, Evangelizing Sisters of Mary; and in Hong Kong, Sisters Announcers of the Lord.

CB (Citizens Band) 2-way radio expands in USA from 200,000 radios (1973) to 10 million (1975) to 20 million (1977) to 30 million (1984).

417.5 million telephones in world (162 million in USA alone, placing 467 million local calls, and 38.8 million long-distance calls, every day).

Conference of World Confessional Families (WCFs) convenes in Rome for first time.

Germany: 17th Protestant Kirchentag, with related Missio Berlin 77 yearlong evangelistic campaign.

250,000 word processors in use in USA offices.

Ethiopia: 90,000 killed in Red Terror 1977-80 including emperor Haile Selassie, patriarch Theofilus and numerous bishops and clergy.

Greece: Orthodox charismatics organize Crusade for Christ in Athens.

Philippines: film evangelism under Philippines Action International Ministries; 143,797 attenders in year, with 8,262 decisions for Christ.

6th Assembly, Lutheran World Federation (LWF), Dar es Salaam (Tanzania), on 'In Christ a New Community'.

Thailand: Every Home Crusade (EHC/WLC) completes Operation Torch with 95% nationwide saturation achieved; 5,975,998 homes reached (77% of total), 38,037 written responses for Christ recorded.

1st Worldwide Chinese Church Growth Seminar (Chinese Coordinating Center of World Evangelism, CCCOWE), near Taipei, with over 400 delegates (November).

1st Latin American Missionary Congress (COMLA-1), in Torreon, Mexico, on 'The Church, the Universal Sacrament of Salvation' (20-23 November).

World's most successful movie 'Star Wars' describes rebellion in totalitarian galactic empire in BC 60 million.

Pan African Conference of Third World Theologians (EATWOT-2), in Accra, Ghana, on 'Emerging themes in African theology' (December).

1978 World Mission 1978-1981 begun as World Methodist Council's 4-year plan of global evangelism.

LCWE Consultation on Gospel and Culture, Willowbank, Bermuda (January).

Congress on Evangelism for Malaysia and Singapore (COEMAS); 300 leaders (April).

2nd World Conference of Baptist Men, Indianapolis, USA (April).

International Conference on the Charismatic Renewal in the Catholic Church, in Dublin: 'You shall be My Witnesses'; 15,000 participants, led by L.-J. Suenens cardinal primate of Belgium (June).

8th International Convention on Missionary Medicine, Wheaton, USA (June).

9th Baptist Youth World Conference, Manila, Philippines (July).

BIMA series (Bishops' Institute for the Missionary Apostolate), sponsored by FABC: BIMA I, Baguio City, Philippines (July, 1978); BIMA II, Kerala, India, on 'The Christian community as the bearer of the Good News' (November, 1978); BIMA III, Changhua, Taiwan (August, 1982).

11th Lambeth Conference, Canterbury, England: 'Today's church in today's world'; 420 Anglican bishops (July-August).

2nd Nigeria National Congress on Evangelization, Ile-Ife; 1,000 participants (August).

4th Conference, International Association for Mission Studies (IAMS), Maryknoll, New York, on theme 'Credibility and Spirituality in Mission' (20-28 August).

Holy Shroud of Turin (Italy) exposed for 43 days (27 August-8 October) ('Exposition of the Holy Shroud'), to 3.3 million pilgrims; followed by Sindonological Conference.

Rhodesia: National Christian Leadership Assembly (NACLA), held in Bulawayo, with 300 delegates (September).

Death of pope Paul VI; succeeded by an Italian champion of the Church of the Poor, Albino Luciani (born 1912), who as John Paul I instigates revolutionary changes over Vatican finances; on his alleged murder 34 days later, cardinals elect a Pole, first non-Italian for 450 years: John Paul II (born 1920), 264th Pope of Rome (110th since 1143, on St Malachy's reckoning), who in 1981 himself survives assassination attempt.

4th Latin American Protestant Conference (CELA IV) at Oaxtepec, Mexico, with 340 delegates representing 110 denominations (September); UNELAM proposes creation of Latin American Council of Churches (in formation) (CLAI); 1982, CLAI officially constituted at Lima, Peru.

International convention series of Jehovah's Witnesses produce 100 'Victorious Faith' assemblies in 45 countries, averaging 25,000 attenders at each.

World Congress of Mission and Migration, Rome (October).

New World Information Order (NWIO) proclaimed by UNESCO in 'Mass Media Declaration' at 21st General Conference, denouncing cultural imperialism and informatics (transborder data flow, TDF).

Ectogenesis ('test-tube babies') achieved, in England (fertilizing of human eggs outside the body).

5.85% of world's total electricity generating power comes from nuclear power stations.

Minerals: over next 30 years, world will consume 3.5 times volume of minerals (copper, bauxite, zinc, nickel, lead, iron ore, petroleum, gas, coal, etc) that it has used up since dawn of civilization.

World export trade rises from $246 billion in 1969 to $1,190 billion in 1978.

Third-World arms imports of major weapons soar from $1.4 billion in 1961 to $9.4 billion in 1978.

Science television 13-part series 'Cosmos' (by astronomer C. Sagan) seen in 60 countries by 140 million people (5.4% of Earth's adult population).

Scandinavia: Skandia '78 evangelistic campaign on radio/TV for Norway, Sweden et alia.

Panama: Africa-Panama Crusade (Mission '78), with evangelists from Africa; 90 supporting churches, 15,000 attenders, 700 decisions.

Colombia: 200,000 decisions for Christ registered during 500,000-pilgrim Easter climb up Hill of the Three Crosses, during Here's Life Cali campaign.

2nd Plenary Assembly, World Catholic Federation for the Biblical Apostolate (WCFBA), in Malta, on theme 'Biblical Spirituality and Biblical Catechesis'.

North American Conference on Muslim Evangelization, Glen Eyrie, USA; 150 participants (October).

Malcolm Muggeridge's lectures *Christ and the media* portray Jesus' '4th Temptation' by Satan offering him prime time on Rome television to preach his gospel to the entire world; offer turned down.

All Asia Lutheran Seminar on Mission, in Hong Kong.

All African Lutheran Consultation on Christian Theology and Christian Education in the African Context, in Gaborone, Botswana (October).

Consultation on Church and Service, in Chania, Crete; 'An Orthodox approach to diaconia' (November).
LWF Consultation for Churches in North America, the Nordic Countries and FR Germany, at Loccum; first specifically designed for 'northern churches' (November-December).
Organization of African Independent Churches (OAIC) inaugurated at Cairo conference, representing 25 million church members from Black indigenous churches throughout Africa (November); 1982, 2nd OAIC Conference, in Nairobi.
1st Norwegian Congress on World Evangelization (related to LCWE), followed about every 2 years by Danvik National Conferences on Evangelization, with 140 church leaders, held in Drammen (Norway) in 1980, 1981, 1982, 1984, 1986.
7th General Chapter, Catholic Foreign Mission Society of America (Maryknoll) issues 'Statement of Mission Vision': 'Our particular task gives special emphasis to the evangelization of the poor, of cultures and of structures'.
Asian Leadership Conference on Evangelism (ALCOE), Singapore: 'Together obeying Christ for Asia's harvest'; 350 leaders from 20 Asian countries (November).
Guyana: mass suicide-murder of 925 followers of People's Temple (90% USA Blacks) at Jonestown in jungle.
Symposium on Mission and Evangelization of Lutheran Churches in Latin America, in Porto Alegre, Brazil (29-31 May).
7th International Lutheran Conference on the Holy Spirit, Minneapolis; 25,000 participants including Belgian cardinal L.-J. Suenens.
Britain: Nationwide Initiative in Evangelism (NIE) launched by all churches (Anglican, Roman Catholic, Ecumenical, Evangelical, Black) as interdenominational program 'to stimulate intelligent and effective evangelism by all Christians'.
10th Mennonite World Conference, Wichita, KS, USA.

1979 Asian Theological Conference (EATWOT-3), in Sri Lanka, on 'Asia's struggle for full humanity' (January).
3rd General Conference of CELAM, in Puebla, Mexico: 'Evangelization in Latin America now and in the Future' (27 January-13 February).
USA: Colloquium on the Church in Future Society, sponsored by Lutheran Brotherhood (January).
Joint Christian Ministry in West Africa (JCMWA: 8 churches from West Africa, 6 European churches and agencies including Anglican CMS), as a new ecumenical and global model for cooperative mission and evangelism, holds consultation in Dakar (January).
West Germany: Conference on 'Unreached Peoples', sponsored by World Evangelical Fellowship, at Bad Liebenzell (January).
Caribbean Lutheran Conference, in St Thomas, US Virgin Islands (30 January-2 February).
LWF Consultation on Global Partnership in Mission in Asia, in Manila (March).
Awesome astronomical phenomenon seen by scientists: on 5 March, the most intense burst of hard x-rays and gamma rays ever observed, a truly enormous explosion lasting only a few seconds, outshining the whole Universe in gamma rays; from a neutron star (supernova remnant) in Large Magellanic Cloud at 180,000 light-years' distance.
National Missionary Congress, Irish Missionary Union, at Knock, with nearly 400 Catholic missioners from every continent; theme 'A New Missionary Era' emerges (April).
Pan-Orthodox Consultation on 'The place of the monastic life within the witness of the Church today' at Amba Bishoy monastery, Egypt (April-May).
ACC-4: 4th Meeting, Anglican Consultative Council, London, Ontario, Canada (8-18 May).
LWF Consultation on Theological Education for the Service of the Church in a Secular Society, in Bratislava (May).
WCC Conference on Faith, Science and the Future, on 'Faith and Science in an Unjust World', at MIT, Cambridge, MA (USA), with over 900 participants (12-24 July).
South African Christian Leadership Assembly (SACLA), Pretoria (July).
Over 10,000 pilgrims attend International Charismatic Pilgrimage to Lourdes on shrine's 100th anniversary (July).
12th Pentecostal World Conference, in Vancouver, Canada: 'The Holy Spirit in the Last Days' (October).
All-India Conference on Evangelical Social Action (AICOESA), in Madras, India (2-5 October).
BIRA series (Bishops' Institute of Interreligious Affairs) sponsored by FABC: BIRA I, Bangkok (October, 1979); BIRA II, Kuala Lumpur (November, 1979); BIRA III, Cochin, India (Hindu-Catholic dialogue, 1981).
2nd Latin American Congress on Evangelization (CLADE II), Huampani, Lima, Peru (October); sponsored by Latin American Theological Fraternity (FTL), promoting Lausanne Covenant but from critical perspective; 266 delegates from 39 denominations in 21 countries.
Canadian Congress on World Evangelization.
8th Assembly, Conference of European Churches (CEC), in Crete, on 'Alive to the World in the Power of the Holy Spirit'.
Asiatic New Religions (New Religious Movements) continue to grow rapidly, with 94 million adherents growing by 2 million a year.
Overthrow of shah Mohammad Reza of Iran by ayatollah Khomeini; emergence of neo-fundamentalist militaristic Islam as a global power.
Conservative Baptist historian T.P. Weber publishes *Living in the shadow of the Second Coming: American Premillennialism, 1875-1925*.
Apostolic Exhortation *Catechesi Tradendae* on 'Catechesis in our time' promulgated by pope John Paul II (16 October).
Quantum physics seen as a new religion by speculative physicists; possibility raised of branching probability universes: an infinite series of real, solid universes fitted into the probability gaps between the quantum events of our own Universe.
'The Source' network (based on USA) founded as world's first popular mass database accessible to personal computers by telephone, which assists users to set up own networks.
Hi-Ovis experimental home service project in Japan: central computer scans every home once every 7 seconds, checking all alarm systems and supplying needs and requests.
Venezuelan National Congress on Evangelization, Caracas (November).
Vast increase in short-term missionary personnel from Western world, including 17,358 young persons from 250 USA agencies.
International Mission Congress (FABC and SC Propaganda), in Manila, on 'Towards a New Age in Mission: the Good News of the Kingdom to the Peoples of Asia' (2-7 December).
USA Evangelical foreign mission leaders issue call for '120,000 missionaries by the year 2000' in order to reach unreached peoples and establish 'A church for every people by AD 2000'.
USA: Angel-I/Angel-II/Angel-III Project to blanket Earth with gospel broadcasts proposed by NRB and WEF: 3 satellites in geostationary orbit filling roles of 3 angels of Revelation 14:6-11, each covering a third of Earth's surface, fulfilling Matthew 24:14 'for a witness unto all nations'; by 1983 proposal passes into oblivion, though use of satellites for USA Christian TV grows.
Computer-aided scripture translation by SIL (Wycliffe) includes program to compile and print scripture concordances for each new language completed; 1984, Bible Society (UK) produces computer concordance of Good News Bible with program applicable also to any language's Bible translation.
USA: New King James Version of Bible published, update of KJV using Textus Receptus by 130 Evangelical scholars: NT 1979, Bible 1982.
Assembly on Dialogue with Islam (Muslim/Catholic) in Kuala Lumpur, Malaysia.
Incidents of international terrorism increase worldwide from 1,550 in 1979, to 1,709 in 1980, to 2,387 in 1981.
Mission '80, 2nd Missionary Congress for European Youth (TEMA, The European Missionary Alliance), in Lausanne, with 3,000 participants.

1980 **Global status:** 64.9 generations after Christ, world is 32.2% Christians (50.5% of them being Whites), 68.4% evangelized; with printed Scriptures available in 1,811 languages.
Soviet Union becomes world's leading military power, replacing earlier goal of economic and ideological supremacy by the pursuit of imperial power, with by 1980 completely novel boldness, efficiency, and intervention capabilities; cost of armed forces 14% of Soviet GNP, but total cost of military empire over 45% of GNP.
USA (now world's 2nd-greatest military power) possesses 9,000 missile warheads and bombs continuously targeted on cities, industrial centers, military installations and major infrastructures of USSR.
60,000 sophisticated industrial robots in Japan (77,000 one year later, 70% of world's total), 3,000 in USA, 105 in Britain.
Sending messages into the past proposed: in physicist Gregory Benford's scenario *Timescape*, doomed inhabitants of a future Earth beam tachyonic (faster-than-light) signals backwards in time to warn present-day Earth-dwellers about imminent doom.
International arms trade climbs from $300 million annually in 1955 to $20 billion by 1980.
Africa: Christians number 203,491,000 in 59 countries, increasing at 6 million a year; African indigenous churches (AICs) number some 6,730 separate denominations with 27,438,000 adherents in 43 African countries.
4th International Ecumenical Congress of Theology (EATWOT-4), in São Paulo (Brazil) with 180 participants, convened by Ecumenical Association of Third World Theologians, on 'Ecclesiology of the popular Christian communities' (20 February-2 March).
Pope John Paul II undertakes global apostolic travels over last 2 years: Mexico, Poland, Ireland, USA, Africa, Brazil et alia; by February 1986, makes 29 official foreign pilgrimages as pope.
LCWE International Consultation on Simple Life-Style, Hoddesden, UK (March).
7th General Assembly, World Evangelical Fellowship, High Leigh, UK; delegates from 50 countries (March).
Stuttgart Congress on World Evangelization, Germany (April).
All Africa Lutheran Consultation on Christian Theology and Strategy for Mission, in Monrovia (April), interrupted by bloody military coup.
UK: National Pastoral Congress of England and Wales (Roman Catholic), Liverpool; 2,100 elected delegates (May).
1st World Missionary Conference on Mission and Evangelism (4th Meeting

of CWME/WCC), in Melbourne, Australia, with title 'Your Kingdom come' and theme 'Good News to the Poor'; 650 delegates representing 300 churches from 100 countries; 'The proclamation of the Gospel to the whole world remains an urgent obligation of all Christians' (12-24 May).

LCWE Consultation on World Evangelization (COWE) in Pattaya, Bangkok: 'How shall they hear?'; 875 delegates from 87 countries; 17 miniconsultations (16-27 June).

1st Global Conference on the Future (3rd General Assembly, World Future Society), Toronto, on theme 'Through the '80s: thinking globally, acting locally'; with 5,000 delegates from over 45 countries (July).

14th Baptist World Congress (BWA), on 'Christ's Presence through the Spirit', Toronto, with over 20,000 attenders from 93 countries (July).

6th Latin American Lutheran Congress, in Bogota, on theme 'Our Faith and Our Mission in Latin America', with 47 delegates (August).

USA: Detroit Conference II of Theology in the Americas, in Detroit (August).

USA: 8th Annual Meeting, American Society of Missiology (ASM), in Wheaton (IL), on theme 'World Evangelization Today: Convergence or Divergence?' (22-24 August).

Conference of Lutheran Churches in Europe, in Tallinn, Estonia, USSR, on 'Proclamation Today' (6-13 September).

Pan-Orthodox Consultation (CWME) on 'Preaching and teaching the Christian faith today' at Zica monastery, Yugoslavia (September).

10th United Bible Societies Council Meeting, Chiang Mai (Thailand), with 68 member societies, on theme 'God's Word: open for all' (September); plan for decade to provide by 1990 common Bible translations in every language with over 1 million literates.

World Evangelization Crusade (Here's Life, Korea), Seoul; 16,500,000 attendances, including largest single meeting in Christian history to date (2.7 million).

5th Ordinary Synod of Bishops in Rome, on the Christian family, with disquiet voiced on nonfulfillment of collegial promise of synods; also 2 Special Synods of Bishops, to deal with problems of (a) conservative/liberal rift in Dutch hierarchy, and (b) Ukrainian Catholic Church (with a second Synod on this latter subject in 1985).

United States Festival of World Evangelization; 50,000 participants (September).

Britain: Assembly on Evangelism, sponsored by NIE (Nationwide Initiative in Evangelism), in Nottingham; 700 attenders (22-27 September).

International Congress on Evangelization and Atheism, Pontifical Urbanian University, Rome (October).

China: Three-Self Patriotic Movement (TSPM) resuscitated after 13-year inactivity, holds 3rd National Conference in Nanjing, with 176 delegates; new pastoral body created, China Christian Council (CCC) (October).

1st World Consultation on Frontier Missions (WCFM), Edinburgh, organized by US Center for World Mission: 'A Church for every People by the Year 2000'; 270 delegates (October).

World Consultation on 'Churches Responding to Racism in the 1980s', at Noordwijkerhout, Netherlands.

Episcopal churches with disputed apostolic succession number 280 in 80 countries, 130 being miniscule autocephalous Catholic churches under 700 bishops-at-large (episcopi vagantes).

Telecommunications: AT&T/Bell survey calculates total telephones in world (1 January 1980) at 472,136,789, with nearly a million telex machines.

In 80 years, annual circulation of complete Bibles in all languages has risen from 5.4 million in 1900 to 36.8 million by 1980.

Christian broadcasting expands from origin in 1921 to global force heard or seen regularly by 23% of world's population.

Urban dwellers rise from 14.4% of world in 1900 to 37.4% (1970), 41.1% (1980), 43.3% (1985), increasing at a million a week.

Total new book titles published each year increase from 269,000 (1955) to 521,000 (1970) to 726,500 (1980); total scientific journals increase every 50 years by factor of 10: from 10 journals in 1750 to 100 (1800) to 1,000 (1850), 10,000 (1900), 100,000 (1950), to a projected total of 1 million titles by AD 2000.

Scientists and engineers engaged in R&D (research and development) increase from (1970) 2,608,100 to (1980) 3,756,100, with annual expenditure increasing from (in 1930) US$1 billion (less than 0.1% of GWP), to (1965) $50 billion (2%), to (1970) $62.1 billion, to (1980) $207.8 billion (2%), of which only 6.0% is spent in developing countries, to (AD 2000) a projected $650 billion (4%), and (by AD 2500) to 15%.

Basic ecclesial communities (*comunidades de base*, grassroots Christian groupings) expand to 200,000 in Latin America.

2nd Norwegian Congress on World Evangelization, in Drammen (November).

World's 10 largest cities: Tokyo/Yokohama 17,670,000, New York/NENJ 15,610,000, Mexico City 14,470,000, São Paulo 12,820,000, Shanghai 11,750,000, London 10,310,000, Buenos Aires 10,060,000, Calcutta 9,540,000, Los Angeles/Long Beach 9,530,000, Rhein-Ruhr 9,300,000.

USA: 'Washington for Jesus 1980' rally brings out 500,000 charismatics and evangelicals.

Social potential movement begins, demonstrating what the human race can do together (Teilhard de Chardin, Sri Aurobindo, A.C. Clarke, Buckminster Fuller, Julian Huxley, et alii); envisages a eupsychian society (composed of self-actualizing people).

24th Annual Conference of Secretaries of Christian World Communions (CWCs), Geneva; 1957-1974 Geneva; 1976 London; 1977 Rome; 1981-1982 Geneva; 1983 (27th) Sofia; 1984 (28th) Geneva; 1985 (29th) Windsor, UK.

1st Asian Leaders Conference, Catholic Charismatic Renewal (ICCRO), on 'Feed My Sheep', Manila.

USA: new generation of charismatic TV evangelists arises, including Oral Roberts (who began Pentecostal TV preaching in 1953) and son Richard, Pat Robertson, Rex Humbard, Jimmy Swaggart, James Robison, Kenneth Copeland, Paul Crouch, Jim Bakker, et alii.

China: 3rd National Conference, Association of Patriotic Catholics, Beijing; forms Church Affairs Commission, and National Bishops' Conference; Catholics in China decrease from 3 million (1949) to 500,000 (1974), then increase to 6 million (1985).

FR Germany: Missionary Year 1980, a coordinated effort to mobilize pastors and congregations of regional churches.

Lausanne Consultation for Jewish Evangelism (LCJE) formed at Pattaya (Thailand) by 14 Jewish-Christian groups.

1981 Asian Lutheran Church Leaders' Conference, in Hong Kong (February).

SEDOS Research Seminar on 'Future of Mission', Rome, with representatives of 45 Catholic missionary institutes from 6 continents; produces 'an agenda for future planning, study and research in mission' (8-19 March).

International Leaders Conference, Catholic Charismatic Renewal (ICCRO) in Rome, addressed by pope John Paul II (May).

Orthodox Consultation on 'Orthodox involvement in the World Council of Churches', Sofia, Bulgaria (23-31 May).

2nd Chinese Congress on World Evangelization (CCOWE), on 'Life and Ministry', with over 1,500 church leaders, Singapore (June).

UBS Common Language translations now available: 107 Bibles, 136 New Testaments.

Planetary Initiative for the World We Choose (UN-related) set up 'to work for a new and unified world order' of New Age socialism; recognized as part of international New Age Movement with network of thousands of organizations and hundreds of millions of members, proliferating in Western world at astounding rate, expecting a new evolutionary development, a quantum leap in evolution towards Point Omega, to Homo Noeticus (Intellectual Man), a new and higher form of humanity.

Supercomputers emerge (Cray-1, Cyber 205) capable of carrying out over 100 million operations per second; total in use, 150 by 1985.

Worldwide telecommunications network is now largest machine in the world, with 480 million telephones, 1.2 million telex terminals, data networks and other special systems.

USA places or receives annually 265 million overseas telephone calls, most by satellite, rising to 370 million by 1983.

American Festival of Evangelism, Kansas City; 14,500 participants including 8,000 pastors, evangelists and church leaders; 200 seminars on evangelism, discipling, and ministry (July).

3rd Norwegian Congress on World Evangelization.

3rd Nigeria National Congress on Evangelism (August).

Delhi Conference of Theology (EATWOT-5), in New Delhi, on 'The irruption of the Third World: challenge to theology' (17-29 August).

August: one year after assembling development team, IBM enters personal computer market; spends $36 million on advertising it; by July 1983 has captured 21% of the $7.5 billion US market for personal computers; 40% of worldwide market for computers, produces 65% of all mainframes; 1982—sells 200,000 PCs, 1983—sells 800,000.

4th Assembly, Pacific Conference of Churches (PCC), in Nuku'alofa, Tonga, on 'The challenge of the '80s and the Pacific churches'.

7th Assembly, Christian Conference of Asia (CCA), in Bangalore, India, on 'Life in Christ with People'.

4th General Assembly of AACC, Nairobi: 'Following the Light of Jesus Christ'; 370 delegates from 95 denominations (August); by 1975, AACC has 114 member churches and associated councils in 33 countries.

World's largest banks: (1) Credit Agricole de France (assets of $105 billion), (2) Bank of America.

Total artificial Earth satellites launched since 1957: 2,725 (70% for military purposes).

Total nuclear explosions since 1945: 1,321 (551 above ground).

Broadcasting: radio receivers increase from 535 million (1965) to 1,320 million (1981) or 293 per thousand people; TV receivers from 186 million (1965) to 546 million (1981) or 121 per thousand.

Human knowledge is now expanding at rate of 200 million words per hour (1,750 billion words per year).

Online bibliographic databases total over 190, with 40 million unique references (books, articles) increasing by 6 million a year; equals 50% of mankind's collective memory.

14th World Methodist Conference meets in Hawaii, endorses WMC's World Evangelism Committee's Continuing Plan for the Mission to the 80s (Decade of Evangelism), founds Institute for World Evangelism

(Atlanta, USA) which holds seminars around world.

Massive increases in business paperwork produced in USA, from 72 billion pieces of office documents in 1981, to a projected 250 billion in 1991 (50% electronic), to 1 trillion by 2000 (93% generated in digital form).

World Conference of Religions held in Cochin, India, with theme 'Religions and Man'; Christians, Hindus, Buddhists, Muslims, Sikhs, Jains, Jews and Baha'is present.

Muslim-Christian dialogue on 'Mysticism in Christianity and in Islam', in diocese of Ajmer (India) under auspices of Catholic Bishops' Conference of India.

Operation Pearl, largest Bible-smuggling operation ever, organized by Open Doors: 200 tons of Bibles illegally landed by barge off Swatow, China, then taken away by 20,000 Chinese Christians.

South Korea: Roman Catholic project 'Year of Evangelization of your Neighbour' in all parishes results in 59% increase in annual baptisms; 57,535 catechumens, 71,005 young people in correspondence courses; slogan 'Two Million by 1984'.

West Germany: large evangelistic rallies continue annually, with huge youth attendance; alternating between Protestant Kirchentagen—1981 Hamburg ('Be ye reconciled to God'), 1983 Nuremburg, 1985 Dusseldorf (130,000 enrolled for 4-day period, 400,000 attenders)—and RC Katholikentagen at Munich and Cologne (1984, et alia); since 1981 East Germans once again permitted to attend.

UK: Evangelical Missionary Alliance sponsors conference on 'Reaching Unreached Peoples: breaking new ground in areas of neglect', at High Leigh, Hertford (November).

4th Consultation of United and Uniting Churches, under WCC sponsorship, held in Colombo, Sri Lanka, on theme 'Growing towards consensus and commitment', with Protestant, Roman Catholic and Orthodox participation (November).

International Consultation on 'The Community of Women and Men in the Church', in Sheffield, UK.

3rd Assembly, Caribbean Conference of Churches, in Willemstad, Curaçao, Netherlands Antilles, on theme 'For thine is the kingdom, the power and the glory'.

LWF/DCC Working Party on Ministry to Migrants in Europe, with its 15 million migrant laborers (5 million in West Germany).

China: Protestant churches mushroom spectacularly from 2 open TSPM churches in 1979 to 3,400 open TSPM churches (parishes with central building) by 1985; and total Christian community of all churches (TSPM, RC, independent) from 2 million to 52 million in 6 years.

1982 'Pentecost over Europe', European ecumenical charismatic congress, at Strasbourg (France); 20,000 attenders, 80% RCs and organized by RCs (held over Pentecost).

5th Conference, International Association for Mission Studies (IAMS), Bangalore, India, on theme 'Christ's Mission to the Multitudes: Salvation, Suffering and Struggle' (4-9 January).

Brazilian National Congress on Evangelization: Commission on Evangelization formed; yearly conferences from 1985-1991 planned and organized.

American Leprosy Missions announces 13-point plan to eradicate Hansen's Disease (leprosy) and to cure world's 11,500,000 lepers by AD 2006; European leprosy agencies demur; 1984, plan abandoned, president and staff resign.

German Association of Evangelical Missions meets on theme 'Hidden Peoples' (February).

1st Conference of Evangelical Mission Theologians from the Two-Thirds World, Bangkok (March); LCWE-sponsored but with critical stance.

Consultation of Evangelicals in Latin America, in Panama, with 200 representatives from 23 countries, resulting in organizing of Confraternity of Latin American Evangelicals (CONELA), of anti-ecumenical stance, linking 98 Evangelical denominations (April).

IIIrd Conference of Religionists on Peace (initiated by Russian Orthodox Church), Moscow (May).

LCWE Consultation on the Relationship between Evangelism and Social Responsibility (CRESR), Grand Rapids, USA (June).

Consultation on 'Just development for fullness of life: an Orthodox approach'; coins terms 'microdiaconia' (service to individuals) and 'macrodiaconia' (service to societies and structures); in Kiev, USSR.

Major document *Mission and evangelism: an ecumenical affirmation* produced in Geneva by CWME and officially promulgated by Central Committee of WCC (July).

African Conference on Evangelism and Education (All Africa Baptist Fellowship and BWA), at Tigoni, Kenya, on theme 'Africa for Christ' (7-9 July).

Asian Conference on Church Renewal, Seoul, Korea (18-22 August); results in inauguration at Hong Kong in July 1983 of Evangelical Fellowship of Asia (EFA) with 12 member bodies (8 being national fellowships).

13th Pentecostal World Conference, Nairobi, Kenya; peak attenders 18,000 (September).

EFMA Missions Consultation on 'The Challenge of Our Task', in Colorado Springs, USA (27-30 September).

International Old Catholic Congress, in Vienna (September).

Pontifical Council for the Laity holds Meeting on 'Men and Women in Evangelization', Rocca di Papa, Rome (2-6 October).

IBM spends $3 billion on research, development and engineering (= 9% of sales), subscribes to virtually every major computer market-research service, and has a worldwide intelligence-gathering network that includes economists and market analysts.

1,440,000 microcomputers sold during year (over 1 million in USA, a 70% leap over 1981 sales).

Largest tent ever (seating 40,000) erected in South Africa for Apostolic Faith Mission evangelists under Reinhard Bonnke (a German).

Thanksgiving '82, yearlong evangelistic crusade ending in Guatemala City Crusade (evangelist Luis Palau) with audience of 700,000, largest crowd for any single evangelistic meeting in Latin America (November).

3rd World Hindu Conference, on 'The Search for Religious Identity and Dialogue'.

2nd Asian Leaders Conference, Catholic Charismatic Renewal (ICCRO), on 'Evangelize Asia for Christ', Singapore.

2nd Japan Congress of Evangelism.

7th World Congress, Theosophical Society, Nairobi (December).

UBS Africa Regional Assembly, Nairobi, Kenya, on theme 'God's Word open for All in Africa', with 170 representatives from 45 countries (1-8 December).

21st General Council, World Alliance of Reformed Churches (WARC), in Ottawa, Canada, on theme 'Thine is the Kingdom, the Power and the Glory'.

Constituting Assembly, Latin American Council of Churches (CLAI), at Huampani, Lima (Peru), on theme 'Commitment to the Kingdom'; 110 member denominations.

Consultation on Mission in the Context of Poverty and Situations of Affluence (sponsored by CCA), in Manila (10-14 December).

Mission '83, 3rd Missionary Congress for European Youth, sponsored by the European Missionary Association (TEMA), on theme 'Let us rise and build', in Lausanne; over 7,000 present from 42 countries (28 December-2 January 1983).

Council of European Bishops' Conferences (CCEE) begins 3-year discussion of 'evangelization in a secularized continent'.

LWF/CCC Interregional Consultation on Mission and Evangelism, Stavanger, Norway, with over 140 participants from 39 countries (18-26 May), after 6 regional Lutheran consultations: 1978 Loccum (Germany), 1979 Caribbean, 1979 Manila, 1980 Monrovia (Liberia), 1980 Bogota, 1980 Tallinn (Estonia).

WCC Faith and Order Commission meets in Lima, Peru, and initiates global 5-year reflection by member churches on BEM (Baptism, Eucharist and Ministry) document.

A.C. Clarke writes sequel to *2001* entitled *2010: Odyssey Two*, in which Chinese, Russian and USA spaceships encounter huge alien monolith in orbit round moons of Jupiter.

1983 6th International Conference, Ecumenical Association of Third World Theologians (EATWOT-6): Dialogue between First and Third World Theologians, in Geneva, on 'Doing theology in a divided world' (5-13 January).

1st World Conference of Religious Workers for Saving the Sacred Gift of Life from Nuclear Catastrophe, in Moscow convened by Russian Orthodox Church for all religions, on 'The economic and moral implications of a nuclear freeze' (March); 1984, 2nd World Conference, in Moscow on 'Space without weapons' (April); 1985, 3rd World Conference, on 'New dangers'.

Mission England, a 2-year evangelistic crusade involving most denominations.

SEDOS Dialogue in Mission, in Rome (March).

Mission Congress '83, sponsored by US Catholic Mission Association (USCMA), Baltimore, on 'Inculturation, Dialogue, Liberation' (17-21 March).

2nd Latin American Missionary Congress (COMLA-2), sponsored by CELAM, in Tlaxcala, Mexico, on theme 'Together with Mary, Missionaries of Christ' (16-21 May).

Canadian Consultation on Evangelism (sponsored by North American LCWE), Waterloo (7-10 June).

Conference on The Nature and Mission of the Church, at Wheaton, IL, USA, convened by World Evangelical Fellowship, with theme 'I will build My Church' (June).

World Baptist Congress on Urban Evangelism, in Niteroi, Brazil (26 June-3 July).

11th World Congress, International Council of Christian Churches (ICCC), at Cape May, USA (June).

Latin American Consultation on Evangelism and Social Responsibility (sponsored by CONELA), Panama (July).

1st International Conference for Itinerant Evangelists, Amsterdam; theme 'Do the Work of an Evangelist'; 3,800 evangelists from 132 nations (July).

IJCIC-LWF Consultation (International Jewish Committee on Interreligious Consultations—Lutheran World Federation), Stockholm (July).

USA president launches 20-year experimental Strategic Defense Initiative (SDI, or 'Star Wars') costing $1 trillion, as shield against USSR nuclear missiles.

6th Assembly of WCC in Vancouver, Canada, on theme 'Jesus Christ the Life of the World'; 900 delegates (300 being women) from 310 member denominations, 850 journalists, 15,000 attenders at opening service (24 July-10 August).
Caribbean Baptist Fellowship Congress of Evangelism, at Moneague, Jamaica (5-13 August).
2nd International Christian Youth Conference, World Methodist Council, in Bahamas; over 1,000 delegates from 47 nations (August).
2nd LCWE Consultation on Jewish Evangelism (LCJE) at Newmarket (UK), with 52 delegates representing 17 Jewish missions (September).
Assembly on Dialogue with Islam (Muslim/Catholic) in Varanasi, India.
All Asia Lutheran Conference, India.
6th General Assembly, Ordinary Synod of Bishops, Rome, on 'Reconciliation and penance in the mission of the Church'; 221 member bishops (September-October); 1983 is celebrated as Holy Year, being Jubilee of the Redemption.
1st Brazil National Congress on Evangelization, Belo Horizonte, with over 2,000 delegates (31 October-5 November).
YWAM (Youth With a Mission, begun 1960) with 14,000 young short-term workers serves as world's largest evangelistic agency.
13 million computers in use in world, worth $200 billion.
Canadian Catholic Mission Congress (Entraide Missionnaire), Montreal.
IRAS project (InfraRed Astronomical Satellite), a US$100-million telescope supercooled to 2° Kelvin above absolute zero, maps massive infrared activity throughout Universe, discovers 20,000 new galaxies (99% of whose energy is infrared), large numbers of planetary systems, starburst galaxies, stars in formation, and vast amounts of cold interstellar dust throughout Galaxy.
SOMA Pan-African Conference (Sharing of Ministries Abroad) for Anglophone Charismatic Renewal Leaders, Nairobi, Kenya (October).
After 14 years' negotiations, United Presbyterian Church in the USA, and Presbyterian Church in the US, formally unite as Presbyterian Church (USA), with 4.8 million members.
SVD Missiologists' Meeting for Asia, in Tagaytay City, Philippines; request by FABC bishops for establishment of an Asian Center of Missiology (11-18 December).

1984 Southern Africa Missiological Society Congress on 'The challenge of the African Independent Churches', at Krugersdorp, Johannesburg; 100 participants (January).
Collective brain power of all computers now doubling every 2 years.
First commercial service of computer-aided translation available (English/French/German/Spanish/other European languages).
USA: computers in homes rise from nil in 1978 to 10 million in 5 years, then by 1995 to 80 million.
Central Asia: Apocalyptic Buddhists propound cosmology of Wheel of Time Tantra (Apocalyptic Vehicle); aggressiveness must be transcended in order to reach Shambhala, the next step in human evolution.
World debt from Western banks loaned to Third-World nations now $700 billion: 30% has been stolen in large amounts and resides in a few personal or numbered accounts in Western world, 30% more has been stolen locally in smaller sums, and 20% more has been deliberately mismanaged for personal gain.
Consultation on Caste and the Church, sponsored by EFI/EFA, with 33 leaders in Bangalore (9-12 February).
India: conclusion of Project Calvary, 2nd Every Home Crusade (EHC) campaign to reach every home in nation.
2nd All-Asian Conference on Christian Art (organized by Asian Christian Art Association), at Mt Makeling, Philippines, on 'The Magnificat in Asia' (23-30 March).
USA: American Museum of Natural History holds exhibition 'Ancestors: Four Million Years of Humanity', in New York (16 April-9 September).
International Festival of Christian Radio, at National Catholic Radio & TV Center, Hatch End, London (29 April-4 May).
Pope John Paul II canonizes 93 Korean and 10 French martyrs at Seoul's Yoido Plaza, in presence of one million faithful (out of 1.7 million Korean RCs) (6 May).
6th International Convention of Life Line (network of telephone counseling services), on 'Perspectives on the human spirit', at Hershey, PA, USA (24-28 May).
Guatemala: DAWN (Discipling A Whole Nation) Congress held as whole new wave of evangelism and church planting sweeps nation; goal to double Evangelical churches from 7,500 to 15,000 by 1990 (May).
5th International Leaders Conference, Catholic Charismatic Renewal, in Rome, attended by pope John Paul II (May); also ICCRO Worldwide Priests Retreat, in Vatican attended by 6,000 priests and 80 bishops and cardinals (October).
SVD Missiological Conference 'First Evangelization Today', St Augustin, Germany (Whitsun).
LCWE International Prayer Assembly for World Evangelization, Seoul, Korea (June); 3,200 participants from 69 nations.
Religious Futurists' Network (RFN) Conference on 'Religious Visions of the 21st Century', at 5th General Assembly, World Future Society on 'A Global Assessment of Problems and Opportunities', in Washington, DC (11-14 June); majoring on global nuclearization, and global economic disparities.
ACC-6: 6th Meeting, Anglican Consultative Council, in Badagry, Nigeria (17-27 July).
Ethnic Chinese Congress on World Evangelization (ECCOWE), in Honolulu, with 144 delegates (5-12 July).
XIth Assembly, Mennonite World Conference, in Strasbourg (France), with over 7,000 participants, on theme 'God's People Serve in Hope' (July).
Over 30 national and 8 regional LCWE conferences on world evangelization, plus intensive prayer, commitment and planning, are organized for 5-year period leading into 1989 ICOWE II.
7th Assembly, Lutheran World Federation (LWF) in Budapest, Hungary, on 'In Christ—hope for the world'; 12,000 attenders (22 July-5 August).
World Methodist Camp Meeting, sponsored by WMC, at Ocean Grove, NJ (USA), led by evangelist Alan Walker; 5,000 present (August).
Congress 1984, International Association for Reformed Faith and Action (IARFA), in Lausanne (2-8 August).
3rd Plenary Assembly, World Catholic Federation for the Biblical Apostolate, in Bangalore, India, on theme 'Would that all of God's People were Prophets'; 120 delegates from 55 countries, representing WCFBA's 61 member national Bible organizations (full members) and 125 associate member organizations (12-25 August).
13th International Lutheran Conference on the Holy Spirit (ILCOHS), in Minneapolis; 12,000 participants (15-19 August).
Conference of the International Council for the Promotion of Christian Higher Education, in Breukelen, Netherlands (15-22 August).
1st World Congress, International Christian Studies Association, in Los Angeles, USA (24-26 August).
2nd International Conference on Christian Parapsychology, sponsored by Churches' Fellowship for Psychical and Spiritual Studies, in London (9-11 September).
6th International Colloquy on Carthusian History and Spirituality, in Grenoble, France (12-15 September).
Middle East Christian Leadership Assembly (MECLA), Cyprus (September).
Congress on the Evangelization of the Caribbean (CONECAR), Kingston, Jamaica, with 600 participants from 29 countries (September).
2nd World Congress on Religious Liberty, Rome (under International Religious Liberty Association); 300 participants from 42 countries (September).
French Catholic Mission Congress, Lisieux (France).
Communist Party of Tibet concedes religion still of key importance, orders immediate rebuilding of 200 temples and reviving of Tibetan culture; 1985, pays for new printings of Buddhist scriptures including 1,100-volume Lamaist Kanjur.
Series of conferences for 5,000 Spanish-speaking evangelists in 15 cities in Central and South America (July-September).
European 3-satellite project studies solar wind, which sweeps through space at over 1 million km/hour.
Since World War II, over 150 small wars have claimed 10 million lives.
8th European Charismatic Leaders' Conference, Nidelbad, Switzerland (19 September).
Nigeria: Mission to the Nation held across Nigeria, sponsored by Methodists under evangelist Alan Walker (October).
Evangelism and Education Conference, Asian Baptist Fellowship, in Penang, Malaysia; over 80 delegates from Asia.
Mexico: 2nd National Youth Conference, Catholic Charismatic Renewal, with 18,000 young people, Guadalajara (November).
Consultation of Christian Councils in West Africa, on Christian-Muslim Relations, in Monrovia, Liberia (25-28 November).
USA: Urbana '84, 14th International Student Missions Convention, at Urbana, on theme 'Faithful in Christ Jesus', with 18,145 students and missionaries (December).
London, Tokyo, Hong Kong open world's first operational teleports (ground control for massive information transportation and routing via satellite); 1985, Texas teleport (San Antonio), followed by 20 others in USA, 10 in Japanese cities, others in 40 other countries.
10th Baptist Youth World Conference (BWA), in Buenos Aires.
Frustration at slow progress towards organic church union leads to federation approaches: (1) Council of Churches in Indonesia, with 54 member denominations, changes name to Communion of Churches in Indonesia; (2) Federation of Christian Churches in Madagascar (including RC Church); (3) 1985, Christian Federation of Malaysia (RC Church, Council of Churches in Malaysia, National Evangelical Christian Fellowship).
Britain: major ecumenical venture 'Not Strangers But Pilgrims' involving over 30 denominations including RCs, Anglicans, Black pentecostals, to formulate ecumenical policy for the future.

1985 **Global status of Christianity:** 65.1 generation after Christ, world is 32.7% Christians (47.5% of them being Whites), 72.1% evangelized; with printed Scriptures available in 1,950 languages; total martyrs since AD 33, 39,500,000 (0.5% of all Christians ever; recent rate 230,000 per year).
Total Christians who have ever lived (New Israel): 8,053 million (23.5% of all persons born since AD 33).
Japanese government injects US$70 billion into its computer industry

from 1975-1985.

600 million telephones in world; 93% can be direct-dialled from London (leading global telecommunications center), and 70% from USA.

4th World Zoroastrian Congress, India; over 1,200 Parsi attenders.

East Java: 9 teams from Every Creature Crusade visit 4,000 homes in 26 different areas; 250 conversions.

Colombia: during International Year of Youth, Catholic Charismatic Renewal undertakes to proclaim Jesus to one fifth of all Colombian youth; each RC diocese allocated large quotas as targets.

'Mission 2000' scheme proposed by missiologists D.A. McGavran and R.D. Winter, aiming to plant a church in each of world's unreached peoples by AD 2000 through formation of 100,000 local church mission fellowships in Western countries.

USSR: Methodists launch evangelistic mission before 3,000 people in St Olous Cathedral, Tallinn (Estonia), led by global evangelist Alan Walker.

Bolivia: New Life For All evangelistic initiative results in 2,000 converts in 1984, and up to 100 a week in 1985.

USA: Northamerican Full Gospel Missions Association formed to promote missions in charismatic churches; name then changed 3 times, finally to AIMS (Association of International Mission Services).

India: 6th National Convention of the Charismatic Renewal, with 15,000 attenders, bishops, 600 RC priests, 1,500 religious personnel, in Madras (January).

African indigenous churches (AICs) number some 7,170 separate and distinct denominations with 29,100,000 affiliated church members and grand total of 32,700,000 adherents of all kinds in 74,000 places of worship, increasing at 850,000 new members a year.

6th Conference, International Association for Mission Studies (IAMS), Harare, Zimbabwe, on 'Christian mission and human transformation'; 160 participants (8-14 January).

Presbyterian Church (USA) sponsors Congress on Renewal (charismatic) in Dallas (Texas), with over 5,000 attenders (January).

1st General Assembly, Evangelical Fellowship of Asia (EFA, formed 1983), in Manila (Philippines), on 'The Holy Spirit and the Church' (30 January-2 February).

3rd World Conference of Religious Workers, in Moscow convened by Russian Orthodox Patriarchate, on 'New Dangers to the Sacred Gift of Life: Our Task', dealing with nuclear winter; 60 religious workers and scientists from 27 countries, including Christians, Muslims, Hindus, Jews, Buddhists (2-13 February).

Fiji: 60,000 attend final rally in Suva of 150th Anniversary Celebrations of Methodism; 6,000 commitments.

International Missionary Congress, on theme 'Bringing Christ to Man', sponsored by Pontifical Urbanian University, Rome (18-21 February).

4th General Assembly, Middle East Council of Churches, in Nicosia, Cyprus (February); 21 member churches.

LCWE Consultations on Radio in Church Planting (RICE): (1) Manila (February), and (2) Kristiansand, Norway (December).

Youth Congress on World Evangelization, Stuttgart, Germany (February).

Philippines: Manila '85 launched (with 188,000 attenders and 18,000 professions of faith) as year-long evangelism/discipleship program aimed at winning one million people through Metro Manila's 400 churches in 1985 (February).

Sierra Leone: Consultation on Muslim Evangelism; 21 churches and missions represented (February).

Interchurch Consultation on Future Trends in Christian World Mission, Maryknoll, New York, on research methodology, sociopolitical issues, and unfinished tasks of world evangelization (15-17 February).

USA: Conference on New Age Issues, sponsored by Evangelical Ministries to New Religions (EMNR), in Denver; over 300 registrants; releases 'Statement on the New Age Movement' (14-16 March).

15th European Pentecostal Fellowship Conference, Naples, Italy (19-21 March).

Zaire National Congress on Evangelism; leaders from 64 denominations plan to plant churches in 10,000 unreached villages and thousands of city neighborhoods by 1990 (April).

Conference of International Interfaith Organizations, convened by World Congress of Faiths, at Ammerdown, Bath (UK), representing over 20 organizations (April).

South Africa: Andrew Murray Consultation on Prayer for Revival and Mission Sending; 800 attenders in Cape Town and Pretoria.

National Convocation on Evangelizing Ethnic America, Houston; over 700 attenders (April).

Italy: 8th National Charismatic Conference, in Rimini; 12,000 participants including several bishops, 500 priests (25-28 April).

European Evangelism Conference, sponsored by International Fellowship of Evangelical Students (IFES), in De Flevohof, Netherlands; 560 students including 50 from Yugoslavia (April).

Conference of National Evangelists (CONE), sponsored by Asia Evangelistic Fellowship, in Singapore; 140 participants from 14 countries (May).

3rd Scandinavian Conference of Catholic Charismatic Renewal, Stockholm, with 150 delegates (16-19 May).

LCWE Conference on the Laity, Denver, surveys evangelism within occupational groups, states 120,000 volunteers work in over 120 Christian lay affinity groups in USA; 40 leaders (21-23 May).

11th Session, Roman Catholic/Classical Pentecostal theological dialogue (begun 1972), on topic 'Communion of Saints'; at Riano, Rome (21-26 May); 1986, 12th Session, in USA (24-31 May).

LCWE/WEF Consultation on the Work of the Holy Spirit and Evangelization, in Oslo, Norway; over 70 participants from 30 countries (May); results in published book 'God the Evangelist'.

Charismatic Retreat for Priests (Polish Bishops Conference and ICCRO) in Czestochowa, Poland (June).

1st Global Evangelization Strategy Consultation, Ridgecrest, NC (USA), with 70 participants from Baptist churches across world associated with Southern Baptist Convention; results inter alia in publication of 'The AD 2000 Series' (25-28 June).

8th Assembly, Christian Conference of Asia (CCA), in Seoul (Korea), on theme 'Jesus Christ sets free to serve', with delegates from its 110 churches in 16 Asian countries (June-July).

Chinese Culture and the Gospel Seminar (CCCOWE), in Hong Kong, with 85 delegates (July).

World Congress on Japanese Evangelism, Los Angeles (USA), with 300 Japanese Christians from 20 denominations and 10 nations.

6th All-Christian Peace Assembly (ACPA), convened by Christian Peace Conference (CPC), in Prague, on theme 'God calls: choose life; the hour is late!'; 800 participants from 90 countries (2-9 July).

9th Latin American Leaders Conference (ECCLA IX), Catholic Charismatic Renewal (ICCRO), for 200 leaders, Costa Rica (July).

Information crimes rise sharply; computer fraud, commercial espionage, software and data theft, sale of disinformation.

35 countries now potentially able to make atomic weapons, though only 11 have actually succeeded.

Electronic warfare: USA and USSR each spend over $1 billion annually on this and its related research.

50 million computers in world (12,000 per million people, or 80 people per computer), with USA having 11 million (55,000 per million, 20 people per computer); 50% of all whitecollar workers own one.

15th Baptist World Congress (BWA) meets in Los Angeles, USA, with theme 'Out of Darkness into the Light of Christ'; 25,000 participants from 127 member bodies (July).

4th Asian Institute for Christian Communication (AICC-4), Chiang Mai, Thailand, for 37 leaders (July).

World Conference of Baptist Evangelists, Bolivar, Missouri (USA): 'Strategies of evangelism to win world cities' (July).

14th Pentecostal World Conference, in Zurich, organized by World Conference of Pentecostal Churches; on 'Jesus Christ—the Hope of the World'; 10,000 participants from 100 countries (2-7 July).

World Christian Peace Conference, London, sponsored by World Methodist Council, on 'Commitment to Jesus Christ the Prince of Peace'; 250 delegates from 32 countries (July).

Salvation Army International Youth Congress, Western Illinois University, USA; 5,000 delegates from 85 nations (17-23 July).

Latin America Chinese Evangelization Conference (sponsored by CCCOWE) held in São Paulo, Brazil (23-27 July).

1st Costa Rican Missions Consultation, with 36 denominations and agencies (July).

5th West Malaysia Chinese Congress on World Evangelization, sponsored by CCCOWE, in Port Dickson (5-9 August).

Chinese Missionary Convention of Canada (CMCC '85), at Guelph; 1,050 registrants (19-24 August).

Uganda: National Catholic Charismatic Leaders Conference, with 130 leaders (22-27 August).

International Christian Zionist Congress, in Basel, Switzerland, with 600 delegates from 27 countries; to show support for the state of Israel (27-29 August).

Friends World Committee for Consultation (FWCC) meets in Cuernavaca, Mexico (August).

Belgium: Colloquium on the Bible and the Computer, at Louvain (August).

43rd International Eucharistic Congress, Nairobi, Kenya, on 'Eucharist and the Christian Family' (August).

Global Simultaneous Evangelistic Missions launched in Indonesia, Nigeria and other countries by World Methodist Council; thousands of local mission outreach campaigns planned across world.

4th Nigeria National Congress on Evangelization, Zaria, on theme 'Arise let us go from here', with 667 participants (August).

Asia Committee for World Evangelization, Hong Kong (3-6 September).

Annual Conference, World Congress of Faiths, Leicester, UK on theme 'The Worshipping Community' (September).

World Consultation on Evangelism, Lake Junaluska (USA), sponsored by World Evangelism (World Methodist Council) (September); 5-year evangelism plan for 1987-1991 adopted.

World Missions Conference, Guadalajara, Mexico (September).

Anglican Renewal Leaders Consultation, sponsored by SOMA (Sharing of Ministries Abroad), in Chorleywood, UK, with 90 leaders (September).

Britain: 5th National Charismatic Conference for Clergy and Leaders (sponsored by Anglican Renewal Ministries), Swanwick (23-26

September).
Project 'The World by 2000' announced by 3 major Christian broadcasting agencies, FEBC, HCJB/World Radio Missionary Fellowship, TWR: to complete by AD 2000 giving everyone on Earth the opportunity to hear the gospel of Christ by radio (September).
1st Pan-African Francophone Leaders Conference, Catholic Charismatic Renewal (ICCRO), on 'A Holy People', with 100 leaders, Kinshasa, Zaire (4-9 October).
USA: Hispanic Congress on Evangelization, at Crystal Cathedral, Garden Grove, CA: 2,000 Hispanic evangelical leaders from 25 countries, 80% being pastors; goals to reach 2 million Hispanics for Christ by end of 1987, and to plant 20,000 new Hispanic churches in USA by AD 2000 (14-18 October).
World Christian Conference for Chinese Graduates, sponsored by NACOCE; 110 attenders.
1st International Youth Leaders Consultation, Catholic Charismatic Renewal (ICCRO), held in Rome, with 500 participants from 100 countries (15-19 October).
1st Venezuelan Congress of World Missions, Maracay, aiming to appoint 500 missionaries by 1987 (15-19 October).
CWME Orthodox Advisory Group meets in Sofia (Bulgaria) on 1,100th anniversary of death of Methodius, criticizes Orthodoxy's failure to fulfil Jesus' Great Commission and 'to reach out to the unreached' (21-26 October).
Amsterdam Prayer Conference for World Evangelization, sponsored by LCWE, YWAM, et alia (November).
3rd Asian Leaders Conference, Catholic Charismatic Renewal (ICCRO), on 'Discipleship in the Holy Spirit', with 100 leaders, Bangalore, India (9-12 November).
Assembly of the World's Religions, in preparation for future World Parliament of Religions; in McAfee, NJ, USA (15-21 November).
Kenya: 6th Workshop of the Apostolate to Nomads, Nairobi; 42 participants from RC dioceses across East Africa (25-30 November).
Macao: Gospel Saturation Campaign (Campus Crusade for Christ, from Korea) reaches 150,000 young people.
Manila: 1st General Assembly, Institute of Foreign Missions of the Philippines, founded in 1965.
Extraordinary Synod of Bishops, in Rome, to reappraise Vatican II and its changes; 150 participating bishops; general opinion that conservatives in Curia's Holy Office have again stifled genuine collegiality (November-December).
World's fastest supercomputer introduced: Cray-2, with 4 main processors working in parallel, 2-billion-byte memory, 1,200 megaflops (floating point, or arithmetical, operations in millions per second); 150 supercomputers (of 6 different makes) now in use around world.
12% of USA's 85 million homes have personal computers; by 1990, 30%.
World's 10 largest cities: Tokyo/Yokohama 18,820,000, Mexico City 17,300,000, São Paulo 15,880,000, New York/NENJ 15,640,000, Shanghai 11,780,000, Calcutta 10,950,000, Buenos Aires 10,880,000, Rio de Janeiro 10,370,000, London 10,360,000, Seoul 10,280,000.
Explosive rise of 121 anti-Christian megacities and 20 supercities hostile to Christian mission, especially 4 Muslim supercities over 6 million each in 1985 (Jakarta, Cairo, Teheran, Karachi), increasing to 5 Islamic supergiants over 10 million each by AD 2000 (Jakarta, Cairo, Karachi, Teheran, Dacca); resurgence of Islamic neo-fundamentalism and sectarian violence.
Total of literary doomsday novels (describing cataclysmic ends of the world) published to date is 260; most written before 1914 postulate natural catastrophes, most written after 1914 postulate man-made catastrophes.
EXPLO-85 global Christian training teleconference organized in 95 locations in 55 countries simultaneously by Campus Crusade for Christ (CCCI), using satellite video relays (6 uplinks, several thousand downlinks), training 550,000 Christian workers from 100 countries worldwide in prayer, evangelism and discipleship, with 4 telecasts reaching 60 million (27-31 December).
Australian Chinese Congress of Evangelism (30 December-3 January 1986).
C. Sagan writes science fiction classic *Contact* predicting contact with extraterrestrial aliens in 1988 and 1999.

1986 1986 is proclaimed International Year of Peace by United Nations
Halley's Comet returns as the final harbinger or portent of impending eco-disaster (Nostradamus).
Astronomers discover most massive object ever, the strongest gravitational lens yet found: either a supercluster of over 1,000 galaxies, or the biggest black hole ever (with mass of 10^{15} stars), or a cosmic string (a defect in the fabric of space-time left over from Big Bang) billions of light-years long but only an atom thick, with mass density 10^{18} tons per inch.
USA: 5 million users send 250 million electronic-mail messages every year; by 1990, 3 billion messages a year.
Spain National Missions Consultation, related to COMIBAM '87.
International Catholic Programme of Evangelization begins functioning, first in Malta, Rome, New Zealand.
Afro-Asian Ecumenical Colloquium on Spirituality and Liberation in Post-Independent Africa and Asia, New Delhi (4-12 January).
Australia: Jubilee 86 United Charismatic Convention, in Adelaide; over 3,000 delegates, 10,000 attenders (7-11 January).
International Conference on Liberation Theology, in Burnaby, Canada (6-8 February).
Australia: 1st National Convention on the Holy Spirit (World Methodist Council), in Sydney (February); followed by regional conferences, then 1987 2nd National Convention.
India: pope John Paul II visits 14 cities on his 29th foreign pilgrimage since 1978 (February).
Guatemala National Consultation on World Missions, related to COMIBAM '87; 129 participants, plus 380 in adjacent meetings (21-26 February).
Consultation on Evangelizing World Class Cities, Moody Bible Institute, Chicago (14-17 March).
General Assembly, World Student Christian Federation (WSCF), in 90th anniversary celebration; in Oaxtepec, Mexico (March).
International Prophetic Ministry Convention, Mount Carmel (Israel) and Jerusalem; 30 modern prophets and 5,000 attenders, at Easter (Christians of all confessions).
1st Catholic FIRE Charismatic Evangelistic Rally, Providence, RI (relayed by satellite to 17 cities), on 'I have come to cast fire on the Earth' (5 April).
USA: 15th World Mission Institute, held in Chicago, on theme 'Trends for the Future and World Mission' (10-12 April).
Conference of Revival Evangelists for Inter-Africa (sponsored by CFAN, Christ for All Nations), Harare, Zimbabwe (April).
7th Latin American Lutheran Congress, in Caracas, on theme 'To be reborn and to grow in hope and peace'; 70 participants from 14 Latin American countries (18-24 April).
1st General Assembly, Latin American Evangelical Confraternity (CONELA, founded 1982, with 225 member denominations, councils, associations and agencies), in Maracaibo, Venezuela; topic, challenge to evangelize Latin America and the world, with 'millions of Latin American missionaries sent to the Muslim world and other regions where they are needed' (M. Ortiz, president); 95 delegates and over 1,000 attenders (22-25 April).
USA: International Conference for Equipping Evangelists (charismatic pentecostal) in Sacramento (CA), 'training thousands of evangelists to equip millions of Christians to reach billions of unbelievers' (5-9 May).
United Bible Societies launches 2-year Youth Advance, providing special translations (May).
World Literature Conference, sponsored by Evangelical Literature Overseas; at Wheaton, USA (27-30 May).
El Salvador: World Literature Crusade plans to make 1 million converts in a year through house-to-house visitation.
2nd Assembly, Ecumenical Forum of Christian Women of Europe, in Jarvenpaa, Finland, on 'Building Hope—a New Vision of Life'; 150 women from 26 countries (2-8 June).
Venezuela: 1st Regional Conference of World Missions, convened by Evangelicals in eastern region of country, at Puerto la Cruz, with over 200 present (96 official representatives of 30 organizations) (10-14 June).
12th World Congress, International Council of Christian Churches (ICCC), Seoul, Korea, with delegates from 93 nations (12-16 June).
Conference on 'A Century of World Evangelization: North American Evangelical Missions, 1886-1986', at Wheaton, USA (17-19 June).
8th General Assembly, World Evangelical Fellowship, in Singapore, on 'Renew the Church—Reach the World', with 250 delegates from 50 WEF member alliances and fellowships (22-27 June).
ASIA 86 radio/videotape preaching mission, from Luis Palau Singapore Mission, largest broadcast outreach to Asia ever, aiming to evangelize in 10 languages through FEBC, HCJB, TWR, and others (23-27 June).
Scandinavian Oasis Conference (Oase; Lutheran Charismatic Renewal), based in Oslo, with 500 pastors and 10,000 others (July).
15th World Methodist Conference, sponsored by World Methodist Council, Nairobi, on theme 'Christ Jesus: God's "Yes" for the World'; further 5-year plan adopted for World Evangelism, 1987-1991; 3,000 delegates (July).
12th Annual Conference, Association of Church Missions Committees (ACMC), in Wheaton and San Diego, USA; 1,300 attenders (9-12 July).
2nd International Conference for Itinerant Evangelists (ICIE), Amsterdam; 8,000 evangelists from 150 countries (12-21 July).
ACTS 86 (European Festival of Faith), an all-Europe charismatic congress on 'Evangelism in the Power of the Holy Spirit', in Birmingham (UK); 20,000 RC/Protestant/Anglican/Orthodox participants from East and West (100 from Eastern Europe), but without formal RC participation (23-27 July).
6th International Seminar of Christian Artists (Europe), Netherlands (3-9 August).
14th International Lutheran Conference on the Holy Spirit (ILCOHS), Minneapolis; 12,000 attenders (5-8 August).
3rd Chinese Congress on World Evangelization (CCOWE '86) sponsored by CCCOWE, held in Taipei (Taiwan), on theme 'Renewal, Breakthrough and Growth'; 1,900 Chinese church leaders from over 20 countries (6-13 August).
15th Annual Conference, Association of Muslim Social Scientists, in Plain-

field, IN, USA (7-9 August).
USA: Aldersgate '86, 8th National Conference on the Holy Spirit (United Methodist, UMRSF), at Savannah, GA, on 'Christ in You, the Hope of Glory' (7-10 August).
Indonesia: LWF Urban Mission Consultation, in Jakarta (7-15 August).
All Africa Congress on Evangelism (under MCWE/Morris Cerullo), Nairobi (11-16 August).
4th Chinese National Christian Conference, Beijing (16-23 August).
12th General Assembly, World Fellowship of Orthodox Youth (Syndesmos), in Effingham, UK; over 100 delegates (17-24 August); 1989, 13th General Assembly, in USA.
2nd World Convocation, Prison Fellowship International (PFI), in Nairobi, Kenya; 200 chaplains and workers.
3rd Lausanne Consultation on Jewish Evangelism (LCJE/LCWE); 300 delegates, at Easneye, Ware, UK (19-27 August).
Honduras: 1st National Missions Consultation, at Lake Yojoa, with 26 churches and organizations (9-11 January); followed by Honduras National Missions Congress (21-25 August).
Paraguay National Missions Consultation (25-27 August); and Uruguay National Missions Consultation (August); both related to COMIBAM '87.
Philippines: National Missions Consultation '86, in Taytay, Rizal, sponsored by DAWN 2000 Continuing Committee; results in goal '2,000 new Filipino missionaries by 2000 AD'; 100 participants (25-28 August).
24th International Old Catholic Congress (International Old Catholic Bishops Conference) in Munster, Germany, on 'Witness and Service in the World' (26-30 August).
4th General Assembly, Caribbean Conference of Churches (with 31 member denominations), in Bridgetown, Barbados, on theme 'Jesus Christ—Justice, Hope, Peace' (September).
LWF/WCC Joint Consultation on New Religious Movements, in Amsterdam (7-13 September).
India: 3rd Every Home Crusade (EHC) campaign (after 1975, 1984 campaigns) to reach 765 million people, in every home in India, with printed gospel messages by 1994.
USA: Youth With a Mission (YWAM) announces goal of fulfilling Great Commission in 25 years, by AD 2011.
Korea: 10th Church Growth International Seminar (P.Y. Cho and Full Gospel Church) in Seoul and Osaka (Japan), with 3,000 attenders (September), bring total attenders since 1976 to 70,000 pastors and leaders from 30 countries; goal announced of winning 10 million Japanese to Christ by AD 2000.
US Society for Frontier Missiology (USSFM) inaugurated in Colorado Springs by leaders from 15 Protestant agencies; goals for AD 2000 planned (19-20 September).
11th International Congress of Christian Archeology, in Aix-en-Provence, France (September).
5th Assembly, Pacific Conference of Churches (PCC), in Apia, Samoa (September).
SOMA Conference for Anglican Diocese of Jerusalem in Old City, Jerusalem, on 'Evangelism in the Power of the Holy Spirit' (22-26 September).
LWF International Consultation on Confirmation, in Geneva (25-27 September).
Annual Meeting, Conference of Secretaries of Christian World Communions (CWCs), in Rome (October).
4th Triennial Convention, Asia Missions Association (AMA), in Pasadena, USA, on 'Thy Will be done on Earth' (6-12 October).
England: widespread growth of local ecumenical projects (LEPs), totalling 460 in number.
'Jesus' film produced by Campus Crusade for Christ (filmed in Palestine in 1979) is circulating in 1986 dubbed in 106 languages; viewers total 275 million, decisions for Christ reach 33 million (12%).
Mandate '86, 1st Annual Mid-West Student Missions Conference, 'to reach the world's unreached', organized in Illinois (USA) with 800 students by IVCF-related students, supported by CCCI, AoG, SBC, IVCF et alia, with 9 related regional meetings; also Mission Advance 86 (Hamilton, Canada, 850 students); 1987, numerous student-run conferences—Mandate '87 (in Muncie, IN; 1,200 students, 23-25 January), Harvest (in Minneapolis, 6-8 February), Vision, Proclaim, Go (Global Outreach), GAP (Global Awareness Project).
USA: 3rd North American Buddhist-Christian Theological Encounter, on 'Notions of Ultimate Reality in Buddhism and Christianity', West Lafayette, IN (10-12 October).
11th International Conference on Patristic, Medieval, and Renaissance Studies, in Villanova, USA; held annually (10-12 October).
1st International Christian Media Conference (ICMC), at Flevohof, The Hague, Netherlands, on 'Partners in Communication', sponsored by WEF, NRB, TWR; 500 participants from 75 countries (13-17 October).
Interfaith 9-hour prayer and fasting summit for world peace at Assisi, Italy, convened by John Paul II for 120 Christian leaders including 2 Orthodox patriarchs, and 80 other religious leaders including Dalai Lama, Buddhists, Muslims, Hindus, Sikhs, Shintoists, Parsis, Jains, Baha'is, shamanists, animists (27 October).
Conference of Lutheran Churches in Europe, in Brezice, Yugoslavia (28 October-4 November).
WCC Consultation on Role of National Councils of Churches in Increasing Christian Cooperation and Unity, in Geneva; representatives of 70 councils (in 35 of which the Roman Catholic Church is a full member) (October).
LCWE Consultation on Conversion and Evangelization.
Congress on Franciscan Witness among Muslims, in Spain.
14th World Congress, International Catholic Press Union (UCIP), in New Delhi (India), on theme 'Church, Culture, Communication'.
USA: Presbyterian Church announces Decade of Evangelism for 1990-2000.
USA spends $8 billion on nerve gases from 1982-86.
60 million microcomputers in world, of which 32% are installed in homes.
Fifth-generation computers using Josephson Effect introduced.
Brazil: Christian TV Network launched, a series of stations covering Latin America with TV programmes in Spanish and Portuguese.
North American Leaders Congress on the Holy Spirit and World Evangelization (RC/Protestant charismatic renewal), New Orleans, with over 7,500 pastors and leaders, also 4,000 other attenders (October); vast numbers of regional and denominational conferences and seminars proliferate.
World Consultation on Inter-Church Aid, Refugee & World Service (sponsored by WCC/CICARWS), in Larnaca, Cyprus, on theme 'Diakonia 2000: called to be Neighbors'; 300 participants (November).
Deadly pandemic of AIDS (acquired immune deficiency syndrome) rapidly sweeps across world: 1986, 1 million cases (Africa, USA) and 10 million carriers infected with virus; 1991, 3 million cases and 100 million carriers (50% of whom will die) in Africa, Asia, Americas, Europe.
Pacific '86 Conference for Evangelists, in Suva, Fiji, on theme 'Let the Islands hear'; 700 evangelists from 23 Pacific nations (12-21 December).
Mission '87, 4th Missionary Congress for European Youth (sponsored by TEMA), at Utrecht, on theme 'I chose You, Jesus Christ'; 10,500 participants (27 December-1 January 1987).
European Open Systems Interconnection (a computer language parallel to Esperanto) operates to enable computers to talk to each other in a common set of languages.
A.C. Clarke writes novel *The songs of distant Earth* about discovery in AD 2008 that Sun will go nova and explode in AD 3620.

1987 John Paul II announces new Office in Rome, 'Evangelization 2000', to prepare for 1990-2000 Decade of Universal Evangelization: comprising retreats, biggest public rally ever, 3-satellite global telecasts, global homilies, conscientization teams, mass video cassette distribution, with as aims (a) to win 1 billion new Christians 'as a present for Jesus on his 2,000th birthday', and (b) to unite all Christians and all churches by AD 2000.
5th Islamic Summit, Organization of the Islamic Conference (OIC), in Kuwait, with official delegates from Islamic nations (26-28 January).
2nd Asia Leadership Congress on World Evangelization (ALCOWE II), under LCWE/ALCOWE auspices, in Singapore, on theme 'Witnessing for Christ through the Local Church' (8-15 January).
6th Annual All India Renewal Conference (charismatic), Kerala, with 300 church leaders and 2,000 attenders (27-30 January).
LWF Consultation on Evangelism in Malawi and Mozambique, held in Malawi (1-3 February).
Consultation on World Evangelization, Singapore, with 31 global charismatic renewal leaders (RC/Lutheran/SOMA-Anglican, et alii) (9-12 February).
European Ecumenical Satellite Conference, in Hilversum, Netherlands (20-21 March).
Taiwan: National Symposium on Evangelization (Roman Catholic).
Asian Lausanne Conference on World Evangelization (ALCOWE/LCWE), in Hong Kong (April).
LCWE International Researchers Consultation, in Zeist, Netherlands (14-17 April).
East Germany: annual meeting, Conference on the Evangelization of the German Democratic Republic.
Zimbabwe: National Church Growth Conference on 'Discipling Zimbabwe'; 30 denominations and all parachurch agencies (20-24 April).
Papua New Guinea: 1st National Evangelists' Conference (April).
International Colloquium on 16th Centenary of the Conversion/Baptism of St Augustine in Milan, held in Milan, Italy (22-24 April).
ACC-7: 7th Meeting, Anglican Consultative Council, in Singapore (25 April-9 May).
National Charismatic Leaders' Conference (North American Renewal Service Committee, NARSC), related to global Charismatic Renewal in mainline denominations (100 million Christians, fielding 60,000 foreign missionaries), meets in Glencoe, MO (USA), appoints World Evangelization Strategy Committee with AD 2000 goal in mind (4-8 May).
World Literature Crusade changes name to Every Home for Christ, proclaims goal 'to systematically place 2 gospel booklets in every home in the world, one country at a time, by AD 2000'; 40% of world's homes reached since 1946; 1986, 21,969,676 pieces of literature distributed,

producing 178,509 written responses (0.8%); 1957-86, tracts distributed total 1,462,406,418, with 14,605,937 responses (1.0%).
Lutherische Europäische Kommission für Kirche und Judentum, in Budapest, Hungary (6-8 May).
6th International Leaders Conference, Catholic Charismatic Renewal (IC-CRO), Rome, on 'The Spirit of the Lord is upon Me' (11-16 May).
ICMM '87, 11th Triennial International Convention on Missionary Medicine (MAP International), on St Simons Island, GA (USA), on 'Christian health care: the challenge of change' (30 May-2 June).
Singapore '87, LCWE International Conference for Younger/Emerging Christian Leaders; 275 leaders (1-10 June).
Pentecost '87: National Satellite Celebration of Catholic Evangelization: one-day 7-hour USA-wide media event (Pentecost Saturday, 6 June) by Paulist National Catholic Evangelization Association (PNCEA), training 60,000 lay, religious and clerical evangelizers in 200 auditoriums; to be repeated every Pentecost Saturday up to AD 2000.
All-Europe Catechetical Congress, in Munich, Germany (8-11 June).
10th World Congress of the Deaf (World Federation of the Deaf, WFD, with 76 countries as members), in Helsinki (June); also World-Wide Symposium on Sign Languages, in Helsinki (June).
USA: 15th Annual Meeting, American Society of Missiology (ASM), in Pittsburgh, on theme 'Forecasting the Future in World Mission' (19-21 June).
All Africa Lutheran Consultation (sponsored by LWF), in Antsirabe, Madagascar (20-28 June).
1st Meeting, Baptist International Conference of Colleges and Universities (BICCU), Amman, Jordan (29 June-1 July).
3rd International Christian Youth Conference, World Methodist Council, in Brisbane, Australia; over 1,000 delegates (30 June-7 July).
LCWE Consultation on Muslim Evangelization, in Zeist, Netherlands, on theme 'Operation Firstborn' (27 June-4 July).
3rd Latin American Missionary Congress (COMLA-3), on 5th centenary of Roman Catholic first evangelization of Latin America; in Bogota, on theme: 'America, the Hour has come for You to be an Evangelizer' (5-10 July).
International Conference on Data Bases in the Humanities and Social Sciences, in Montgomery, AL, USA (11-13 July).
North American General Congress on the Holy Spirit and World Evangelization, in New Orleans (successor to 1977 Kansas City ecumenical charismatic rally); over 75,000 participants (RC/Protestant charismatic renewal); theme 'Power Evangelism' (22-26 July).
Uniting churches (churches negotiating toward organic union) suffer more setbacks than in previous decades, collapsing in England and Ghana, in difficulties in New Zealand, Tanzania, South Africa and Scotland; with recent successful unions achieved only in USA (1983 Presbyterians, 1988 Lutherans) and in Canada (1985 Evangelical Lutheran Church in Canada).
5th International Consultation of United and Uniting Churches, sponsored by WCC Faith and Order Commission, in Potsdam (GDR), dealing with models of unity, new forms of mission (July).
Pentecostal European Conference (PEC/PEK), in Lisbon (22-26 July).
3rd Consultation of Evangelical Missiologists from the Two-Thirds World, in Kenya (August).
Poland: Youth Congress '87 (Protestant), in Warsaw, with 5,000 attenders (August).
LWF Consultation on 'The Church and Civil Religion Worldwide—The Importance of Religion and Basic Values for Nation and State', in Bossey, Switzerland (31 August-5 September).
USA: EFMA-IFMA Joint Triennial Conference, on 'Focusing the Vision', in Orlando, FL (21-25 September).
2nd Annual Meeting, US Society for Frontier Missiology, in Orlando, FL (USA), on strategy for world evangelization by AD 2000 (25-26 September).
5th Assembly, Association of Evangelicals of Africa and Madagascar (AEAM), in Zambia; on theme 'Following Jesus in Africa Today' (September).
USA: Ecumenical Mission Consultation (USCMA/DOM-NCCCUSA), on 'Divided Churches/Common Witness: an Unfinished Task for US Christians in Mission', in Madison, CT (27 September-3 October).
1st Meeting, Commission of Third World Missions (related to AMA), São Paulo, Brazil.
7th General Assembly, Ordinary Synod of Bishops, Rome, on 'Vocation and Mission of the Laity in the Church and in the World'.
World Consultation on Ecumenical Sharing of Resources (sponsored by WCC), to seek guidelines for a radical new pattern of resource sharing between churches, missions, development agencies, etc, each transferring 50% of its resources ecumenically (October).
Ecuador: SOMA International Conference, Quito, on 'Evangelism in the Power of the Holy Spirit in Latin America', for Anglican bishops, clergy and lay leaders (8-11 October).
Britain: joint BCC/RCC conference (British Council of Churches, Roman Catholic Church) to consider nature of church and mission in light of Lima (BEM), ARCIC and Vatican II documents.
Japan: National Incentive Convention for Evangelization (NICE '87), held by Catholic Church in Japan after extensive preparations in all Japan's dioceses (November).
1st Ibero-American Missions Congress (Congreso Misionero Ibero-Americano, COMIBAM '87), in São Paulo (Brazil), with 3,500 Evangelical representatives from across Latin America, and preceded by series of national missions consultations in 23 countries; goal to generate 10,000 vocations to full-time service (24-29 November).
USA: Urbana '87, 15th International Student Missions Convention; 17,200 delegates.
3rd Japan Congress on Evangelism, Kyoto, with 4,500 delegates.

STATUS OF THE COSMOS, 1988

1988 *Galactic civilizations.* Scientists estimate our Galaxy with its 400 billion stars has (1) some 300 billion planets suitable for life, (2) 100 billion inhabited worlds on which life forms have actually arisen, (3) 600 million planets that are Earthlike, bear life and are suitable for habitation by man, (4) between 1,000 and 1 billion developing planetary communicative civilizations with intelligent lifeforms, (5) between 100 and 1 million technical civilizations (those capable of interstellar radio communication) now existing out of 1 billion ever, increasing at rate of up to one new one every decade, with nearest one around 100 light-years from Earth, and (6) between 10 and 100,000 civilizations substantially or vastly in advance of Earth's. (C. Sagan, *Cosmos*, 1980).
Extragalactic civilizations. Whole Universe with its 100 billion galaxies contains between 10 trillion (10^{13}) and 10,000 trillion (10^{16}) of these more advanced civilizations, with unimaginable technologies, together with between 100 trillion (10^{14}) and 10^{20} developing civilizations; however, none of all these extraterrestrial civilizations is likely to have produced anything resembling Homo Sapiens; all almost certainly have totally different lifeforms.
New worlds. New suns (stars) are forming or being created across the Universe at a present rate of 10,000 suns every second, new planetary systems at 10 a second, new worlds with life on at 100 a day, and new technical civilizations at one a day.
Cosmic violence. Our Galaxy experiences from 20-100 novas (binary hydrogen-fusion stars which explode) every year and one supernova (a single silicon-fusion star which explodes) every 30 years; whole Universe experiences vast, chaotic cosmic violence with 2 trillion novas a year, 2 billion supernovas a year (which then collapse into pulsars, spinning neutron stars, or black holes) also 10 million quasars (massive exploding galaxies, each destroying millions of stars and planets).
Ends of worlds. This cosmic violence destroys related or nearby planetary civilizations at rate between 10,000 and 10 billion a year (27 a day to 300 every second), and vastly advanced civilizations at between 3 a day and 2 every minute.
Self-destroyed worlds. Advanced technical civilizations across Universe last on average less than 10,000 years; before that time, at least 1% destroy themselves in wars or nuclear explosions, at rate of between 1 a year and 12 an hour.

STATUS OF THE WORLD, 1988

Global categories. World comprises 9 continents or continental areas, 25 regions, 252 countries with 2,000 major civil divisions; 3,200 rapidly growing metropolises (mother cities) of over 100,000 population each, housing 1.4 billion people, of which 300 are megacities (over 1 million population) housing 800 million souls; world consists of 11,000 distinct ethnolinguistic peoples speaking 7,000 languages.
Megacrises. Earth and its peoples and civilizations are progressively engulfed by massive crises in energy, pollution (water, air, soil), overpopulation, in a rushing vortex of convulsive social and ecological change causing dislocations globally and engendering widespread future shock.
Ecosystem. Earth's capacity to support people is being irreversibly reduced by overpopulation and overconsumption.
Species. Of world's present 8 million species (mostly invertebrates, with 500,000 plant species), 9,000 a year are being destroyed by man; rising by AD 2000 to 50,000 a year, with a million more at risk.
Millions of new species of life now being created artificially by man through insertion of genes from one species into another.
Environment. Desertification spreads as world's great forest areas are destroyed (Sahara advances by 40 km a year); 25 square miles of arable land are engulfed by deserts every day; in last 100 years, 50% of virgin equatorial rainforest of Africa destroyed by man; in Amazon river basin, 1 million trees a day felled by man (1980), 62,000 square miles of forest disappear a year; present global rate 50 hectares per minute (2.5% of remaining forests per year).
Climate. Greenhouse effect: since 1960, unregulated burning of fossil fuels increases carbon dioxide in atmosphere, heating it by 1 °F more every 8 years; by AD 2045, reaches 7 °F hotter at which point polar regions begin to thaw, ice caps melt, ocean levels rise 200 feet and flood much of Europe, UK, US Gulf states, eastern China, et alia.
Demographics. World population (mid-1988) 5,085,910,000, increasing at 1.61% per year; birth rate 2.61% per year, death rate 1.00% per year, life expectancy at birth 60.4 years.
Tourism. International tourists per year rise from 25 million arrivals (1950)

to 93 million (1963) to 141 million (1968) to 285 million (1980) to 350 million (1987); total domestic as well as international movements per year, 3,500 million (1980).

Networking. Widespread phenomenon of innovating networks of shared attraction in all fields: health, space, human potential, environment, consciousness expansion, etc.

Megapoverty. 2.1 billion people (46% of world) live in poverty, of whom 800 million live in absolute poverty; 1.1 billion without adequate shelter, 2.1 billion without adequate water supply, 3 billion with unsafe water and bad sanitation, 800 million adults illiterate, 850 million with no access to schools, 1.5 billion with no access to medical care, 500 million on edge of starvation (20 million starvation-related deaths a year), 1.5 billion hungry or malnourished.

Handicapped. World contains 1.6 billion disabled persons (80% in developing countries, a third being children, mostly among absolutely poor in Africa, Asia, Latin America): 13 million lepers, 21 million totally blind persons, 48 million psychotics (with severe mental disorders), 85 million severely handicapped children, 205 million partially handicapped children, 450 million deaf (320 million being partially deaf), 950 million psychoneurotics.

Abortion. 75% of world's population live in countries where abortion is legal, though regarded by most Christians as murder; 25% of all pregnancies worldwide end in abortion, resulting in 65 million abortions a year of which 38% are illegal.

Urbanization. Greatest migration in history under way, in Third World, by 400 million underprivileged country-dwellers streaming into urban centres; urban dwellers rise to 44.3% of world, increasing by 1.2 million a week.

Skyscrapers. Largest under development: 2,000-ft Braced Towers, New York; 2,500-ft 210-storey World Trade Center, Chicago; and 6,864-ft (1.3 miles) 500-storey Houston Tower, Houston, Texas.

Government. Military coups and armed forces' takeovers of governments escalate to over 50% of world's countries.

Multinationals or TNCs (transnational corporations) with affiliates outside their own countries number over 10,000, increasing annually, of which 250 are Communist transnationals; total short-term liquid assets (1971) $268 billion; a major political challenge to the world's 200 sovereign nation-states.

Transnational associations. Global 'T-Net' grows from 1,300 transnational bodies in 1963 (political, cultural, ethnic, religious groupings, trade unions, non-governmental associations with millions of members) to 2,600 by 1975 and to 4,700 by 1987.

Inter-governmental organizations (IGOs). Supranationals, largest of which is EEC (Common Market), coordinate global transport, communications, meteorology, atomic energy, free trade, oil, patents, etc; number grows from 139 in 1960 to 262 in 1977.

International non-governmental organizations. Total NGOs across world number over 1,000 (800 in consultative status with United Nations Economic and Social Council, some 15% being Christian agencies).

Mega-industries. 300 multinational corporations produce goods and services totaling US$300 billion a year (largest being General Motors USA with $25 billion annual sales); destabilizing effect on smaller and poorer nations.

Megafinance. World largely controlled by money and power of the international banking community and gigantic oil companies with their allied banks through multinationals, controlling and even creating depressions, recessions, prosperity, inflation, money supply, interest rates, taxation, profits, losses, loans, localized conflicts and even full-scale wars; seeking the enormous profits to be made from a new world economic order and world socialistic government dominated by international finance.

International electronic fund transfers (EFT) total US$5 trillion per year ($14 billion a day).

Debt. Third World owes First World more than $1 trillion; corporate debt exceeds $1.5 trillion; possibility of global crash imminent.

Bureaucratization. Political chaos spreads worldwide as corrupt bureaucracies strangle political leadership, orderly government, democratic procedures, and economic progress; popular outcry for tough, take-control, messianic global leader figures.

Human rights. Increasing vulnerability of human rights; widespread government use of torture, increasing from 98 countries in 1980 to 110 countries, especially in South America (Colombia, Peru, Paraguay, Chile), Africa and Asia (Syria, Pakistan, Iran, etc). (Amnesty International).

Refugees. World total of refugees of all kinds in asylum countries fluctuates around 20 million from 1965 to 1987.

Palestinian Arabs number 5.3 million, 36% in Palestine (West Bank) and 64% in exile in 25 other countries.

Pain. 20% of human race (900 million persons) experience persistent or recurrent chronic pain (cancer, arthritis, migraine, shingles, sciatica, gout, etc).

Computers. Total computers in world 80 million, some 30 million owned and operated by Christians and churches (98% in Western churches, 2% in Third-World churches mostly in Latin America); large number of Christian networks.

Supercomputers (4th-generation very large-scale integrated VLSIs, performing 2 billion operations per second) now operating at 180 sites in Western world; average cost $12 million each.

Databases. Commercially available databases accessible online grow from 20 in 1965 to 320 in 1979 and to 900 by AD 2000 (on a wide spectrum of subjects).

Information processing now a $200-billion per year industry ($88 billion in USA); in USA and Europe, 86% of workforce involved in information gathering/processing/disseminating.

Electronic mail. 300,000 systems (distinct company-wide organizations) in place in USA offices, rising by 1990 to 1.7 million systems (used by 1 million organizations).

Electronics. As a Third-Wave industry, annual sales rise from $100 billion in 1977 to $400 billion by 1987; world's 4th-largest industry after steel, cars, and chemicals.

Communications. 650 million telephones in world, 95% being direct-dial from London (72% dialable from USA).

Electronic bulletin boards number 1,700, covering every interest, rising to over 2,500 by 1995.

Broadcasting. Total radios in world 1,600 million.

Space industries. Manufacture, in space factories, of a thousand alloys and countless products that cannot be made in presence of Earth's gravity.

Informatics (transborder data flow, TDF: computerized management techniques employed to transmit and use information without reference to national borders) assumes massive proportions, accounts for 90% of total worldwide information flow (other 10% being international news services); causes major Third-World discontent.

Counterfeiting. Some 9% of all international trade ($36 billion in 1984) involves counterfeit products.

Megacrime. International crime now costs $400 billion a year: megafraud and computer crime $44 billion; illegal hard drug industry and traffic $110 billion, representing 38% of all organized crime; includes 25 million cocaine users in USA ($25 billion), 60 million marijuana users.

Secret police. Scores of national police forces around world (KGB, DINA, SAVAK, BOSS, SIS, as well as in less recent history OGPU, NKVD, Gestapo) use surveillance, terror, imprisonment and torture to destroy human rights and to persecute alleged enemies of state.

Absolutism. Number of citizens killed by totalitarian or extreme authoritarian governments reaches 130 million since 1900 (1918-53, USSR kills 40 million citizens, China under Mao 45 million, 1975-79 Cambodia 2 million, et alia), far greater than 36 million combatants killed in wars since 1900; absolutist governments now mankind's deadliest scourge.

Warfare. Persistent wars continue: since dawn of first literate civilization in BC 3500, historians have recorded a total of 14,500 wars (defined as armed conflicts each with over 50,000 combatants) with only 250 years of complete worldwide peace in the millennia since; during these wars 1,240 million people have been killed (2.9% of all humans born in this period).

Armed forces. Total military in uniform: 26 million (18 million full-time soldiers); total combat aircraft 60,000; lethal poison-gas stockpiles include USA's 42,000 tons and USSR's 200,000 tons; in China, Peoples' Militia numbers 200 million part-time (75 million being women).

Strategic warfare. USA's strategic plan designates 40,000 targets worldwide (60 within Moscow alone).

Strategic defense plans take account of nuclear weapons delivery by ballistic missiles, cruise missiles, stealth technologies, bombers, small planes, terrorist groups; all defenses coordinated by huge battle management computers capable of tracking 20,000 strategic warheads and 1 million decoys likely to be used in a nuclear exchange.

Arms. Worldwide annual military expenditure (arms race) rises from $2 billion in 1969 to $650 billion in 1982, to $940 billion in 1985, with $4 trillion from 1983-88.

40 million engineers and a million scientists work on Earth, of whom 40% are engaged in military/defense research and development.

25 nations possess chemical or biological weaponry.

Twelve countries achieve nuclear bomb capability; global arsenals now total 65,000 nuclear warheads or weapons (25,000 strategic, 35,000 tactical; USA 26,000, USSR 34,000) equivalent to 25 billion tons of TNT (2 million times size of Hiroshima bomb); scientists calculate world could not survive nuclear war if more than 1,000 warheads detonated.

International arms trade in major weapons sold abroad now $40 billion per year, through 6 major exporters: USSR 36.5%, USA 33.6%, France 9.7%, Italy 4.3%, UK 3.6%, West Germany 3.0%.

Global terrorism. International terrorism proliferates around world: blackmail, bombings, kidnappings, assassinations, hijackings.

Local terrorism. Left-wing and right-wing terrorist gangs, political toughs, storm-trooper thugs, and paramilitary private armies proliferate across world's cities.

Religion. Global status: 85% of world are religionists, 15% atheists (anti-religion) or agnostics (no religion).

Religious pluralism widespread and accepted as the norm in most countries, cities and towns.

Quasi-religions. Rapid increase in secular movements which are partly or virtually religions, whether anti-religious (atheism, communism, Leninism, Stalinism, etc) or non-religious (agnosticism, fascism, humanism, nationalism, etc).

Messiahs. 75% of human race expects advent of a messiah figure: either Lord Maitreya as Boddhisattva (by Buddhists, numbering 6.2%), Kalki or Kalkin (the coming 10th Avatar/Incarnation of Vishnu, after Krishna the 8th and Buddha the 9th) (by Hindus, 13.5%), Jesus Son of Mary as Judge (by Muslims, 17.1%), Jesus Son of God as Judge (by Christians, 33.0%), Aquarian messiah (by New Age cultists, 0.6%), tribal messiahs (by 1.9%), New-Religionist messiahs (2.2%), Jewish Messiah (0.4%), et alia.

False messiahs or would-be Christs (several with millions of followers) become a hundred times as numerous as in any previous era.

Global status of Christianity, 1988

Christians number 33.0% of world, receive annual income of $8.6 trillion (62% of entire world's annual income), spend 97% of it on themselves; donate 1% to secular charities and 2% ($160 billion) to operate global organized Christianity.

Massive global growth of electronic Christianity: the electronic church, electronic evangelism, electronic worship, electronic religious education, electronic administration, electronic research, electronic communication.

Pentecostal-charismatics. 12% of organized Christianity are now charismatics (6% of RCs, 34% of all Protestants, 5% of Anglicans); of world's 250,000 foreign missionaries, 25% are charismatics (20% of RCs, 40% of Protestants, 60% of Third-World missionaries).

Christian groupings. Evangelicals worldwide number 221 million, neopentecostals (charismatics) in mainline denominations 70 million, premillennialists 90 million.

Ministries. Christian experimental ministries multiply to cover whole range of human activity and human need: ministries to structures, discipling/equipping models of pastoral leadership, whole-Body ministries.

Women. Major increases in pastoral and other church leadership by women, also in seminary enrollment and ordained ministries of most major denominations.

Youth workers. Western world's foreign missionary agencies send abroad, to 220 countries, 50,000 short-term young persons a year for evangelism (YWAM: 15,000 a year, total 100,000 since 1967).

Ecumenical conferences. Total held under WCC auspices since 1948, at all levels, across world: 810 distinct consultations.

Conferences on evangelization. Since 1945, some 5,510 conferences on mission and evangelism (at international, continental, regional or national level) have been held, via 5 groupings: 1,050 by Roman Catholic agencies; 1,100 by Ecumenical Movement agencies; 2,100 by Protestant and Anglican mission agencies; 840 by Evangelical mission agencies; and 420 by Charismatic Renewal agencies.

Unevangelized world. 25.5% of world, or 1.3 billion, are unaware of Christianity, Christ or the gospel; in metropolises, 13%; unreached peoples (no disciples, no churches, no witness, no scriptures, no broadcasting) fall from 1,300 ethnolinguistic peoples in 1970 to 520 by 1988; no Christian broadcasting exists in 30 major languages with from 5 to 85 million native speakers each.

Pilgrims. Some 7% of all Christians (108 million), of all traditions, are on the move as pilgrims every year, visiting national and international shrines; also 80 million Hindu, Buddhist, Muslim and other non-Christian pilgrims.

Christian lifestyles. 52% of all Christians live in affluence, 21% are comparatively well off, 14% live in moderate poverty or near-poverty, and 13% (195 million) live in absolute poverty.

Churches of the poor spread gospel in almost every corner of Earth.

New construction of religious buildings in USA peaks at $1.2 billion in 1965, falls to $0.9 billion in 1970, rises to $1.6 billion in 1980, and to $2.5 billion in 1987.

Megachurches. Rise of huge individual local churches mostly in megacities: all over 5,000 members each, some with over 100,000; with multiple ministries of all kinds.

Christian activism. Rapid spread of activism among Christians, especially in regard to pro-life issues, abortion, poverty, injustice, pornography, nuclear weaponry, war, euthanasia, child abuse, human rights, environment, et alia.

Christian unity. Global Christian interest in church union plans declines as number of involved denominations and Christians in process of uniting decline drastically by comparison with mushrooming of 500 new denominations coming into existence each year; global ecumenical movement rejects model of 'reconciled diversity', in favor of 'conciliar fellowship', i.e. united local churches forming a universal fellowship excluding confessionalism.

Internal disarray. Polarization between conservative/fundamentalist and liberal/radical constituencies grows rapidly worldwide in largest denominations, especially Roman Catholic, United Methodist, Presbyterian, Anglican, Lutheran and Southern Baptist.

Megaparachurch agencies. Rise of ultralarge Christian transnationals—service agencies outside the control of churches or denominations, with global operations and huge though precarious annual budgets.

Scripture translation. Total Common Bibles (interconfessional RC-Protestant collaboration) in preparation: 172 current active projects in 172 languages.

Christian literature. New commercial book titles per year in all languages 22,000 (rising to 25,000 by AD 2000); new titles including devotional 63,200 (75,000 by AD 2000); Christian periodicals 20,100 (35,000 by AD 2000).

Literature on evangelization. On narrower definition, titles strictly on 'evangelize', 'evangelism' or 'evangelization' total 400 new books and articles every year; on broader definition, titles on evangelization and synonyms total 10,000 a year.

Theological education by extension. TEE organizations worldwide number over 300, with over 500 programs and 100,000 extension students in 120 countries.

Christian research. Vast, loose network of 950 Christian or church-related research centers across world, very few controlled by denominations.

Church-member Christians pay out of their pockets 7,000 times as much for secular research (including on the arms race) as they pay for specifically Christian research to advance the kingdom of God.

Christian outreach. Global foreign missions of Christian world operate on $8 billion a year; rest of organized Christianity's annual income, $152 billion (95%), goes on home church and its ministries.

Evangelistic mass campaigns. Several hundred organized campaigns, usually multidenominational, are held in cities across the world each year.

Geostrategy. Of 300 plans since AD 33 for completing world evangelization, 250 have fizzled out; of 50 plans extant now, 30 are in trouble; little or no cooperation between plans, nor any geostrategic framework for realistic planning.

Eschatology. Popular books on premillennialist position (held by 41% of Evangelicals) sell 30 million copies in USA and a million copies abroad, 1970-85, especially H. Lindsay's 9-title series beginning with *The late great planet Earth* (19 million copies sold); these all however dismiss global mission and world evangelization after only miniscule passing mention (less than 1% of text).

Christian prophecy. Millions of predictions, prophecies and proposed scenarios have been made throughout history; Catholic prophecy alone, not officially acknowledged by Rome, has produced over the centuries several thousand collected prophecies about End of World and the Antichrist, some by laypersons, some by clergy, some by monks and nuns, some by bishops, and some by popes.

Ecclesiastical gangsterism proliferates in Third World: 5% of all churches' top leadership posts now occupied by corrupt accountants, embezzlers, swindlers, pirates, blackmailers, extortioners, liars, adulterers, thieves, thugs, vandals, even murderers; church and mission properties and funds regularly seized or looted (though still under 1% of the whole); vast increases in litigation and in illegal dealings.

Post-Christianity. New Age Movement expands rapidly across world to embrace 1,100 million people (22% of world), based on self-realization, divinity of man, denial of Christ's bodily Incarnation, Hindu/Buddhist occultism, made up as follows: 16.4 million Christians as members in 176 countries in 1,500 marginal Christian denominations and churches; 25 million members of non-Christian religions, pseudo-churches and New Age cults; 60 million worldwide who dabble in the occult arts (witchcraft, black magic, orgies) of whom 15 million are devotees, with a further 80 million sympathetic and interested onlookers; 672 million Hindus in 84 countries, 12.0 million shamanists, 18.1 million Tantric Buddhists, 4.0 million Afro-American low spiritists, 3.1 million high spiritists in 20 countries, plus 200 million or so secularists committed to New Age philosophies.

COSMIC ERA III: THE FUTUROLOGY OF WORLD EVANGELIZATION

An eschato-scientific scenario

This chronology divides its presentation of possible, probable and preferable future events into 2 distinct sections: (a) the elements of the Christian eschatological scheme as contained in the biblical materials, and (b) a religio-scientific composite scenario of alternative futures, derived from secular, religious, ecclesiastical and other non-biblical sources.

(a) The Christian Eschatological Schema of the Biblical End-Time

Notes.

1. In keeping with Christian tradition, no exact dates can be given for events in this short 4-page sequence here in section (a). No detailed apocalyptic timetable is possible. However, the scenario as a whole, which is a composite made up of numerous convergent and divergent alternative miniscenarios, may be compared with the dated sequence from 1988 onwards in section (b) entitled 'A Religio-Scientific Composite Scenario of Alternative Futures'.
2. The sequence contains (1) biblical material (followed by abbreviated scriptural references), plus (2) additional theological and other interpretative material that reasonably can be or has been attached to the biblical data by way of explanation and elaboration. Related scriptural references are given so that the reader may study them himself to see if particular scenarios best represent likely or probable or accurate exegesis. These scenarios embody the varying eschatological interpretations proffered by scholars throughout Christian history: chiliasm (millennialism), amillennialism, nonmillennialism, postmillennialism, historic (posttribulational) premillennialism, dispensational (pretribulational) premillennialism, realized millennialism, inaugurated imminency, other varieties of tribulationism, and so on.
3. The End-time portrayed below can be interpreted as being either (a) allegorical, or spiritual, or symbolic, or (b) literal, or a mixture of all of these. It can be seen as either (1) a series of apocalyptic vignettes or spiritual lessons in no particular order in time, or (2) a series of events in approximately chronological order. To the extent that this whole sequence is, or was, or is intended to be, a literal chronological sequence, the whole of this biblical End-time scenario, from its start (after Signs of the Times) to the onset of the Millennium, is usually regarded as occupying only a short 5-year, 7-year or 10-year period. Throughout Christian history, as described in the preceding pages of Cosmic Era II, Christian thinkers and ecclesiastics have imagined it as about to happen in their own immediate or near-term or middle-range future from one to 20 years ahead.
4. For purposes of understanding, interpretation and speculation, therefore, we can imagine this climactic period being placed at various concrete future points in our chronological scenario of the future, e.g. at AD 1990, or 2000, or 2050, or 2300, or 10,000, or 100,000, or 1 million, etc. We thus proffer below 2 alternative scenarios, combined for convenience into a single sequence. (1) Our Total Discontinuity scenario (nuclear holocausts or natural cataclysmic ends of the world) then envisages Christ returning in the aftermath of world annihilation and creating an entirely new world de novo. (2) More plausible is our Partial Continuity scenario which envisages Christ returning at one particular future date (unknown to us at present, of course), intervening in time to avert possible or even inevitable or imminent global disaster, and then taking control over the world in all its future aspects as shown below, thereby inaugurating a period we can recognize as the biblical Millennium, and controlling and guiding in person all the world's developments and potentialities as detailed below in section (b) 'A Religio-Scientific Composite Scenario of Alternative Futures', especially in the realms of science, technology, space, society, politics, government, human evolution et alia.

Epoch Omega
THE BIBLICAL END-TIME: A COMPOSITE SCENARIO

The Signs of the Times

Signs and portents arise in profusion, all being evangelistic, hortatory, warnings to rebellious mankind; Bible contains at least 22 major signs signalling the End-time, including international (wars), cultural (interest in occult), natural (famines, drought), mysterious (UFOs, etc), satanic (devil worship), et alia. (Mt 16:3, Mt 24:4).

Increasing global population mobility, global strife, disintegrating social order, vast increases in knowledge in all subjects. (Dan 12:4).

Jerusalem the Holy City trampled by Gentiles (Times of the Gentiles, under hostile Gentile powers from BC 586 and AD 135 up to state of Israel (1948) and future Advent). (Lk 21:24).

Wars and rumours of wars (cold wars), famines, earthquakes, epidemics, terrible sufferings, celestial portents. (Mt 24:6-7, Lk 21:9-11).

Beginning of the 2 great End-time revivals: (1) of good, (2) of evil. (Joel 2:28-29).

Revivals and rapid church growth with mass acceptance of gospel in some parts of the world, with mass rejection of gospel in others: millions converted in last great global spiritual revival; worldwide signs and wonders accompany proclamation of the gospel in every land.

Spread of false gospels increases, with rise of false prophets, false christs, false messiahs, and antichrists. (Mt 24:5,11,14, 1 Tim 4:1, 2 Pet 2:1, 1 John 1:18).

End-time apostasy within Christendom (represented by the 7 churches of the Apocalypse, Rev 1-3); abandonment of biblical Christianity by millions of nominal church members; polarization of global Christianity into the affluent middle-class Western-world Church of the Rich ('the Laodicean Church'), the Church of the Poor (Africa, Latin America), and the Church of the Absolutely Poor (South and Central Asia) ('the Smyrna/Philadelphia Church'). (Mt 24:10-12, 2 Thess 2:3, Rev 2:9, 3:17).

Failure of the church to evangelize the world, part remaining still unevangelized until the Tribulation. (Mt 10:23b).

Rise of a charismatic leader within 10-nation confederacy (European Economic Community, or a Mediterranean Confederacy, as revived Roman Empire), who seizes power and sets up a ruthless, totalitarian world government; who further is (a) a political genius with vast organizational and leadership abilities who creates a world socialist order, and a psychic genius who creates a new universal world religion (based on occult Hinduism), mastery of secret cosmic forces, tremendous hypnotic powers; frightening display of psychic force, attempt to convert the whole world forcibly to occultism; later, ruler is revealed to be the final Antichrist, the Ultimate Antichrist, the Universal Monarch. (2 Thess 2:3-4).

THE SECRET PRETRIBULATION RAPTURE SCENARIO

First or Secret Coming of Christ on the clouds of heaven (the private or invisible Coming 'for' his Saints) in his imperishable immortal resurrection body, imminent, sudden, unexpected, without prior signs or warnings, 'as a thief in the night'; announced with trumpet to the church but not publicly to the world. (1 Thess 4:16, 1 Cor 15:52).

First stage of calling out of the Elect (the Body of Christ): Translation of the Saints; imminent, sudden, secret Rapture of the Church, or part of it (only those prepared, worthy and expectant; or only the Confessing Church of prophets, apostles, martyrs, confessors and witnesses; or, 'God's preferential option for the poor', i.e. only the downtrodden, the persecuted, the deprived, the oppressed, the marginalized, the Church of the Poor, or the Church of the Absolutely Poor as the most faithful or most deserving Remnant), with the dead in Christ preceding them (the Church of the Martyrs, in the Out-Resurrection); Age of Grace with offer of salvation still open however until end of Great Tribulation. (1 Thess 4:16-17).

The Rapture, with sudden disappearance of millions of Christians, is interpreted by hostile antichristian New Age Movement leaders as a mighty evolutionary quantum leap to a higher consciousness, the Cosmic Mind ejecting laggards of the species as a body rejects unwanted cells. (2 Peter 3:4).

On other scenarios, no secret coming or rapture takes place, but entire church moves forward as the suffering Body of Christ as it passes into and through the Great Tribulation.

Inauguration of New Age order and religion

Global inauguration of this-worldly New Age (the New Genesis), a pseudo-New Age biblically termed 'The Great Delusion', or 'The Lie', or the 'wicked deception', a 'false gospel', being widespread irresistible religious disinformation and deception as a 'Sign of the Times'; long period of unprecedented peace, prosperity and plenty, sharing and global euphoria on Earth, as satanic counterfeit and parody of promised Millennium; Western wealth redistributed among poorest countries; miracles, signs and wonders performed; millions of New-Agers agree to cooperate

with newly-emerged World Ruler (the Antichrist) in building New Age Paradise on Earth. (Mt 24:24, 2 Thess 2:9-12).
Antichrist proclaims lasting and permanent peace settlement in Middle East including alliance with Israel; rebuilds great cities including Tyre as political capital. (Ezek 28).
Rebuilding of Temple in Jerusalem permitted and resumption of its sacrifices begun. (Dan 9:27).
New Age world order inaugurated: Antichrist regulates international and local commerce and finance by ordering every person to have indelibly impregnated into his body an identifying number accessible to scanning devices, thus controlling all buying and selling; computer-controlled cashless society; total control of all personal and corporate wealth; ruler embraces number 666 to show rejection of Bible as myth. (Rev 13:2b,4b,7b,14-18).
New Age world religion inaugurated: blend of Western science and ancient Eastern wisdom or Hinduism/Buddhism/Lamaism/Tantrism, i.e. of elements of Hindu or Eastern philosophy, astrology, astral projection (out-of-body experiences), ancient pagan occultism, spiritism, medium religion, metaphysics, apostate modern or secular religion, denial of Incarnation of Christ, rejection of Bible as ultimate authority, mind power, self-realization (realizing one is God), deification of man, ESP, psychokinesis, psychology, parapsychology, telepathy, clairvoyance, precognition, hypnosis and hypnotherapy, autosuggestion, yoga, biofeedback ('electronic yoga'), witchcraft, shamanism, voodoo, satanism, chakras, reincarnation, vegetarianism, zen, demon possession, necromancy, overwhelming sense of universal consciousness.
Concrete embodiments of New Age religion, or Aquarian Age religion, include: Unity School of Christianity, Religious Science, Mind Science, Christian Science, Divine Science, Great White Brotherhood, Church Universal and Triumphant, White Eagle Brotherhood, Theosophical Society, Rosicrucians (AMORC), Human Potential Movement, TM, et alia; with elements of religious deception, delusion of divinity or godhead, higher or altered states of consciousness, exploitation of consciousness (inner space), based on belief in the oneness of all life and in themselves as part of the Universal Self or Consciousness, the Self's infinite potential, expecting an Aquarian messiah/saviour (Lord Maitreya, etc).
Mass media, computers, communications technology, artificial intelligence, mind control, hypnosis, drugs etc, all utilized by Antichrist to propagate pseudo-evangelization worldwide within days, i.e. establishment of the New Age world religion (based on man's divinity, self-realization, self-sufficiency, denial of Christ's bodily Incarnation).
Period of peace, plenty, prosperity under New Age world order begins to disintegrate as realities of human evil surface.

The Tribulation

Global peace and prosperity shattered in first half of a 7-year period of unprecedented terror, turmoil and bloodshed (the 'Great Disaster', the 'Great Chastisement' to Catholics, the 1st half of Daniel's 70th Week). (Dan 9:24, Mt 24:9, 2 Tim 3:1).
Northern power (Russia) launches all-out invasion of Middle East to obliterate Israel, but armies suddenly and inexplicably destroyed in northern Palestine; burial of corpses takes 7 months. (Ezek 38-39).
Antichrist renounces defense pact with Israel, breaks covenant with Jews, causes Temple sacrifices to cease, enters Temple and in Holy of Holies announces he is God (Abomination of Desolation, the Final Blasphemy), demands worship by whole world, sets up his own image as Prince of Peace in every city. (Mt 24:15, Ascension of Isaiah 4:11).
Vision of scroll or book of human destiny (God's purpose in judgment), sealed with 7 seals. (Rev 5, being Revelation's 1st of 7 groups of 7 visions each).
The 7 Seals opened by all-powerful and all-seeing Lamb: (1) conquest, (2) war, (3) famine, (4) death, (5) martyrdom, (6) anarchy, (7) judgment. (Rev 6:1-17, 8:1-2).
The Four Horsemen of the Apocalypse (opening of the first 4 Seals), white, red, black, pale: (1) war/conquest/deception/false religions/cults/pseudo-messiah/antichrist, (2) slaughter, (3) famine, (4) death (or (1) missionary preaching of the gospel, (2) civil war/bloodshed, (3) famine/hunger/disease/poverty, (4) terror/pestilence/death/destruction); 25% of world slaughtered. (Mt 24:7, Rev 6:1-8).
1st Persecution: storm of religious persecution sweeps across globe resulting in martyrdoms of vast numbers of Christians, especially in Western world's Church of the Rich (the Laodicean church), but including multitudes of new converts (after 5th Seal opened); persecuted Christians about to be martyred are told to be patient until foreordained total of all martyrs is completed. (Mt 24:9, Rev 6:9-11).
Collapse of governments—world, regional, local—into unprecedented global anarchy (after opening of 6th Seal); universal mass hysteria, total terror. (Rev 6:12-17).
False gospel of religious disinformation and deception now accepted worldwide: false christs and false prophets deceive vast mass of mankind by stupendous signs and wonders. (Mt 24:24).
Sealing begins of overcoming Christians and future martyrs on Earth; all 144,000 prospective martyrs are now permanently sealed for spiritual protection as the New Israel as Great Tribulation approaches. (Rev 7:1-8).
7th Seal opened: 7 Trumpet Woes herald plagues and curses: (1) natural calamities, (2) ships and seas destroyed, (3) rivers and water supplies ruined, (4) celestial bodies disorganized, (5) locusts from the Abyss (the bottomless pit), (6) Eastern army of 200 million kill a third of mankind; the 2nd Persecution. (Rev 8:1-9:21, being Revelation's 2nd group of 7 visions).
Sufferings of the church multiplied as it prophesies and witnesses to the world. (Rev 10:9-11).
Times of the Gentiles (period for God's punishment of Israel and their repentance and conversion) conclude with vicious persecution of Israel for three and a half years (literal or figurative) until end of Tribulation. (Lk 21:24, Rev 11:1-2).
The Two Witnesses (Olive Trees, Lampstands: Moses and Elijah, Law and Prophecy; Joshua and Zerubbabel the anointed religious and civil leaders; the witness-bearing two-sevenths of the universal church about to be martyred), after 42 months or three and a half years (literal or figurative) of preaching the gospel and opposing New Age philosophy, complete their task of world evangelization through bearing witness to claims of Christ, are slain by Antichrist symbolizing near-obliteration of the church, in 3rd Persecution; but then are raised from dead, symbolizing final global revival of faith in Christ with millions converted. (Zech 4:11-14, Rev 11:3-14).
Great Commission of Christ fulfilled in the sense that universal preaching of the gospel to all nations (world evangelization, discipling of the peoples) has been finally accomplished by the church militant on Earth, with disciples and witnesses found in every race and people and language. (Mt 24:14, 28:19-20).
Penultimate direct supernatural work of the Holy Spirit in proclamation, evangelization and conversions throughout world as Church Age draws to its close.
Midtribulation Rapture of the Saints: removal of confessing church before Great Tribulation escalates into total horror. (1 Thess 4:17).

The Great Tribulation

Second half of the Tribulation (2nd half of Daniel's 70th Week) eclipses terrors of first half now past. (Dan 9:24, Mt 24:21-28, Rev 11-18).
7th Trumpet sounds, announcing imminent end of present satanic world age and imminent commencement of Reign of Christ on Earth, with God's impending assumption of all power, preceded by second and more terrible half of the Great Tribulation. (Rev 11:15-19).
The Restrainer (=Holy Spirit; or Church before final rapture; or orderly process of government; or missionary preaching of the gospel) is removed from Earth, allowing evil full sway. (2 Thess 2:6-7).
The 7 significant Signs of Revelation: woman clothed with Sun, Satan, war, 1st beast, 2nd beast, Lamb, harvest. (Rev 12:1-14:20).
War in heaven (a legal battle between opposing counsel over the claims of Christ to be Lord and Messiah) between archangel Michael and the great blood-red 7-headed Dragon (the Devil or Satan, world deceiver, prince of the present world-system), who with his angels is then thrown down to Earth with great wrath; three and a half years (literal or figurative) of violent persecution of Israel and the Remnant and reign of terror against remaining Christians. (Rev 12:1-17, being Revelation's 3rd group of 7 visions).
Emergence of Trinity of Evil (Satan, Antichrist, Pseudo-Christ): (1) rise of the Dragon (Satan) as final authority of evil; (2) rise from the sea ('the seething cauldron of unregenerate humanity') of 7-headed hydra, the beast Leviathan with blasphemous Name claiming Deity, the Antichrist as world political ruler over a global government (representing all such rulers and antichrists in history from 1st-century Roman emperor worshipped as divine, to Nero Redivivus, to final ruler of one last terrible empire, head of 10-nation confederacy of Europe or Mediterranean as revived Holy Roman Empire, one of whose 7 heads is killed but then resurrected); and (3) rise from the earth of the beast Behemoth, the False Prophet, religious incarnation of the final Antichrist, the Pseudo-Christ (the False Christ), the False Lamb (parodying Christ's death and resurrection), the Man of Sin, the Lawless One, the Little Horn, the Son of Perdition, the Pseudo-Messiah (symbolizing a long sequence from 1st-century imperial priesthood in charge of rites of emperor-worship), whose cipher is 666; vicious religious persecution (the 4th Persecution) under universal world religion, psychotic hatred of Israel, totalitarian economic enslavement; Antichrist demands all take the mark of the Beast or die; millions slaughtered. (Rev 13:1-10, Mt 24:15-21, Mk 13:14-19, 2 Thess 2:3-12, Rev 13:11-18, 16:13, 19:20).
New Age world religion, which initially has been a universal religious movement emphasizing peace and prosperity, degenerates under control of Antichrist as supreme head; obligatory entry, on pain of death, by means of ancient Luciferic initiations; cult of worship of Antichrist enforced on all. (Rev 13:4,8,13-14).
Image of the Resurrected Beast made and animated; huge size, utters oracles, universally believed. (Rev 13:14-15).
As full foreordained number of Gentile Christians is reached, mass conversion of Jews begins: a Remnant of 144,000 is converted out of Israel, together with vast numbers of new Gentile converts; all 144,000 pros-

pective martyrs being sealed for spiritual protection against forces of evil. (Rom 11:25-27, Rev 7:1-17, 14:1-5).

The 144,000 converted Israelites become end-time evangelists who reach world's last unreached people groups and so complete task of world evangelization.

Vast worldwide satanic activity, under Antichrist as the Great Dictator (political tyrant with worldwide power); terrifying worldwide destruction.

Three-and-a-half-year (literal or figurative) reign of terror: (a) the 5th or Great Persecution, one last worldwide persecution, worst in history; ruthless persecution of Israel and Jews, as ultimate scapegoat for ills of Earth, as Antichrist turns to 'the final solution' — total genocide; (b) the Great Falling Away (the Great Apostasy): millions of Christians from former Church of the Rich abandon their faith; and (c) on some scenarios, total destruction of the whole church with entire body of believers martyred. (Mt 24:10, Lk 18:8, 2 Thess 2:3, Rev 13:7a).

Last days of the Age of Grace

Last supernatural proclamation from heaven of Everlasting Gospel of love in all its fullness to every nation, and kindred, and tongue, and people, either to convert or to seal doom of mankind; last appeal and announcement of final chance for repentance and salvation, imminent end of Age of Grace with following judgment upon wicked in climax of Great Tribulation. (Rev 14:6-7, being Revelation's 4th group of 7 visions; Lk 16:31).

Reaping of the harvest of Earth's peoples, and treading of 'the great winepress of the wrath of God', with total bloodshed throughout Israel. (Joel 3:13, Mk 4:29, Rev 14:14-20).

The 7 Last Plagues (the 7 Bowls of the wrath of God; terrible judgments, not chastisement but final and punitive): (1) foul bodily sores, (2) death of all seas, (3) pollution of all water supplies, (4) heat and fire, (5) darkness, (6) drought and plague of demons, (7) hail, thunder, lightning, mega-earthquakes. (Rev 15:1-16:21, being Revelation's 5th group of 7 visions; Mt 24:7).

Destruction of Great Babylon, city of Antichrist, the Great Harlot (Rome, the goddess Rome, et alia) seated on her paramour the 7-headed Dragon: (a) Religious Babylon (the apostate religious world, or the one-world religious system); (b) Secular Babylon (civilized, urbanized man organized apart from God, man in organized but godless community); and (c) its destroyer, and usurper of its religious primacy, Political Babylon (the Antichrist's confederated 10-nation empire, the ruthless secular world of luxurious commerce, or the one-world politico-commercial system). (Rev 17:1-18:24, being Revelation's 6th group of 7 visions).

THE DAY OF THE LORD

End to 20 centuries of delay over Parousia, a delay due to God's patience and forbearance 'not wanting anyone to perish but everyone to come to repentance'. (2 Peter 3:9).

The Day, the Day of Christ, the Great and Terrible Day of the Lord, the Last Day, the Day of Wrath. (Rev 6:17, 19:11-21, being Revelation's 7th group of 7 visions; Mal 4:5).

Massing of 4 great confederations of Gentile nations: North (Russia and allies, Ezek 38-39) and South (Egypt and Arabs, Dan 11) mass to finally destroy Israel and God's people; opposed by West (10-nation confederation of Europe, Dan 2), with kings of the East (China and allies, Rev 16:12) also involved (USA having been destroyed after Rapture of church, on current premillennialist interpretation). (Mt 24:7, Rev 16:12-16, 19:17-19).

Battle or war of Armageddon (at Megiddo, scene of many decisive battles in history); the ultimate world war, greatest in history, with hundreds of millions of combatants, the entire armed might of the world, deployed for several hundred miles around Megiddo; last cataclysmic struggle between good and evil on the Day of the Lord, the Great Day of God's Wrath; slaughter of armies of Antichrist. (Rev 16:16, 19:17-19).

Total discontinuity scenario: complete destruction of old world

Celestial cataclysms, woes and terrors: Sun, Moon and stars disappear, 'great noise', 'fervent heat', 'earth burned up': a great celestial conflagration. (Mt 24:29, 2 Peter 3, Rev 6:12-14).

Jerusalem the scene of unparalleled warfare, with house-to-house fighting in streets; Mount of Olives suddenly splits with east-west chasm as Christ returns. (Zech 14:2,4).

The Last Trump: final consummation of all things in Christ, ending of all human history. (Mt 24:31a, 1 Cor 15:52).

Second Advent of Christ (Second Coming, Parousia, Arrival, Appearing, Return, Disclosure, Revelation, Revealing, Unveiling): premillennial, sudden, unexpected, public, visible Return of Jesus Christ as lightning with power and glory ('with' his saints, 'revealed from Heaven with his mighty angels in flaming fire'), to Mount of Olives to establish the Millennial Kingdom, as king and great High Priest. (Mt 24:27, 2 Thess 1:7, Rev 19:11-16).

Final close of Age of Grace; universal mourning, and completion of number of the Elect (Body of Christ) who have come through the Great Tribulation and their gathering in from 4 quarters of Earth after Last Trump (Posttribulation Rapture of the Saints). (Mt 24:31b).

Judgment of All Nations on Earth: i.e. of living Gentile believers ('sheep'), of Israel's Gentile persecutors ('goats'), and of Israel itself and the Jews ('brethren'); the great eschatological reversal of fortunes. (Mt 25:31-46, Rom 14:10, 2 Cor 5:10).

The Last Day reveals final outcome of God's age-long cosmic dispute/controversy/lawsuit against nations of the world and their gods or idols to establish the claims of Jesus Christ. (OT, Jn 1-12, Jn 13:17, et alia).

Overthrow of Beast and False Prophet, cast into Lake of Fire with their followers. (Rev 19:20).

Satan bound and thrown into Abyss (the bottomless pit); consummation and close of Age of Grace; 'End of the World' (end of entire satanic world-system). (Rev 20:1-3).

First Resurrection from the Dead (the resurrection of the just, the martyrs, the dead in Christ), who will live and reign with Christ 1,000 years (literal or figurative). (Rev 20:4-6).

THE MILLENNIAL AGE: THE MESSIANIC KINGDOM

The Millennium is inaugurated, either (a) spiritual (allegorical, symbolic, nonmillennialist, amillennialist) i.e. the Church Age from AD 33 to Second Advent, with new birth as First Resurrection; or (b) literal transitional period of either 1,000 years, or 400 years, or 40 years, or a complete period of some sort, or one generation, or 1,000 generations, or 1,000 eras, or 1,000 ages; or (c) Sabbath Day lasting a literal 1,000 years, after preceding 6 Days (6,000 years) of recorded secular history and Heilsgeschichte (salvation history); or (d) both spiritual and literal overlapping where Church Age overlaps with eternal Kingdom of God. (Rev 20:3-7).

Partial discontinuity scenario: Christ takes over existing world

The Messiah restores throne of David and sets up Millennial Kingdom at Jerusalem, over a restored Israel and subdued Gentile nations; Jews as a nation accept Jesus as their Messiah; earthly Jewish kingdom with restoration of Israel as God's people, rebuilt and restored Temple, daily sacrifices, annual feasts; but curse on humanity only partially lifted, people still born in sin, even allowing a small satanic following eventually to emerge.

Pacification, conquest and restoration of divine authority over entire world-system and all its peoples; gradual but final conquest of death, disease and sin; evil present but held firmly in check since Satan has been bound; all surviving persons and Christians on Earth at time of Parousia enter Millennium retaining their natural (mortal) bodies to repopulate the world, but Christians formerly raptured retain their heavenly bodies; eschatological union of Christ with Israel and Gentiles in his body, the church.

Universal spread and acceptance of the Kingdom of God (as envisaged by Irenaeus in AD 180); gradual conversion of vast numbers to Christ.

Conversion of the entire world (remaining humankind of all other religions, including 'anonymous Christianity'), under direct leadership of the Messiah, to open Christian faith; 'at the name of Jesus every knee would bow, every tongue confess that Jesus is Lord'; end of institutionalized Christian religion and worship. (Phil 2:10-11, Rom 14:11).

The Messianic Banquet (Marriage Supper of the Lamb, the Great Feast), attended by nations from North, South, East and West. (Mt 26:26,29, Lk 13:29, 14:15-24, 22:16-18, Mt 24:31, Rev 19:7-9).

Reign of Christ on Earth, presiding over annihilation of time itself, with resurrected apostles and martyrs from every race and people and culture and language as co-rulers, as a new species of Homo Sapiens i.e. immortal humans in the New Age (Mt 19:28, GNB), 'sitting on thrones ruling over the 12 Tribes of Israel'; the Golden Age of the Church, Reign of the Church in Society, the Eternal Sabbath rest of Creation, an earthly kingdom of peace, righteousness, justice and plenty, in which however flesh and blood (human nature in its weakness) cannot inherit the Kingdom of God. (Lk 22:30, Rev 20:4,6, 1 Cor 15:50, Heb 4:9).

The Last Judgment: the Eschaton

Recapitulation of entire period since Jesus' Cross and Resurrection: Satan loosed from prison (the Abyss) to foment one last rebellion with vast host 'as the sand of the sea' led by the great persecutors Gog and Magog (Rome and Babylon); Satan finally overthrown and destroyed by fire. (Rev 20:7-9).

Postmillennial coming of Christ: final destruction of Satan with Beast and False Prophet in Lake of Fire. (Rev 20:10).

Second or General Resurrection of the Dead, for judgment of the wicked, idolators, worshippers of the Beast, Christian apostates. (Rev 20:12-13).

Last Judgment (Last Assize, Day of Judgment, Final Judgment, Great White Throne) invoking Lamb's Book of Life, based on people's response to persecuted church's witness and on loyalty to Christ under persecution. (Rev 20:11-15, Rom 14:10).

Death and Hades with their followers are cast into Lake of Fire; 'This is the Second Death'. (Rev 20:14).

End of space-time continuum; specifically, end of 7 evils: death, mourning (sorrow), weeping (tears), pain, curse, night, and the sea (the unregenerate world of evil). (Rev 20:15; 21, 22).

CONSUMMATION OF THE NEW CREATION: GOD CREATES NEW HEAVENS AND A NEW EARTH

Final fulfillment and completion of God's promise 'Behold, I create new heavens and a new earth'. (Isaiah 65:17, RSV).

Beginning of the genuine New Age, the eternal state, the everlasting Kingdom of God, the Paradise of God, the New Eden, the New Jerusalem (1,500 miles cubed, an eternal Holy of Holies), 12 gates never closed (free access to God), River of Life and Tree of Life (knowledge of how creation works, with fruit conferring immortality), a place of light, glory, splendor, truth, universality, salvation, security, worship, work, service, responsibility, abundance, health, joy, enjoyment, the vision of Christ as Alpha and Omega; 12 zodiacal signs of the Old Age permanently reversed (Rev 21:19-20); a renovated Universe, a renewed Galaxy, a transformed Earth, built on Earth's different peoples (races), Israel and the church, and 'the unsearchable riches of Christ'. (Eph 2:7, Rev 2:7; 21-22).

(b) A Religio-Scientific Composite Scenario of Alternative Futures

Notes.

1. To assist us comprehend the study of the future, it is helpful to recognize 10 basic periods of the future, as follows. Of these, everybody is interested in periods (1) and (2); most futurists study periods (3) and (4); futurists involved in medicine and the sciences often make forecasts in periods (4) and (5); ecologists study periods (3) to (6); and astronomers and cosmologists specialize in periods (7) to (10).

   (1) The immediate future (up to 1 year from now),
   (2) The near-term future (1-5 years from now),
   (3) The middle-range future (5-20 years from now),
   (4) The long-range future (20-100 years from now, i.e. up to AD 2100),
   (5) The distant future (100-1,000 years from now, i.e. AD 2100-3000),
   (6) The far distant future (over 1,000 years hence, i.e. after AD 3000),
   (7) The megafuture (after AD 1 million, up to end of Solar System),
   (8) The gigafuture (after AD 1 billion, up to death of stars),
   (9) The terafuture (after AD 1 trillion, up to supermassive black hole),
   (10) The eschatofuture or exafuture (after AD 1 quintillion or 10^{18} years, up to end at 10^{100} years).

   This schema is not superimposed in toto on the future chronology below, but the reader can do so if he finds it helpful.
2. The following single continuous chronology is not intended to in any sense imply prediction, prophecy or predestination, nor should it be construed as presenting only one single coherent and consistent scenario. It combines numerous overlapping scenarios and miniscenarios and single scientifically-predicted or forecasted events with the entire range of possible and probable events envisaged by technological-social optimism, limits-to-growth secular pessimism, and extrabiblical Protestant and Catholic prophecy. In consequence, particular items or scenarios will often be inconsistent or even appear to be contradictory. The sequence should therefore be regarded as simply what it is: a set of possible or probable or preferable alternative futures, not necessarily connected or consistent.
3. A large number of Christian events, particularly international conferences, have already been arranged and announced for the period 1988-2000. They are here included together with places and themes and other details as planned and anticipated in 1987.
4. The years shown at the left margin are simply those forecasted or suggested by specialists in the particular items enumerated. They should be regarded not as exact predictions but as approximate milestones, probabilistic forecasts, or only conditional forecasts, claiming accuracy perhaps to 20% of the time distance from the year 1988 (thus the year '2088' below would mean somewhere between 2068-2108).
5. A large proportion of these items are secular events or situations. They are included here because all have ethical, theological and missiological significance, hence are given so that the reader can himself consider and assess their implications for global mission and world evangelization.
6. None of the individual items below should be taken as necessarily the personal opinions or position of the author, who is here simply bringing together significant items from the vast extant literature on futurology, forecasting and alternative scenarios—possible, probable or preferable.

The Information Civilization: Fourth Industrial Revolution

1988 After 1st Industrial Revolution (1775), 2nd (1901), and 3rd (1950, nuclear power, microchips, genes), 4th revolution from 1988 on is noological, knowledge-based, information-based; with people-supervised cybernated machines based on inexhaustible resources in space.

Knowledge explosion: the stock of human knowledge increases phenomenally each year; contents of Library of Congress (world's largest), and other major libraries, available to all via personal computers.

Five dominant technologies drive progress for next 40 years: computers, automation, space colonies, energy, communications.

First USA 5th-generation ultracomputers: supercomputers using multiprocessing (hundreds of microprocessors linked together).

Supercomputers increasingly used for international sabotage via software bombs (programmed booby traps).

Robotics revolution, with large numbers of industrial robots, begins to dramatically alter economy of Japan and then of Western world; 20% of all industrial mass production now carried out by robots.

Critical 100-year phase in human existence is now recognized to be the century 1950-2050: nuclear annihilation of all life on Earth possible and therefore of entire human race, until humans begin to spread out into space colonies.

New Transcendentalism: new interest in meditation and other New Age self-exploratory techniques; growing global drug addiction.

USA: new uniting denomination, Evangelical Lutheran Church in America, formally inaugurated by 3 bodies with 5.3 million members: American Lutheran Church, Lutheran Church in America, Association of Evangelical Lutheran Churches (1 January).

Explosive growth of charismatic, evangelical and fundamentalist 'video churches', video denominations and video mission agencies; vast rash of house-church networks begins to spread in all countries with large denominations.

International Theological Consultation on Religious Conversion (sponsored by LCWE and WEF), in Hong Kong (4-8 January).

2nd All India Congress on Missions and Evangelism (AICOME '88), sponsored by indigenous-mission body India Missions Association, IMA (successor to AICOME in 1977); in Pune, India; 350 participants (4-8 January).

1st World Meeting, Global Network of Centers for World Mission, in Singapore (May).

USSR places permanent space stations in orbit for military purposes.

First success in repairing a human genetic defect.

Third-World nations led by Mexico repudiate $1,000 billion debts to Western banks; West and USSR retaliate, Latin American economy collapses, starvation sweeps Africa and Asia; huge Third-World terrorist operation smashes Western electronic economy, stock market crashes, world community disintegrates in chaos. (W. Clark's 1984 scenario *Cataclysm: the North-South conflict of 1987*).

Specialized space telescopes put in orbit: SIRTF (Spacelab Infrared Telescope Facility), COBE (Cosmic Background Explorer), GRO (Gamma Ray Observatory).

NASA's Hubble Space Telescope launched by Space Shuttle in 320-mile-high orbit; 14-feet diameter, 12 tons; 10 times better viewing than on Earth, sees as far as 14 billion light-years, enables unprecedented census of the Universe planned by AD 2010; solves mystery of quasars (galaxies forming or dying which each emits more light than 100 billion stars, and many with superluminal parts moving demonstrably faster than light).

Hipparcos (High Precision Parallax Correcting Satellite) launched by European Space Agency, results in most accurate star map in history.

Computers widely used in automatic document translation and multilingual instantaneous interpreting.

Automatic computer self-programming using plain ordinary language replaces 30% of all human programming of computers.

World's fastest supercomputer introduced: Cray-3, with 16 main processors working in parallel, 8-billion-byte memory.

Technological disasters proliferate: nuclear mishaps, chemical spills, virus escapes, major air and shipping accidents, structural failures, industrial sabotage, unstoppable pest attacks on crops and animals or people.

Estimated date for Prayalog, Hindu end of the world, at end of present Kali Yuga of decay, degeneration and guilt (Kali Age or Dark Ages, for last 5,000 years since Flood over whole Earth); final act of Lord Brahma's wrath; whole world disintegrates in chaos in natural disasters (according to 'Bhagwat' in *Mahabharata*), new life arises after Brahma completes 100,000 years of meditation.

11th United Bible Societies (UBS) Council Meeting, Budapest/Vienna (May).
5th Nigeria National Congress on Evangelization, Zaria.
7th General Congress, International Association for Mission Studies (IAMS), in Rome, on theme 'Christian Mission towards a Third Millennium: a Gospel of Hope' (29 June-5 July).
Urban Evangelism Conference, sponsored by Baptist World Alliance, in Panama/Mexico/Costa Rica (2-4 July).
USA: Leadership '88, LCWE Conference for Emerging Younger Christian Leaders, in Washington, DC; 1,500 participants (5-8 July).
Canterbury '88: Anglican Spiritual Renewal Conference, Canterbury (UK), organized by SOMA, for leaders of leaders on 'The Church in the Valley of Decision'; 350 present including many bishops (3-7 July); followed by SOMA open conference for 1,500 (9-12 July).
12th Lambeth Conference of Anglican Bishops, Canterbury (UK); 450 bishops from 420 dioceses (16 July-7 August).
1st International Congress for the Evangelization of the Spanish World, in USA, sponsored by Evangelicals, with 4,000 Hispanic leaders (25-29 July).
11th Baptist Youth World Conference (BWA), Glasgow, on theme 'Jesus Christ rules'; 10,000 youth participants from over 100 countries (27-31 July).
World Conference on the Christian Approach to Poverty 1986-1991 (World Methodist Council), in Latin America; on Methodism's social witness.
International Evangelical Bible Consultation/Conference (sponsored by LCWE, BGEA et al), in Amman, Jordan, stressing biblical position on justice and human rights.
World Conference on Religious Liberty, Jerusalem.
USA: Congress 88, A National Festival of Evangelism, sponsored by all major mainline denominations (PCUSA, UMC, SBC, RCC, et alia); 15,000 church leaders present; aim, to reach all unchurched and unreached Americans; title, 'That the World May Believe'; in Chicago (4-8 August).
13th World Congress, International Council of Christian Churches (ICCC), in Amsterdam; 40th anniversary of founding there during 1st Congress (August).
15th Pentecostal World Conference, in Kuala Lumpur, Malaysia, on 'Behold the Glory of the Lord', with emphasis on strategy for global evangelization (5-9 October).
World Wesleyan Conference on Witness and Evangelism, sponsored by World Methodist Council, on 250th anniversary of John Wesley's conversion.
1st International Meeting, Theological Students for Frontier Missions.
2nd World Consultation on Frontier Missions (WCFM).
Enzyme processing (a chemical synthesis system) becomes fastest-growing industry on Earth.

1989 VATs (voice-activated speech-recognition typewriters and word-processors), introduced 1988, begin to displace 3 million typists and secretaries worldwide; sales in USA alone reach $3.5 billion a year by 1989.
Scientists perfect art of cloning (reproduction of infinite number of genetically identical people from cells of a single person, whose human body consists of 10^{28} atoms); first human is cloned.
New weather patterns produce global crop failures and lead to megafamines, with hordes of starving people marching across continents in search of food.
Synclavier invented: minicomputerized synthesizer capable of duplicating sounds of 25 musical instruments individually and as an orchestra; 1995, 'Music Minus One' company produces recordings leaving out one instrument for any amateur to join in.
2nd World Conference on Mission and Evangelism (5th Meeting of CWME/WCC, Commission on World Mission and Evangelism), São Paulo, Brazil, or Cyprus; theme 'Your Will be Done: Mission in Christ's Way'; distributes pan-Orthodox missionary icon widely (February).
1st World Congress on Evangelization of Portuguese-speaking Peoples, in Brazil.
Brazil, Mexico, Philippines and other Third-World countries default on total of $400 billion of international indebtedness; dozens of Western corporations, banks and cities go bankrupt.
Soviets develop psionics (science of electronics dealing with psychic phenomena) and place psionic weapon in orbit around Earth; Western world reacts belatedly by opening parapsychology laboratories.
Mission World '89 (International Satellite Mission) sponsored by Billy Graham Evangelistic Association, originating from a major city and beamed by satellite to hundreds of others across the world (Summer).
Titanic nuclear accident as nuke (power plant) melts down in populous area: tens of thousands of casualties from radiation and mass panic; public outcry to shutdown all nukes.
International Bishops' Retreat 2000 for world's 3,500 Roman Catholic bishops, to inaugurate decade of evangelization 1990-2000.
World Evangelization Conference on Liberation Theology and Personal Salvation (sponsored by World Methodist Council), in Latin America.
World Conference of Methodist Fulltime Evangelists, sponsored by World Methodist Council.
2nd International Congress on World Evangelization (ICOWE II) convened by Lausanne Committee (LCWE), in Singapore; 6,000 attenders (July).
Computer robot designed to understand all major languages.
Satellites enable living maps (animated color displays, movie x-rays in motion) of any city or area on Earth to be inspected for activities as they take place.
OPEC cartel of oil-producing countries, which has rapidly accumulated unprecedented vast wealth, suddenly collapses and goes bankrupt.
Second Western Asia-Southern Asia war, spreading from Iran-Iraq war begun in 1980: both sides use nuclear weapons, destroying major cities.
USA stock market crashes, annihilating US economic stability; US economy destroyed, no longer a superpower.
Data-broadcasting stations begun, regularly transmitting all forms of data for personal computers and others to pick up; global electronic church arises, broadcasting daily all data, teaching and communications necessary for the day-to-day functioning of organized Christianity.
A radical communications invention makes it possible to see, touch and speak with anyone in the world.
Worldwide financial collapse scenario: world's greatest economic depression begins, lasts until 1994; Third-World debt wipes out hundreds of major Western banks and institutions.
Terrorists in Africa seize and dominate world's supply of gold, diamonds and strategic metals.
Consultation on Dimensions of Christian Martyrdom, sponsored by Evangelicals, dealing with effects of martyrdom on upbuilding and evangelistic growth of whole church.
Global oil war erupts as Arabs cut off oil to USA: USSR's oil reserves also rapidly running out.
The long-predicted Great Earthquake, centered on San Andreas Fault, California, followed by unprecedented natural disasters including a Universal Famine leading to mass cannibalism. (Nostradamus).
Biomedical technology: predetermination of sex and intelligence of children before birth achieved.
All cancers can now in principle be instantly arrested, cured and eliminated through reprogramming of DNA in individual body cells.
Bacterial and viral illnesses fall to new drugs.
Timolol and other drugs greatly reduce danger of heart attacks.
HALO (High Altitude Large Optics) military satellite places 10 million no-blink infrared detectors in space to protect USA from sneak missile launchings.
Earth receives first extraterrestrial contact: a complex coded radio message is received from star Vega, being instructions to build an interstellar starship; 1999, dodecahedron Machine completed and activated, travels instantaneously to center of Galaxy and back via vast disused network of space wormholes in star systems with small double black holes (built by galactic civilization defunct 5 billion years ago) (C. Sagan, *Contact*, 1985).
Universe now found by astronomers to be not open (expanding forever) but closed, i.e. to have sufficient mass and energy for its receding galaxies to collapse back when expansion limit reached.
Education explosion across world as electronic tutors make programmed instruction available on any subject at any level of difficulty.
Soviets develop operational ground-based particle-beam accelerator, making missile attack against USSR impossible; USA counterpart (orbiting laser weapon) beaten in race for time, so USA turns to nerve gas as final deterrent.
Secret preparations by USSR for first-strike nuclear attack on USA discovered; USA strikes first, destroys most Soviet centers along with 100 million citizens.
New religions arise based on psychobiological-chemical altered states of consciousness: ecstatic experiences, trance, dissociation, spirit possession, soul loss, astral projections, faith-healing, mysticism, glossolalia, occult, shouting, visions, out-of-body experiences, et alia.
Creation of primitive form of artificial life (in form of self-replicating molecules).
Anti-christian bodies hire (1) gangs of thugs, and (2) organized terrorist groups, specifically to harass and disrupt Western foreign mission operations and to kill their missionaries.

EPOCH X: THE FINAL THRUST OF WORLD EVANGELIZATION 1990-

1990 **Global status of Christianity:** 65.2 generations after Christ, world is 33.2% Christians (44.5% of them being Whites), 75.9% evangelized; with printed Scriptures available in 2,200 languages.
World's 10 largest cities: Mexico City 20,250,000, Tokyo/Yokohama 19,280,000, São Paulo 18,770,000, New York/NENJ 15,690,000, Calcutta 12,540,000, Shanghai 11,960,000, Bombay 11,790,000, Buenos Aires 11,710,000, Seoul 11,660,000, Rio de Janeiro 11,370,000.

Global Christianity launches Decade of Universal Evangelization

Vast increases in all types of evangelization and of evangelistic activity:

virtually all Christian denominations and agencies announce programs leading up to AD 2000.
'Evangelization 2000' inaugurated by John Paul II and other world Christian leaders, calling all Christians to a decade of mission, with as aims to unite all churches and to bring the total of Christ's disciples to over 50% of world (3.1 billion) by AD 2000.
International Priests' Retreat 2000 on 'Evangelization 2000', in Rome; 9,000 RC priests attend.
Round the World Prayer Event, organized by World Evangelism (World Methodist Council), to inaugurate evangelism in decade of 1990s.
8th General Assembly, Ordinary Synod of Bishops, Rome (25 years after Vatican II), on theme 'The Word of God'.
4th International Christian Youth Conference (World Methodist Council).
Peace Council/Convocation of Christians: World Convocation on Justice, Peace, and the Integrity of Creation (JPIC), a worldwide ecumenical event, convened by RCC, WCC et alia, to oppose injustice, war and environmental destruction.
USA: Joint IFMA/EFMA Conference approves specific allotments for 1995 schedule for reaching all peoples on Earth with gospel.
USA: after 30 years of negotiations, 9 major Protestant denominations within the organic union scheme COCU (Consultation on Church Union/Church of Christ Uniting) finally agree to establish 'covenanting relationship' with 'councils of oversight' at all levels handling ordination, mission, et alia.
Worldwide medical consultation networks and data banks.
Daily body checkups by computer provide ample early warning of any impending illness.
Establishment of national computerized human organ banks for transplants; organ procurement from neomorts (brain-dead persons) now a major industry; by 2000, transplantation of all organs possible except central nervous system.
Substitutive medicine (replacement of defective parts by implants or transplants) replaces drug treatment; kidney dialysis patients wear device internally; by 2000, people being kept alive by spare parts number 1% of population in Western world.
Ten million transistors (equivalent) now on a single microchip; data transfer (bubble) 10 million bits per second.
Videotex (viewdata and teletext: consumer-oriented 2-way interactive electronic distribution services) supplies 8 million USA homes with vast array of computerized information data banks; similarly in Europe.
Genetic manipulation allows humans to create evolutionary change: creating pilots with faster reaction times, workers happy with monotonous work, cloned soldiers to fight wars.
Massive urban growth (7,000-year-old trend of urban flow or clustering) slows and reverses in most high-technology developed countries as offices and factories relocate in countryside, taking vast populations with them; large numbers of computerized 'intelligent buildings' arise, controlled by information management systems.
Automated highways with central computer control of all vehicles moving at same speed at much greater densities than previously; all vehicles now have electronic collision-avoidance hardware.
Particles discovered capable of travelling faster than light: tachyons.
Virtually all crime rates increase massively in Western societies for next 30 years, until crime eliminated by computerized surveillance by AD 2022.
Battle of Armageddon (as anticipated by Jehovah's Witnesses); 2 billion people killed, 144,000 Witnesses go to heaven with Christ, rest of Witnesses remain on Earth during Millennium and then on into eternity.
One billion telephones in world, nearly all direct dial; everyone in world has UN-designed 17-digit personal number, making him accessible wherever he travels to.
Inexpensive wrist televisions with hundreds of channels available.
IBM places world's first ultrahighspeed Josephson Junction computer online (super-cold superconducting switches); world's largest computer memory sits in 14 cm cube; one result, weather forecasting of superb accuracy for months into future.
Ultrafast optical (fibre-optic) computers (for speedier informational transmission than by wires) produced by Bell Laboratories, IBM et alia.
Worst natural disaster of century as massive earthquake devastates most of Iran.
16th Baptist World Congress (BWA) meets in Seoul, Korea (10-15 July).
World Congress on the Holy Spirit and World Evangelization, in Seoul, on 'Power Evangelism'; over 2 million attenders (Catholic/Protestant charismatic renewal).
Explo '90 global Christian training teleconference organized by Campus Crusade for Christ (expanded version of Explo '85).
'Jesus' film (Campus Crusade for Christ) becomes after 10 years translated into world's 270 languages each with over 1 million mother-tongue speakers, and is being shown to 10 million persons every night, of whom 2 million become converts or enquirers each night.
2nd General Assembly, Latin American Evangelical Confraternity (CONELA).

1991 World Congress of Charismatic Leaders for World Evangelization, in Singapore, to usher in decade of evangelization before AD 2000; 10,000 renewal leaders.
Definitive cures for cancer found in principle; universal cancer vaccine comes into wide use.
Pocket-sized portable dators (radio/computer/database/phone) widely in use as universal personal accessory for instant information.
First commercial computer to be completely conceived, designed, and manufactured by other computers and robots.
Cosmology revolutionized through discoveries made by space-borne telescopes and instruments: riddles of quasars, black holes, et alia all solved, but other more massive riddles arise as discoveries proliferate.
Holovision (life-size 3-dimensional pictures through use of laser holography) replaces television in homes.
400 million computers in world, 350 million being personal computers (with 11 million sold worldwide during year), many able to run hosts of expert systems.
Prototype 5th-generation computer produced in Japan, handling artificial intelligence, knowledge bases and ultracomplex expert systems.
Haiti becomes virtually barren of all trees, resulting in massive soil erosion.
Food riots, mass starvation, in Africa and India.
Time shown by scientists to be flowing at different rates in different parts of the Universe, including tachyons (particles that move faster than light) for which time moves backwards.
Workers at nuclear reactors stage major controlled accidents to protest unsafe conditions.
Muslim end of world, as prophesied by traditional Islam: coming of Antichrist into godless world, Kaaba vanishes from Mecca, all copies of Quran suddenly become blank paper, all Quran's words disappear from human memory, final Mahdi appears, then Prophet Isa (Jesus) ushers in Islam as sole global religion, followed by Last Judgment.
7th Assembly, World Council of Churches (WCC), in Canberra, Australia, with delegates from 350 member denominations.
4th Chinese Congress on World Evangelization, CCOWE '91 (sponsored by CCCOWE/LCWE), in Hong Kong.
Sudden growth and mushrooming worldwide of youth churches completely outside control by denominations: loosely-organized churches begun and run by charismatic under-25s, meeting at lunchtimes in hotels, theaters, cinemas, shops, anywhere; huge growth of converts.

1992 NASA (USA) places Space Station in orbit, permanently-manned research laboratory, observatory and factory in space, involving 12 countries.
Lethal new space weapons introduced, including gamma-ray lasers (grasers) able to blow up planets and stars; arms race between Superpowers escalates.
USSR wins complete dominance of Middle East oil fields.
Nuclear crime, blackmail and terrorism become rampant on all continents, especially in megacities and supercities.
National Computer Mercantile Network established, with superconducting supercomputers monitoring and recording every commercial and mercantile transaction in USA, including personal tax files, credit records.
Diagnosis of almost any illness possible in a few hours by examining patient's Human Protein Index (human body contains 50,000 different kinds of protein).
USA: illiteracy rises to 27% from low of 1% in 1980, due to mass immigration from Third World and decline of books and reading.
Beginning of freefly (flying for individuals) by means of jetpacks or rocket belts.
40% of all Western world's 230 million homes have a general computer for home management and cottage industry.
Schisms or secessions out of major Western denominations since 1975 amount to 10% of membership (ex LCMS, PCUSA, ELCA, ECUSA, CofE, EKD, UMC, SBC, et alia).
Public deliberately-staged TV trials and martyrdoms of Christian workers and leaders by fanatical Muslim and Communist regimes.
Organized hostage terrorism turns against foreign missionaries: scores rounded up as hostages, ransoms demanded, many murdered.
Global killer pandemics arise, sweeping across (a) Third World with 'diseases of poverty' (malaria, bilharzia, filariasis, et alia) as parasites achieve full resistance to present drugs, and (b) rest of world with revived deadly ancient diseases (smallpox, bubonic plague, pneumonic plague, et alia) as world loses its herd immunity and abandons vector control and vaccination; hundreds of millions die.
Reemergence in Atlantic Ocean of part of lost continent of Atlantis.
A newscaster using very powerful personal computer gets access to, and finally control over, all data banks in world. (A. Budrys' scenario *Michaelmas*, 1977).
Coming of Antichrist to power at age 30, followed in 2001 by Second Coming of Christ and End of World, as envisioned by internal architecture of Great Pyramid of Giza (alternate dates: 2030, 2090, 2444).
Conversion of Jewish race to faith in Christ takes place, during pontificate of last pope before Peter the Roman. (St Malachy).
Project Space Voyage, a low-Earth-orbit popular tour organized by Society Expeditions: 4 days' briefing, 12-hour trip, 2 days' debriefing.
Latin American Catholics celebrate '500 Years of Evangelization', with overall Evangelization 2000 plan.

1993 Definitive alleviation of mental illness attained.
5th-generation Japanese megacomputers with artificial intelligence introduced and put on market: a staggering extension of human intellect.

Knowledge-intensive expert systems now widespread: a species of knowledge-based computer program performing at the level of, and replicating, human experts in professional fields.
First prototype SPS (solar-power satellite) successfully beams energy from space to Earth, relaying solar power via low-density microwaves to become DC electrical current; 2021, over 20 SPS in geosynchronous Earth orbit each producing 10 gigawatts (10 billion watts) microbeamed to Earth to join existing electric-power grids; 2028, SPS supply 90% of Earth's energy requirements.
USSR approaches hegemony over most of world.
Memory metal Nitinol (and similar alloys) remembers its previous shape before crashes, etc; on heating, snaps back to its original shape, exerting enormous force in the process.
Customized electronic newspapers become widespread.
'Green machines' constructed: engineering systems using biological and biochemical processes or their human-made analogs to create materials, food, energy or other goods and services.
Superconductivity: room-temperature superconductors (transmitting electricity without any resistance) transform all human energy usages.
World Congress of Faiths (WCF, headquartered in London) meets on centenary of 1893 World's Parliament of Religions (Chicago), attempts to create an interreligious World Council of Faiths.
Human race enters Sign of Aquarius, embarks on Aquarian Age (Age of Aquarius, the Watercarrier, interpreted by Christians as Age of Christ the Giver of the Water of Life); 6,000 years of human history are now completed, Sabbath rest of 1,000 millennial years is about to begin.
Last Pope of Rome elected, Peter II (Peter the Roman, 266th Pope, Pope of the Apocalypse; on St Malachy's reckoning, 112th since 1143); when he flees Rome, rival antipopes emerge over a Church of Darkness, as the Great Tribulation begins.
Several communications satellites vital to global economy and nuclear balance of power are seized, disabled or taken over by techno-terrorists until demands met.

1994 Iran starts global conflict in Muslim world centered on Middle East by invading Macedonia and North Africa; Arab invasion of Europe, France, Italy. (Nostradamus).
Routine use of microcomputer implants in human brain to control epilepsy, psychoses and other diseases.
Horrifying forms of warfare unleashed: nerve and other poison gas, biochemical weapons, immense swarms of killer bees, acid rain, artificially-induced earthquakes and volcanoes.
Enormous increase in all kinds of organized evangelism attracts heavy infiltration by nihilists, terrorists, antichristian fanatics, bounty seekers, criminals, rival government agents.
Development of 'cottage theology' via microcomputer networks, cottage electronic mission think-tanks, cottage Christian teleconferencing, cottage accessing of global Gallup sample of population on religious subjects, cottage Christian research units tapping into databases across the world.
Rise of final Antichrist III (also known as Eighth & Final Antichrist), either (a) a polylingual ruthless Jewish despot from Israel's tribe of Dan posing as Messiah, (b) a blue-turbaned tyrant from Arabia espousing militaristic Islam and wielding the oil weapon, or a professedly-Christian European dictator dominating 10-nation confederacy; each wielding nuclear weapons, global terror, and mass destruction. (Nostradamus).
Bionic eyes: artificial eyesight invented for blind people (the nonsighted); alternatively, whole-eye transplants become possible.
USA: computers now reach 70% of population (60 million terminals or screens).
First wristwatch computer perfected, accepting and imparting spoken instructions in English or any other language.
Hospital (computerized health-care facility) opened in space by NASA (USA).
Maglev (magnetic levitation) track reduces travel time from Los Angeles to Las Vegas (282 miles) to one hour, in trains flying on invisible magnetic cushion two-thirds inch off ground.
Final decade of 20th century proves to be greatest decade in Christian history for signs and wonders, miracles, conversions, evangelism and evangelization: greatest sign or wonder being Christians loving one another and gathering in unity everywhere.

WORLD WAR III: NUCLEAR HOLOCAUST SCENARIO

1994 World War III erupts: Western world and organized Christianity versus Communist world and militant Islam; nuclear holocaust and chemical/biological warfare drag on for 27 years until 2021. (Nostradamus).

1995 Hyperinflation leads to general breakdown of world monetary system.
Control of human obesity attained.
Biotechnologists succeed in mapping the complete neural signature of the entire human brain.
Mexico City (23.1 million inhabitants) has now overtaken Tokyo/Yokohama (19.7 million) as world's largest supercity, maintaining this rank on into the indefinite future.
Self-replicating machines, computers, and factories begin to be produced in Japan, reproducing exact copies of themselves (initially for a limited range of products).
Some 50% of world's nations have become Marxist, mainly in Third World.
Inexorable increase in number of countries closed to organized foreign Christian mission; 75% of world's populations become inaccessible in this way.
3rd World Consultation on Frontier Missions (WCFM), specifically for mission executives.
Travel and tourism become world's major industry, growing at 10% a year to reach 400 million foreign tourists a year; in North America, 7 million foreigners visit each year (1978, 2 million), 23 million citizens a year go abroad (1978, 10 million); foreign students 1.3 million (1978, 350,000); 1998, tourist services to space begin; 2010, packaged vacations in space available.
Accurate long-range weather forecasts now available over telephone, custom-made to any individual's or organization's detailed requirements.
Vegetarianism adopted worldwide, with more vegetarians than meat-eaters in Western world.
Mass production of implantable miniaturized artificial kidneys.
People assisters (computer-assisted hydraulic mover systems with powered arms) worn by infirm or handicapped people to give them increased mobility; also, for healthy persons, personal manoeuvering units (in space), Moon bugs, Mars rovers, submersibles, solarsail kites; also lighter-than-air skyships.
People amplifiers (PAs) in use: portable computerized devices which assist average person perform as a pseudoexpert in several different spheres at once (e.g. law/accountancy/mathematics/astronomy/theology/missiology/homiletics).
Experience-amplifiers in use, for magnifying human experiences: emotion-amplifiers, sensation-amplifiers, awareness-amplifiers, intelligence-amplifiers.
Intelligence-amplifiers (resulting in enhanced intelligence) create artificial personalities for secretaries, assistants, technicians et alii.
Context-recognition chips (anti-advertising modules) marketed: Adnix which mutes TV set when commercials begin, and Preachnix which switches channels when doctrinaire religious programs appear (at preselected keywords like 'Advent', 'Rapture', etc).
Luggage, parcels, valuables and eventually all people are electronically tagged so that none can be lost or ever disappear.
International terrorist gang seize nuclear weapons, devastate a major capital city of over 5 million population.
Self-replicating factory placed on Moon, produces first exact copy in one year, and 1,000 replicas by 2025 thus creating major lunar manufacturing center.
NASA Shuttle passenger liner begins 74-passenger trips, ferrying 10,000 people into space annually.
6th-generation computers with artificial intelligence emerge, equaling human brain in any intellectual activity.
First submotel (submarine hotel) opens, with parking for tourist minisubmarines.
Machines scan foreign-language newspapers and journals daily, then translate and archive materials for later retrieval.
Race and class wars erupt across Southern Africa, Middle East, northern India, together with mass urban terrorism in urbanized Northern half of planet.
City of Rome devastated by nuclear bomb; flight and murder of Peter the Roman, end of Roman papacy; Paris and cities across Europe also devastated. (St Malachy; Nostradamus).
Computer-generated holocaust: all-out nuclear war erupts as superpowers' huge computer networks overreact.
World's greatest denominations begin to disintegrate through violent internal radical/liberal/moderate/conservative/fundamentalist controversies: Roman Catholic Church, UMC, CofE, SBC, EKD, et alia.
In democracies, citizens govern by televoting regularly every Sunday at noon.

1996 Holocaust recovery scenario: due to warhead detonation patterns in global nuclear war, initial deaths 10% of world (including 50% of USA) but 90% of world survives (including 50% of USA) and 90% of world's surface remains unaffected; secondary deaths from fallout, wind-borne radiation followed by radiation sickness, contaminated food and water, breakdown of civilization, and decreased fertility, all kill another 10% of world; animal and plant life only marginally affected; world recovers fully within 20 years (USA 40 years).
Holocaust median scenario: nuclear war between USA and USSR leaves initially 50% of both populations dead and all major urban cities destroyed; full-scale thermonuclear attack immediately kills 88% of USA and 50% of USSR; a new Dark Ages era begins.
Cold apocalypse scenario: pitch-dark bone-chilling nuclear winter brought on by limited nuclear war using 5,000 megatons (20% of USA and USSR arsenals) in which 1.2-billion-ton cloud of dust (black snow) and smoke envelops northern hemisphere first, then southern; world freezes or starves to death except for bands of hunter-gatherers in south.

Extinction scenario: nuclear war results in 6 billion deaths (6,000 megadeaths), end of civilization, destruction of the North, destruction of all global infrastructures, destruction of knowledge and know-how, mankind reduced to handful of demoralized tribal savages; eventually, final extinction of all human and animal life.

Divine intervention scenario: Christ appears and intervenes at last minute to save mankind from certain imminent self-destruction by nuclear holocaust; role as Savior now universally understood and acknowledged; evil held firmly in check as Millennium begins.

Goal redefinition scenario: all 200 major Christian denominations and parachurch agencies which have previously, over last 30 years, announced separate grandiose goals for reaching the entire world for Christ by AD 2000, suddenly realize that there is too little time left to do so; 'redefinition of the task' is therefore publicly announced, postponing target date by a further 20 years or changing 'By AD 2000' to 'Within this generation'.

Total-information technologies and world evangelization

1997 Media revolution ushers in new era in total evangelization: instant communication, total knowledge, total teaching on any subject at any time; universal, continuous, non-stop, round-the-clock preaching and witnessing; global witness in all languages; full evangelization achieved in nearly all situations whether local, national, regional, continental or global.

Popular religion (popular religiosity, popular piety), a christianized phenomenon, sweeps civilized regions of world in vast, rank growth effecting over 400 million church members.

Direct communication with computers by speech achieved by humans; talkwriters (transcribing speech) replace human transcribers.

USA and USSR engage in unpublicized robotic war in space as both try to establish networks of laser-armed anti-ballistic-missile satellites.

Sudden global power failure and total breakdown of sociosphere as domino effect destroys global infrastructures.

Invention of programmable sound silencer to eliminate noise far better than brick or stone.

Artificial wombs widely available for women unable to bear children naturally.

Genetic transcription provides first genetic map of healthy human cells, opens up new science of genetic markers (diagnosing at birth all of a person's future illnesses in order to prevent them).

Manned expedition to Mars launched by NASA (20 years after first landing of unmanned robot probe Viking).

Unified field theory finally constructed by physicists, a mathematical model tying together the 5 basic forces holding the Universe's particles together: gravity, electromagnetism, weak nuclear force, strong nuclear force, hypercharge.

Synthetic blood in wide use.

World Convocation of Christianity convened on initiative of Vatican.

Proliferation of local organic church unions begins around world, as hostile governments order or force all churches in their countries, of totally different confessions, to unite under one single name in order to exercise total control over them.

1998 Plans for organized world evangelization (as the church's responsibility) run into major obstacles: internal management fiascos, shortages of resources, shortfalls in personnel, secular urbanization, confessional disagreements, ecclesiastical schisms and secessions, theological disarray, mushrooming secularism and materialism, proselytism, ecclesiastical gangsterism and corruption, terrorism, insoluble complexities produced by world's 7,000 languages, disinformation, mass religious espionage, antichristian infiltration, unexpected prophets and seers, breakdowns in health care, failures of communications, collapse of education, global religious persecution, natural disasters, famines, popular hostility to Christianity, total state opposition, uncontrolled wars and warfare, collapses of infrastructures, universal chaos and terror.

Proselytism (sheep-stealing from other churches) becomes widespread, though denounced in theory by all major church bodies.

Worldwide disintegration of ecclesiastical coherence and centralized control.

All overt evangelistic activity prohibited or suppressed in over 50 countries.

Schisms out of major Western churches proliferate, numbering 20% of all church members since 1970.

World's greatest denominations finally self-destruct over insoluble internal controversies: RCC, CofE, EKD, UMC, SBC, et alia.

Churches forced underground in many countries, into clandestine or illegal existence.

Global collapse of organized faith in Christ.

Planetran world transportation network transports millions daily in electromagnetically-propelled cars travelling at 14,000 mph through evacuated tubes in underground tunnels.

Collapse of most major currencies, with runaway global inflation.

Soviet Union tests propulsion drive for speed-of-light starship; pilot ship said to be being readied to set out for Proxima Centauri star system.

Most large enterprises managed largely by artificial intelligence.

Majority of countries enforce strict population control, including contraceptive injections and forced abortions.

Automatic language translation for telephone users, enabling speakers worldwide to converse each in his own language.

Nuclear reactor disaster in Western capital city; millions killed, huge area contaminated; headquarters of major church and mission organizations there permanently abandoned.

United Religions Organization (URO) bought into being to parallel United Nations, to provide visions and moral power for world faiths; based in Jerusalem.

Mind-reading computers invented, with direct telepathic reading of thoughts in the brain; telepathic machines pick up human thoughts, place them on screen in front of the thinker.

TECHNOLOGICO-SOCIAL UTOPIA SCENARIO

1999 Global energy crisis finally solved as SPS (Solar Power Satellite) comes online; by 2021 becomes world's major energy source.

Earth unexpectedly enters dense belt of cosmic dust; temperatures fall catastrophically, new ice age begins.

90% of all governments in world have now become totalitarian, exercising total control over their own citizens.

World-level conference convened by Evangelicals with a representative from every people group on Earth, in last-minute attempt to complete evangelization of *panta ta ethne* by AD 2000.

Catholics begin preparations to celebrate Jubilee Year of AD 2000, in the Holy Year series, with pope to telecast on 25 December 2000 to 6 billion viewers via network of satellites.

Human transplant surgery multiplies; vast organ banks set up for freezing and storing of human organs, limbs, and undiseased youthful cadavers.

All known human infectious diseases successfully eradicated in principle.

Reunion of churches: faced with the world ridiculing the scandal of Christianity's fragmentation into 26,000 separate denominations, and under heavy governmental pressures, the world's largest churches (with 95% of all Christians) agree to begin immediate, loose, de facto reunion embracing intercommunion, fellowship, acceptance of ministries and a common shared name, the Church of Jesus Christ, or The Body of Christ.

Professional consultation on any subject available to all in any language at low cost by telephone, provided by computer expert systems.

Two-way wrist or pocket telephones/TVs/pagers/maintenance-free wrist computers/translatorfones in widespread use across globe.

Ecological warfare perfected, including deliberate induction of earthquakes by triggering vibrations from a distance.

World's greatest natural explosion, of submerged volcano Krakatoa off Java, far larger than first cataclysm in 1883.

Huge numbers of Asian, African and Latinamerican youth converts reject or ignore historic and Western Christianity; on world level, Christians henceforth align themselves not on confessional or denominational lines but on racial lines in 10 vast ethnolinguistic megaclusters.

Emergence of hundreds of new shortlived millennial religions or belief systems at local, national and global levels; ultra-fast-growing religious cults and revivals, millions joining and leaving in rapid succession.

Antichrist III annihilates city of New York by missiles, reveals self's true identity in Horror of Horrors (Abomination of Desolation). (Nostradamus).

Collapse of political Communism begins as both an ideology and a system, due to spread of Islam in Soviet Central Asia. (Nostradamus).

All sizeable nations and many private groups have nuclear weapons or can easily purchase them.

Global panic spreads as end of millennium approaches, widely believed to be 31 December 1999 (wrongly, since 20th century ends on 31 December 2000).

STATUS OF THE WORLD IN AD 2000

2000 *Postindustrialism.* 25% of mankind live in societies with postindustrial (transindustrial) economies, where producing necessities of life becomes trivially easy technologically, and in which therefore knowledge and information replace capital as society's most important resource.

Demographics. World population 6.1 billion (30.7% under 15, median age 26.1, life expectancy 63.9 years); 20-year period begins of probable population megadisasters due to famine, drought, crop failures, mismanagement, corruption, warfare (Neo-Malthusianism).

Urbanization. Supercities (urban agglomerations with over 4 million inhabitants) total 79 (59 in developing countries); megacities (with over 1 million) 433; urban dwellers number 51.2% of world, increasing by 1.6 million a week; urban slums expand far faster than cities, producing 'a planet of slums'.

World's 10 largest cities: Mexico City 25,820,000, São Paulo 23,970,000, Tokyo/Yokohama 20,220,000, Calcutta 16,530,000, Bombay 16,000,000, New York/NENJ 15,780,000, Seoul 13,770,000, Teheran 13,580,000, Shanghai 13,260,000, Jakarta 13,250,000.

Industrialization. World industrial robot population 35 million: Japan 11,000,000 (and a million new ones a year), USA 7,500,000, USSR 5,600,000, FR Germany 3,600,000, France 1,620,000, Italy

1,600,000, German DR 1,000,000, UK 820,000, Sweden 650,000, Brazil 550,000, others in 100 other countries.

Industry. Only 4 automobile firms remain in world as all smaller ones consolidate into global giants, with production centered in Korea, Italy and Latin America.

Work. USA: 35% of all paid work is now done from people's homes.

Transportation. Linear-motor trains become standard means of intercity transportation up to 1,000 km; ultra-highspeed, magnetic-levitation.

Society. Mankind now more unified than at any time in the past; more standardized (English as lingua franca), more affluent, longer lived, more mobile, less religious, better educated; tourism by now world's largest industry, with 470 million foreign tourists a year.

USA colleges host 1 million foreign students from abroad.

Cashless society in place, using a single world monetary unit for trade and exchange.

Creation of one single planetary culture and civilization finally achieved on Earth; planetization of human race well under way.

Geopolitics. Farthest extent of global penetration of Marxism, covering 90% of world including Australia and Canada; massive decline in influence suddenly begins; world Communism disintegrates by 2010.

Politics. Instant polling of viewers' opinions and election choices over viewer-interactive cable TV.

Evolution of synocracy—government by synergy, by multiple mutual attraction not coercion.

Psychology. Future shock becomes worldwide: breakdown of civilization because society's sub-systems no longer function and people can no longer cope with accelerating change (pace of life too fast).

Ecosystem. Human pressure on natural systems of Earth (consumption of raw materials) multiplies 70-fold in last hundred years.

Agriculture. 30% of world's arable land destroyed by human encroachment in last 20 years; 20% of world's population are subsistence farmers, 20% more are poor farmers responsible for spread of desertification.

Mariculture. Ocean farming begins to produce more food than agriculture, including 900 million metric tons of meat annually.

Biosphere. 10% of world's 10 million animal and plant species destroyed in last 20 years due to deforestation, desertification and destruction of habitats; by AD 2030, possibly as high as 40%; since Earth's biosphere is a single complex system similar to a living organism (the Gaia theory), this extinction has vast adverse effects on human prosperity.

Evolution. Two new human species of genus Homo with own distinct cultures begin to evolve and become recognized: (a) Homo Solaris, humans who function predominantly off-Earth in space, dependent on technology and alien life-support environments; and (b) Homo Posthumanus, arising from coalescence of humans and ultra-intelligent machines.

Next stage or giant leap in evolution begins to be manifested: the New Man in Christ (with resurrection body similar to Christ's), which will coexist on Earth with genus Homo during the Millennium.

Language. New universal language evolves due to automated communication.

Medicine. Drugless medical treatment attacks all illnesses electromagnetically, making body cells produce antibodies, new tissue, et alia.

Human hibernation developed for extensive periods (months to years).

Disease. Global pandemics sweep across continents wiping out millions every few days; rapid destruction of Earth's ozone layer by aerosols (freon gas) results in increase in ultraviolet radiation, causes widespread cancer.

Pollution. Urban pollution becomes deadly: Mexico City (largest in world with 26 million population and 1,100,000 influx each year) is world's most polluted city, with 6 million cars; Tokyo (20 million) next; also Cubatão (Brazil), world's most polluted petrochemical center; and Cairo (11 million) has world's worst noise pollution.

Communications. Vast expansion of telephone systems: e.g. in Brazil, from 500,000 phones in 1967, to 7.6 million (1982) and to 125 million (AD 2000); total worldwide 2.2 billion, 98% being direct-dial.

Rapidly-growing global telecommunications network in its entirety now equals human brain in complexity.

Computerization. World's 700 million computers, from micros to mainframes, become connected to each other in a single global network.

Broadcasting. Radios number 2.5 billion worldwide.

Subliminal TV in widespread use by countries for mass mind control.

Cable TV (CATV) reaches 100 million households in USA (up from 14 million in 1982).

Data broadcasting widespread, becomes norm for many professions.

Publishing. Computer printout terminals in every neighborhood in Western world will publish and bind on demand any book requested before customer's eyes while he waits.

Litigation. Disputes escalate over rights to information (copyrights, patents, industrial espionage, personal rights).

Energy. Widespread use of renewable energy sources (invariant energy systems), i.e. solar energy (99.98% of all the energy Earth receives), geothermal energy, tidal energy; also, wireless transmission of energy comes into operation.

Commercial energy consumption increases from 0.5 billion tonnes oil equivalent (1900) to 1.667 billion (1950) to 5.6 billion (1974; 1.4 tons per capita) to 15.5 billion (AD 2000; 2.5 tons per capita).

Warfare. Inner solar system becomes vast arena for nuclear confrontation with locating dark or hidden satellites, and nuclear missiles on Moon.

Nuclear power. 100 large power plants worldwide become due for retirement after full working life, but their dismantling and disposal pose major problems.

Weaponry. Countries owning nuclear power facilities proliferate, though over 100 exhausted or terminated nuclear plants exist, remaining lethally radioactive for thousands of years into future; total plutonium produced as by-product of global nuclear power reaches equivalent of one million atomic bombs; illegal nuclear weapons result, with disastrous consequences.

Nuclear powers. Countries possessing clearcut nuclear weapons and means of delivery rise to 35, including Argentina, Egypt, Iraq, Israel, Kuwait, Libya, Saudi Arabia, Turkey, Zaire.

China now one of the world's 3 military and nuclear superpowers (with USSR and USA); latter 2 each have laser arsenals.

Biological warfare. First use of deadly bacillus botulinus to destroy entire populations in a few hours.

Ethics. Human selfishness and greed lead world inexorably towards eventual catastrophe or self-destruction.

Age of manufactured experience begins: experiences of any kind (religious enlightenment, perception, insight, mystic contemplation, planetary consciousness, moods, orgasm, wellbeing, etc) available on order using chemical, physical and psychological stimulants (LSD, marijuana, peyote, mescaline, hallucinogenic drugs, etc).

STATUS OF RELIGION AND CHRISTIANITY IN AD 2000

Non-Christians. 83% of world's 4.0 billion non-Christians now reside in 120 nations closed to traditional crosscultural foreign missionary endeavor and also to internal home mission or evangelism by nationals.

Agnosticism. Abandoning of religion worldwide results in 260 million antireligious or atheists (4.2% of world) and 1,048 million non-religious or agnostics (17.1%); USSR over 50%, Europe 17.5%.

Primal religion. Despite attempts of missionary religions to convert them, adherents of traditional tribal religions (animism, shamanism, polytheism, pantheism, folk religion, fetishism, et alia) number 110 millions, almost exactly the same as in year 1900.

Mass movements. Nativistic, messianic, cargo-cult and other mass religious movements of popular syncretism mushroom across Third World.

Global status of Christianity: 65.6 generations after Christ, world is 34.8% Christians (39.9% of them being Whites, 60.1% Non-Whites), and 83.4% of all individuals are now evangelized; with printed Scriptures available in 2,800 languages.

Respect for Christ. Person of Christ now widely known and respected throughout world, by all world religions, even among atheists and agnostics; also his teachings and his gospel (but not his church) are understood and valued, though not accepted or implemented, almost universally.

Churchmanship. Churches tend increasingly to combine 3 traditions or streams: (a) Catholic (liturgical or sacramental), (b) Protestant (Bible-based), (c) pentecostal (Spirit-filled, charismatic).

Christians. At world level, Christians are now 60% Non-Whites, 55% Third-Worlders, 18% pentecostal-charismatics (5% in pentecostal denominations, 3% charismatics, 2% in Chinese house churches, and 8% inactive or unaffiliated); or, on maximum-growth scenario, 22% pentecostal-charismatics.

Pentecostal-charismatics. Organized Christianity's 22% charismatics constitute 12% of all RCs, 65% of all Protestants, 10% of Anglicans; of world's 400,000 foreign missionaries, 40% are charismatics (25% of RCs, 50% of Protestants, 80% of Third-World missionaries).

Entire world finally reached with Christian gospel for first time in history, in the sense that everyone everywhere has heard or hears the gospel in depth with understanding and has access to Scripture, churches, missions, Christians, Christian broadcasting (with 4,000 Christian radio and TV stations worldwide), movies, literature and other means of grace.

Global church-planting goal completed: at least one fellowship or church or congregation or nucleus of disciples has been planted as an ongoing indigenous witness in each of the world's 11,500 ethnolinguistic peoples and 4,000 metropolises of over 100,000 population.

Foreign missionaries engaged in crosscultural ministries worldwide number 400,000, including citizens of 200 countries.

Spirituality. Widespread revival of monasticism both eremitic (hermits) and cenobitic (communities), among young people of all churches across world, especially in Third-World countries.

Many segments of global church adopt radical and revolutionary personal, congregational and denominational lifestyles.

Growth. Christianity and other world religions survive and flourish, also mysticism, magic, divination, cults, occult, astrology, numerology.

Mormonism (Church of Jesus Christ of Latter-day Saints), as USA's fastest-growing religion, reaches 20 million members worldwide, with 30,000 foreign missionaries abroad, global television programs from Salt Lake City, et alia.

Theology of mission. 100 years after J.R. Mott, Christian theology of religions, mission and evangelization (Protestant, Orthodox and Catholic) is still centered on Christ as sole Savior but has shifted radically towards a new universalism and recognition of value of world religions as ordinary or common ways of salvation, albeit incomplete without God's grace in Christ and his extraordinary or special way of salvation; world religions and Christianity are therefore widely regarded by many RCs and liberal Protestants (but denied by conservative evangelicals) as parallel paths to salvation, with final convergence reserved for the Eschaton.

21st CENTURY BEGINS PERIOD OR AGE OF CRISIS, AD 2001-2180

2001 Third Millennium of Christian era begins (on 1 January 2001).

Three-quarters of world's nations involved in wars; fate of Earth lies in balance for 2 centuries more until nuclear disarmament with nations finally abandoning warfare. (First of 4 periods envisaged in B. Stableford & D. Langford, *The Third Millennium: a history*, 1985).

Major energy crisis with worldwide exhausting of fossil fuels and essential minerals.

Japan becomes most informationized society on Earth, based on massive mainframe megacomputers storing vast data/information/knowledge banks; Japan now world's leading nation in design, manufacture and export of communications technology.

Normal human lifespan extends to 150 years for 50% of Western world, but increased longevity only viable for future Homo species voyaging beyond Solar System.

Human migration into space begins: origin of astroculture

Chemists create staggering compounds for every area of human experience, including the ultimate glue (adhesives that replace all existing fasteners).

Most human genes now mapped (100,000 genes to build a human being), due to gene-splicing technology; many of medicine's problems and mysteries solved.

Ocean level rises gradually by 50 feet until 2120 then falls, stabilizing from 2200-2400.

First true space colony (High Frontier or O'Neill-type) built and inhabited in orbit between Earth and Moon; first children born off-Earth; 50,000 people now live and work in space.

Towing of asteroids Earthwards for mining planned, using mass driver (cost for 3-km-thick asteroid: $200 billion); over 60 asteroids are known to cross Earth's orbit; but whole scheme delayed.

Wars fought with mercenary replicants (cloned humanoids with silicon intelligence), intelligent weapons, robot tanks, smart missiles, RPVs (remotely piloted vehicles), et alia.

2002 One vast megacomputer established under UN auspices, with centralized global data facility giving wide public access to library, business and home terminals.

Emergence of 7th-generation computers, powered not by electricity but by light beams.

Alien virus brought back by interplanetary spaceprobe wipes out 10% of population of Earth.

Startling influence of Christian world confessionalism continues to spread, at expense of world interdenominationalism, ecumenism and conciliarism; decline of WCC and its 200 associated continental and national councils of churches, under charges of having stood for ecumenical imperialism.

2003 90% of all world's first-class mail now transmitted electronically (electronic mail).

Third-generation artificial experience developed through mammoth artificial-intelligence computer systems creating 3-dimensional holograms of any historical or future reality or event in the Universe.

Corporate commercial warfare: giant multinational conglomerates engage in worldwide organized espionage, intimidation, threats, fraud, violence and terrorism to discourage competition.

Full-immersion video rooms in homes for families to surround themselves with tropical rain forest, a Mars landscape, a movie epic, et alia.

The 7 major obstacles to Christian world mission become megamaterialism, mega-affluence, megapoverty, megapollution, megacrime, megaterrorism, megapersecution.

Postindustrial societies and transindustrial economies

2004 As result of microelectronics revolution, 50% of all jobs in industrial world have been eliminated over last 25 years; robots run 50% of world's industrial mass production.

Research on control of aging well on way to perfection.

Hydrogen now the most popular small-scale energy source, powering commercial vehicles et alia.

Seminaries, missionary training colleges, TEE et alia revolutionized by chemical transfer of learning: memory pills, knowledge pills, new languages learned by injection.

Orient Express, or TAV (transatmospheric vehicle, a hypersonic space vehicle) takes off from and lands on conventional runways, deploys SDI payloads in space.

Gigantic electromagnetic railguns, mounted on mountainsides, accelerate cargo-carrying missiles to hypersonic speeds out into space.

European vigilantes' group called Speedwatch systematically assassinates dangerous, drunk or speeding car drivers.

Massive pentecostal-charismatic latter-rain revival sweeps across whole of Asia due to power evangelism with signs and wonders, with 150 million converts in Korea, Japan, China, Viet Nam, Thailand, Malaysia, Indonesia, Burma, Cambodia, India, Sri Lanka and Pakistan.

2005 Eco-collapse scenario: initial worldwide eco-catastrophe due to unabated population growth, resource depletion, pollution of the biosphere, destruction of the ecosphere and the sociosphere, crop failures, starvation, megafamines, et alia. (Club of Rome).

Development of direct brain-computer interfaces as means of extending human mental capacity; human brains linked to supercomputers; also direct communication between computers and human central nervous system.

Cures found for every known 20th-century illness.

Polio as a children's disease is eliminated throughout world (goal of Rotarians since 1985).

Centennial celebrations of Baptist World Alliance (BWA) held at 19th Baptist World Congress.

First commercially viable biochip interface, linking a human by wire to multilingual interface computer.

Total strategic nuclear warheads rise from 14,000 in 1982 (USA 9,000, USSR 5,000) to 35,000 by 1995, then fall to 24,500 (USA 13,500, USSR 11,000) by 2005.

Tourism continues as world's biggest industry, with 700 million people travelling abroad for pleasure each year.

Telepathy in use for some types of communication, criminology, diplomacy, military intelligence, espionage.

Parapsychology comes into use as a military weapon used by terrorists, private armies, vigilantes, and military regimes.

Biotechnological disaster through a microbe spill: creation and accidental release of virulent microbes wipes out entire populations.

Medical advances: antiviral drugs and vaccines wipe out communicable diseases; genetic manipulation removes congenital defects; lung and brain-cell transplants become routine; nerve tissue regenerated to rehabilitate paraplegics and quadriplegics.

2006 Blatant state disinformation tactics cause havoc with organized Christianity: religious espionage, thefts of strategic plans, computerized embezzlement of funds, false accusations, forged documents, blackmail, heretical literature, pseudo-Christian broadcasting, terrorism falsely ascribed to Christian bodies.

Accepted safeguards for religious liberty begin to collapse worldwide; as persecution spreads, bulk of local churches cut all ties with centralized denominational control, break all conciliar links, and retreat into nonconciliarism and ecclesiastical isolationism.

International telephone system finally has enough switches (10^{10}) to become a conscious system, a giant brain similar to human brain (which has over 10^{11} or 100 billion neurons or cellular building blocks). (A.C. Clarke, 'Dial F for Frankenstein', 1965).

Earth invaded from outer space by Overlords in giant spaceships, who then assist humanity to continue its evolution into a Galaxy-wide and ever-expanding Overmind; but in the end humans reactivate volcanic energies of Earth's core and destroy planet. (A.C. Clarke's scenario, *Childhood's end*, 1953).

Conflict between science and religion finally disappears; physicists and biochemists become more concerned about questions of spirit, soul and creation than many theologians.

Neurotransmitters activate human brains and change mental performance; brain radios communicate with electricity in brain, enabling people to dial into any emotional, mental or sensual experience.

Declining Euroamerican denominations in Western world spark off itinerant tourist churches, groupings of believers ceaselessly travelling and witnessing around the Earth; Latin Americans form itinerant pilgrim churches which multiply phenomenally across world.

2007 Development of vast single computer which runs world, world economy and world government and monitors and controls all other computers. (I. Asimov, *The life and times of Multivac*, 1975).

All Persian Gulf states run out of oil; virtual exhaustion of petroleum reserves; Saudi Arabia, Gulf states, Iran, Libya et alia lose accumulated oil wealth, revert to pauper status.

Establishment of first nonterrestrial permanent resource base, either on Moon or Mars or in space.

21st-century epidemic Plague Wars, with appalling variety of new lethal diseases, begin with 15 million killed by influenza virus in southern Africa, leading to violent overthrow of White rule in South Africa; 2015, deliberately-engineered plague in Los Angeles, USA, kills 1 million; 2024, VD virus kills 5 million in Poland; 7 million in outbreak in Brussels; 2049, 38 million killed in China by lightning hepatitis; finally checked by 2060. (*The Third Millennium*, 1985).

Computer work stations in offices equipped with expert systems function as dictionaries, directories, telephones; office typists and secretaries replaced by managers.

Passive entertainment, passive listening to radio, passive TV watching, passive observing all disappear as reality becomes widely synthesized to give people active participation in sports, arts, wars, thrills et alia via sensavision head fittings.

2008 Terrorist outrages against strategic Christian gatherings in church headquarters: Vatican devastated during conclave of 150 cardinals, Ecumenical Center (Geneva) destroyed with heads of 300 major denominations, Canterbury Cathedral razed with 700 bishops at 14th Lambeth Conference, scores of cathedrals bombed during Easter services; end of mass public leaders' conferences.

Fanatical religious terrorism turns against Christian missionary bodies: selective or same-time assassinations of whole mission societies, or of all top mission executives.

Soviet Union attempts for political reasons to alter the past using scientific information carried by tachyons (particles that move backwards in time).

Global church research project to determine which major events or situations in past history of evangelization should be changed by messages or messengers sent from today, as soon as science invents method of tachyonic time travel and alteration of the past; preference for rectifying the great missed opportunities of Christian history (as with China in 1266, 1644, 1843).

Final Return of Mahdi (Mirza Ghulam Ahmad), regarded as Christ/Vishnu/Mohammed in Ahmadiyya belief, on centenary of his death; huge crowds of Ahmadis wait expectantly across world.

Scientists at International Astronomical Union announce Sun will go nova and explode in AD 3620; by 2553, 4 km-long seedships packed with data, life (species, DNA), technology and a million hibernating humans each, depart for Alpha Centauri A and 50 other planetary systems with oxygen; 3450, quantum drive invented making perpetual travel without fuel possible; 40 seedship voyages fail but 10 succeed including Mormon 'Ark of the Covenant' and other religious ones; 3617, starship Magellan leaves doomed Earth, 4135 arrives to begin life on planet Sagan Two. (A.C. Clarke, *The songs of distant Earth*, 1985).

2009 China invades Russia; nuclear exchange, then ground warfare drags on for 12 years.

Terrorist outrages against world religions: Kaaba in Mecca razed with 1.8 million Muslim worshippers killed (700,000 inside); Kumbh Mela (Hindu 12-yearly festival at confluence of Ganges and Jumna) annihilated with 16 million worshippers present.

Ecumenical Sharing of Resources (WCC program transmitting $65 million in 1983, $400 million in AD 2000) collapses catastrophically as banks disintegrate.

Organized global moves against all Christian foreign missions: expulsions, prohibitions, seizure of properties, trials, assassinations, executions, massacres, eradication.

Majority of global organized Christianity becomes underground or catacomb church as state surveillance, interference, persecution and suppression spread.

Space-com wrist-radios enable user to speak with anyone in world; by 2010, 50 million users across globe.

Cataract system, a network of orbiting nuclear mines, launched by USA to blind all enemy satellites before a nuclear preemptive first strike.

Total global charismatic worship of Christ introduced, in which at a fixed time each Sunday one billion living believers across world are holographically present visibly at same location; the ultimate in inspiration and evangelistic converting power.

2010 Post-nuclear human mutants multiply and spread, with telepathic powers; several bizarre civilizations develop: telepathic societies, high-technology societies, barbarisms, dictatorships.

Death of oceans scenario: terminal process leading to death of world's seas and oceans due to massive and irreversible pollution by industrial poisons, chemicals and sewage, leading to global disease, epidemics, famine, warfare and extinction.

Technological collapse scenario: beginnings of collapse of global technology due to overload, exhaustion of minerals, warfare, terrorism; technological civilization disintegrates into barbarism.

Private transport severely restricted, even abolished by law in many vast areas.

All information in a large library storable on machine the size of a postage stamp and instantaneously retrievable.

Psychiatry and medicine can now call on vast arrays of drugs.

Anti-aging drugs available on prescription to arrest and reverse aging in humans.

Governments drug reservoirs and all water supplies with contraceptives to control population explosion.

Intelligent machines tackle all mental activities somewhat better than humans can.

World government arises as vastly complex polynucleated or decentralized matrix organization or network rather than all power being centrally concentrated.

Mind-control and behavior-control chemicals widely used (via water and food supplies) by authoritarian governments to suppress dissension and unrest.

Rise of totalitarianism produces mass religious revivals; bogus robot evangelists seduce ignorant with promises of immediate salvation.

Vast growth of magical and pseudoscientific cults; governments use androids (chemically constructed beings) to deceive and manipulate religious followers.

Increasing influence of Christianity on secular worlds of science, politics, society, ideas; scientists in particular openly become more religious.

Roman Catholic pope, a Black African, transfers Vatican to Jerusalem; church ends opposition to contraception, compulsory clerical celibacy, and ordination of women to priesthood, and seeks full rapprochement with separated Christians.

Historic discovery: brain code deciphered, showing how human brain (most efficient and compact information storage system ever) works; direction communication with human minds achieved.

A new Golden Age of peace and prosperity begins.

World's 10 largest cities: Mexico City 30 million, São Paulo 28 million, Tokyo/Yokohama 21 million, Calcutta 20 million, Bombay 20 million, Teheran 17 million, Delhi 17 million, Jakarta 16 million, New York 16 million, Dacca 15 million.

Widespread genetic engineering (gene splicing) to fix deformed arms or legs; all childhood diseases eliminated, also skin, breast and cervical cancer; by 2020, 90% of all forms of cancer eliminated, regeneration of fingers and toes accomplished, also plastic surgery without scalpel; by 2050, regeneration of human internal organs.

2011 Revolution and civil war in South Africa finally lead to Black majority rule over White remnants and a shattered nation.

Major shortages of vital metals (mercury, cadmium, copper, tin, silver) result in political blackmail and miniwars.

Most forms of mental retardation now curable.

Collapse of organized secularism, agnosticism (non-religion), atheism (anti-religion), and rise of spiritual movements with vast rash of sects and cults of all kinds.

Religious pilgrims become a major force in world, over 400 million religious zealots (50% being Christians) constantly on move from shrine to shrine and country to country, ignoring secular and state restrictions; Christian pilgrims form a vast unorganized network of continuously itinerant pilgrim churches.

All texts published in English routinely put on electronic deposit; 2030, this becomes sole form of publication for scientific papers and other reference items, reproducible by printer only at point of consumption.

All radio, telephone and televisual communication becomes integrated in single worldwide information-transfer network; satellite-relayed entertainment, English-language teletext library services, even for poorest nations; 2150, full integration universal.

Great Cycle of the ancient Mayas of Meso-America due to be completed, ushering in end of whole Cosmos.

First of only 3 hostile nuclear incidents since 1945; 2011, Israelis destroy Libyan city, killing 78,000; 2020, Zaire accident detonates missile killing 7,000 with fallout throughout equatorial Africa; and 2079, city of Buenos Aires destroyed by Brazilian air force; thereafter, all nuclear weapons seized by superpowers, worldwide nuclear peace enforced. (*The Third Millennium*, 1985).

SPACE COLONIZATION SCENARIO

2012 Orbital colonies commenced: one-mile-diameter Stanford torus space stations with living space for 10,000 people permanently resident (no return to Earth possible), each weighing 500,000 tons (materials from the Moon) and costing $30 billion and 10 years to build; several hundred artificial colonies around Earth by 2050, some 10,000 within Solar System by 2100, many millions throughout Galaxy by 2500, billions across Universe by AD 4000; but on other scenarios, endless delays and obstacles cause entire program to be abandoned until resurgence of interest in AD 2250.

Space wars: incidents, conflicts and full-scale warfare in space erupt and proliferate.

Long-predicted great earthquake in northern California strikes, with incredible force.

Solar Army (antinuclear movement) grows as quasi-religious movement with massive rallies, protests, lobbying.

2013 Church of the Absolutely Poor (260 million Christians in South Asia) finally revolts against all other churches; blackmail, hostages taken, forced reparations, arson, seizure of properties and money, thefts, violence, mass arming of members with weapons, sackings of mission stations and churches, massacres of missionaries and affluent Christians, immense armies on rampage across continent; huge guerrilla churches likewise arise on all other impoverished continents.

Beginning of protracted development of nuclear fusion power; 2039, fuser technology born in Spacelab IV orbiting laboratory; 2054, prototype fusion cell; 2070, first fusion reactors feeding power into national grids; 2090, true fusion-energy economy becomes widespread, world electrical grid set up, global use of fossil fuels abandoned.

2014 Controlled thermonuclear power extracted from hydrogen isotopes; huge

fusion power plants come online across world.
On optimistic scenario, 1 million people now live permanently in space colonies.
Manned exploration of Solar System expands to first human landing on planet Mars; no evidence of life found.

2015 Weather control on Earth achieved.
Gradual military ascendancy of the North (Western world in new alliance with northwestern USSR) versus Islam and the South. (Nostradamus).
Art of bodily healing becomes centered in self-regulation and self-regeneration, training our brains to produce exactly the right chemicals needed to heal the body of every disease including aging, and to develop optimal health and well-being.
Pollution spreads: Caribbean Sea reduced to an ecological sewer.
Catastrophic breakdown of world trade system.

2016 NASA launches 'Ambassador I', first robot interstellar data-gathering spaceprobe, on 20-year mission to Alpha Centauri star system; 2030, results in evidence of life there.
Colonies of Earth move out from Moon to be set up on Mars, Venus and other planets of Solar System, including moons of Jupiter (Europa, Titan).
After 2,000 years of predominance over 99% of all Catholics, Roman Latin rite breaks up and declines to 10% of all Catholics as hundreds of ethnolinguistic cultures defy Curia to form their own ecclesio-liturgical rites.

2017 Nighttime eliminated from Earth through solar satellites.
Tooth decay, dental cavities and pyorrhea eliminated for 95% of all persons accepting pre-decay treatment including vaccines.
Biological computers developed as 8th generation of computer technology, with biochips and genetic codes assembling fully operational computers inside a cell each; computers increasingly participate in their own evolution.
Medical science perfects implanting of silicon chips with over 10^{12} memory (greater than human brain), surgically linked to the brain, giving mankind a totally new order of development.

2018 Affiliated Christians (church members) reach 2.5 billion worldwide, heavily infiltrated and monitored in most countries by police operatives, spies, informers, world government agents, computers, bugs and robots.
Massive series of earthquakes over 50 years including in Greece, Turkey, Japan, China, Ecuador et alia.

2019 Global megafamine sweeps Earth due to deliberate mismanagement and embezzlement; 2 billion die.
Completion of Project Daedalus (British Interplanetary Society): unmanned spaceship accelerates to 13% of speed of light, in 50 years reaches Barnard's star (with view to possible space colonization) and sends back information.

2020 World's 10 largest cities: Mexico City 33 million, São Paulo 31 million, Bombay 24 million, Calcutta 23 million, Tokyo/Yokohama 22 million, Teheran 21 million, Delhi 21 million, Jakarta 19 million, Dacca 19 million, Karachi 18 million.
Robots and self-reproducing (self-replicating) machines go out in space to mine Moon and asteroids.
Self-replicating uncrewed spaceprobes (von Neumann probes) embark on consecutive self-multiplying space exploration, taking 300 million years to explore entire Galaxy (2% of its lifetime).
Regeneration medical techniques, by electrical stimulation of regenerative growth (e.g. new kidneys, amputated limbs), begin to replace substitutive medicine (replacement of defective parts by implants or transplants).
Widely-developed urban systems of (a) covered cities on unused land masses, (b) subterranean cities especially in desert regions, (c) underwater cities in tropical and arctic regions, and (d) floating cities in mid-ocean.
Major climate-control accident: attempts in upper levels of atmosphere to bring rain to desert areas get out of control; within 4 years a new catastrophic Ice Age has begun, obliterating 15 nations including Canada, UK, Scandinavia, Switzerland, New Zealand, with 2 billion deaths from starvation, panic and inability to flee.
Worldwide fragmentation of global Christianity over last hundred years results in 32,000 distinct and separate denominations, as centralization and coordination become less possible.
Widespread thought control and control of people's minds by drugs, subliminal techniques, psychological methods, and psychosurgery.
Average lifespan in West increases to 97 years from 90 years in AD 2000, and to 200 years for large numbers of people.
Final destruction of world's great forests by human encroachment.
Nations possessing nuclear weapons total 50, including Libya, Cuba, Saudi Arabia, Nigeria, Indonesia, Zaire and Angola, all with long-range ballistic missiles.
Overthrow and death of Antichrist III; end of militaristic Islam; conversion of Islam to Christianity. (Nostradamus).
Alien civilization sends out probes to millions of planets, locates life on Earth, laser-transmits biological clones of its members (10^{17} bits of information per individual), beaming them across space to Earth.

2021 Final end of World War III as result of unexpected alliance between Western world and European Soviet Union. (Nostradamus).
Voluntary surrender of sovereignty by all 250 previously independent nations to an enlarged United Nations organization, leading to a de facto world government.
First manned interstellar expedition, intending only to explore nearest star systems.
Electronic transfer of funds (ETF) largely replaces cash, but cash still valued for the privacy its use gives.
Emerging worldwide data net reduces need for face-to-face communication in international business.

2022 Authoritarian/totalitarian/dictatorial world state arises after global nuclear war and famine kill over 600 million people (600 megadeaths); wields total world domination. (J.B.S. Haldane, H. Kahn, M. Bundy).
Crime wiped out due to mind-reading police, telepaths, parapsychologists, psychiatrists, forensic scientists, and universal computerized surveillance.

2023 Demographic megacatastrophe scenario: massive 30-year population crash begins due to (a) mankind becoming sterile after nuclear testing or warfare, or (b) worldwide famine and drought catastrophe; 7 billion die from 2020 to 2050, leaving 3 billion alive.
A free democratic United States of the World is established; all war finally outlawed; wars and threats of war disappear for first time in human history.
Mass state expropriations globally of church institutions, properties, privileges, premises, plant, possessions, programs, and funds.

2024 After nuclear holocaust, Christians regroup as Luddite church savagely opposed to technology and machines. (E. Coopers's scenario, *The cloud walker*, 1973).
Worldwide Authority set up after 65 million killed by nuclear war and famine; population control enforced by withholding food supplies. (McGeorge Bundy's 1974 scenario 'After the Deluge, the Covenant').
Asian New Religions, and secular quasi-religions, with world government support sweep across entire world destroying infrastructure of global organized Christianity.

2025 Communications satellites (a) enable instant global surveys of agriculture, minerals, hydrology, et alia, and (b) enable people to live anywhere they please, work anywhere including in electronic cottage industries, doing 90% of their business electronically at speed of light.
Robots of human complexity produced, with IQ of over 100. (A.C. Clarke).
Lethal new influenza virus appears in India, decimates continents before burning out after 6 months.
Final demise of denominational Christianity and its complete abandonment by vast mass of rank-and-file lay Christians (99.8% of world Christianity), replaced by local combined approaches by all Christians together to local problems of the times, a diaspora church of small minority groupings, a future world utopian community. (J.C. Hoekendijk, Harvey Cox, et alii).
Centralized world government arises, based heavily on artificial intelligence.
Control of behaviour by computerized monitoring of brain waves with automatic intervention to prevent misdeeds.

2026 Common world language (evolved English) understood by 90% of Earth's people; also constructed languages (Esperanto, Glossa, Suma).
9th generation of computers shift away from digital processing to analog processing whereby light waves are used to compute.
Space industrialization: heavy industry and power generation relocated off Earth's surface so that waste heat and pollution can be harmlessly dissipated into space.

2027 Christian broadcasting (overt and clandestine) utilizes vast range of 3,000 major languages, programs of every type; reputation for truth results in 90% of world as regular audience; but dangerously exposed to disinformation tactics and terrorism.

2028 New religious awareness results in interfaith convergence and union of all major world religions, despite core Christian opposition; emergence of totally new religions, cults, and messiahs using electronic communications techniques to gain power.

2029 In capitalist societies, most goods and services now distributed and supplied free of charge; also, children attain virtually true equality with adults.

UNIVERSAL PEACE SCENARIO: NEW AGE OR PLANETARY CONSCIOUSNESS AGE

c2030 Church of the future plays dynamic part in the evolution of mankind, bringing the world to final perfection in Point Omega. (Teilhard de Chardin).
Point Omega reached in noogenesis, emergence of a completely new evolutionary level (Fifth Level of Evolution: supermind): human minds of new species Homo Noeticus (Intellectual Man) become progressively integrated into some form of planetary consciousness or global social superorganism or supermind, a single living system or interthinking group or mind-linking process (Teilhard's noosphere, comprised of all consciousness minds; or, planetary Gaiafield; or, high-synergy society; or, New Age movement); expressed as synergy, syntony (superconscious learning), suprasex (empathy, mutual love for whole creation and minimal conflict between all, merging not of bodies for procreation but of minds).

2030 Age of universal peace begins: long period of global peace, the Millennium. (Nostradamus).

After Holocaust, Christianity spreads again around world in global revival led by 'an ancient, Black and primitive Church'; ascendancy of Non-White indigenous Christianity.

Capitalism now seen to have virtually destroyed itself as a viable ideology.

Conversion of China to Christianity through multitude of Chinese house-church evangelists and witnesses, resulting in 1.5 billion zealous, charismatic, nondenominational Christians, who then launch their own global mission without reference to Western or Eastern churches and missions.

Large-scale terraforming of other planets begins (transforming them to be habitable by humans).

Western world relies on sun, wind and water for 60% of all power and heating needs.

Continuing decline in rainfall by 55% over Africa; Sahara Desert, world's largest, advances 300 km farther south.

Nations in space are set up, living on very large orbiting space colonies, 20 miles long, 4 miles in diameter, 10 million population each; eventually 30% of human population lives in space by 2200.

Multinational companies of 20th century evolve into huge global corporations, each using a single global marketing strategy; top 50 are bigger and richer than many nations.

World's 10 largest cities: Mexico City 36 million, São Paulo 33 million, Bombay 27 million, Calcutta 26 million, Teheran 25 million, Delhi 24 million, Tokyo/Yokohama 23 million, Dacca 22 million, Jakarta 21 million, Karachi 20 million.

2031 Advanced extraterrestrials, who have discarded biology in favor of electronics, become one gigantic collective intelligence, with immense computer as its only body; machine uses lasers to transmit instructions for its own replication on Earth.

2032 Telemedicine and computer diagnosis: computer replaces physician as primary agent of health care.

Biological research extends possible normal human life-span to 800 years; by transcending nature, disease and death, man becomes potentially an immortal species.

2034 Manipulation of genetic material (pantropy): genetic packages of fertilized human eggs begin to be altered before birth to fit alien environments, e.g. zero-gravity or high-gravity conditions, or deep water, or speed-of-light travel.

2035 Holography comes into universal use (projecting image of a 3-dimensional object in space); laser holography expands, replacing and duplicating museums and exhibitions; specialized museums now display holograms of priceless art treasures while originals remain securely stored; also 4-dimensional dynamic holograms for science and research.

Invention of time-machine capable of viewing any event in history, in complete 3-dimensional color with stereophonic sound.

Computers and robots become more intelligent than humans, make all major decisions.

First major space city opened, on Moon; HQ of United Nations moves there.

First Declaration of Independence by Spacekind from Earthkind: space colonies in orbit between Earth and Moon set up own government.

2036 In barbaric aftermath of 30-year world war, altruistic scientists help launch world's first space flight. (H.G. Wells' scenario and film, *The shape of things to come*, 1934-5).

2038 Over 250 million people live on High Orbital Mini Earths (HOMEs), 100 million having been born there; majority leaving Earth are female; majority can never return to Earth; violent competitive theocracies emerge, also varieties of crime.

Scientific recognition of spiritual dimension in world; power of prayer explained in terms of Heisenberg's Uncertainty Principle.

End of world, one of several dates predicted by Nostradamus (his earlier date: 1943).

2039 Earth's colonies on other planets rebel; brief battle between their forces and Earth's, then their independence is recognized.

2040 Magnetic floaters in operation: high-speed underground transport systems travelling in vacuum at 2,000 km per hour through Earth propelled by magnetic fields.

Accelerating change, increasing since beginning of Industrial Revolution in AD 1775, now becomes critical (as measured by statistical indicator—growth of mass of knowledge, doubling every 10 years in 1980 and every 2 years by 2040).

Decline of great religions and quasi-religions, including Marxism.

Worst anti-Christian persecution in history, involving terrorism, huge mob riots, fanaticism, racism, all instigated and coordinated by hostile world government.

World's 10 largest cities: Mexico City 38 million, São Paulo 35 million, Bombay 30 million, Teheran 28 million, Calcutta 28 million, Delhi 27 million, Dacca 25 million, Jakarta 23 million, Karachi 22 million, Tokyo/Yokohama 22 million.

TERMINAL ECO-CATASTROPHE SCENARIO

2040 Limits-to-growth end scenario: final collapse of world civilization (as predicted by Club of Rome in 1972) due to population increase and poverty in sociosphere, pollution and industrialization in ecosphere; supplies of many minerals and food items exhausted; freak weather conditions; collapse of world transport systems; famine among urban populations; runaway greenhouse effect on Earth, leaks of radioactive waste, pesticide-immune insects, corrosive rain, et alia.

Universal information system on Earth: single global telephone and videophone system; instant access by all to contents of any book, magazine, document, program or fact ever published.

Moon (Luna) acquires colony of several hundred thousand human contract workers (not permanent colonists, due to its low gravity) mining aluminum, iron, silicon.

Earth's resources of numerous important essential minerals and metals finally exhausted.

In climax of hostility, world government turns definitively against churches, orders all followers of Christ worldwide without exception to identify themselves publicly and then to proceed within next 6 months to one central location (an island) where they will then be exterminated by nuclear device, in ultimate act of deliberate and voluntary martyrdom; Christians refusing to do so being officially pronounced to have denied Christ and then rewarded with massive material benefits.

2045 Global Bible distribution reaches optimal maximum level of 10 billion Scriptures per year (whole Bibles, NTs, portions, selections), in languages understood by whole world's population; but highly susceptible both to antichristian terrorism and also to world government edicts.

Breeding of intelligent animals (apes, cetaceans, et alia) for low-grade labor.

First humans land on Mars.

2049 Gantz organic homes produced by genetically-engineered bacteria manufacturing organic glues binding soil together; lifestyles transformed in crumbling Third-World cities.

2050 **Global status of Christianity:** 67.2 generations after Christ, world is 37.0% Christians, 99.0% evangelized; with printed Scriptures available in 5,000 languages.

50% of all Christians are charismatics (pentecostals, neo-pentecostals, apostolics, et alii), as are 70% of all church workers and 90% of all foreign missionaries.

World's 10 largest cities: Mexico City 40 million, São Paulo 37 million, Bombay 32 million, Teheran 31 million, Calcutta 30 million, Delhi 30 million, Dacca 27 million, Jakarta 25 million, Karachi 24 million, Bangkok 24 million; all but 2 being non-Christian or anti-Christian.

After 200 years of attempts, world at last adopts a single constructed international auxiliary language, a variant of Glossa, Suma or English. (A.C. Clarke).

World's private cars and aircraft travel (latter at 350 mph) entirely under control of central traffic computers.

Control of gravity on Earth achieved. (A.C. Clarke).

Risk of total destruction of human race through nuclear war recedes as vast numbers emigrate to distant space colonies.

'Freedom IV', first interstellar starship carrying humans intending to seek planets to colonize, departs for Alpha Centauri star system 4.3 light-years from Earth. (L.S. Wolfe & R.L. Wysack's scenario).

Experimentation with human DNA reaches peak, leaving behind freak individuals, freak groups, freak colonies, freak races.

World adult literacy rises from 15% in 1800, to 55% in 1960, to 70% by 2000, to 90% by 2050.

Computer-controlled commercial factory farms become universal.

Mankind's basic character fails to improve despite scientific advances; life still disrupted by greed, lust, dishonesty, corruption, and desire for power.

Christianity now dominated worldwide by Third-World indigenous pentecostal-charismatic bodies, spreading like wildfire through unorganized self-replicating media churches.

Multigeneration starships (taking several generations, e.g. 200 years, to reach destinations) built, with nuclear fusion reactors, travelling at 10% of speed of light (with continuous 1g acceleration, speed after 1 year = 95% of speed of light).

Relativistic spaceflight makes entire Universe accessible to those on the journey: starships that accelerate continuously at 1g reach 95% of speed of light within one year, reaching center of Galaxy in apparent 21 years (for an elapsed time of 30,000 years), circumnavigating entire Universe in 56 years ship time.

Rise of eccentric religious cult, Neo-Manichees, an orbital religion with no meeting places except television screens; their 'statistical theology' disproves, and destroys faith in, a personal God.

2055 Cybernetic Wave (A. Toffler's Fourth Wave) arrives, based on artificial intelligence, brain-computer linkups, biochips, instant creativity.

Cyborg minds widespread, through implanting electronic accessory brains in human brains, including biocomps (bionic-implant computer terminals) which monitor, calculate and advise the host brain.

Religions become closely influenced by, even based on, chemistry once chemical basis of all life is understood.

Human normal lifespan extends to 250 years for 75% of human race.

Urban dwellers number 80% of world's population, 80% of them being in Third World.

Plagues due to viruses from space ravage Earth killing billions. (M.

Crichton, *The Andromeda strain*, 1969).

2060 Reunion of all major separated branches of Christianity achieved: Catholic, Protestant, Anglican, Orthodox, organically united in 'the Coming Great Church'.
Medical means discovered to achieve earthly immortality, even circumventing accidental death; open to 95% of Western world's population; also ability of individuals to change sex at will.
Population increase deliberately reduced to near zero by proception, the procedure whereby every child born is deliberately chosen, wanted and adored; birth defects a nightmare of the past.
Synthetape replaces film: sophisticated software available for synthesizing visual images; human actors no longer necessary; 2120, 3-D holographic epics made using 3-dimensional synthetape.
Bus, subway and other transportation services in most of world's large cities are now provided free of charge.

2065 World population, on mediodemographic scenario, levels off at around 12 billion, well below Earth's absolute capacity. (*Interfutures* OECD Project, 1979).
Small handheld pocket computers serve as audio translators into 300 different languages for instantaneous spoken translation, also for instantaneous transcribing and translated printout.

2070 Combining of ectogenesis with eugenics so that only superior humans can propagate.
Europe and Eurasia become 70% nonreligious or antireligious.
The Lost Billion: a 1,000 million subsistence farmers, displaced from their land, become religious cultists and urban guerrillas dedicated to mass assassination before being gradually destroyed.

2075 Human beings control spaceships via skull sockets linked to ships' computers.
Man reaches travel at near-light speeds; participants' apparent longevity increases markedly.

2080 Transporting and storing of energy done through liquid hydrogen as preferred medium.
Human race uses 15 times as much energy annually as it did in 1980.
Stable world government in place: either a Soviet empire, or an American empire, or joint Soviet/American, based on English and/or Russian; or the Millennial kingdom.
Criminal procedures of all nations standardized everywhere.
Uniform world monetary system established and enforced.
All persons everywhere required to furnish total personal data annually for police work, social research, eugenic reform, et alia.
Eugenic infanticide widespread (killing of handicapped children at birth).
English becomes sole international language of science, technology, scholarship, culture, diplomacy, and Christianity.
Spread of Christianity throughout Chinese and Arab races generates vast missionary zeal to point where both launch independent schemes for total world evangelization and conversion.

2082 Moon is now settled by humans, with 50,000 Lunarians (5,000 born on Moon, who have never visited Earth); at height of tourist season, total population rises to 110,000.
Escalating arms race halted and finally terminated by (1) new generation of ultra-sophisticated computers in spy satellites, and (2) economic decline among superpowers, who finally hound international arms merchants into extinction.

EXTRATERRESTRIAL INTELLIGENCE AND INTERSTELLAR NEGOTIATION SCENARIO

2085 First verifiable alien contact with extraterrestrial intelligence among our Galaxy's (Milky Way's) 400 billion stars, where between 100 and 1 million other advanced technical civilizations (capable of interstellar radio communication) probably exist, as well as up to 1 billion lesser communicative civilizations (none resembling humanity); nearest, possibly only 100 light-years distant.
Existence discovered of vast star empires, great civilizations and alien cultures unimaginably far advanced.
Planetary war scenario: alien beings from planet Mars, emotionless Martian killers, invade Earth; Darwinian struggle for survival of human race until Martians finally killed off by microbes. (H.G. Wells' scenario, *The War of the Worlds*, 1898).
Alien religion (religion of extraterrestrials, very popular theme of science fiction) found to take many bizarre forms: worship of sentient crystals, worship of intelligent polished black monoliths, etc.
Holy Bible available translated into all 7,000 human languages, in numerous forms: print, comics, audio, video, drama, pictodrama, psychodrama, holographic, telephonic, and computerized forms; with instant holographic commentary by galaxy of scholars, Bible teachers and preachers from throughout history.
Biggest earthquake ever recorded devastates Japan, breaks Honshu in two, blasts Shikoku apart, killing 15 million; most Japanese emigrate worldwide to form a global technological diaspora.

2090 Mass global transportation systems, with zero energy loss, in operation: (a) through Earth in vacuum tubes; superspeed floater vehicles travelling at 7 miles a second, 39 minutes from one side of Earth to the other; and (b) into space, either using balloon-borne floater guideways, or space elevators riding up on superstrength cable.
Military expenditures, 10% of world income in 1980, fall to 2% by 2090, eventually to 1% by 2200 and to 0.1% by 2500.
Military arsenals include ultra-sophisticated weaponry: antimatter beams, laser rays, bullets near speed of light.
Vast volumes of galactic space regularly monitored by remote sensing instead of by direct patrolling.
First manned starship sent to nearby stars within 40 light-years known to have planets; interstellar manned flight within 1% of speed of light achieved, using ion drive, carbon-dioxide laser, composite optics, and immensely potent energy source—reaction of matter with antimatter. (A.C. Clarke, G.K. O'Neill).
Self-reproducing replicator factories, replicating exact copies of original machines/electronics/cybernetics; by 2380, up to any complexity reproducible within 10 years.
New-style religions and mystical nature cults arise opposing biotechnology.

2095 Superpowers, faced by omniscient presence of alien beings of vastly superior technology, agree to abandon war and destroy all armaments.
Church of the martyrs: on one scenario, ruthless 80-year persecution by world government reaches climax, decimates global Christianity, reduces churches to a tiny minority, then liquidates all churches, which thus follow their Master to final execution and martyrdom.

THE DISTANT FUTURE (beyond 21st century AD)

2101 **Global status of Christianity:** 68.9 generations after Christ, world is 40% Christians (75% of them being Non-Whites), 99.5% evangelized; with printed Scriptures available in all 7,000 languages.
World population reaches a peak of 8,250 million, then starts to decline. (C. McEvedy & R. Jones scenario).
World becomes either high-technology, ample-energy utopia, or a low-technology, overcrowded, energy-poor dystopia.
First space arks begin to be made from hollowed-out asteroids.
Some 10,000 orbiting space colonies exist around Earth; 100 million to 2 billion permanent population, including more USA citizens than remain in USA; after 5 generations their cultures draw apart even to mutual linguistic unintelligibility.
Vast dispersion of human race into colonies across Galaxy makes humankind invulnerable to any single future disaster.
Decline of industrial espionage, software sabotage, and computer crime, due to proficiency and omnipresence of police forces.

A new Dark Age begins

A new Age of Barbarism arises, with world ground underfoot by war, religious fanaticism, neo-Islamic domination, terror, and Antichrist for 2 centuries before final advent of the Golden Millennium in AD 2300. (Nostradamus).
Cities of over 100 million inhabitants built, completely 3-dimensional and soundproofed, with varieties of transport on many levels; eventually cities each with over 1 billion residents, each with hundreds of thousands of museums, theaters, aquatic centers, recreation centers, universities, libraries, research institutes.
Global dictatorship established under guise of a religious cult, the Prophets; a theocracy enforced by watchful 'Angels of the Lord'. (R. Heinlein, *Revolt in 2100*, 1940).

2102 Manufacture of androids: artificially-produced human creatures made out of organic materials.
Immense macro-engineering projects arise: space elevators (skyhook), with 100-ton cars climbing cable at 3,700 miles per hour for 22,300 miles to satellite; 150-foot plastic pipe diverts Rhone river under Mediterranean to irrigate North African desert; shipment of Antarctic icebergs to Sahara desert.
World's population rises to 10,185 million (Africa 2.5 billion, Latin America 1.3 billion, South Asia 3 billion, East Asia 1.8 billion, Northern America 400 million, Europe (stabilized since 2050) at 500 million. (UN projections 1984).
'Blade runners' (replicant-killers) widely employed to kill or 'retire' renegade Nexus-6 replicants (4-year-life androids). (Movie 'Blade Runner', 1982).

2110 Whole world now follows essentially a planned economy, due to proliferating UN agencies.
Global sea-farming: seaweed becomes one of world's major food crops; 2130, Pacific coast of South America hosts long chain of kelp farms; vast regions of oceans sown with enriched plankton harvested by huge factory ships; 2180, whole ocean industry under UN control.

2112 'Albert Einstein', first faster-than-light starship, departs on exploratory mission to 10 star systems. (L.S. Wolfe & R.L. Wysack's scenario).

2120 Spacetorium, an orbiting clinic, established in space where 900 ultra-wealthy geriatrics with heart and degenerative problems can retire.
Rising ocean levels finally destroy Shanghai, one of world's greatest trading cities.

2130 Starship drives include (a) nuclear ion-drive, (b) propulsion by pressure of light, (c) pulsed fusion-bomb explosions at 250 per second, (d) Bussard ramscoop starship (designed in 1960), (e) antimatter/photon drive; at acceleration of 1 Earth gravity, ship reaches center of our Galaxy in 20 years (ship time) and any point in Universe within one lifetime; use of hyperspace and time warps developed.

2140 Federation of Galactic Civilizations proposed but comes to nothing.

2150 Widespread development of extrasensory perception (ESP), telepathy, telekinesis, teleportation (instant communication and transport), clairvoyance, precognition, remote viewing.
Minute computer (size of a pinhead) stores for instant retrieval every word in every book entire human race has ever published.
Universal use of synthetic foods.
Free mass passenger transport provided universally: not only within large cities, but also globally and extraterrestrially.
First manned long-distance starship leaves Earth for stars beyond 40 light-years distant, seeking any planets of theirs; millions of humans subsequently are transported across interstellar space.

2160 Definitive, permanent and universal cures finally achieved for cancer, aging, and all other human ailments; with bionic aid, man becomes virtually immortal either in same body or in succession of bodies; final end, after previous 2 billion years of evolution of life, of programmed death and also sexual reproduction to replace deaths.
Greenhouse scenario: despite all precautions since 1987, vast production of carbon dioxide from burning of fossil fuels since AD 2000 leads to marked rise in Earth's temperature; 'greenhouse effect' then results in initial melting of polar ice caps and raises level of globe's seas by 18 feet, submerging New York, London and other great coastal cities.

2170 Several varieties of humans exist: those with prosthetic limbs or bodies, robots run by disembodied human brains, extraterrestrial humans, clones, cyborgs, androids, wholly artificial humanoids, replicants, mutants, et alii.
Internationalists (people working for UN agencies) become major influence in world at all levels.
Non-urgent flight including freight shifts to ubiquitous airships affordable by even poorest countries; widespread use in agriculture, reclaiming deserts et alia.

2175 Population of Earth 15 billion, gross world product US$300 trillion, per capita income $20,000 (at 1980 values).

PERIOD OR AGE OF RECOVERY, AD 2180-2400

2180 Human beings are everywhere numerous, rich, and in control of forces of nature; by contrast in AD 1780 human beings were relatively few, poor, and at mercy of forces of nature.
UN's Land Use Committee attempts to turn entire world into a planned Garden of Eden, but thwarted by national jealousies.

2190 North America approaches 10-fold population increase (over 1980) to 2 billion persons in massive high-rise blocks.
Explosive growth of cryonics corporations begins; 2210, over 10,000 persons 'frozen down'; 2214, lotteries offering treatment a huge success; 2230, 30,000 a year frozen down; 2244, massive electrical power failure in USA kills most off; cryonics industry finally collapses.

2200 Post-holocaust life on Earth now stabilized with, on minidemographic scenario, 2 billion population, homogeneous, largely self-supporting, no energy shortage, limited technology.
On mediodemographic scenario, world population now 25 billion (or even as high as 75 billion in mile-high high-rise blocks, orbiting colonies and undersea city habitats), according to technological-social optimism scenario; world now in quaternary postindustrial phase, with all primary and secondary activities fully automated; many people in tertiary activities (research, industrial planning, operating the single world government, medicine, education).
On maxidemographic scenario, population expands to 1,000 billion, crammed into 100,000 cities of 10 million people each, with thousand-storey tower blocks each housing a million people. (J. Blish & N.L. Knight, *A torrent of faces*, 1967).
30% of humanity now lives in orbiting space colonies.

2210 Computers designed and built with sense of identity, of self, of consciousness, self-designing, self-programming, self-maintaining and self-replicating.
Disembodied human brains function at center of machines, computers, vehicles, factories, spaceships.

2217 Space explorers from Earth encounter first spaceship of an alien species.

2220 First ectogenetic baby born from artificial womb; by 2300, 20,000 ectogenetic births in USA alone; 2302, Crusade for Moral Rearmament launched against ectogenesis.

2223 UN's Council of Justice set up; 2236, publishes its first Code of Rights.

2245 Deadly Sealed Laboratory in Antarctica, producing lethal microorganisms in genetic research, relocated out in space.

2248 First successful experiments in large-scale human total rejuvenation.

2250 Americanized world state founded (First Men, on O. Stapledon's 1930 scenario); lasts until 6250, becoming rigidly stratified and regimented; power failure, breakdown of law and order, succeeded by Dark Age of semi-barbarism for 10,000 years; new civilization arises, destroyed by nuclear chain reaction.
High Frontier (space colonization) makes comeback after 300 years' procrastination; 2285, O'Neill-I opened as first residential microworld, for 15,000 people; future of industry gets under way in space with specialist industrial microworlds; 2350, first lunar mass-driver (electromagnetic cannon on Moon accelerating buckets to escape velocity).
Rapid growth of new mysticism and new monasticism.

2271 UN passes resolution enforcing universal sterilization to control population explosion; Ireland and Italy refuse, so are flooded with fanatical immigrants.

2275 Von Neumann machines (VNMs) or self-reproducing robot probes are despatched beyond Solar System, mapping Universe and producing growing cloud of VNMs throughout space.

2282 SAP (solid artificial photosynthesis) results in colossal food-yields from restricted areas of land.

2285 Mauritania offers sanctuary to rival Roman papacy (conservative, anti-sterilization), which then builds headquarters at Kiffa, 300 miles inland in Sahara desert.

2289 Earth humans' first contact with an alien race, the Vegans; 2310, first interstellar war.

2291 Earth and 2 alien civilizations form Galactic Association of Intelligent Life.

2293 World divided into 3 distinct communities: Eternals, who rule; Brutals, poverty-stricken peons who worship a giant stone god, Zardoz; and Exterminators, barbarians trained by Eternals to restrict Brutals by killings and slavery. (J. Boorman's film *Zardoz*, 1974).

2300 Easily reachable coal reserves of world now all used up.
Advent of Golden Millennium, on Nostradamus' predictions.

2305 Earth under complete control of a debased religion using science and psychology to keep man in subjection; rebellion comes via underground satanic cult with witches and warlocks. (F. Leiber, *Gather, Darkness*, 1943).

2310 First successful human analogues (artificial humans, sentient humanoids); 2325, wave of luddite or mechanophobic paranoia sweeps world as people smash robots, computers, androids.
Personal contact easier to avoid then ever before in history; people program electronic analogues of themselves to handle routine contacts.

2316 US Maglev Subway links east coast to west, with cars running in elevated transparent tubes floating on web of electromagnetism.

2350 A file on every known person in Galaxy exists in every starship's data bank.
Universal immunization available; sophisticated cancer treatments available to half world's population; rejuvenation available only to the rich.

2360 Humans now live dispersed in microworlds across Solar System.

2364 Totalitarian coup by admiral Hrunta who proclaims self emperor of all colonies; 3089, assassinated after 725 years of arbitrary personal rule. (J. Blish, *Cities in flight*, 1962).

2367 Tetroli disaster: first deaths of a microworld's entire complement: 615 perish in bacterial outbreak.

2380 Automation results in self-replicating devices of great complexity capable of self-reproduction, reproducing any apparatus no matter how complex, without human intervention, in under 10 years.

2390 Humans have now discovered and colonized 8 planets within 78 light-years of Earth; outward migration continues across Galaxy's 100,000 light-year diameter.
World population nearly homogenized into a single race (neo-Mongoloid) with a single culture and language (25th-century English); entire world urbanized, industrialized, homogenized, wired as a single global village.

PERIOD OR AGE OF TRANSFORMATION, AD 2400-2650

2400 World 95% urbanized and industrialized with all industries organized as monopolies.
Aggregate households (6 adults and 3 children) replace nuclear family and become widespread, and by 2500 become the norm; by 2650, old-style 'family life' and biological parenthood abandoned worldwide except in space microworlds.
Medical advances include repair of brain damage, regeneration of severed limbs, and regular body-scanning of entire populations in Western world (but only 1 in 10,000 in Third World).

2419 Date of Armageddon battle as postulated in original Buck Rogers stories and scenarios. (P.F. Nowlan, *Armageddon 2419 A.D.*, published 1928-29).

2433 Ceres, largest asteroid of the Belt (760 km radius), cracked (blown apart) by engineers to provide 10^{18} tons of valuable mass (metals, ores); mass and energy now everywhere the key to space.

2460 Personality analogue transfer (PAT): people in distant space communicate with Earth via updated personality analogue constructs of themselves on Earth, who can converse with Earthdwellers with no time lag.

2465 Jupiter Bridge shuttle: fleets of robot shuttle-scoops transfer mass from Jupiter to moon Ganymede and its microworlds, making them refuelling bases for transJovian travellers.

2482 All world's nations merge into 12 large superstates (including North American Nation), governed by social scientists, under World Federal Union (world government) with world capital in Honolulu, using new language Voca scientifically designed to be easily teachable and learnable.

2485 Humans now diversified into 5 distinct species: (1) Homo Sapiens, or sapients, the 'ordinary humans' or 'normals'; (2) by 2485, merpeople as first radically modified humans, with gills, flippers etc; (3) by 2505, space-adapted humans (fabers, or ETs) with spaceships manned entirely by ETs in regular service by 2528, and nearly 3,000 ETs in Solar System by 2600; (4) by 2581, life-extended humans (emortals, or ZTs) interbreed successfully and thus become a new species; (5) by 2700, starpeople (emortal fabers); with further species being developed.

2500 800-year decline of scientific profession, from overinflated novelty alone able to save the world, to more modest role in society: from AD 1740 to 1965, 90% of all scientists who ever lived were alive; by AD 2200, 45%; AD 2500, 18%; thereafter, further decline.

Roofing-in of whole Earth as in effect a single several-mile-high tower block, housing around 400 billion people, fed either by artificial production or from extraterrestrial sources.

2510 Instantaneous teleportation now normal: all transport obsolete since people travel instantly by mind alone. (A. Bester's novel *The stars my destination*, 1956).

2512 Massive experimental manned ramjet starliner 'T.E. Lawrence' (6,000 feet long, with hydrogen funnel propulsion) travels around Sun and returns with more fuel than it began with.

2520 Daedalus-class robot starprobes, weighing 50,000 tons at departure, routinely make one-way exploratory trips to nearer stars.

2530 World rulers use genetic engineering to perpetuate society stratified by intelligence and physique; scheduled sexual orgies substitute for both marriage and religion. (Aldous Huxley's scenario, *Brave New World*, 1931).

Whole ecosystems of genetically-engineered species assembled (Hanging Gardens of New Babylon, giant insect islands); genetic scientists recreate living monster dinosaurs by cloning from fossilized bones of extinct species, and place them in tropical neosaurian game parks; also herds of woolly mammoths for commercial meat industry.

2550 Laser lightsails in use: 60 starships without main engines, each with 1000-km sail driven at half lightspeed across space by light from 10 laser stations in close orbit around Sun.

2565 Interstellar ramjet 'Columbus', an entire microworld powered by cold-fusion torch using galactic hydrogen clouds for fuel, becomes first manned vehicle to orbit a star, averaging 20% of lightspeed; time of trip, 30 years; numerous microworlds established around Sirius and other stars; interstellar trade begins and flourishes.

2630 Gigantic spaceships or space arks begin to leave Earth on mission of 'zygotic evangelism': supermicroworlds each peopled by thousands of space-adapted humans, each cruising forever on its funneldrive at near-lightspeed, carrying (1) millions of frozen zygotes (life-building information in DNA coils), and (2) rest of entire human knowledge in its computer banks; also (3) Christian teams with full biblical and other materials.

2639 Antarctica becomes first genuinely international territory; 2650, Amundsen City built there as UN headquarters; whole continent and its resources rapidly developed.

CREATION OF THE NEW WORLD, AD 2650-3000

2650 Life-extension technology available to every living person, through rejuvenation (NAR, nucleic acid renewal) or engineered longevity (Zaman transformation, ZT); all political power passes to rejuvenates, i.e. the old inherit the world; by 2700, over 99% of UN Council Chamber seats are occupied by NAR rejuvenates, and by 2950 by emortals (ZTs).

UN decides all human embryos everywhere have right to engineered longevity free of charge.

2700 Very little now proves to be impossible; almost everything is now practicable: e.g. faster-than-light travel, instantaneous matter transmission (teleportation), time travel, personality and memory transfer between humans, widespread telepathic communication.

2750 Dominant religion now neo-Stoicism, but fragmented into rival schisms and cults; on other scenarios, Christianity dominant.

2800 Totality of human knowledge readily and instantly available to all human beings; life far more complex than in 20th century; life spans up to 900 years; no language barriers.

World population restabilizes, at 2.5 billion, with global average life expectancy at birth of 180 years.

Worldwide equalization of economic opportunity arrives; age of universal abundance for all begins; money no longer matters.

Some 500 self-sufficient human communities live out in Solar System; by 2900, some 2,000, with 200 independent microworlds (population 100,000 starpeople) en route to other stars, and a dozen already arrived.

2900 More human beings live in space than on Earth.

2967 Robot probe from Earth intercepted by alien sentients 75 light-years from Earth.

THE FAR DISTANT FUTURE (everything beyond 30th century AD)

3001 Interstellar distances finally recognized as too great to sustain any meaningful galactic communications or communities; no viable galactic empires or federations therefore possible; on alternative scenarios, however, humans discover flight at 30,000 times speed of light, quantum drives, and then instantaneous travel throughout Universe via black and white holes.

Construction of a Dyson sphere (built from disassembly of gas giant planet Jupiter) enclosing everything within Earth's solar orbit (186 million miles diameter with Sun at center), in order to (1) gather up all the Sun's energy, and (2) provide living space for a million Earths with 400 trillion humans; creates vast civilization unique in history; but massive engineering know-how required also carries enormous potential for blackmail, evil, warfare and chaos.

No religions remain for human race except Christianity and materialism. (L.E. Browne, 'The Religion of the World in AD 3000', 1949).

Extraterrestrial end scenario: human race wipes itself out by inept handling of alien (extraterrestrial) technology.

3450 Geodynamics of superspace discovered; scientists find out inconceivably dense yet bubbling, foamlike structure of superspace: every empty space or vacuum contains massive infernos of energies and seething violence; harnessing these enormous subatomic quantum fluctuations leads to invention of ultimate propellant, the quantum drive; mankind now free to roam the Universe for ever. (A.C. Clarke 1986).

3500 Cosmic collision scenario: large astral body crashes into Earth catastrophically; previously, 500 meteorites crash annually, one asteroid collides every 1,000 years, and one comet (out of 100 billion circling the Sun) strikes Earth every 100,000 years.

3781 Monks of Order of Leibowitz, who have preserved knowledge through Dark Ages after 20th-century World War III nuclear holocaust, eventually see civilization rebuilt by AD 3100 to point where, again, a new industrial-scientific age culminates by AD 3781 in imminent nuclear World War IV; just before outbreak, discredited Order launches an ecclesiastical starship through which Church of New Rome transfers authority of St Peter from Earth to Alpha Centauri. (W.M. Miller's novel, *A canticle for Leibowitz*, 1960).

3797 End of world in cosmic explosion (as envisioned by Nostradamus as finale of his prophecies).

3936 End of world as predicted by Spanish Dominican monk Vincent Ferrer (c1350-1419).

4000 Human race is still Homo Sapiens Sapiens but has become alien by 1980 standards: communication and mutual understanding with humans of 1980 probably would be very difficult; no race problem since only one race (Mongoloid, tan); lifespans average several thousand years, with large numbers taking immortality drug or injection to become immortal at any particular age they wish.

4100 Ice Age scenario: after interglacial (mild period) of 15,000 years, Earth enters new ice age, with famine reducing population from 10 billion to 1 billion, and freezing the rest to death by AD 12,000.

4104 Cosmos ends in stupendous collision of matter and antimatter, after which new Universe is created. (J. Blish's tetralogy *Cities in flight*, 1955-62).

4500 Cosmic rays scenario: Earth's magnetic field declines gradually to zero leaving humans unprotected for 500 years from cosmic radiation; a giant solar flare from Sun, or a star within 30 light-years which then explodes as a supernova, destroys Earth by radiation.

4600 Intelligent machines control world after outstripping now extinct creators. (O. Johannesson, *The great computer*, 1966).

5000 Instantaneous communicators (superluminal faster-than-light connectors) across Universe include Dirac transmitter, sending messages that can be picked up by any Dirac receiver past, present, or future. (James Blish's scenario, *The Quicunx of Time*, 1973).

Material from planets is used to construct immense spherical floor around Sun enclosing entire Solar System, with area of 160 quintillion (1.6×10^{20}) square miles, capable of supporting human population of up to one septillion (10^{24}).

Supercivilizations are installed on rigid shells around black holes, extracting energy from hole by space-rubbish shuttle.

Black holes prove to be time machines, wormholes or gravity tunnels providing a kind of instantaneous interstellar and intergalactic subway, emerging in remote parts of space-time through white holes (quasars); or even star gates out of this Cosmos and into totally different cosmoses.

6000 Intergalactic space-travel and time-travel underway using space and time machine: men construct a spinning or rotating black hole just outside Solar System, which instantaneously transports men and matter across millions of light-years, or across millions of years in time, spewing them out through white holes. (A. Berry's scenario, *The Iron Sun*, 1979).

6250 World supplies of energy finally fail; long Dark Ages of savagery begin, with scores of major disasters. (O. Stapledon's epic chronicle of future history, *Last and First Men*, 1930).

8000 Asteroidal collision scenario: large asteroid Ceres collides with Earth with 12,000 billion megatons impact energy, sterilizes Earth and shifts its orbit significantly.

9500 Planet Jupiter (a star that failed) supports human colonies in great balloon cities permanently floating in upper atmosphere.

10,000 Human race begins to evolve from Homo Sapiens Sapiens into a more advanced species Homo Noeticus Noeticus (Pan-Intellectual Man); evolution of humanity into a Galaxy-wide and continuously-growing cosmic Overmind.

10,150 Commission of Ecumenical Translators attempts to unite peoples of Universe, results in galactic Holy War. (F. Herbert, *Dune*, 1965).

12,000 Post-catastrophe scenario: 10,000 years after nuclear holocaust, sparsely-populated pastoral utopian matriarchy on Earth, with communal living, personal longevity, eugenics, superintelligent domestic animals. (W.H. Hudson's scenario, *A Crystal Age*, 1887).

20,000 Rise of pantropy, i.e. spread of human race throughout Galaxy, invading countless different environments by adapting mankind genetically to suit new conditions (life under sea, in flight, or on Mars, etc).

30,000 Supercivilizations move out to colonize whole galaxies at rate of 10 million years a galaxy; intergalactic travellers learn to utilize space warps and time warps (irregularities in space-time continuum) to traverse immense distances involved.

50,000 Exploding Sun scenario: a hostile alien civilization deliberately triggers solar cataclysm, Sun explodes as nova, flaring up in millionfold increase of brightness and heat to burn all Earthly life and vaporize the planet.

c100,000 New Homo species, interstellar man (Homo Superior), evolves and outnumbers Homo Sapiens populations of Earth and its immediate colonies.

200,000 Mining of heaviest elements in Sun, by large magnetohydrodynamic machines built from Mercurian ores, provides Earth with unlimited energy for 300 million years, at the same time extending natural life of Sun from 8 billion years to 20 trillion years.

800,000 Human race degenerates by devolution into racial decadence with 2 separate races, the childish Eloi and the troglodyte cannibalistic Morlocks; humanity finally proves to be just another of Nature's unlucky failures; time travellers visiting them then move on to visit far future's last days of humanity and Earth. (H.G. Wells' scenario, *The Time Machine*, 1895).

THE MEGAFUTURE (after AD 1 million)

1 million Mankind evolves to Homo Galacticus: great unemotional intelligences, large-headed beings retaining no bodily parts except hands, 'floating in vats of amber nutritive fluid', doing little but think; a global brotherhood of enlightened supermen living in strongholds deep inside Earth whose surface is thickly mantled with ice at absolute zero temperature. (H.G. Wells' scenario, 'The Man of the Year Million', 1893).

2 million Point Omega finally reached and consummated (as envisaged by Teilhard de Chardin), with Christ as Cosmocrat and perfector of human evolution.

Humanity completes its colonizing spread across the Galaxy, settling it in 2 million years.

3 million Man's body height evolves to some 8 feet tall; tongue, palate and larynx increase in size to handle rapid complex speech.

10 million Superintelligent Second Men evolve, plagued by cloud-intelligences from Mars, then gradually stagnate. (O. Stapledon 1930).

15 million Next scheduled mass collisions of Earth with comets/asteroids (every 26 million years, last being in BC 11 million), resulting in mass extinction of majority of remaining species including genus Homo.

40 million Third Men evolve, midgets with massive ears, music as their religion, biogenetic control; then Fourth Men (Great Brains many feet across), who then design Fifth Men (huge intellectuals who migrate temporarily to Venus); AD 100 million, Sixth Men evolve, a barbarous throwback, also on Venus; AD 300 million, Seventh Men evolve: pygmy flying men uninterested in science or material progress. (O. Stapledon 1930).

100 million Sun cools past point where it is visible from Earth, whose surface is too cold to support life; last human beings live 100 miles below surface in Pyramid (8-mile-high metal scientific marvel), with monsters outside in volcanic fireholes. (W.H. Hodgson's scenario *The night land*, 1912).

400 million Eighth Men evolve, physically larger; science and progress resumed; they escape collision between Sun and gas cloud by migrating to planet Neptune; Ninth Men evolve as dwarfs, developed to survive on Pluto, but become degenerate and collapse. (O. Stapledon 1930).

500 million Human race evolves into wealthy, powerful, coordinated universal society reaching across Galaxy and also across Universe; humans finally discover ultimate secrets of the Cosmos.

Emergence of Sixth Level of Evolution: galactic mind, i.e. galactic consciousness, with transition to a galactic superorganism; inter-Gaian interaction and communication reach sufficient complexity and synergy for all 10 billion Gaias (planets with life) in our Galaxy to integrate into a single system, a galactic society of communicating civilizations.

THE GIGAFUTURE (after AD 1 billion)

1 billion Sun begins to expand and turns Earth into tropical nightmare, with fantastic array of carnivorous and poisonous jungle plants and insects seizing telepathic control and destroying remaining civilization of devolved green-skinned descendants of Homo Sapiens. (B.W. Aldiss' scenario *Hothouse/The long afternoon of Earth*, 1962).

2 billion Supernova end scenario: final extinction of human race by supernova, with Last Men (18th race after Homo Sapiens as First Men) as final form of civilized humanity, living on Neptune in virtual Paradise, one trillion strong; telepaths, virtually immortal, group mind. (O. Stapledon 1930).

3 billion Disintegrating Moon scenario: Earth gradually pulls Moon closer, triggering earthquakes, volcanos, tidal waves engulfing continents; when Moon reaches 5,000 miles out, it disintegrates totally into planetary ring bombarding Earth with huge chunks.

4 billion Final shape of man scenario—Homo Universalis, a non-material being with enormous powers, a sphere of force able to travel instantaneously across Galaxy or Universe at will; on this scenario, church of Jesus Christ now numbers 1 decillion members (10^{33} persons, or 1 billion trillion trillion).

5 billion Emergence of Seventh or Final Level of Evolution: cosmic mind, i.e. universal consciousness, with all 100 billion galaxies or galactic superorganisms in Universe evolving into one single universal superorganism or being, the perfect Cosmos.

6 billion Sun evolves into luminous red giant with radius reaching planet Mercury; Earth's oceans and atmosphere have long since disappeared in intense heat; most stars very old, Galaxy (and most other galaxies) becoming a graveyard of stars at endpoint of stellar evolution; human race, if not yet extinct, embarks on its last journey.

7 billion Sudden ice death of Earth scenario: huge alien star appears, loops around Sun, draws Earth off into icy depths of space.

8 billion Solar end scenario: Sun, gradually expanding over last 13 billion years, engulfs Earth and all its related colonies, then collapses as a degenerate white dwarf and then finally a dead black dwarf.

15 billion Universe's disorganization or entropy ('anti-information', e.g. decay, rusting, pollution, growing old, accumulated rubbish, deaths of stars, black dwarfs, neutron stars, dead hulks, multiple collisions, intergalactic chaos, supermassive black holes) rapidly increases with every energy transfer. (2nd Law of Thermodynamics).

Black holes engulf entire Cosmos

25 billion Black hole at center of Galaxy (Milky Way) which has been devouring matter and stars for 40 billion years, emitting ever more intense radiation (and reaching a billion miles wide by AD 1987), finally consumes whole of Galaxy; most other galaxies similarly eaten up until all matter has been sucked into a number of gigantic black holes.

50 billion Period of star formation ends, majority of stars begin to go out, whole Universe gradually becomes a graveyard of stars.

100 billion After 100 billion (10^{11}) years, life and intelligence continue after end of Homo Sapiens (since essential feature of consciousness is, not cells or DNA, but structural complexity) in forms of sentient computers, sentient clouds and other vastly complex structures.

THE TERAFUTURE (after AD 1 trillion, or 10^{12} years)

10^{14} years After 100 trillion (10^{14}) years, last remaining stars run out of nuclear fuel, contract and collapse under their own weight; all lose their planets through close encounters with other stars.

10^{17} years Dead stars break up, evaporate and are swallowed by massive black holes (one at center of every galaxy), which then all finally coalesce into one immense supermassive black hole coextensive with the still-expanding Universe.

Alternative end-time scenarios, after 10^{18} years: (1) Universe is *open* (with insufficient mass to halt expansion of galaxies, which thus continues for ever); or (2) Universe is *flat* (exactly flat, with just enough mass to halt expansion but not to reverse it), or (3) Universe is *closed* (with sufficient mass, especially nonluminous mass (cold dark matter) in haloes around galaxies, to halt expansion and reverse it).

THE ESCHATOFUTURE — 1: ENDLESS EXPANSION OF OPEN UNIVERSE (The Expansion Heat Death scenario)

10^{18} years In the eschatofuture or exafuture (after 10^{18} years), Universe gradually runs down in energy and temperature.

10^{30} years Some 40% of all matter in Universe with its 10^{80} elementary particles (protons, neutrons, electrons) has now totally decayed.

10^{32} years Life-span of all protons and neutrons ends as they disintegrate and all long-lived matter decays; nothing left in Universe except electrons, positrons, photons, neutrinos and black holes.

10^{50} years Universe continues expanding for ever; as its heat death approaches, humanity builds its own computer-god which duly creates another universe. (I. Asimov's scenario 'The Last Question', 1956).

10^{95} years Despite dying Universe, many advanced long-lived civilizations manage to maintain themselves by constructing rigid shells around rotating supermassive black holes and living off their energy until they decay and evaporate after 10^{100} years.

10^{100} years Final evolutionary heat death of Universe as entropy (disorder or chaos) reaches maximum: disappearance by quantum evaporation of all supermassive black-hole relics of collapsed galaxies, and elimination of all solid matter; lastly, remaining diffuse gas of low-energy particles vanishes, leaving nothing except cold, thin, expanding sea of radiation.

THE ESCHATOFUTURE — 2: GRADUAL DEMISE OF FLAT STATIONARY UNIVERSE
(The Motionless Heat Death scenario)

10^{18} years Expansion of Universe slows, gradually comes to a permanent halt, declines toward ultimate heat death as entropy (disorder, chaos) approaches maximum.

10^{20} years Humans, huddled in space colonies across icy Universe, create new life forms based on plasma (remnants of interstellar gas), resulting in structured, constantly evolving plasmoid society and plasmoid creatures each living 10^{15} years in Universe's freezing night, using energy from black holes.

10^{31} years Final civilization: before plasmoid society disintegrates as protons decay, it creates enormously sluggish creatures of new kind of atom, positronium (orbiting electron and positron), forming its own vastly more diffuse plasma, powered by electron-positron antimatter clashes.

10^{99} years Space temperature only 10^{-60} degrees above absolute zero in stationary and motionless Universe.

10^{100} years Photons (light from earlier epochs) as only remaining entities in motion continue to expand, carrying the entire record of the Universe, galaxies, humanity and all creation, across limitless reaches of empty space.

THE ESCHATOFUTURE — 3: GRAVITATIONAL COLLAPSE OF CLOSED UNIVERSE
(The Big Crunch or Big Squeeze scenario)

10^{25} years At its maximum expansion, Universe is made up of dead stars, supermassive black-hole remnants of collapsed galaxies, and low-energy particles; gravity of Universe, especially nonluminous matter (over 80% of all matter), halts expansion and reverses it; dead stars begin to burn up and explode.

After expansion of Universe is halted and recession of galactic systems reversed, Universe begins to collapse rapidly and catastrophically.

10^{32} years A million years before the Big Crunch, photons dissociate interstellar hydrogen atoms into electrons and protons; one year before, stars break up; supermassive black holes swallow up matter and radiation; 3 minutes before, black holes coalesce, Universe becomes a single monster supermassive black hole.

The Big Crunch: in final collapse of Universe, at first galaxies then stars and lastly atoms, particles and quarks are crushed into each other in one overwhelming cataclysmic inferno, with collapsing Cosmos approaching a singularity of infinite density and temperature and reverting to primal chaos of original cosmic explosion and fireball, the primordial monobloc.

GOD CREATES SUCCESSIVE OSCILLATING UNIVERSES
(The Big Bounce scenario)

After final collapse of our contracting Universe, a new and mightier Big Bang occurs and a totally new, more immense universe commences its vastly faster expansion; and ditto, in due course, for an endless sequence of progressively vaster universes. (Landsberg-Park model of universe bigger with each succeeding bounce).

GOD CREATES INFINITE PARALLEL CYCLIC UNIVERSES

Numerous cycles or bounces: present Universe is no more than 100 bounces from cycle which lasted just long enough to create a single generation of stars.

Our Universe and its successors turn out to be only one bubble in a froth of a billion trillion parallel sequences of infinitely evolving universes in superspace; awesome might, majesty, dominion, power and glory of God as Creator finally fully unveiled.

APPENDIX 1: A Statistical Overview of World Evangelization, BC 13 Million to AD 4 Billion

YEAR	GLOBAL POPULATION: LIVE POPULATION Total	Increm	ALL PEOPLE EVER Since AD 33	All Homo	GLOBAL CHRISTIANS: LIVE CHRISTIANS Total	%	Increm Xtns	ALL CHRISTIANS EVER All Since AD 33 Total	%	% all Homo	MARTYRS Total (ever)	% (ever)	Per year (recent)	GLOBAL EVANGELIZED: LIVE EVANGELIZED Total	%	Increm	ALL EVANGELIZED EVER All Since AD 33 Total	%	% all Homo
COLUMN: 1	2	3	4	5	6	7	8	9	10	11	12	13	14	15	16	17	18	19	20
(m=millions)	m	m	m	m	m	%	m	m	%	%	m	%		m	%	m	m	%	%
COSMIC ERA I: THE PREHISTORY OF WORLD EVANGELIZATION																			
BC																			
13 million	0.1	-		-	First hominids														
5,500,000	0.2	-		0.0	Origin of genus Homo														
4,500,000	0.3	10000.0		10000.0	Homo Habilis														
1,700,000	0.5	44800.0		54800.0	Homo Erectus														
500,000	0.7	28800.0		83600.0	Homo Sapiens														
150,000	1.4	14700.0		98300.0	Homo Sapiens Neanderthalensis														
100,000	1.5	2900.0		101200.0															
45,000	2.0	3850.0		105050.0	Homo Sapiens Sapiens														
10,000	4.0	4200.0		109250.0	5 modern human races														
8000	5.0	360.0		109610.0															
4000	7.0	960.0		110570.0	God's Old Testament People:														
2000	27.0	1360.0		111930.0	0.0	0.0	0.0	0.0											
1000	50.0	1540.0		113470.0	0.5	1.0	4.0	4.0											
500	100.0	1500.0		114970.0	0.9	0.9	17.5	21.5											
0	165.0	2650.0		117620.0	2.1	1.3	28.0	49.5											
30	169.7	200.8	0.0	117820.8	2.3	1.4	3.0	52.5											
COSMIC ERA II: WORLD EVANGELIZATION IN CHRISTIAN HISTORY																			
AD																			
33	170.2	20.4	0.0	117841.2	0.0	0.0	0.0	0.0	0.00	0.00	0.000	-	-	0.8	0.2	0.0	0.0	0.00	0.00
100	181.5	471.3	471.3	118312.5	1.0	0.6	1.3	1.3	0.28	0.00	0.025	1.92	500	50.8	28.0	69.1	69.1	14.66	0.06
200	190.0	743.0	1214.3	119055.5	6.6	3.5	15.2	16.5	1.36	0.01	0.080	0.48	1,000	60.8	32.0	223.2	292.3	24.07	0.25
300	192.0	764.0	1978.3	119819.5	19.9	10.4	53.0	69.5	3.51	0.06	0.410	0.59	1,540	67.2	35.0	256.0	548.3	27.71	0.46
400	190.0	764.0	2742.3	120583.5	35.3	18.6	110.4	179.9	6.56	0.15	1.950	1.08	5,310	74.1	39.0	282.6	830.9	30.30	0.69
500	193.4	766.8	3509.1	121350.3	43.4	22.4	157.4	337.3	9.61	0.28	2.540	0.75	5,440	81.2	42.0	310.6	1141.5	32.53	0.94
600	200.0	786.8	4295.9	122137.1	48.0	24.0	182.8	520.1	12.11	0.43	2.700	0.52	1,000	78.0	39.0	318.4	1459.9	33.98	1.20
700	210.0	820.0	5115.9	122957.1	50.0	23.8	196.0	716.1	14.00	0.58	3.000	0.42	1,000	73.5	35.0	303.0	1762.9	34.46	1.43
800	219.9	859.8	5975.7	123816.9	49.5	22.5	199.0	915.1	15.31	0.74	3.300	0.36	3,100	68.2	31.0	283.4	2046.3	34.24	1.65
900	240.0	919.8	6895.5	124736.7	50.0	20.8	199.0	1114.1	16.16	0.89	3.700	0.33	3,000	67.2	28.0	270.8	2317.1	33.60	1.86
950	250.0	490.0	7385.5	125226.7	50.4	20.2	100.4	1214.5	16.44	0.97	3.930	0.32	3,090	65.0	26.0	132.2	2449.3	33.16	1.96
1000	269.2	519.2	7904.7	125745.9	50.4	18.7	100.8	1315.3	16.64	1.05	4.200	0.32	3,200	67.3	25.0	132.3	2581.6	32.66	2.05
1100	320.0	1178.4	9083.1	126924.3	60.0	18.8	220.8	1536.1	16.91	1.21	4.400	0.29	4,000	81.6	25.5	297.8	2879.4	31.70	2.27
1200	361.9	1363.8	10446.9	128288.1	70.1	19.4	260.2	1796.3	17.12	1.40	4.700	0.26	3,000	94.1	26.0	351.4	3230.8	30.92	2.52
1300	360.0	1443.8	11890.7	129731.9	86.0	23.9	312.2	2108.5	17.73	1.63	5.200	0.25	5,000	97.2	27.0	382.6	3613.4	30.39	2.79
1350	359.7	719.7	12610.4	130451.6	86.6	24.1	172.6	2281.1	18.09	1.75	5.510	0.24	3,950	100.7	28.0	197.9	3811.3	30.22	2.92
1400	350.0	709.7	13320.1	131161.3	84.0	24.0	170.6	2451.7	18.41	1.87	8.800	0.36	90,000	94.5	27.0	195.2	4006.5	30.08	3.05
1500	425.3	1550.6	14870.7	132711.9	81.0	19.0	330.0	2781.7	18.71	2.10	9.200	0.33	24,600	89.3	21.0	367.6	4374.1	29.41	3.30
1550	485.0	910.3	15781.0	133622.2	92.5	19.1	173.5	2955.2	18.73	2.21	9.600	0.32	5,000	106.7	22.0	196.0	4570.1	28.96	3.42
1600	545.0	1030.0	16811.0	134652.2	103.0	18.9	195.5	3150.7	18.74	2.34	10.100	0.32	4,000	125.4	23.0	232.1	4802.2	28.57	3.57
1650	552.2	1097.2	17908.2	135749.4	116.9	21.2	219.9	3370.6	18.82	2.48	10.400	0.31	6,000	136.4	24.7	261.8	5064.0	28.28	3.73
1700	610.0	1162.2	19070.4	136911.6	136.0	22.3	252.9	3623.5	19.00	2.65	10.900	0.30	20,000	153.7	25.2	290.1	5354.1	28.08	3.91
1750	720.7	1330.7	20401.1	138242.3	160.0	22.2	296.0	3919.5	19.21	2.84	11.280	0.29	8,320	185.9	25.8	339.6	5693.7	27.91	4.12
1800	902.6	1623.3	22024.4	139865.6	208.9	23.1	368.9	4288.4	19.47	3.07	11.800	0.28	10,000	245.5	27.2	431.4	6125.1	27.81	4.38
1815	989.0	567.5	22591.9	140433.1	229.4	23.2	131.5	4419.9	19.56	3.15	12.030	0.27	11,540	299.7	30.3	163.6	6288.7	27.84	4.48
1850	1203.9	1535.0	24126.9	141968.1	330.0	27.4	391.6	4811.5	19.94	3.39	13.000	0.27	20,000	458.7	38.1	530.9	6819.6	28.27	4.80
1900	1619.9	2823.8	26950.7	144791.9	558.1	34.4	777.1	5588.6	20.74	3.86	14.100	0.25	30,000	831.0	51.3	1289.7	8109.3	30.09	5.60
1914	1870.0	879.5	27830.2	145671.4	664.0	35.5	299.4	5888.0	21.16	4.04	15.551	0.26	35,600	991.1	53.0	459.2	8568.5	30.79	5.88
1950	2504.2	2716.4	30546.6	148387.8	854.0	34.1	819.7	6707.7	21.96	4.52	30.760	0.46	422,500	1452.4	58.0	1583.4	10151.9	33.23	6.84
1970	3683.5	1918.2	32464.8	150306.0	1216.6	33.0	683.3	7391.0	22.77	4.92	38.000	0.51	300,000	2261.7	61.4	1225.7	11377.6	35.05	7.56
1975	4076.0	572.3	33037.1	150878.3	1316.8	32.3	209.0	7600.0	23.00	5.04	38.500	0.51	200,000	2645.3	64.9	368.0	11745.6	35.55	7.78
1980	4453.2	607.7	33644.8	151486.0	1432.7	32.2	226.8	7826.8	23.26	5.17	39.000	0.50	210,000	3046.0	68.4	426.8	12172.4	36.18	8.04
1985	4842.0	627.4	34272.2	152113.4	1583.3	32.7	226.2	8053.0	23.50	5.29	39.500	0.49	230,000	3491.1	72.1	457.6	12630.0	36.85	8.30
COSMIC ERA III: THE FUTUROLOGY OF WORLD EVANGELIZATION																			
(m=million (10^6), b=billion (10^9), t=trillion (10^{12}), q=quadrillion (10^{15}), s=septillion (10^{24}), d=decillion (10^{33}))																			
1990	5248 m	631 m	34903 m	152744 m	1742 m	33.2	232.8	8286 m	23.74	5.42	40.725	0.49	249,100	3983 m	75.9	485.8	13115.8	37.58	8.59
2000	6127 m	1365 m	36268 m	154109 m	2130 m	34.8	503.4	8789 m	24.23	5.70	50.000	0.57	500,000	5110 m	83.4	1045.7	14161.5	39.05	9.19
2025	8177 m	3579 m	39847 m	157688 m	2944 m	36.0	1332 m	10121 m	25.40	6.42	60.000	0.59	600,000	7605 m	93.0	3178.8	17340 m	43.52	11.00
2050	9 b	3654 m	43501 m	161342 m	3330 m	37.0	1569 m	11690 m	26.87	7.25	90.800	0.78	835,000	8910 m	99.0	3096.6	20437 m	46.98	12.67
2100	10 b	7125 m	50626 m	168467 m	4 b	40.0	2749 m	14439 m	28.52	8.57				10 b	99.5	6146 m	26583 m	52.51	15.78
2200	20 b	15 b	65626 m	183467 m	9 b	45.0	6500 m	20939 m	31.91	11.41				20 b	99.8	15 b	42 b	64.00	22.89
2500	50 b	34 b	99 b	217467 m	25 b	50.0	26 b	46939 m	47.41	21.58				50 b	99.9	34 b	76 b	76.77	34.95
4000	200 b	188 b	287 b	405467 m	120 b	60.0	109 b	156 b	54.36	38.47				200 b	100.0	188 b	264 b	92.00	65.11
10,000	1 t	3600 b	3887 b	4005 b	650 b	65.0	2310 b	2466 b	63.44	61.57				1 t	100.0	3600 b	3864 b	99.41	96.48
100,000	1 q	5 q	5 q	5 q	850 t	85.0	4 q	4 q	85.00	85.00				1 q	100.0	5 q	5 q	100.00	100.00
1 million	1 s	7 s	7 s	7 s	1 s	99.0	7 s	7 s	99.00	99.00				1 s	100.0	7 s	7 s	100.00	100.00
4 billion	1 d	10 d	10 d	10 d	1 d	99.9	10 d	10 d	99.90	99.90				1 d	100.0	10 d	10 d	100.00	100.00

NOTES, ASSUMPTIONS AND METHODOLOGY

PHASES. This table is divided vertically into 3 chronological phases following exactly the 3-phase arrangement of the chronology. Cosmic Era III describes the numerical developments most likely if the Parousia/Eschaton is delayed and if nuclear and cosmic holocausts are avoided.

SOURCES. Data come either from the chronology or from other original compilations produced specifically for this analysis of evangelization.

YEARS. The first column refers to particular years, either BC (before Christ) or AD (after Christ), covering the entire span of the existence ofgenus Homo (the human race), from its creation in BC 5,500,000 to its ultimate extinction as described in our chronology under the scenario for AD 4 billion. For queries or further details concerning any particular year, consult first the chronology for that identical year.

STATISTICS. The 19 columns of statistics are divided into 3 distinct sections across the page, separated by heavy vertical lines. The first section (columns 2-5) deals with global population since the origin of genus Homo in BC 5,500,000. The second section (columns 6-14) gives global statistics of Christians (followers of Jesus Christ) since AD 33, preceded by a small box giving statistics of the pre-Christian People of God. The third section (columns 15-20) gives global statistics of all persons evangelized by the gospel of Christ since AD 33.

POPULATIONS. The 3 columns in bold italic type (2,6,15) give, for each year shown,live populations (i.e. world or human population alive in that year), live Christians (i.e. Christians alive in that year) and live evangelized (i.e.evangelized persons alive in that year). Totals for future years include humans living off-Earth on space colonies. Population projections for the future and megafuture have to balance the possibilities of enormous numerical expansion across the Galaxy and Universe with the possibilities of enormous numerical reduction due to disasters and cataclysms. Our figures here are very conservative, i.e. at the lower end of current forecasts.

CHRISTIANS. Enumeration of Christians in the table starts in AD 33. The 2 boxes in the space above the AD 33 line do not refer to Christians: the top box depicts the years of origin of the various Homo species at the time, and the second box gives parallel statistics of the People of God in Old Testament times (the Israelites).

PERCENTAGES. All columns in medium type are percentages(7,10,11,13,16,19,20). Columns 7 and 16 are % of world population alive at that year; columns 10 and 19 are % total all world population who have ever lived since AD 33; and columns 11 and 20 are % total all persons who have ever lived on Earth, as given in column 5.

INCREMENTS. Columns in italic type headed 'Increment' (columns 3,8,17) are included to enable the reader to follow the methodology used in computing the following 1, 2 or 3 columns. These figures refer to new persons (new souls) born since the previous line's year. Human birth rate has dropped from around 4% per year in prehistoric times to 3.6% per year for the world's populations from 1900 on (3.5% from 1850 on for Christians),to 2.8% per year by 1980; we estimate it will be 2.3% by 2000, 1.7% by 2030 (UN estimates, 1980), and so will average 2% p.a. from 2000-2100, 1% p.a. after 2100, to 0.1% p.a. after 2500 as longevity turns gradually into immortality. After AD 3000 we can anticipate massive growth and expansion due not only to natural births but far more to artificial births, artificial creations of new human species, mass clonings with geometric progression, genetic multiplications of whole populations and races and worlds, vast varieties of immortality, and so on. The reader can, of course, supply whatever other assumptions he prefers and work out the corresponding figures. Each figure gives the increment in population, or Christians, or evangelized persons, up to the year indicated (column 1) from the preceding year indicated in column 1.

POPULATIONS EVER. Columns 5,9,18 give, for each year shown, the grand-totals of, respectively, all persons of genus Homo who have ever lived on Earth and its colonies to date (live and dead), all Christians ever from AD 33 to date (live and dead), and all persons ever evangelized from AD 33 to date (live and dead).

MARTYRS. Column 12 gives the total number of martyrs worldwide since AD 33 up to the year shown (source: global survey to be published in The AD 2000 Series). Column 13 gives the same total as a percentage of all Christians ever since AD 33. Column 14 gives the average number of martyrdoms each year based on the recent situation at the dates indicated. After AD 2050, no attempt at a possible scenario is made here.

VERY LARGE NUMBERS. In Cosmic Era I and Cosmic Era II above, numbers (apart from percentages) are all given as millions, as shown by the abbreviation *m*. In Cosmic Era III, 5 larger measures are used with abbreviations (b,t,q,s,d) as given under Cosmic Era III's title line. The largest, 1d = 1 decillion, is 10^{33} or 1,000,000,000,000,000,000,000,000,000,000,000 (10 followed by 33 zeroes).

BC 5,500,000. Origin of human race, genus Homo (see chronology), after 45 billion hominids have lived on Earth.

AD 30. Beginning of ministry of Jesus of Nazareth; AD 33, resurrection of Jesus and beginning of Christian church.

AD 2100. World population (column 2) estimated by United Nations projections at 10,185 million.

AD 2200. Human population could be as low as 2 billion or as high as 1,000 billion (see alternative scenarios in chronology), with 30% living off-Earth on space colonies.

AD 2500. Human population 25 billion (or as high as 400 billion) on Earth and a similar number off-Earth on space colonies; or, human population very small because of disastrous wars or cataclysms.

AD 4000. Majority of human populations now off-Earth on space colonies.

AD 10,000. Homo Sapiens evolves into Homo Noeticus (Intellectual Man). Note that by now the church of Christ has grown to 650 billions.

AD 100,000. Homo Superior (Interstellar Man) evolves and expands rapidly across Solar System, with possible population of the order of 1 quadrillion (10^{15} persons). The scenario envisages at this time a church of 850 trillion Christians.

AD 1 million. Homo Galacticus evolves and spreads out to populate entire Galaxy, with possible population of the order of 1 septillion (10^{24} persons). Virtually everyone is now a follower of Christ — a church of 1 septillion members.

AD 4 billion. Final age of man as Homo Universalis, able to traverse Galaxy or Universe instantaneously at will; with possible population of the order of 1 decillion (10^{33}) persons throughout the Universe. Ultimate size of the church of Jesus Christ, on this scenario: 1 decillion believers.

APPENDIX 2: Status of Global Mission, 1987, in Context of 20th Century

Year:	1900	1970	1980	**1987**	2000
WORLD POPULATION					
1. Total population	1,619,886,800	3,610,034,400	4,373,917,500	**5,004,622,800**	6,259,642,000
2. Urban dwellers	232,694,900	1,354,237,000	1,797,479,000	**2,187,850,500**	3,160,381,900
3. Rural dwellers	1,387,191,900	2,255,797,400	2,576,438,500	**2,816,772,300**	3,099,260,100
4. Adult population	1,025,938,000	2,245,227,300	2,698,396,900	**3,072,585,800**	3,808,564,300
5. Literates	286,705,000	1,437,761,900	1,774,002,700	**2,060,565,100**	2,697,595,100
6. Nonliterates	739,233,000	807,465,400	924,394,200	**1,012,020,700**	1,110,969,200
WORLDWIDE EXPANSION OF CITIES					
7. Metropolises (over 100,000 population)	400	2,400	2,700	**3,050**	4,200
8. Megacities (over 1 million)	20	161	227	**296**	433
WORLD POPULATION BY RELIGION					
9. Christians (total all kinds)	558,056,300	1,216,579,400	1,432,686,500	**1,646,007,800**	2,130,000,000
10. Muslims	200,102,200	550,919,000	722,956,500	**854,094,000**	1,200,653,000
11. Nonreligious	2,923,300	543,065,300	715,901,400	**819,201,800**	1,021,888,400
12. Hindus	203,033,300	465,784,800	582,749,900	**658,592,100**	859,252,300
13. Buddhists	127,159,000	231,672,200	273,715,600	**312,491,700**	359,092,100
14. Atheists	225,600	165,288,500	195,119,400	**224,182,900**	262,447,600
15. Tribal religionists	106,339,600	88,077,400	89,963,500	**99,086,300**	100,535,900
16. New Religionists	5,910,000	76,443,100	96,021,800	**111,308,600**	138,263,800
17. Jews	12,269,800	15,185,900	16,938,200	**18,278,300**	20,173,600
18. Sikhs	2,960,600	10,612,200	14,244,400	**16,427,700**	23,831,700
19. Other religionists	400,907,100	246,406,600	233,620,300	**244,951,600**	143,503,600
GLOBAL CHRISTIANITY					
20. Total Christians as % of world	34.4	33.7	32.8	**32.9**	34.0
21. Affiliated church members	521,563,200	1,131,809,600	1,323,389,700	**1,519,585,400**	1,967,000,000
22. Practicing Christians	469,259,800	884,021,800	1,018,355,300	**1,159,000,000**	1,377,000,000
23. Charismatics in Renewal	0	1,587,700	11,005,390	**19,830,400**	55,000,000
24. Crypto-Christians	3,572,400	55,699,700	70,395,000	**121,537,000**	176,208,000
25. Average Christian martyrs per year	35,600	230,000	270,000	**334,900**	500,000
MEMBERSHIP BY ECCLESIASTICAL BLOC					
26. Anglicans	30,573,700	47,557,000	49,804,000	**51,627,900**	61,037,200
27. Catholics (non-Roman)	276,000	3,134,400	3,439,400	**3,667,600**	4,334,100
28. Marginal Protestants	927,600	10,830,200	14,077,500	**16,503,900**	24,106,200
29. Nonwhite indigenous Christians	7,743,100	58,702,000	82,181,100	**125,512,800**	204,100,000
30. Orthodox	115,897,700	143,402,500	160,737,900	**173,349,900**	199,819,000
31. Protestants	103,056,700	233,424,200	262,157,600	**305,478,800**	386,000,000
32. Roman Catholics	266,419,400	672,319,100	802,660,000	**907,536,700**	1,144,000,000
MEMBERSHIP BY CONTINENT					
33. Africa	8,756,400	115,924,200	164,571,000	**202,844,000**	323,914,900
34. East Asia	1,763,000	10,050,200	16,149,600	**71,228,100**	128,000,000
35. Europe	273,788,400	397,108,700	403,177,600	**407,464,500**	411,448,700
36. Latin America	60,025,100	262,027,800	340,978,600	**401,592,400**	555,486,000
37. Northern America	59,569,700	169,246,900	178,892,500	**185,874,500**	201,265,200
38. Oceania	4,311,400	14,669,400	16,160,600	**17,218,600**	21,361,500
39. South Asia	16,347,200	76,770,200	106,733,200	**130,325,900**	185,476,700
40. USSR	97,002,000	86,012,300	96,726,500	**104,429,400**	118,101,000
CHRISTIAN ORGANIZATIONS					
41. Service agencies	1,500	14,100	17,500	**20,100**	24,000
42. Foreign-mission sending agencies	600	2,200	3,100	**3,700**	4,800
43. Institutions	9,500	80,500	91,000	**98,000**	103,000
CHRISTIAN WORKERS					
44. Nationals	1,050,000	2,350,000	2,950,000	**3,747,700**	4,500,000
45. Aliens (foreign missionaries)	62,000	240,000	249,000	**250,400**	400,000
CHRISTIAN FINANCE (in U.S. $, per year)					
46. Personal income of church members	270 billion	4,100 billion	5,878 billion	**8,191 billion**	12,700 billion
47. Giving to Christian causes	8 billion	70 billion	100.3 billion	**139 billion**	200 billion
48. Churches' income	7 billion	50 billion	64.5 billion	**79 billion**	80 billion
49. Parachurch and institutional income	1 billion	20 billion	35.8 billion	**60 billion**	120 billion
50. Ecclesiastical crime	300,000	5,000,000	30,000,000	**115,000,000**	550,000,000
51. Income of global foreign missions	0.2 billion	3 billion	5 billion	**8 billion**	12 billion
Giving per church member per week					
52. to all Christian causes	$0.29	$1.19	$1.46	**$1.82**	$2.09
53. to global foreign missions	$0.01	$0.06	$0.07	**$0.10**	$0.10
54. Computers in Christian use	0	1,000	3,000,000	**29,000,000**	340,000,000
CHRISTIAN LITERATURE					
55. New commercial book titles per year	2,200	17,100	18,800	**21,600**	25,000
56. New titles including devotional	3,100	52,000	60,000	**62,800**	75,000
57. Christian periodicals	3,500	23,000	22,500	**20,400**	35,000
SCRIPTURE DISTRIBUTION (all sources)					
58. Bibles per year	5,452,600	25,000,000	36,800,000	**45,763,200**	70,000,000
59. New Testaments per year	7,300,000	45,000,000	57,500,000	**66,801,200**	110,000,000
CHRISTIAN BROADCASTING					
60. Christian radio/TV stations	0	1,230	1,450	**1,620**	4,000
61. Total monthly listeners/viewers	0	750,000,000	990,474,400	**1,132,556,300**	2,150,000,000
62. for Christian stations	0	150,000,000	291,810,500	**406,857,200**	600,000,000
63. for secular stations	0	650,000,000	834,068,900	**956,802,300**	1,810,000,000
CHRISTIAN URBAN MISSION					
64. Non-Christian megacities	5	65	95	**131**	202
65. New non-Christian urban dwellers per day	5,200	51,100	69,300	**86,300**	140,000
66. Urban Christians	159,600,000	660,800,000	844,600,000	**1,003,887,300**	1,393,700,000
67. Urban Christians as % of urban dwellers	68.8	47.8	46.3	**46.0**	44.5
68. Evangelized urban dwellers, %	72.0	80.0	83.0	**87.0**	91.0
CHRISTIAN MEGAMINISTRIES					
69. World total all persons reached per day	250,000	10,000,000	30,000,000	**48,000,000**	70,000,000
WORLD EVANGELIZATION					
70. Unevangelized population	788,159,000	1,391,956,000	1,380,576,000	**1,317,486,600**	1,038,819,000
71. Unevangelized as % of world	48.7	38.6	31.6	**26.6**	16.6
72. Unreached peoples (with no churches)	3,500	1,300	700	**530**	100

METHODOLOGICAL NOTES ON TABLE (referring to numbered lines on facing page). Indented categories form part of, and are included in, unindented categories above them. Definitions of categories are as given and explained in *World Christian Encyclopedia* (1982), with additional data and explanations as below. Sources include in-process world surveys by author.

8. Megacities are also metropolises ("mother cities") so are included in line 7.
9. Widest definition: professing Christians plus secret believers, which equals affiliated (church members) plus nominal Christians.
16. Adherents of Asian so-called New Religions.
19. Mainly Chinese folk religionists.
20. Definition as in 9.
22. Church attenders, by churches' own definitions.
22–24. These entries are selected subgroups of 21 and are not intended as a complete breakdown of 21.
23. Active members of the Renewal in older mainline denominations (Anglican, Catholic, Orthodox, Protestant).
24. Secret believers.
25. World totals for all confessions (from survey by author, forthcoming).
26–32. The total of these entries can be reconciled to line 9 by referring to *WCE*, Global Table 4. To the total of these entries, add the category "nominal Christians," and subtract "doubly-affiliated" and "disaffiliated" members, as found in *WCE*, Global Table 4.
33. Definitions of the eight continents or continental areas follow exactly United Nations' practice.
41. Including 42.
46–53. Defined as in article "Silver and Gold Have I None," in *International Bulletin of Missionary Research*, October 1983, p. 150.
49. As distinct from churches' (denominational) income.
50. Amounts embezzled (U.S. dollar equivalents, per year).
54. Total computers and word processors owned by churches, agencies, groups, and individual Christians.
55. On strict UNESCO definition of book (over 49 pages).
56. As 55, but adding the mass of smaller devotional literature (prayer books, service books, liturgies, hymnbooks, choruses, etc.).
61. Total of audiences in 62 and 63, excluding overlap.
63. Total regular audience for Christian programs over secular or commercial stations.
64. Megacities with long non-Christian or anti-Christian tradition (Hindu, Muslim, Buddhist, etc.), under 25% Christian, and usually hostile to Christian mission.
69. Megaministries are defined here as ministries which each reach over 1 million persons every day. Total includes Scripture distribution, literature, tracts, broadcasting, mass media, films, audiovisuals; it also includes duplications and overlap.
70–71 (also 68). Defined as in *WCE*, parts 3, 5, 6, 9.

Reproduced with permission from author's article in *International Bulletin of Missionary Research*, January, 1987.

Fission and fusion diagrams have a long and distinguished history in the study of how and when Christianity's vast number of denominations have arisen. All the major Christian traditions have them, explaining how today's denominations have evolved out of yesterday's. Here we show a comprehensive diagram illustrating the whole of Christian history up to the present, this being given in identical form in the following 4 diagrams as the lefthand part of each diagram.

We then show 4 possible alternate futures for Christianity. These 4 miniscenarios are shown as the righthand part of each diagram, covering the period 1987-2100, i.e. the next century.

The flow chart or development diagram on the next 4 pages, with its 4 alternate futures, illustrates the Chronology on the previous pages. It can be divided into 2 stages, (1) the past and present (illustrating Cosmic Era II) and (2) the future (illustrating Cosmic Era III).

1. THE PAST AND PRESENT: Cosmic Era II

The lefthand half of the diagram shows the expansion of Christianity over the centuries, and sketches its fragmentation or fission into 7 major blocs or streams, 156 different ecclesiastical traditions and 22,200 separate and distinct denominations or churches. It also illustrates recent movements towards church reunion or fusion. The diagram should be studied in conjunction with the detailed statistics of the evolution of these phenomena given in Global Tables 1, 2, 9, 26, and 27 in the *World Christian encyclopedia* (1982). The various concepts and schemata in this diagram may be explained as follows.

THE 7 MAJOR BLOCS. As set forth in this Encyclopedia, all Christians can be divided into the following 7 major blocs or streams of Christianity: Orthodox, Roman Catholics, Catholics (non-Roman), Protestants, Anglicans, Non-White indigenous Christians, and marginal Protestants. In the diagram, the boundaries of these blocs are shown by heavy full lines.

THE 156 TRADITIONS. The 7 major blocs can be further subdivided into around 156 ecclesiastical traditions, by which are meant the various confessions, families or types of Christianity. In the diagram, the boundaries of a selection of these traditions are shown by light full lines.

MAJOR DENOMINATIONS. Within the 156 traditions there have been formed over 22,200 separate autonomous denominations or churches. A detailed analysis of the location of these denominations by bloc and continent is given in *WCE*, Global Table 26; but this evolution is not shown here.

CHURCH REUNIONS. Since the year 1900, at least 180 denominations including some of the largest have merged to form over 60 united churches. Where a vertical line is shown not full but broken, it indicates a continuity of communion from the left side through to the right. This means the formation of either united churches, or uniting churches (in process or under way), or internal realignments, or the eventual single reunited world church.

ORIGINS. The diagram depicts in brief the origins and development of blocs and traditions on the world scene over 20 centuries, shows where they came from and how they have fared, and indicates, schematically and relatively, the numerical strength of each over the centuries up to the year 1987.

CHRONOLOGY. The horizontal scale represents time, or chronology. The lefthand half of the diagram covers, from left to right, the period from AD 33 to 1987, with projection to the year AD 2000 shown by the major vertical line.

NUMERICAL SIZE. Vertical scale represents, approximately or schematically, the numerical size of Christians affiliated to the various traditions or blocs at any particular year up to the present.

CENTRALIZATION. Across the centre of the page a horizontal axis can be envisaged, which represents the concept of centralization, including the concepts of unified control, uniformity, and collaboration. It represents schematically the position of churches with centralized structure, centralized hierarchy, centralized organization, centralized administration, and centralized tradition, doctrine, ritual and liturgy. As the most centralized of all churches, the Roman Catholic Church therefore straddles this axis in the diagram.

DECENTRALIZATION. The position of a tradition (or bloc, or denomination) above or below this central axis represents the concept of decentralization, which includes the concepts of local congregational autonomy, departure from centralization, ruptures of relations, splits, schismatic movements. Traditions (or blocs, or denominations) which have separated from or moved away from the Church of Rome in order to decentralize some aspect of their church life are thus found above or below the central axis. The same is true for subsequent divisions from other churches.

STRUCTURALISM. The position of a bloc or body vertically on the diagram also stands for what may be called the concept of relative ecclesiastical or structural conservatism or liberalism: from conservative at the top to liberal at the bottom. At the top are right-wing or conservative structures such as the Oriental Orthodox or monophysite churches which still largely use ancient dead languages in worship. Along the central axis is the Roman Catholic Church. Below the axis are Protestant churches and others in what may be called left-wing or liberal structures adapted to their eras. Going down the page are found increasingly left-wing or liberal or radical traditions rejecting centralization or uniformity of structure, hierarchy, tradition, doctrine, ritual or liturgy. Next below follows the range of Non-White indigenous churches across the world which have rejected Western and Eastern Christianity along with all attempts at control by these latter blocs. Finally, along the extreme lower edge of the diagram is a fringe of free-thinking or radically heterodox bodies originating in the Western Protestant world. These are here termed marginal Protestant bodies because of their peripheral nature in relation to mainstream or mainline or orthodox Christianity.

EVOLUTION. Lines across the diagram from left to right indicate evolution, i.e. the way in which the 7 major blocs (separated by heavy lines) and the 156 traditions (separated by light lines) have evolved and crystallized out over the centuries. At first sometimes the lines are dotted, illustrating how new traditions begin to form within existing traditions and exist therein for a time before rupture of relations with the parent or adjacent traditions takes place. Sometimes a dotted line means the first stage in the parting of the ways when a large body begins to divide into two. If and when a rupture or schism eventually takes place, this is shown at that point by the line changing from dotted to full. If the rupture is later healed, and the schism is reabsorbed into the parent, the line stops at that point in its movement across the page. Church unions or mergers can be illustrated by such lines, with the original separate traditions shown bounded by full lines; then after union the lines are dotted until the traditions begin to lose their original identity in the new united body and eventually disappear.

SCHISMS OR FISSIONS. Full lines drawn vertically indicate the clearcut formation of a schismatic or separate body out of an existing body, or the breaking of communion with those on the left by those on the right of the line. In most cases such schisms have been a small or minority part of the existing body. When a large parent body splits into 2 or more parts of comparable size, however, the vertical line covers all of the parts.

2. THE FUTURE: Cosmic Era III

ALTERNATE FUTURES. The righthand half of the 4 diagrams that follow represent 4 different, possible alternate futures, covering the whole range or spectrum of possibilities ahead for Christianity. These start with the year 1987 and become crystallized at the heavy vertical line (full or broken) representing AD 2000. They then extend to the righthand edge of the diagram, which represents approximately AD 2100. Lines, rules and scales all have the same meanings as described above for the lefthand half of the diagram. Notes under each diagram explain the details and differentia of each case.

FOUR SCENARIOS. It is possible to envisage a large range of possible alternate futures for Christianity. The 4 chosen here can be labelled as follows: Monodenominationalism, Nondenominationalism, Postdenominationalism, Martyrdom.

NON-CHRISTIAN MOVEMENTS. The entities shown outside the heaviest lines delineating the edges or boundaries of Christianity properly so called, fall into 6 categories as follows: (1) churches which cannot, or can no longer, be called Christian, as a result of abandoning or denying the centrality of Christ as Savior, Lord and God; (2) bogus churches, often allied with anti-Christian infiltrators; (3) non-Christian cults including New Age movements; (4) non-Christian religions; (5) secular creeds (secularism, agnosticism); and (6) anti-Christian creeds (atheism).

DEFECTIONS. The arrows from within Christianity to outside its boundaries stand for losses or defections from Christianity into the above-described non-Christian entities.

TYPES OF FUTURE CHURCH. Superimposed on each diagram's future part is a series of popularly-used or often-used titles or names for the church in the future. These names are all shown in the same type size and style, each within an oval or ellipse.

MAJOR DATES OR YEARS. Dates (years) in the text under each diagram indicate major times or turning points or watersheds in the future when significant events seem likely to occur. Each date refers the reader to the text of the Chronology itself, where he will find a brief descriptive entry with additional details.

FOOTNOTES. On each diagram will be seen a small number of capital letters, thus: A, B, C, D, etc. These represent important situations or developments at the points indicated. Each is explained in a short sentence or phrase below the diagram.

3. DESCRIPTION OF THE SCENARIOS

From some points of view, the 4 scenarios are similar to the story of Creation and the range of possible alternate subsequent fates of the Universe. First, the church comes into existence as suddenly and dramatically as in the Big Bang. Second, the church is still expanding fast today. Third, in the future the church (like the Universe) could either turn out to be *open* and continue expanding indefinitely (as Scenarios 2 and 3 suggest), or it could turn out to be *flat* and plateau at a certain level (Scenario 1); or it could turn out to be *closed* and reverse its growth and collapse in a catastrophe parallel to the Big Crunch (Scenario 4).

Here are brief descriptions of the scenarios.

SCENARIO 1: MONODENOMINATIONALISM

In his High Priestly prayer, the Lord Jesus prayed 3 times (John 17:21,22,23) for his disciples 'that they may all become perfectly one' (Latin 'Ut omnes unum sint'), 'so that the world may believe.' Subsequently, however, his followers have formed themselves into, by 1987, the 22,200 distinct and separate religious denominations, which often fight or war or compete with each other. Most have nothing to do with most of the rest. This scandal of disunity and fragmentation has been widely seen over the centuries as a major obstacle to evangelizing or converting the world.

All down the ages Christians have longed and prayed to be united as Christ prayed, with the resultant converting power. This first scenario therefore sets out, as a possible future, a situation in which this actually takes place. It envisages all the major denominations of the world finally agreeing in 1999 to begin an immediate, loose, de facto reunion of the churches, thus forming one single denomination. This might come about, no doubt, in reaction to growing world ridicule or to heavy pressures from political regimes (as happened in Japan in 1940, or Zaire in 1970). At the least, it would encompass mutual fellowship, joint recognition, intercommunion, acceptance of ministries, joint evangelization and a common shared name—perhaps 'The Church of Jesus Christ', or 'The Body of Christ'.

One result might well be that Christianity, as today, continues to just hold its own numerically in a hostile world, neither expanding nor declining noticeably.

Despite governmental pressures and demands, full organic union might well then take a further 60 years to evolve. There would certainly be internal opposition, not least from former Protestants.

SCENARIO 2: NONDENOMINATIONALISM

A second possible alternate future envisages the vast mass of ordinary Christian believers finally losing patience with the scandal of denominational fragmentation. They take drastic action; they simply disown the structures of centralized Christianity. By 2000, the groundswell of irritation has reached massive proportions. The laity everywhere (who form 99.7% of all Christians) now break ties with denominational headquarters, ignore confessional pretensions, and concentrate solely on local worship, fellowship, witness, service and evangelism. They still retain their denominational identities and traditions, but recognize no central offices or agencies.

The scenario sees all Christians then as clustering into 5 loose, decentralized, unorganized, lay megaclusters: ritualists, traditionalists, charismatics, indigenous and marginals. In particular, huge charismatic revivals sweep across Asia, winning hundreds of millions from the great non-Christian world religions. Centralized denominationalism withers and dies out. Spontaneous Christianity surfaces everywhere with vast numbers of ceaselessly itinerating churches of pilgrims, tourists, et alii.

SCENARIO 3: POSTDENOMINATIONALISM

A third possible alternate future sees the huge mass of dynamic Christianity as largely made up of Third-World charismatic youths who operate only through their own racial and linguistic identities. Disillusioned with both centralized ecclesiastical organization, and also the whole traditions and identities of denominationalism and confessionalism, they reject all ties with Western Christianity and ignore or brush aside all aspects of traditional or historic Christianity. Denominations now become part of the forgotten past. Instead of aligning themselves with historical divisions, these future Christians operate on the de facto, natural lines of language, ethnic and racial affiliation. This results in 10 unorganized ethnolinguistic megaclusters whose vastly divergent socioeconomic status or plight characterizes them as follows (in order of affluence in AD 2000): Euroamericans (the Church of the Rich); Arab-Asians and the newly-converted Jewish race (the Church of the Biblical Lifestyle, i.e. the original cradle or arena or context of biblical Christianity in which Arab and Jewish converts are neither rich and affluent nor desperately poor); Amerindians, Australasians and Aboriginals (the Church of the Powerless); Afro-Americans (the Church of the Poor, mainly in Africa); Asiatico-Chinese (the Church of the Masses, with mind-boggling numbers of new converts); Latinamericans (the Church of the Desperately Poor); and lastly, Indo-Iranians (the Church of the Absolutely Poor). A peripheral category must be added, namely marginal Protestants in churches holding as revelation both the Bible and also a second source; these are largely elite affluent Euroamericans (in what, by comparison, we may call the Church of the Megarich).

Despite these unforgivably and violently opposed lifestyles, on this scenario Christianity as a whole continues its massive expansion across the globe, throughout the 21st century.

SCENARIO 4: MARTYRDOM

The fourth possible alternate future depicts Christianity as a whole being extinguished. Rather than continuing its missionary expansion across the world (as with Scenarios 2 and 3), or barely holding its own (as with Scenario 1), global Christianity could be definitively wiped out by deliberate intent. At present, most of Christianity today (around 84%) is recognized as legal by secular governments, with only 16% being illegal or banned and so forced to exist clandestinely. But this proportion of legal Christianity is rapidly decreasing. This diagram portrays the worst-case scenario which some biblical exegetes see the Scriptures as envisaging: the church is declared totally illegal and banned, then goes into the Great Tribulation and is totally destroyed by the ruthless world system, with all believers being martyred to the last individual, making the ultimate and final witness to Christ.

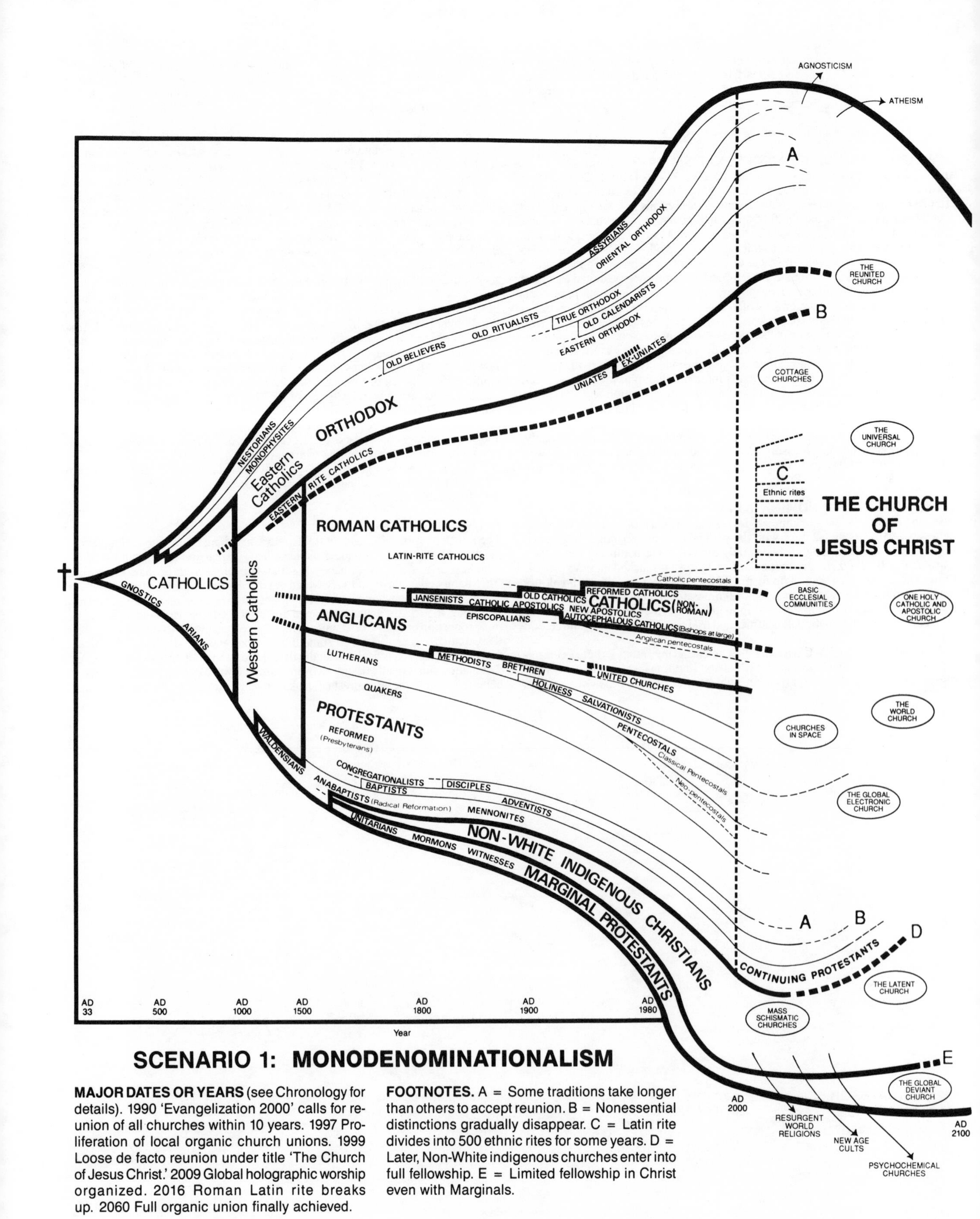

SCENARIO 1: MONODENOMINATIONALISM

MAJOR DATES OR YEARS (see Chronology for details). 1990 'Evangelization 2000' calls for reunion of all churches within 10 years. 1997 Proliferation of local organic church unions. 1999 Loose de facto reunion under title 'The Church of Jesus Christ.' 2009 Global holographic worship organized. 2016 Roman Latin rite breaks up. 2060 Full organic union finally achieved.

FOOTNOTES. A = Some traditions take longer than others to accept reunion. B = Nonessential distinctions gradually disappear. C = Latin rite divides into 500 ethnic rites for some years. D = Later, Non-White indigenous churches enter into full fellowship. E = Limited fellowship in Christ even with Marginals.

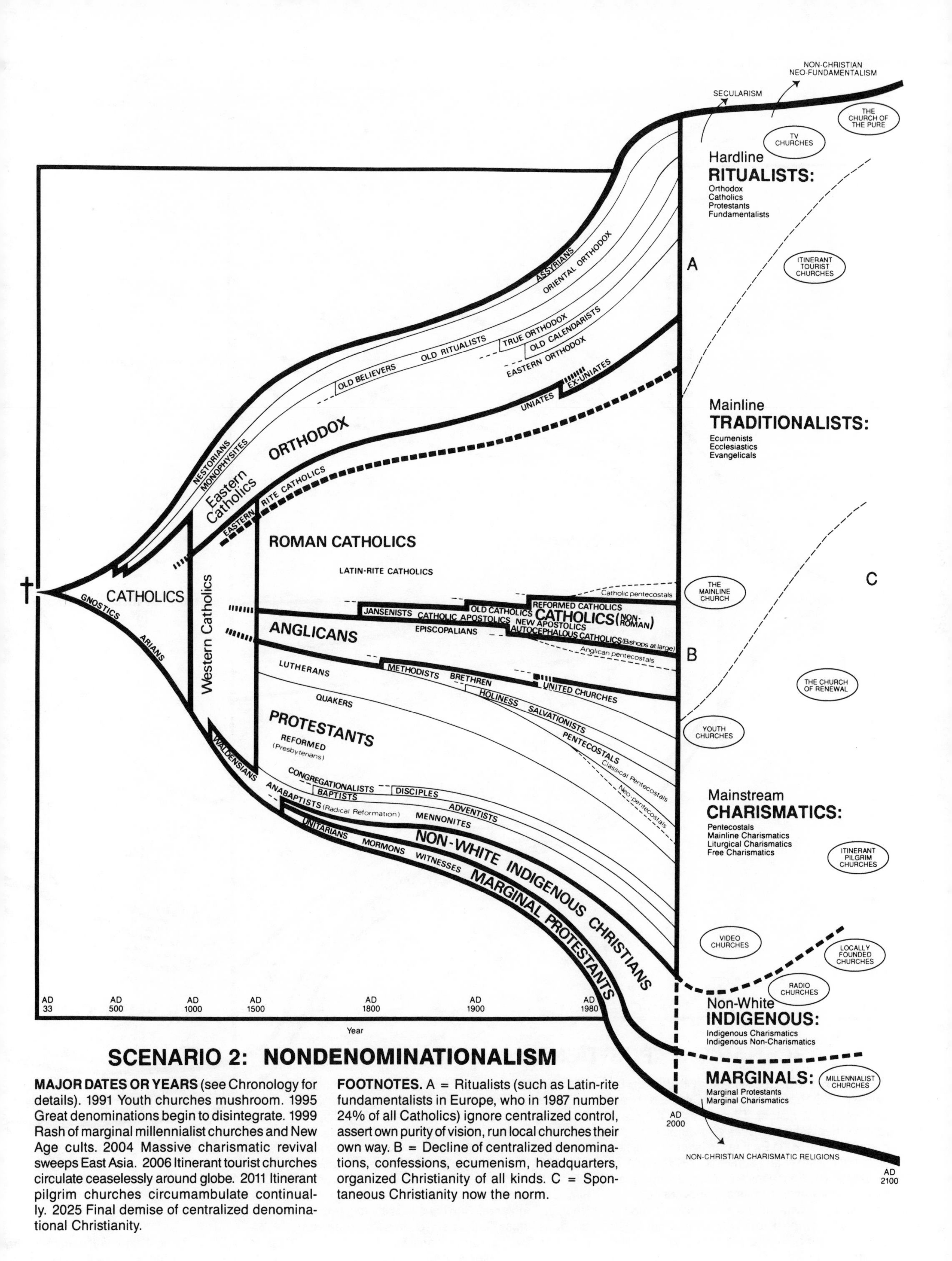

SCENARIO 2: NONDENOMINATIONALISM

MAJOR DATES OR YEARS (see Chronology for details). 1991 Youth churches mushroom. 1995 Great denominations begin to disintegrate. 1999 Rash of marginal millennialist churches and New Age cults. 2004 Massive charismatic revival sweeps East Asia. 2006 Itinerant tourist churches circulate ceaselessly around globe. 2011 Itinerant pilgrim churches circumambulate continually. 2025 Final demise of centralized denominational Christianity.

FOOTNOTES. A = Ritualists (such as Latin-rite fundamentalists in Europe, who in 1987 number 24% of all Catholics) ignore centralized control, assert own purity of vision, run local churches their own way. B = Decline of centralized denominations, confessions, ecumenism, headquarters, organized Christianity of all kinds. C = Spontaneous Christianity now the norm.

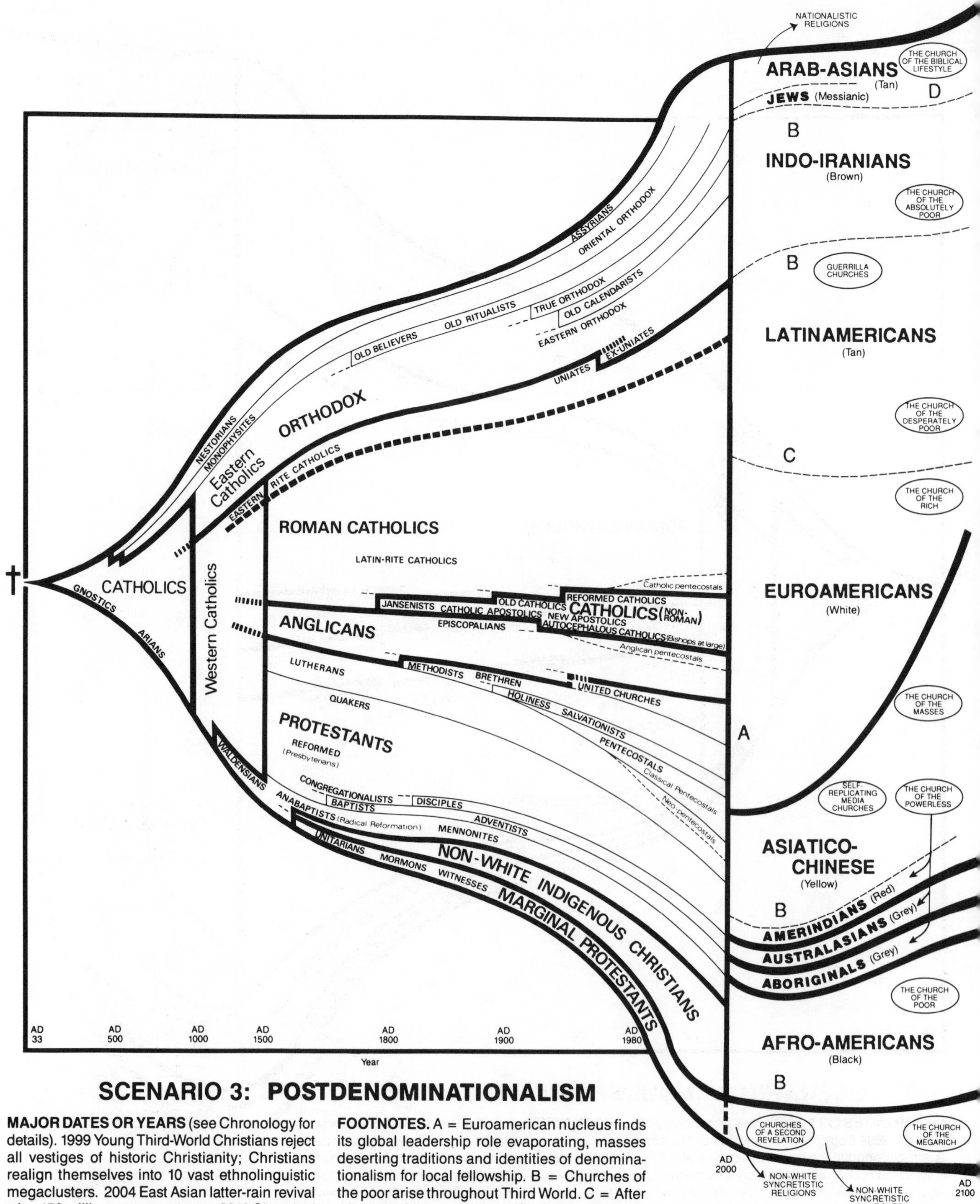

SCENARIO 3: POSTDENOMINATIONALISM

MAJOR DATES OR YEARS (see Chronology for details). 1999 Young Third-World Christians reject all vestiges of historic Christianity; Christians realign themselves into 10 vast ethnolinguistic megaclusters. 2004 East Asian latter-rain revival wins 150 million young converts. 2013 Church of the Absolutely Poor goes on rampage; huge guerrilla churches arise across all impoverished continents. 2030 One and a half billion Chinese Christians embark on world mission. 2050 Self-replicating media churches spread like wildfire. 2080 Chinese and Arab Christians independently launch world conversion schemes.

FOOTNOTES. A = Euroamerican nucleus finds its global leadership role evaporating, masses deserting traditions and identities of denominationalism for local fellowship. B = Churches of the poor arise throughout Third World. C = After AD 2000, Christians split into the 5 basic races (shown bounded by heavy lines: from top to bottom, Caucasoid, Mongoloid, Australoid, Capoid, Negroid. Lighter dashed lines indicate racial subdivisions (thus, 'Caucasoid' covers Arabs, Jews, Indo-Iranians, Latinamericans, Euroamericans). The words for color are purely stylized, as explained in *World Christian encyclopedia,* Part 4 'Culture.' D = Biblical lifestyle becomes the model, making churches of the poor violently opposed to all churches of the rich.

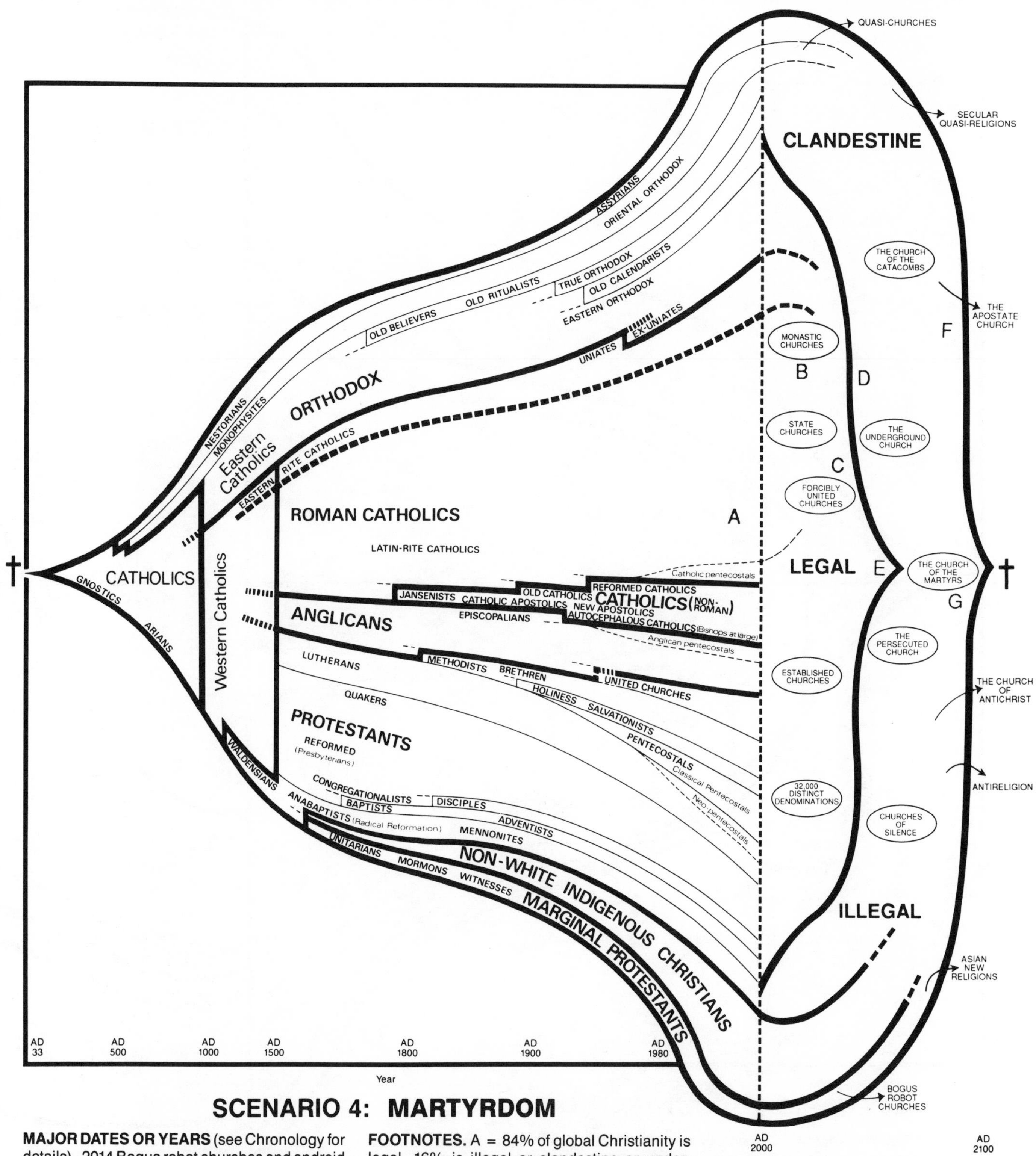

SCENARIO 4: MARTYRDOM

MAJOR DATES OR YEARS (see Chronology for details). 2014 Bogus robot churches and android evangelists controlled by political regimes attempt to infiltrate and destroy the Body of Christ. 2020 Christianity's 32,000 fragmented denominations provoke regimes to interfere once and for all. 2024 Asian New Religions and secular quasi-religions join with political regimes to destroy global Christianity. 2040 (on another miniscenario, 2095) World government obliterates Church of the Martyrs with one final worldwide blow.

FOOTNOTES. A = 84% of global Christianity is legal, 16% is illegal or clandestine or underground. B = Vast numbers of young Christians withdraw from world into monastic life of prayer. C = Groupings of denominations forcibly united by governmental edicts. D = Severe persecution by fanatical regimes. E = All churches and Christians are pronounced illegal and totally banned. F = Massive worldwide coordinated repression and persecution force apostasy by whole churches. G = Final extinction: the church follows her Master to execution and martyrdom.

DAVID B. BARRETT studied aerodynamics at Cambridge University, England, and worked for the period 1948-52 as a scientific research officer for the British government. In 1954 he was ordained in the Church of England. Since 1956 he has served as a missionary with the Church Missionary Society (London) in East Africa, Central America and other areas. As a missiologist he has written some 80 books, articles and publications on the global mission of Christianity in the modern world. Barrett is the editor of the *World Christian Encyclopedia: a Comparative Study of Churches and Religions in the Modern World AD 1900-2000* (Oxford University Press, 1982). He is a contributing editor to the *International Bulletin of Missionary Research.* He now works as research consultant to the Foreign Mission Board of the Southern Baptist Convention.

With his wife, Pam, Barrett has three children; Claire, Luke and Timothy. They live in Richmond, Virginia.